DISCARDED

COMMUNITIES OF INDIVIDUALS

This book examines the liberal-communitarian debate from a new perspective. Communitarians argue that liberal theory neglects the significance of communities for the lives of their members. An examination of that argument reveals that there are deficiencies in the communitarian account of community. Identifying and remedying those deficiencies is the key concern of this book.

Uniquely, this book addresses the deficiencies using Sartre's anarchist theory derived largely but not exclusively from an interpretation of the Critique of Dialectical Reason. Sartre champions the individual yet criticises liberalism. The tension arising from these two apparently disparate positions makes for a fruitful argument, enhanced by the connections made with Aristotelian and feminist theory, Hobbes and Rousseau. Finally, a method is developed for inquiring into the nature of associations which, it is argued, should interest communitarians concerned to avoid deficiencies in their account of community.

ASHGATE NEW CRITICAL THINKING
IN PHILOSOPHY

The *Ashgate New Critical Thinking in Philosophy* series aims to bring high quality research monograph publishing back into focus for authors, the international library market, and student, academic and research readers. Headed by an international editorial advisory board of acclaimed scholars from across the philosophical spectrum, this new monograph series presents cutting-edge research from established as well as exciting new authors in the field; spans the breadth of philosophy and related disciplinary and interdisciplinary perspectives; and takes contemporary philosophical research into new directions and debate.

Series Editorial Board

Professor David Cooper, University of Durham, UK
Professor Peter Lipton, University of Cambridge, UK
Professor Sean Sayers, Kent at Canterbury, UK
Dr Simon Critchley, University of Essex, UK
Dr Simon Glendinning, University of Reading, UK
Professor Paul Helm, King's College London, UK
Dr David Lamb, University of Birmingham, UK
Dr Stephen Mulhall, University of Oxford, UK
Professor Greg McCulloch, University of Birmingham, UK
Professor Ernest Sosa, Brown University, Rhode Island, USA
Professor John Post, Vanderbilt University, Nashville, USA
Professor Alan Goldman, University of Miami, Florida, USA
Professor Joseph Friggieri, University of Malta, Malta
Professor Graham Priest, University of Queensland, Brisbane, Australia
Professor Moira Gatens, University of Sydney, Australia
Professor Alan Musgrave, University of Otago, New Zealand

Communities of Individuals
Liberalism, communitarianism and Sartre's anarchism

MICHAEL J. R. CROSS
St Martin's College, Lancaster, UK

Ashgate
Aldershot • Burlington USA • Singapore • Sydney

© Michael J. R. Cross 2001

All rights reserved. No part of this publication may be reproduced, stored in a retrieval system, or transmitted in any form or by any means, electronic, mechanical, photocopying, recording or otherwise without the prior permission of the publisher.

The author has asserted his moral right under the Copyright, Designs and Patents Act, 1988, to be identified as the author of this work.

Published by
Ashgate Publishing Ltd
Gower House
Croft Road
Aldershot
Hants GU11 3HR
England

Ashgate Publishing Company
131 Main Street
Burlington, VT 05401-5600 USA

Ashgate website: http://www.ashgate.com

British Library Cataloguing in Publication Data
Cross, Michael James Rixon
   Communities of individuals : liberalism, communitarianism and Sartre's anarchism. - (Ashgate new critical thinking in pilosophy)
   1.Sartre, Jean Paul, 1905-1980 2.Liberalism 3.Communitarianism
   I.Title
   303.3'72

Library of Congress Cataloging-in-Publication Data
Cross, Mike, 1949-
   Communities of individuals : liberalism, communitarianism, and Sartre's anarchism / Michael James Rixon Cross.
      p. cm. -- (Ashgate new critical thinking in philosophy)
   Includes bibliographical references and index.
   1. Liberalism. 2. Communitarianism. 3. Sartre, Jean Paul, 1905---Political and social views. I. Title. II. Series.
   JC574.C76 2001
   307'.01--dc21

2001033679

ISBN 0 7546 0546 9

Printed and bound in Great Britain by
Antony Rowe Ltd, Chippenham, Wiltshire

Contents

Acknowledgements	viii
Foreword	ix
1 Introduction: an overview of the argument	1
2 Praxis, needs, scarcity and methodology	12
3 The communitarian case for community	39
4 Associations and the natural environment	79
5 Forms and terms of association: series	103
6 Forms and terms of association: groups	138
7 Praxis, communitarianism and beyond	203
8 Conclusion: the dialectic and the communitarian community	243
Bibliography	249
Index	259

To Sue, Joe and the memory of my mother

Acknowledgements

This book owes much to the support, guidance, inspiration and encouragement of a number of individuals and groups. The philosophy department of the University of Lancaster deserves a mention, particularly the invaluable contributions of John O'Neill and especially Michael Hammond. My own institution, St Martin's College, Lancaster, is to be thanked for supporting this project, with this time a special mention to colleagues in the Department of Religion and Ethics, not least for covering my sabbatical absence. Maria Chippendale, the department secretary, stands out because although I still type with two fingers, thanks to her I now know which keys to press.

Of course, learning and the development of ideas does not occur only in the setting of academic institutions, it can occur also in the context of, for example, friends and family. With regard to the latter, I should mention my father and the frequent, lengthy, occasionally heated but always fruitful discussions that we had and continue to have.

Foreword

The name of Jean-Paul Sartre is linked irrevocably with existentialism. This is to be expected. Of all Sartre's philosophical works, the one that has been read by the most people must surely be *Existentialism and Humanism*. It is short and it is accessible. Moreover, in tune with the spirit of the age, it dismisses the view that human beings are beings with a fixed nature, a given purpose and for whom moral agency consists of the proper application of universal and independently valid principles, independent, that is, of any particular social setting. Instead, it posits human freedom as the most important value and as the only authentic source of both moral agency and human fulfilment.

During the 1950s, Sartre's work became more explicitly political leading, in the *Critique of Dialectical Reason*, to his attempt to reconcile existentialism with Marxism. One outcome of that attempt was his own version of dialectical thinking. Another, connected, outcome was a clear statement of certain anarchist ideas. The argument is that human freedom is enhanced and thus human fulfilment most effectively attained by co-operative action within the context of certain sorts of communities, specifically, non-hierarchical communities.

In its celebration of both human freedom and, as a condition for its enhancement, certain sorts of communities, the *Critique* is well-placed to serve as a source for an examination and extension of the liberal-communitarian debate. Liberalism asserts the priority of the individual over any community and communitarians argue that in making that assertion, liberalism diminishes the significance that communities have for their individual members. In essence this is, of course, an age old debate. Yet it is still resonant not only in the politics and philosophy departments of universities but also in contemporary practical politics. However, one would like to see even more resonance, particularly in connection with criticisms of certain aspects of liberalism and, relatedly, the more secure establishment of the communitarian case for community than communitarianism itself has yet achieved. This book is written as a contribution to that end.

CHAPTER ONE

Introduction: an overview of the argument

The communitarian account of community is deficient in a number of important respects. The purpose of this work is to expose those deficiencies and remedy them. The communitarians who are to be the focus of this work, namely, Michael Sandel, Alasdair MacIntyre and Michael Walzer, have argued that liberal political theory has neglected the significance that communities have for the lives of their members in three main ways. These are, with respect to the three named writers, first, as constitutive of the identity of individuals; second, as a source for the conception and the pursuit of the good life for human beings; third, as a forum for the generation of shared meanings concerning social goods and their just distribution. The argument in this work will be that, in their own way, the communitarians, and not just the three who have been named for the sake of providing a focus, have also neglected the community.

The communitarian attack on liberal political theory, and particularly the Kantian-Rawlsian strain of that theory, has largely been met by a defence that has turned on arguments demonstrating, more or less successfully, that the communitarians had neither fully nor correctly understood the aspect of the liberal position that has been attacked. That defence of liberal theory has been mounted by, amongst others, Amy Gutmann (1985), Gerald Doppelt (1988, 1989), Will Kymlicka (1989, 1990, 1991), Allen Buchanan (1989) and, of course, Rawls himself (1985, 1988, 1993). However, a large part of the communitarian campaign consists of a number of assertions about the nature of community and about the nature of the relationship between the community and the individual. It is this aspect of the debate that will be examined in this work. So it is that the focus in this work will be on the understanding that communitarianism has of itself as a theory of community. The argument will be that in extolling the virtues of community, the communitarians have not fully understood their own position, or at least that they have failed to convey that understanding in the fullest sense. Varieties of liberal theory, having been briefly described, will be directly addressed only in as much as communitarian criticisms of that theory are, in themselves, revealing of the communitarians' views of community. This will serve the purpose of developing those criticisms and, relatedly, views of community.

In order to establish and remedy the deficiencies in the communitarian account of community, communitarian criticisms of liberalism and claims for community will be examined from what might, as a first impression, be regarded as an unusual perspective. The perspective will be that provided by an interpretation of Volumes 1 and 2 of Jean-Paul Sartre's *Critique of Dialectical Reason*. Central to this perspective will be an interpretation of Sartre's notion of praxis, understood as a way of portraying certain dimensions of human activity, which not only points to, as Sartre says, a dialectical process but which is also, as he does not say, one that is normative in character. The argument will be that one particular way of understanding the natures of different sorts of communities can be achieved through the application of this interpretation of praxis and understanding the different sorts of relationships that it yields. Moreover, what will emerge is a dialectical method of inquiring into the nature of different sorts of communities and it will be argued that this method of inquiry should be of interest to the communitarians.

Why use the argument in the *Critique* as the basis for correcting the communitarian idea of community? There are four answers to that question. First, it will be seen that the *Critique* does address particular issues that are neglected by the communitarian account of community. Indeed, although it is not immune from criticism, the extent to which the *Critique* is, through its employment of a view of praxis in order to address those issues, seen to be adequate to the task of addressing that which communitarianism neglects, and has been selected for its adequacy, is the extent to which a critique of the *Critique* will not be developed. However, in order to achieve the aim, what will be developed, in ways that will be specified, are certain themes in the *Critique*. Second, Sartre is interesting because, like certain communitarians, he is critical of classical laissez-faire liberalism, or what he and others call bourgeois liberalism, on the grounds that it leaves individuals isolated and powerless. Yet he remains a champion of the individual and of individual freedom and thus has something in common with the tradition of which he is so critical.[1] This is interesting because the tension generated by these two positions yields a sensitivity in understanding the status of individuals and communities relative to each other that is greater than that to be found in much of communitarian writing. Third, it will be seen that the communitarian project can be supported by other, ostensibly non-Sartrean, schools of thought. However, it will also be seen that these schools of thought can themselves be informed by a view of praxis that is derived from the *Critique* and, moreover, that they also have something to offer this view of praxis. Fourth, what emerges from the *Critique* is a particular view of a dialectical method of inquiring into social experience and specifically into the nature of associating and associations. As has been said, it will be argued that this is a method of inquiry that should be of interest to communitarians.

The tension that is mentioned in the second of the points given above is particularly significant in that it reveals the existence of the very clear arguments

---

[1] The use of 'bourgeois' is retained because it is used particularly by Jean-Paul Sartre and as used by Sartre refers both to a particular class and a particular form of association.

from anarchism that are to be found in the *Critique*. The usual literal meaning of anarchy, absence of rule, is ambiguous. It is, however, a useful ambiguity for those critics of anarchism who, seizing upon a particular understanding of the absence of rule, are able to point out that anarchism in practice would literally mean living in a condition where nobody acknowledged any rules, a state of lawlessness, a state of chaos. To define anarchy as the absence of a ruler or a sovereign is only a little more helpful, even though that is precisely the definition supplied by Pierre-Joseph Proudhon.[2] Crucially, there is the identification of a ruler with a sovereign. So what anarchism opposes is the domination of society by a sovereign body, for example, a monarch, a president or a ruling central government and since a ruling central government can be regarded as the personification of the State[3] then it also opposes the idea and the existence of the State. It is, in fact, the idea of domination combined with coercion that is crucial. Sovereign bodies can and do impose their wills on others but it is the mere fact that they can that renders them anathema to anarchists.

A society that is ruled by a sovereign body will, more probably than not, be a society in which the involvement in that society's political affairs by the citizens is minimal. The citizens of that society may, at times determined by the sovereign body and within the parameters that it controls, vote. However, as we shall see, the purpose and the practice of voting in that context is not unproblematic. Other forms of involvement in political affairs, for example, through the media, are also likely to be controlled. In the case of involvement through the media the control could be exercised by the owners of the medium in question or by whoever can influence the owners, such as central government. So, moving away from what anarchism opposes, what anarchism proposes is the maximum involvement of the citizens in political affairs.

Maximum involvement in political affairs on the part of the citizens is thought to be the antidote to the authoritarianism that anarchists believe to be inherent in rule by a sovereign body of the type just described. This is not to say that anarchism opposes all forms of authority. As Errico Malatesta explains,

> *Anarchism is society organised without authority*, meaning by authority the power to *impose* one's own will and not the inevitable and beneficial fact that he who has greater understanding of, as well as ability to carry out, a task succeeds more easily in having his opinion accepted, and of acting as a guide on the particular question, for those less able than himself.[4]

It is acknowledged, therefore, that someone can be an authority on a particular question. Michael Bakunin makes the same point, though with even more caution. In 'God and the State' he writes,

---

[2] Pierre-Joseph Proudhon, 'What is Property? First Memoir', in Stewart Edwards (ed.), 1970, p. 89.
[3] Enricco Malatesta, 1942, p. 3.
[4] Malatesta, in Vernon Richards (ed.), 1965, p. 20.

> Does it follow that I reject all authority? Far from me such a thought. In the matter of boots, I refer to the authority of the bootmaker; concerning houses, canals, or railroads, I consult that of the architect or engineer. For such a special knowledge I apply to such and such a *savant*. But I allow neither the bootmaker nor the architect nor the *savant* to impose his authority upon me. I listen to them freely and with all the respect merited by their intelligence, their character, their knowledge, reserving always my incontestable right of criticism and censure. I do not content myself with consulting a single authority in any special branch; I consult several; I compare their opinions and choose that which seems to me to be the soundest. But I recognise no infallible authority, even in special questions.[5]

Anarchists reject dominating, coercive, authoritarianism of all kinds but especially of the kind that it believes to be inherent in rule by a sovereign body. This is because, like liberals, they are champions of individual liberty. However, and here we must identify the anarchism that is of interest to this work, the insights from certain types of anarchism are valuable in the context of the liberal-communitarian debate because they come from types of anarchism that also champion community. In fact, it is precisely because they are the champions of one that they are also, at the same time, the champions of the other. So, what might loosely be called social anarchists can be identified by their recognition of the need for voluntary associations, since it is within those associations that the freedom of all the associates can be guaranteed. Malatesta argues that it is, 'By the free association of all, a social organisation would arise through the spontaneous grouping of men according to their needs and sympathies ... This organisation would have for its aim the greatest good and fullest liberty of all.'[6] Bakunin provides an explanation. He argues that, 'Man completely realizes his individual freedom as well as his personality only through the individuals who surround him and thanks only to the labor and collective power of society.'[7]

The arguments of Malatesta and Bakunin are endorsed by Proudhon who also reminds us of a useful distinction. Proudhon argues that, 'political theory will for us be the result of mutual guarantees. It is through guaranteeing each other's liberty that we will be able to do without this government'.[8] At this point an objection in the form of a question could be, "What is distinctly anarchistic about the connection between community and liberty?" After all Karl Marx argues that,

> Within communist society, the only society in which the original and free development of individuals ceases to be a mere phrase, this development is determined precisely by the connection of individuals, a connection which

---

[5] Michael Bakunin, 'God and the State', in Arthur Lehning (ed.), 1974, p. 132.
[6] Malatesta, 1942, p. 18.
[7] Bakunin, 'God and the State', in Sam Dolgoff (ed.) 1973, p. 236.
[8] Proudhon, 'Confessions of a Revolutionary', in Stewart Edwards (ed.), 1970, p. 95.

consists partly in the economic prerequisites and partly in the necessary solidarity of the free development of all.[9]

This is confirmed in *The Communist Manifesto* where we read that, 'In place of old bourgeois society, with its classes and class antagonisms, we shall have an association, in which the free development of each is the condition for the free development of all.'[10] However, the distinction of which Proudhon reminds us concerns his desire to do without the government and the State which it personifies. Each of the anarchists with which I am concerned favours voluntary associations, associations formed out of the free actions of individuals, associations which leave individuals free to join or not. Each of these anarchists opposes the State. When Peter Kropotkin defined what I have called social anarchism as 'the No-Government system of Socialism'[11] he was, because he regarded the government and the State as synonymous, referring to his opposition to the State. Marx did not oppose the idea of the State. He thought that the State would be a necessary condition for the development of the kind of society that he envisioned. It would be a communist State, certainly, but a State nonetheless.

So, in addition to opposing rule by a sovereign body and proposing the maximum participation by individuals in the governance of their community, a further distinctive characteristic of the anarchism with which we are concerned is that it advocates the free association of people agreeing to associate and agreeing to co-operate. It is in such associations that, to paraphrase an earlier quotation from Malatesta, needs can be satisfied and beyond that the good for human beings, including the good of liberty, can be pursued. Notions of agreement and co-operation in order to satisfy needs and pursue the good introduce two other characteristics of this species of anarchism.

The first of those other characteristics is that anarchism does not mean the absence of all forms of government, but it does mean self-government. The forms of government that are acceptable according to anarchism are those that are not authoritarian and coercive and self-government is most likely to fit the bill. Self-government implies self-regulation and that in turn implies that, contrary to critics of anarchism, there will be rules. Moreover, practically, where there are rules there will be sanctions for breaking the rules. However, in line with the notion of maximum participation in associations, these will be rules and sanctions which people will formulate for themselves and which they will, actually and freely, agree to abide by. Indeed, introducing the second characteristic and in a desire to avoid the imposition of rules and sanctions by a sovereign body, every competent adult would have an equal opportunity to take part in the formulation of rules and sanctions. Perhaps not everybody would

---

[9] Karl Marx, *The German Ideology*, in David McLellan (ed.), 1977, p. 191.
[10] Marx and Engels, *The Communist Manifesto*, in McLellan (ed.), 1977, p. 238.
[11] Peter Kropotkin, 1913, p. 5.

want to take advantage of that opportunity but those who do will be able to do so as the equal of everyone else.

The second of those other characteristics of this species of anarchism, therefore, concerns a certain kind of equality. The equality that is at issue concerns the sameness of people regarding the possibility of their participation in the government of the community and so also regarding their exercise of power. Consequently, in this regard, everyone has equal status. In this regard, there is no hierarchy. It has been acknowledged that some people may be better than others at making boots or building houses. However, achievements in those arenas do not in themselves assure those achievers greater power when it comes to the government of the community.

Eventually, the characteristics that have just been described point to government arising out of the form of association as an expression of the terms of that association. This is as opposed to a government imposing its terms indiscriminately on different forms of association. However, on the back of that observation a further characteristic emerges. The notion of equality of participation leads us to interdependency. Interdependency recognizes diversity. People who make boots need houses to live in and people who build houses will have need of boots. Yet the idea that one person needs another has, in itself, no connection with equality. A person who builds houses can admit to needing boots yet still argue that building houses is a more important, skilful, or whatever, function than making boots. Kropotkin addresses the issue by considering whether, among others, the most necessary person in the coal mine is the person who operates the machine that makes the cage go up or down, the mine owner, or the miner. He argues that all have contributed to the extraction of the coal in proportion to their strength, their energy, their knowledge and so on. Moreover, he goes on to argue that the coal they have extracted is not, in fact, entirely their work. It is also the work of the people who built the railway leading to the mine and the roads that radiate from the railway stations and those who built the machines that burn the coal. He concludes that,

> It is utterly impossible to draw a distinction between the work of each of these men. To measure the work by its results leads us to an absurdity; to divide the total work, and to measure its fractions by the number of hours spent on the work also leads us to an absurdity. One thing remains: to put the needs above the works, and first of all to recognize the right to live, and later on the right to well-being for all those who took their share in production.[12]

As David Miller notes, a criticism of capitalism that is made by social anarchists in general is that capitalism confers individual titles on things that are, in fact, the collective products of the community. The skills and the knowledge, the

---

[12] Kropotkin, 1995, p. 154.

tools and the other equipment which the capitalist uses to make his products are the outcomes of collective and cumulative human endeavour.[13] In the face of such interdependency, the first priority in determining the distribution of resources is need.

Now, Sartre's view of anarchism appears to be hedged with ambivalence. In 'The Itinerary of a Thought' it is recorded that Sartre is asked, 'What sort of political organisation do you judge to be the appropriate instrument today?' He replies, 'It is obvious that anarchism leads nowhere, today as yesterday.' However, he immediately goes on to say that,

> The central question is whether in the end the only possible type of political organisation is that which we know in the shape of the present CPs: hierarchical division between leadership and rank-and-file, communications and instructions proceeding from above downwards only, isolation of each cell from every other, vertical powers of dissolution and discipline, separation of workers and intellectuals?[14]

Moreover, Sartre claims that the *Critique* as a whole is anti-hierarchical. He endorses the conception of interpersonal relationships to be found in libertarian socialism. Consensus and small groups are the sole guarantors of shared sovereignty. In an interview in May 1975, Dr Michel Rybalka observes that, 'In recent interviews, you seem to have accepted the term "libertarian socialism".' Sartre responds by saying, 'It is an anarchist term, and I keep it because I like to recall the somewhat anarchist origins of my thought.'[15] In fact, it will become apparent the *Critique* as a whole contains the characteristics of anarchism that have been described. It can be understood as a statement of anarchist philosophy. Part of the interpretation of the *Critique* will, therefore, be a focus on those characteristics and their contribution to remedying the deficiencies in the communitarian account of community.

Interpretation is also required because, as I have said, the *Critique* is itself not immune from criticism. The criticisms that are of concern to this work cover four themes. The first concerns Sartre's use of terror as a device for maintaining cohesion between people. Pietro Chiodi draws attention to the fact that in Sartre's usage terror knows no limits.[16] The second concerns Sartre's use of scarcity as a device to explain conflict. Raymond Aron, taking the Marxist view, argues that it is not scarcity but surplus and the manner by which it is distributed that causes conflict[17] and Ronald Aronson argues that Sartre has made too much of

---

[13] David Miller, 1984, p. 47.
[14] Sartre, 'The Itinerary of a Thought', in *Beyond Existentialism and Marxism*, 1974, p. 60. First published as an interview in *New Left Review*, no. 58, November–December, 1969.
[15] This was an interview that took place on 12 and 19 May 975. The interviewers were Dr Michel Rybalka, Dr Oreste F. Pucciani and Miss Susan Gruenheck. This portion of the interview is recorded in Paul Schilpp (ed.), 1981, p. 21.
[16] Pietro Chiodi, 1978, pp. 75, 98.
[17] Raymond Aron, 1975, p. 36.

scarcity and has ignored the extent to which people co-operate.[18] William McBride makes the point that Sartre's notion of scarcity is too vague and being too vague there is a difficulty in envisioning how it may be overcome.[19] The third, identified by George Stack, is that Sartre 'fails to present an adequate account of the role of leadership in social organisations'.[20] Each of these themes will be addressed in this work not only through an interpretation of Sartre's position as it appears in Volume 1 of the *Critique* which is the inspiration for the criticisms that have been described, but also through the use of Volume 2. However, it is in respect of the fourth theme that interpretation is especially required. This concerns Sartre's style of writing. As Wilfrid Desan notes, 'One of the most frequent criticisms of Sartre's book is that he has shown an utter disregard for his reader.'[21] Anthony Manser described the writing as 'turgid'[22] and Aronson declares that 'by and large it is undisciplined, self-indulgent, confused and confusing'.[23] Those comments are also directed at Volume 1 of the *Critique*. However, Volume 2 does not escape censure. Although Aronson praises Sartre's use of the example of the boxing match to explore the issue of conflict, which occupies the first fifty pages of volume two, for the 'remarkably persistent and clear logic running through the argument,'[24] Aronson also refers to the last two hundred pages where 'it becomes clear that Sartre has gone astray' and has produced 'an unstructured analysis' lacking in 'clarity and penetration'.[25]

Since what is finally to emerge will be a particular view of a dialectical method of inquiry based on the working of praxis some might wonder why the particular view has to be derived from Sartre. Why not develop a dialectical method on the basis of Hegel or Marx? This question also admits of a number of answers. First, although he is openly indebted to both Hegel and Marx, Sartre employs his dialectical view of praxis to investigate a greater variety of forms of association than do either of them. Sartre is able to do this because, second, his notion of the dialectic is different from that of both Hegel and Marx. Sartre's dialectic is, in ways that will be examined, more open than that of either Hegel or Marx and it is, therefore, better suited to the task of investigating a variety of forms of association. Third, another difference between Sartre's dialectic and that of Hegel and Marx is that Sartre's dialectic contains a motivational aspect. This means that Sartre's dialectic is sensitive to the motives of the individuals who constitute and who are constituted by communities. Each of these reasons makes Sartre's dialectic, suitably modified, a particularly appropriate tool to be used in the liberal-communitarian debate.

---

[18] Ronald Aronson, 1980, pp. 254–56.
[19] William McBride, 1991, p. 110.
[20] George Stack, 1971, p. 408.
[21] Wilfrid Desan, 1965, p. 209.
[22] Anthony Manser, 1967, p. 206.
[23] Aronson, 1980, p. 249.
[24] Aronson, 1985, p. 150.
[25] Aronson, 1980, p. 284.

If it is possible to question the choice of Sartre as the basis for the argument then it is also possible to question the choice of Sandel, MacIntyre and Walzer as representatives of communitarianism. The choice is informed by the fact that each employs different arguments as characterized in the opening paragraph of this introduction, and each has different targets. Sandel's target is what he calls 'deontological liberalism,'[26] which he identifies as the Kantian-Rawlsian strand of liberalism. MacIntyre's target is all forms of liberalism. Walzer's target is the manner by which goods are distributed and hence the way in which justice is administered and thus, although he has liberal sympathies, he can be said to be critical of a particular aspect of laissez-faire liberalism.

The next chapter sets the scene by interpreting the basis of Sartre's argument. This will involve an examination of the relationship between needs, scarcity and praxis. From this examination it will emerge that praxis is both normative and dialectical in nature and operates according to a two-way movement by which people are mediated by things to the extent that things are mediated by people. The results of the examination of the relationship between needs, scarcity and praxis understood as normative and dialectical in nature will further our understanding of the ways in which the communitarian notion of community has been neglectful and, since, in the context of this work, such a theory requires a normative notion of praxis, ways in which a normative theory of associations might be developed will start to become apparent. The discussion of scarcity will include the introduction of a comparison between the ideas of Thomas Hobbes and Sartre which is included to clarify some of Sartre's arguments and locate them alongside a particular tradition in political philosophy.

In chapter three, following some brief distinctions between the forms of liberalism that are to receive attention in this work, there will be an examination of the work of Sandel, MacIntyre and Walzer in order to establish why it is thought that communities have a significant part to play in the lives of their members. Although the focus of attention will be on those three writers, reference will also be made to other communitarian writers or writers with communitarian sympathies. The concluding part of this chapter will be a survey of the ways in which communitarianism has been neglectful of community and will be presented in terms of deficiencies in the communitarian account of community.

An understanding of the nature of the relationship between needs, scarcity and praxis understood as normative and dialectical is necessary background for the argument in the fourth chapter. This argument arises from the communitarian failure to appreciate that an understanding of community requires an understanding of the relationship that individuals who constitute communities have with their natural environment. Despite the fact that Sartre is not best known as an environmentalist, the argument that can be derived from the *Critique* will be that the way that individually and collectively people relate to the natural

---

[26] Michael Sandel, 1982, p. 1.

environment affects the way that people relate to each other as members of a community and the way that people relate to each other as members of a community affects the way that individually and collectively people relate to the natural environment. This argument will reveal certain understandings about the satisfaction of needs and from that understandings about two different sorts of alienation.

The comparison between Hobbes and Sartre that began in the previous chapter will be complemented in chapter four by the beginnings of a comparison between Sartre and Jean-Jacques Rousseau and for the same reason. In fact, Sartre's ideas in the *Critique* may, to a greater extent than is generally realized, usefully be compared with those of Hobbes and Rousseau. This is unsurprising given the commonality of their concerns. Therefore, this comparison will form a significant part of this work. The significance resides not only in the fact that all three address similar issues but also in the fact that they address issues that are avoided by the communitarians.

Chapters five and six examine different forms and terms of association. "Forms of association" refers to the nature of the association as indicated by the relationship between an individual and the other individuals who constitute the community to which that individual belongs. This relationship reveals the terms of association, that is, the understandings that people have about their particular community. There is, in fact, a dialectical relationship between forms and terms of association. Each form of association will be accompanied by and sustained by its particular terms of association. The forms and terms of association are instigated by praxis and each type of association is distinguished by its own praxis. The dialectical nature of the praxis that instigates and distinguishes each type of association is such that it will be argued that not only do communities constitute individuals but also that individuals constitute communities. The form of association studied in chapter five is the series. This is the form of association to be found in liberal, particularly laissez-faire liberal, societies. This chapter can, therefore, be regarded as providing reasons which communitarians themselves do not provide for the communitarian criticism of a certain sort of liberalism and hence, by implication, reasons for desiring an alternative form of association. Chapter six can be regarded as a return to the correction of communitarian negligence for it is the chapter that examines Sartre's view of different types of groups.

Chapter seven reviews the deficiencies in the communitarian account of community and reviews the ways in which the interpretation of praxis that is offered in this work can remedy those deficiencies. With that review completed the communitarian account of community is then scrutinized through the lens of another school of thought, that concerned with the psychology of moral agency and in particular with the importance of the dispositions for moral agency. This will involve an examination of Aristotle's notion of the good life and the community. This scrutiny is conducted with the intention of discerning if, from an apparently different perspective, further amendments to the communitarian position can be made. It will be seen that such amendments are possible. It will also be seen both that the interpretation of praxis developed in this work can offer some insights to that school of thought and that insights from that school of thought can serve to emphasize aspects of praxis that hitherto have been acknowledged but not explored in detail. Having, in that way, extended the interpretation of praxis it will now be seen that an understanding of praxis can make a contribution to the work of other critics of certain sorts of liberalism, again not normally associated with Sartre, namely, those feminist theorists who espouse an ethics of care. However, it will also be seen that the work of those feminist theorists can make a contribution to an understanding of praxis not by adding anything new but again by emphasizing what has already been said. Having established a developed view of praxis it will be argued that this view can in itself reveal the existence of a dialectical method of inquiry into social experience in general and into the nature of associations in particular, and also a dialectical structure for reasoning.

With all of the parts of the argument now in place, there is a return to the communitarian notion of community in the concluding chapter. This is in order to subject that notion to the dialectical method of inquiry revealed in the previous chapter and hence to demonstrate that it is a method of inquiry that should be of interest to communitarians.

This work, therefore, uses the *Critique* to remedy deficiencies in the communitarian account of community. In order to do this it will, as has been indicated, move beyond the *Critique*. It will move beyond the *Critique* in five particular ways. First, as was mentioned earlier, by showing that praxis is not only dialectical in nature but also normative. Second, the dialectical and normative nature of praxis will reveal that associations have a variety of forms and each form is accompanied by its particular terms. Third, the normative nature of praxis will provide a basis for a normative theory of associations. Fourth, a dialectical method for inquiring into the nature of social experience and in particular the nature of associations will be established solely on the basis of the process of praxis. Fifth, on the basis of that method, a structure for dialectical reason will be revealed.

CHAPTER TWO

Praxis, needs, scarcity and methodology

The first step is to present a theory of praxis based on Jean-Paul Sartre's *Critique of Dialectical Reason* and so begin the examination of the nature of associating. The argument in this chapter has three related strands, namely, that praxis stems from human need, occurs in a milieu of scarcity and gives rise to certain understandings. An examination of the three related strands of the argument will show that in its immediacy, at the level of operation, praxis is both normative and dialectical in nature and it is the normative and dialectical nature of praxis at the level of operation that, in this and in the following chapters, will yield understandings about the nature of associating and hence of forms and terms of associations. We should remember that the form of an association is the nature of an association as revealed by the relationships that exist between the individuals who constitute a community. The terms of association are the understandings that people have about their community and those relationships and which are manifested by such items as customs, contracts, constitutions, rights and shared meanings in general. The discussion of scarcity will introduce a comparison between Sartre and Hobbes which will clarify some of Sartre's arguments and provide them with a context.

A sense of the meaning of 'need' is supplied by Garrett Thomson. According to Thomson, 'The objects of fundamental needs are necessary in the full-blooded sense of the term: these are things that we cannot do without, or that we must have ... in most circumstances, we have no option but to try to obtain what we need.'[1] I am not at all certain about the absence of an option but Thomson may well be correct to talk of serious harm occurring in the event of needs remaining unfulfilled. Len Doyal and Ian Gough argue that an example of the serious harm that can occur if needs remain unfulfilled is that one becomes disabled in the 'pursuit of one's vision of the good'.[2] This is an idea that will be pursued in this chapter and in the chapters that follow. 'Le besoin', 'need', can also mean 'want'. However, Sartre talks of need in the full-blooded sense and argues that need involves both a lack and a determination to overcome that lack. It is from that determination, where it occurs, that praxis arises. The mere fact of a lack of something will not, in itself, give rise to praxis. On its own, the absence of yesterday's newspaper, let us say, is not a matter of any great concern. The lack becomes a need and gives rise to praxis thus: there is a lack, a negativity, and

---

[1] Garrett Thomson, 1987, p. 27.
[2] Len Doyal and Ian Gough, 1991, p. 50.

this becomes a need if it is important for the organism's well-being to overcome that negativity, or, in other words, negate the negativity. Need, therefore, is experienced as a negativity to be negated. Praxis is the activity of overcoming or negating the lack. It is in this sense that praxis stems from need. It is also the case that needs can be regarded as indicators of certain values. Only indicators because although needs themselves are always experienced in a particular sort of way, nothing necessarily follows from the experience.

Sartre's interest in needs was neither new nor peripheral. There is, for example, evidence of that interest in the *Notebooks for an Ethics* where he writes that, 'A need is one of the many expressions of a lack and is itself a lack'[3] and where he acknowledges the universality of needs in the sense of the 'nonindividuality of man in relation to his needs'[4] and in the sense that 'everyone gets hungry'.[5] When Sartre writes about need he is writing about a lack of something which had best be overcome because something important is missing. However, in Volume 1 of the *Critique* he writes of the need to survive which he regards as the most basic of individual needs and in the second volume of the *Critique* he writes of the need to survive in connection with a community. In talking of the need to survive, the nature of what it is that is lacking is not obvious. To survive is to continue to have something that one has already. Sartre may, therefore, mean that need also refers to the anticipation or fear of a lack, either that of life or possibly that of the means for life to continue. Sartre does in fact talk of the organism facing a threat.[6] It is not clear, however, whether the threat refers to the anticipation or fear of a lack or whether threat is in itself a lack, as with a lack of security.[7] The notion of a fear of a lack will be seen to be a reasonable notion in the light of the discussion on scarcity which is to follow shortly.

Kropotkin also emphasises the significance of needs. I recognise the need for caution here. Just because someone who is known as an anarchist says something, it does not follow that what is said is an aspect of anarchism.

---

3   *Notebooks for an Ethics*, p. 537. Henceforth, the abbreviation NE will be used to refer to the English edition of *Cahiers pour une morale*.
4   NE, p. 66.
5   Ibid., p. 71.
6   *Critique of Dialectical Reason*, Volume One, p. 83. Henceforth, the abbreviation CDR I will be used to refer to the English edition of *Critique de la raison dialectique*, Tome I.
7   This raises the issue of whether all needs are in fact lacks. One can need something even though it is not lacking. It makes perfectly good sense to say that people need oxygen. That is simply a fact about people. Following Sartre's account, however, the need for oxygen is realised or felt as a need when the organism has run out of oxygen and is about to inhale. The same could apply to survival. However, when Sartre talks of the need to survive he presumably means the need to continue to survive since the fact that we have the need to survive means that we already have survival but may lack or fear that we will lack whatever is necessary for survival to continue.

Of course, it does not follow that because someone needs something they therefore ought to have that thing. Someone may need something yet be undeserving. In Sartre's case, however, it is the needy individual who is seeking to satisfy his needs and the extent to which he seeks to do so is presumably the extent to which he feels he deserves to do so.

Kropotkin's recipe for apple pie would, in the absence of instructions on how to obtain the ingredients, simply be a recipe for apple pie. Nevertheless, what he has to say about needs is illuminating. He points out that most texts on economics, from Adam Smith to Marx, begin with production. Only towards the end of most texts does attention turn to consumption. He writes,

> Perhaps you will say this is logical. Before satisfying needs you must create the wherewithal to satisfy them. But before producing anything must you not feel the need of it? Was it not necessity that first drove man to hunt, to raise cattle, to cultivate land, to make implements, and later on to invent machinery? Is it not the study of needs that should govern production?[8]

Kropotkin concludes that the aim of production should be 'the satisfaction of the needs of all'.[9] The essential point, however, is that activity is engendered by need.

Sartre too argues that everything can be explained through need because 'need is the first totalising relation between the material being, man, and the material ensemble of which he is part. This relation is *univocal*, and *of interiority*. Indeed, it is through need that the first negation of the negation and the first totalisation appear in matter'.[10] At this point an explanation of some key ideas is necessary. 'Totalising' is the activity of unifying the human or non-human environment, or some aspect of that, into a coherent whole. A totality is a coherent whole and so too is a 'totalisation' with the difference that a totalisation is a wholeness created or imposed by someone whereas a totality refers to the wholeness of something in itself or as a characteristic of its being. This is not to say that a totality cannot change or develop. As we shall see, Sartre talks of a totality under threat, argues that a lack is defined in relation to a totality and talks of a totality being transcended. So, an individual can be thought of as a totality. A crowd of Derby County supporters is a totalisation. Very few people go for a drink in the 'Punch Bowl' on Monday nights. They are, however, the same few people and have come to be called the 'Monday Night Club', another totalisation. Totalisation can also refer to the dynamic process or activity whereby individuals or groups organise parts or elements into wholes.

The reference to interiority invokes Sartre's process of interiorisation. Sartre's process of interiorisation and the Freudian process of internalisation, spoken of in connection with the development of the super-ego, are similar.[11] However, although the French 'intériorisation' can be translated by both interiorisation and internalisation, in the current context interiorisation is the better translation and this is due to Sartre's particular view of psychodynamics. In the second volume of the *Critique*, for reasons that will become clear in the

---

[8] Kropotkin, 1995, pp. 158–59.
[9] Ibid., p. 160.
[10] CDR I, p. 80.
[11] See, for example, Richard Gross, 1987, p. 659.

examination of his methodology towards the end of this chapter, Sartre indicates the importance of the use of a psychodynamic method within the predominantly Marxist framework of analysis that he both uses and amends.[12] He talks of the praxis of Stalin and describes it as a sovereign praxis. The sovereign, that is to say, parental, praxis is interiorised by the worker, that is to say, the child, and this interiorisation is supported by the interiorisations of other workers.

The major difference between the process described by Sigmund Freud and that described by Sartre concerns the fact that the mechanics of internalisation and interiorisation are different, even though both are instrumental in enabling the individual to acquire a sense of meaning. By its nature Freudian internalisation is an unconscious process. It involves taking in something from the outside, such as ideas or perspectives, which becomes part of the person, for example, as a value. Interiorisation has a volitional aspect. It also involves the assumption of something from the outside but in order to go beyond that thing. Therefore, it must be known and understood. This is not to say that there is no such thing as a process of internalisation, although Sartre might have argued otherwise.[13] It is simply to say that the process of interiorisation is not the same thing. Thus interiorisation can be thought of as part of the process by which praxis becomes intelligible to itself even as it makes the interiorisation intelligible and which, as a feature of the process of praxis, alerts us to what in the course of this chapter will emerge as the dialectical nature of praxis. It is part of the process by which praxis becomes intelligible to itself because, as will become clear, praxis contains within itself its own mode of comprehension and it is a feature of the process of praxis because the complete dialectical process of praxis involves re-exteriorisation and that too is part of the intelligibility of praxis to itself and an expression of that intelligibility. An example of the complete process would be involvement in research which results in the production of a work of philosophy. The interiorisation refers to the recognition of a new idea, recognised as such on the basis of previous work and developing the intelligibility of current work which in the fullness of time is re-exteriorised as the finished product. This in turn, as we will see, becomes the occasion for new praxis both for oneself and for others. It is interiorisation and re-exteriorisation that constitutes the dynamics of what will become known as the transcending movement of praxis. The transcending movement of praxis will be a way of thinking about the development of the moral sensitivities of the individual. However, whether or not this is the equivalent of, or perhaps even an explanation for, the development of the super-ego is an issue that goes beyond the scope of this inquiry.

Need itself as the negation of a negation is explained in terms of the 'univocal', that is one directional or unilateral, relationship between the organic

---

[12] *Critique of Dialectical Reason*, Volume Two, p. 216. Henceforth, the abbreviation CDR II will be used to refer to the English edition of *Critique de la raison dialectique*, Tome II.

[13] See Sartre's discussion of bad faith and existential psychoanalysis in *Being and Nothingness*.

and the inorganic. The organic needs the inorganic but the converse is not the case. Sartre argues that,

> The original negation, in fact, is an initial contradiction between the organic and the inorganic, in the double sense that lack is defined in relation to a *totality* . . . and that, in the last analysis, *what is lacking* can be reduced to inorganic or less organised elements . . . From this point of view, the negation of this negation is achieved through the transcendence of the organic towards the inorganic.[14]

Sartre's use of the word 'organic' creates the possibility for confusion. By organic Sartre means the organism. In other words, the organism constantly requires the inorganic in order to survive. Here Sartre is establishing a particular kind of relationship between the individual and that which is not the individual. This is an idea that occurs in the *Economic and Philosophical Manuscripts* where Marx argued that, 'Hunger is a natural need; so it needs a natural object outside itself to satisfy and appease it. Hunger is the objective need of a body for an exterior object in order to be complete and express its being'.[15] The unity or well-being of the organism is maintained by constantly using the inorganic, that is, that which is not the organism. Thus need is the lack of that which is not the organism. However, Sartre's juxtaposition of organic with inorganic, identified as less organised elements, and talk of only a one directional relationship seems rather narrow. In short the organism might need another organism.

Although further elaboration will be required, as a first step praxis can be thought of as an organising project directed towards some end. Mary Warnock observes that, for Sartre, 'the word "praxis" means very much the same as it meant for Aristotle, who used it to mark off purposive goal-directed activity from random activity'.[16] Aristotle's view of praxis was that it constituted the free man's moral and political life and it was possible because of phronesis which can be understood as prudence, practical wisdom or common sense. This voluntary, purposeful activity was the way in which male citizens distinguished themselves from animals, slaves, manual workers, people engaged in trade and women. A distinction was made between the life of praxis and the life of theoria but it was not the same as the contemporary distinction between theory and practice since, as has been indicated, praxis requires its own mode of knowing, judging and intellectual discipline. It is, therefore, in praxis that the distinction between theory and practice breaks down.

For Sartre the goal or end is the organising project itself. We read that, '*praxis*, in the first instance, is nothing but the relation of the organism, as exterior and future end, to the present organism as a totality under threat'[17] and

---

[14] CDR I, p. 80.
[15] Marx, *Economic and Philosophical Manuscripts*, in McLellan, 1977, p. 104.
[16] Mary Warnock, 1965, p. 147.
[17] CDR I, p. 83.

'*praxis*, born of need, is a totalisation whose movement towards its own end *practically* makes the environment into a totality'.[18] 'Towards its own end' refers to the needs that are satisfied by a praxis, to sustain an end which is the organism thought of as free praxis. Thus '*praxis*, as the *praxis* of an organism which reproduces its life by reorganising the environment, is man – man making himself in remaking himself'.[19] Ross Fitzgerald argues that need statements 'are intelligible only against a background of assumed ends, goals or purposes'.[20] The connection between needs and goals provides labour, or praxis as labour, with meaning. Sartre argues that the meaning of labour is provided by an end. Need is the revelation of an end, namely, the restoration of the organism to a condition of wholeness. The individual defines the means to that end according to what is needed. Thus, 'the hunter or fisherman *lies in wait*; the food-gatherer *searches*'.[21] In other words, given by the end, praxis comes from and is in itself an expression of the end. Praxis is the end in itself expressing itself. Sartre is also arguing that human beings totalise their environment through praxis as labour which is to say that the environment is controlled and organised with future goals in mind.

A question that arises is, are all ends predicated in the light of certain needs? If there are ends that are not predicated upon certain needs then there will be occasions when praxis will not stem from need. However, it would be hard to understand how anything could count as an end, or a goal, if it was not also an expression of a need. Sartre argues that,

> just as according to Kant the dove thinks it would fly more easily without the air which supports it, so it is often thought that the act would be purer – and its end more rigorous – without its dependence, direct or indirect, [upon] the organism and its needs. But exactly the opposite is the case. There would be no acts without ends (at least in the present state of organisms and things) – not even any dream of acting. The most abstract, autonomous end ultimately derives its content and its urgency from needs. It would vanish along with them, and its autonomy would vanish with it.[22]

So it is that according to Sartre all ends and thus all praxis stems from human need and the purpose of praxis is contained within praxis itself. I pick up a pen and I start to write. The purpose of the activity is contained within the activity. So it is that needs are indicators of values in so far as they identify a lack that is to be overcome. It is praxis that reveals that the thing indicated really is a value and it is praxis that realises the value.

Sartre argues that need 'is the organism itself, living itself in the future, through present disorders, as its own possibility and, consequently, as the

---

[18] Ibid., p. 85.
[19] Ibid., p. 330.
[20] Ross Fitzgerald, 1977, p. 197.
[21] CDR I, p. 90.
[22] CDR II, p. 390.

possibility of its own impossibility'.²³ The connection with the future end is significant in that it is a connection that makes the negative intelligible. Negation always presupposes something that is. Sartre writes that, 'The only possible use for the order of negation is to distinguish one direction from an other.'²⁴ Praxis is, therefore, a movement. Consequently, the negation of a negation indicates the direction of a process rather than simply the mutual elimination of opposing forces.

Therefore, in the process that Sartre is describing, the negation of the negation involves a 'totality being transcended towards a totalising end'.²⁵ Totalisation can thus be regarded as the activity that transforms a number of different parts into an entirety which serves as the goal of the activity. Praxis is, therefore, like 'project' in *Being and Nothingness*. It is directed towards a goal which it seeks to attain by using matter and bestowing upon it, from its own perspective at least, a sense of unity.²⁶ It is in that context that a positive is pursued. In other contexts the negation of a negation could simply produce a new negation or, alternatively, a return to the starting point. In other words, what is at stake is not the operation of a mathematical law which states that two minuses make a plus. For all that the negation of the negation produces a positive, in so far as the attainment of a goal is a positive, it does so under certain conditions and in a certain way. In this case the negation of the negation is a movement into the future. For Sartre, therefore, the production of a positive is a consequence of the process of praxis which is a process of transcendence. In *Hope Now* Sartre observes that 'Human action is transcendent – it always aims at a future object from the present in which we conceive of the action and try to realize it. It situates its end, its realization, in the future, and hope is in the way man acts, in the very fact of positing an end as having to be realized.'²⁷ It is, therefore, by

---

23 CDR I, p. 83.
24 Ibid., p. 84.
25 Ibid., p. 90.
26 The similarity of praxis to project has been commented upon by Maurice Cranston who says that praxis is 'more or less identical with the existentialist notion of the project' (Cranston, 1973, p. 100) and by Mohammed Valady who notes that 'The role of praxis in the *Critique*, is . . . comparable to that of consciousness or free project in *Being and Nothingness*'. (Valady, 1988, p. 97)
27 *Hope Now*, p. 53. *Hope Now* is the collected edition of the interviews that Sartre conducted with Benny Levy. They were first published in *Le Nouvel Observateur* on 10, 17, and 24 March 1980 and subsequently *Dissent* obtained the copyright and a translated edition by Adrienne Foulk appeared in *Dissent*, vol. 27, no. 4, Fall, 1980, pp. 397–422. To the chagrin of *Dissent*, *Telos* no. 44, Summer, 1980, pp. 155–81 published an unauthorised translation. Benny Lévy, or Benni Lévi, formerly known as Pierre Victor, is an Egyptian Jew who, when Sartre became blind, was employed as Sartre's secretary. The result of their collaboration was the transcription of a collection of taped conversations into 800 pages of text. This is the book, *Pouvoir et Liberté*, which Sartre discusses in an interview with Leo Fretz to which reference is made later in this chapter. *Hope Now* is the only portion of those conversations to be published. In *Adieux. A Farewell to Sartre*, Simone de Beauvoir reports that she was 'horrified' (1984, p. 119) with these conversations and attributed Sartre's

being a transcending movement that praxis is a totalising activity. In fact Sartre thought that praxis had two aspects, immanence and transcendence, what is and what is to be. In his *Notebooks for an Ethics* he writes of 'the indistinction of immanence and transcendence' and of transcendence as a negation by writing that a human being is a being for whom 'transcendence *is not* but has to be'.[28] The notion of praxis as a transcending movement, the indistinction of immanence and transcendence and transcendence as a necessary negation for human beings are ideas that will have a central part to play in this work.

Thomas Flynn claims that 'Sartre credits Marx with demonstrating that proletarian praxis is a negation of negation.'[29] This is because Sartre conceives of the group as arising from a negation of what he calls the practico-inert. The practico-inert is Sartre's term for the material conditions on which praxis must work in order to satisfy needs and which exist as a consequence of the past praxes of both individuals and groups. These material conditions are said to include aspects of the non-human environment and aspects of the human environment such as social structures, traditions, forms of communication and institutions. Thus class, exploitation and other such negative manifestations of the practico-inert are negated by the group. This negation of a negation is, therefore, an expression or an example of proletarian need. In chapter four there will be an examination of how praxis, stemming from need, can create a negation and then negate it in order to satisfy that need.

The practico-inert realm can prove to be a hindrance to praxis in so far as it sets limits or parameters within which praxis must work. Yet despite those limits Sartre stipulates that praxis itself is essentially free. This has implications for the relationship between cause, motive and effect which will be examined in chapter four. Praxis has to be able to institute change, work on matter and transcend that matter, perform a function in its own way, even go wrong. The insistence on freedom enables Sartre to contrast his dialectic with that of Marxism so that for Sartre the individual is not the passive victim of dialectical processes over which he has no control. A free, creative, praxis can account for

---

'passion for drinking' (1984, p. 118) to his own dissatisfaction with them. Thomas Busch reports that, 'The publication of the interviews finalized a break between, on the one side, Levy and Arlette Elkaïm (Sartre's adopted daughter), and on the other, Simone de Beauvoir and the *Les Temps modernes* group. The latter considered that Sartre was an old man who was being victimized into betraying the powerful edifice of the work of a lifetime'. (Busch, 1990, p. 98) Simone de Beauvoir relates that Benny Lévy/Benni Lévi/Pierre Victor 'was supported by Arlette, who knew nothing whatsoever about Sartre's philosophical works and who sympathized with Victor's new tendencies – they were learning Hebrew together'. (1984, p. 120) In his introduction to *Hope Now*, Ronald Aronson argues that Sartre was not as mentally feeble as Simone de Beauvoir claims. In this judgement, Aronson follows Busch who notes that Sartre may well have been genuinely involved in the transformation of his ideas arguing that, 'It was Sartre, ever open to the new, who by transforming his thought until the end demonstrated in a more powerful way than his books ever did the capacity of a human being to learn and grow, to transform'. (Busch, 1990, p. 100) It was Arlette Elkaïm-Sartre who edited the second volume of the *Critique*.

[28] NE, p. 356.

the new. While the individual's situation influences him and informs his possibilities it is the individual who gives his situation a meaning by making choices. Praxis freely recognises certain exigencies and freely responds to them. On Sartre's account, praxis is a 'free temporalisation and *effective* reorganisation of the practical field in relation to aims discovered and posited in the course of *praxis* itself'.[30] Praxis is 'a free productive dialectic'[31] and this is one way in which Sartre's dialectic is more open than that of Marx. Sartre speaks of praxis as 'the free, re-organising transcendence of particular conditionings'.[32] He points out that the word free throughout the *Critique* 'refers to the dialectical development of an individual *praxis*, born of need and transcending material conditions towards a definite objective'.[33] Sartre explains that, 'I have called this *praxis free* for the simple reason that, in a given set of circumstances, on the basis of a given need or danger, it creates its own law, in the absolute unity of the project (as a mediation between the given, past objectivity and the objectification which is to be produced).'[34] The note in parentheses and the earlier references to particular conditionings, material conditions and need indicates the conditions circumscribing the freedom of praxis and these conditions will be explored in more detail as this work proceeds. There is, however, a further condition that relates to the freedom of praxis. Praxis stems from needs and needs can be regarded as indicators of values. Therefore, although praxis is free, it is a free activity that is constantly seeking and confirming as a value that which has been indicated as a value.

Where the practico-inert is certainly a hindrance to praxis it is because praxis has sought to satisfy needs in a world in which the means to that satisfaction are scarce. Thus where the needs that human beings have cannot readily be satisfied due to scarcity, praxis has produced hindering or even alienating practico-inert structures. The means by which this happens will soon become apparent. The hindrances of the practico-inert would not be so wide-ranging or influential if scarcity was only a temporary or partial phenomenon. According to Sartre, it isn't. Scarcity is all-pervasive. However, even if it was not all-pervasive scarcity would still be a phenomenon that communitarians should take seriously if they hope to provide an adequate account of community. It is a phenomenon that impacts upon individual identity, it gives rise to certain relationships between people in terms not only of the likelihood of conflict but also in terms of the possibility of co-operation and it affects the way that people view the world and in particular the meanings that they give to social goods.

---

29 Thomas Flynn, 1984, p. 88.
30 CDR I, p. 247.
31 Ibid., p. 235.
32 Ibid., p. 160.
33 Ibid., p. 422.
34 CDR I, p. 549.

Sartre asserts that 'the whole of human development, at least up to now, has been a bitter struggle against *scarcity*'.[35] In the interview referred to earlier that he gave in 1975, he argues that 'scarcity is a phenomenon of existence'.[36] In fact, by scarcity, what Sartre also means is a kind of social atmosphere, or climate, which Sartre calls a 'milieu', within which people as individuals or as groups operate in such a way that their actions can and usually do conflict with each other. This atmosphere has created the conditions whereby history has developed in the way that it has, the argument being that it has made us what we are. It is scarcity that has produced the fundamental structures of society, such as society's institutions. This is not because scarcity is a real force and that it has of itself produced those structures but because those structures were produced 'in a *milieu of scarcity* by men whose *praxis* interiorises this scarcity even when they try to transcend it'.[37] Therefore, it is not the practico-inert as such that is alienating, even in unalienating societies people might have to communicate with each other in various ways, but the practico-inert as mediated by scarcity that turns people into competitors. Sartre maintains that others are a threat in so far as they consume the goods that the individual needs. Their praxis is a threat to the individual as the individual is to them. Furthermore, in as much as he is a threat to others who in their turn become a threat to him, he becomes a threat to himself. Joseph Catalano presents the threat that we pose to ourselves in a different way by arguing that 'as a potentially starving and homeless person, I am a threat to my fellow human beings. I am even a threat to myself, because I never know what I might do because of scarcity. I thus always face myself as *other*; that is, as nonhuman'.[38] Therefore, 'scarcity must be seen as that which makes us into *these* particular individuals producing this particular History and defining *ourselves* as men'.[39]

It is not important, for Sartre, to deliberate on how the milieu of scarcity came into being. What is important is that this milieu did come into being and has affected us ever since. However, he does argue that,

> Need is natural . . . Scarcity is social to the extent that the desired object is scarce for a given society. But strictly speaking, scarcity is not social. Society comes after scarcity. The latter is an original phenomenon of the relation between man and Nature. Nature does not sufficiently contain the objects that man demands in order that man's life should not include either work, which is struggle against scarcity, or combat.[40]

The Hobbesian tone is clear. Scarcity comes before society. Interpreting Sartre

---
35 Ibid., 123.
36 Interview, May 1975, in Schilpp (ed.), 1981, p. 31.
37 CDR1, p. 127.
38 Joseph Catalano, 1986, p. 111.
39 CDR I, pp. 123–24.
40 Interview, May 1975, in Schilpp (ed.), 1981, pp. 31–32.

correctly, Gila Hayim explains that, 'scarcity is a basic human relation to nature . . . However, [Sartre] feels that beyond a primary dependence on nature, additional and new forms of scarcity have been unnecessarily produced'.[41] Hazel Barnes agrees saying that the field of scarcity 'which at first was simply there . . . has from the beginning of history been organized and to some extent deliberately perpetuated'.[42] It is not clear in what sense it can be said that scarcity was 'simply there'. Until it was discovered, Pluto was 'simply there'. It is not clear that scarcity was simply there in that sense. As Anthony Waters says, 'scarcity does not have a reality independent of praxis'.[43] Scarcity emerges as a result of praxis attempting to satisfy need. Now people have turned scarcity into a phenomenon of social existence. Malatesta writes of the 'artificial scarcity of goods' which he says is a characteristic of the capitalist system.[44] Kropotkin explains that the owners of capital constantly reduce output by restraining production, by dumping food into the sea, by forbidding miners to work more than three days a week 'because, forsooth, the price of coal must be kept up!'[45] Therefore, scarcity, which was originally a relation between man and nature, has become a relation between man and man. So it is that now scarcity is produced. It is, says Sartre, a value 'transmitted to matter through men and returning to men through matter'.[46] The medium for that transmission remains praxis. In other words, scarcity, in one or another of its many guises, recognised as such through praxis, gave rise through praxis to certain forms and terms of association and those in turn, through praxis, can sustain scarcity. Conjecturally, it can be said that scarcity and forms and terms of association now have a dialectical relationship with each other.

However, without compromising anything that has been said, for Sartre scarcity does not simply refer to a shortage of material goods. Hazel Barnes explains that, 'When he speaks of scarcity, Sartre means both the lack of the most immediate things which enable men to stay alive and the lack of those other things which are necessary to make people's lives satisfying once they have got beyond the problem of mere subsistence'.[47] Certainly for much of the time scarcity refers to the idea that there are not enough goods to go round, or that there are too many people competing for the goods that are available. At other times it is people themselves, as consumers and especially in the second volume of the *Critique*, as workers, who are scarce. Sartre even talks of a scarcity of time and of understanding in the second volume of the *Critique* and of understanding again in the interview, already mentioned, that he gave in 1975

---

[41] Gila Hayim, 1980, p. 78.
[42] Hazel Barnes, 'Sartre as Materialist', in Schilpp (ed.), 1981, p. 675. See also Catalano, 1986, p. 255.
[43] Anthony Waters, 1976, p. 99.
[44] Malatesta, in Vernon Richards (ed.), 1965, p. 93.
[45] Kropotkin, 1995, pp. 22–23.
[46] CDR I, p. 123.
[47] Barnes, 'Introduction' to *The Problem of Method*, 1963, p. xvi.

where he says that, 'Even here, among ourselves, there is scarcity in our conversation: scarcity of ideas, scarcity of understanding. I may not understand your questions or may answer them badly – that, too, is scarcity'.[48] Therefore, scarcity of means may be most obvious but Sartre argues that there is a 'triple *scarcity*: scarcity of time, scarcity of means, scarcity of knowledge. They are *grounded* upon a more *fundamental* scarcity, which conditions and *grounds* the conflict . . . (this scarcity, variable in nature, concerns the material conditions of their existence)'.[49]

Moreover, it is not simply scarcity itself that is significant but also the fear of scarcity. This fear reflects Hobbes's view concerning war and violence. As Hobbes points out, the condition of war does not necessarily consist of actual fighting but the awareness of its possibility. Thus, 'the nature of War, consisteth not in actual fighting; but in the known disposition thereto, during all the time there is no assurance to the contrary'.[50] Similarly for Sartre, scarcity refers not only to the absence of goods but also to the fear of such absences.

It seems that there will always be scarcity of one sort or another. Buchanan argues that it is not clear that scarcity in all its forms can be overcome entirely no matter what social arrangements are in place. For example, medical research can always use more money.[51] David Gauthier also argues that scarcity is an inescapable feature of human life. Even if material scarcity could be overcome, scarcity in respect of opportunities for self-realisation would remain. Gauthier argues that, 'Scarcity in the form of human fulfilment seems a fixed feature of human life. Each of us can realize in herself only one of the many possible lives that together make up human flourishing.'[52] Certain forms of scarcity, therefore, cannot be overcome. However, it may be possible to overcome other sorts of scarcity, those that are phenomena of social existence. There is, as Chiodi has noted, a vagueness in Sartre's thinking on this issue.[53] What can be said is that if it is not scarcity itself that can be overcome, it is certainly the effects of scarcity, of at least the sort that has become a social phenomenon, that may be overcome under certain social conditions.[54] Moreover, it is not impossible that, under certain social conditions, some of the effects of even those sorts of scarcity that are inevitable might also be overcome.

---

[48] Interview, May 1975, in Schilpp (ed.), 1981, p. 30.
[49] CDR II, p. 9.
[50] *Leviathan*, chpt. 13, p. 71.
[51] Buchanan, 1982, p. 157.
[52] David Gauthier, 1986, p. 334.
[53] Chiodi, 1978, pp. 100–101.
[54] In the 1975 interview recorded in Schilpp (ed.), 1981, Dr. Michel Rybalka asks Sartre, 'do you consider the notion of scarcity to be ontological?' Sartre replies, 'No, nor is it anthropological. If you like it, appears as soon as there is animal life'. (Schilpp ed., 1981, p. 13) Later Sartre argues that it 'is impossible to suppress it without changing the conditions of existence'. (Schilpp (ed.), 1981, p. 30)

Earlier it was noted that praxis interiorises scarcity. Praxis interiorises scarcity in that, where it occurs at all, it stems from human need. In a milieu of scarcity that which is needed is scarce, or feared so to be. It is in the recognition of this that praxis interiorises scarcity. Moreover, by making good the absence with something that is scarce, or feared so to be, praxis creates scarcity or the fear of scarcity. In other words, praxis by its very action creates that which it is determined to eliminate and in so doing creates the conditions for certain sorts of human associations. This explains why people are a threat to each other. Praxis stemming from need simply creates need. Every effort to transcend scarcity can succeed only by creating scarcity. As Catalano comments, 'I may wish only to buy food, be employed, buy a house or have a friend, and I find that I have taken something from someone else. Even if I buy a house that no-one else wants, I have a home amid the homeless.'[55] In other words, everything that everyone has is in a sense taken from someone else, or at least denied to them.

Thus scarcity is interiorised. This interiorisation provokes a further praxis as a re-exteriorisation and that praxis itself produces scarcity which affects everyone and which is in turn, in an atmosphere of antagonism, re-interiorised. This, as it turns out, is a continuous process. Therefore, we encounter not only movement into the future but also circularity. Ultimately, the goal of praxis is the continuation of life. This can occur only as a result of the integration of the interior with the exterior and that integration can occur only through praxis. The organism is incapable of spontaneously reproducing its own life and praxis originates in this fact. Thus the interiorisation of scarcity is re-exteriorised as scarcity which affects everyone and which is in turn, in an atmosphere of antagonism, re-interiorised. The point here is that praxis does not simply create scarcity for others it also creates scarcity for oneself. Thus one's activity is turned against one and returns through the social milieu.

The important thing about scarcity, therefore, is not so much it being an objective fact, it may or may not be for different people at different times, but the fact that it is lived and interiorised. Inhumanity does not arise from any fixed human nature; it arises from interiorised scarcity. As Aronson explains, 'Scarcity need not even be directly involved for the Other to become a terrifying enemy. In a general environment of scarcity there is always someone who does not have enough, someone who is treated as, and therefore becomes, an antiman.'[56] Furthermore, according to Sartre, for scarcity to have its terrible effect direct violence need not be necessary, 'It merely means that the relations of production are established and pursued in a climate of fear and mutual distrust by individuals who are always ready to believe that the Other is an anti-human member of an alien species.'[57]

---

[55] Catalano, 1986, p. 111.
[56] Aronson, 1980, p. 253.
[57] CDR I, p. 149.

It has been argued that scarcity does not have the explanatory force that is attributed to it by Sartre, that relative abundance generates more praxis than scarcity.[58] However, it is important to notice that it is not scarcity itself that motivates praxis. Praxis stems from need. Therefore, the true motivation is praxis's own understanding of the existence of a lack. It is true that Sartre's explanation of the force of scarcity differs from the usual Marxist understandings. Sartre admits that scarcity is not a Marxist idea when he says that, 'It is not a Marxist thought. Marx did not think that primitive man or feudal man lived under the rule of scarcity. He believed that they did not know how to use resources, but not that they were living in scarcity.'[59] For Marx, scarcity is the result of exploitation rather than a characteristic of nature. Alienation is the outcome of that exploitation. Marxist critics of Sartre point out that modes of production produce conflict because they create a surplus, not scarcity.[60] This surplus is appropriated by the ruling class. Therefore, there is an unjust distribution of surplus goods, people are exploited, and from that comes alienation. Sartre's counter argument is that exploitation is the outcome of alienating conditions, the most pervasive of which is scarcity. This argument is explored in more detail in chapter four.

In fact, Sartre's concept of scarcity does not deny the exploitative characteristic of class society. He is concerned to know how such a characteristic originated and is sustained. For example, Mark Poster argues that Sartre's concept of scarcity is directed at 'a different level, one concerning the relation of the whole society to nature'.[61] Moreover, unlike classical economic theorists, Sartre does not posit an external scarcity which requires the regulation of capitalism. Scarcity is contingent upon praxis. We have already seen that scarcity is not a simple natural fact but a human project. Thus 'scarcity is prevalent in human history only because human beings have decided to totalise the social field as one in which there is not enough'.[62] Looked at in this way a further criticism of Sartre's concept of scarcity, that it is a useful weapon in the ideological armoury of liberalism, is no longer tenable. The criticism is that the assumption of a world of scarce goods legitimates classical economic theory's view that since the market is the best mechanism for the distribution of such goods, competition is justified. This criticism is no longer tenable because on Sartre's account scarcity is not something that is somehow out there but it is instead the result of human agency, including competition. Furthermore, Sartre's critics on this matter have, by and large, concentrated on Volume 1 of the *Critique* and have, therefore, assumed that scarcity refers to the absence of material goods only whereas it refers also to time, people, both producers and consumers,

---

[58] See, for example, Stack, 1977, p. 112.
[59] Interview, May 1975, Schilpp (ed.), 1981, p. 30.
[60] See, for example, Aron, 1975, p. 36.
[61] Mark Poster, 1979, p. 54.
[62] Ibid., p. 55.

and knowledge. Sartre maintains that conflict comes from all of these scarcities. Sartre's critics also neglect to mention that it is not simply scarcity itself but the fear of scarcity, that is, the milieu of scarcity, that affects everyone, even those who are not, at this time, suffering from scarcity.

However, it is not necessary to agree with Sartre in ascribing to scarcity the force that he ascribes. Neither do other people have to be as antagonistically competitive as Sartre maintains. All that is necessary is to acknowledge that people have needs which have to be satisfied in a world that is already materially and socially constituted, that is, with the practico-inert in place and which will, therefore, present hindrances not least because people are, on occasion, less co-operative than they might be and where there is evidence of different sorts of scarcity. In short, all that is necessary is an acknowledgement of something akin to David Hume's circumstances of justice, those being scarce resources and limited benevolence. As Aronson says, 'Scarcity appears as one decisive factor of a matrix which contains, in the most intimate interconnection, other decisive factors.'[63] The other factors in the matrix, according to Aronson, include co-operative praxis, the distribution of social goods and particularly the criteria that are used to make decisions about that distribution, and the level of the production of goods for meeting needs and combating scarcity. We can admit that Sartre's claims are too strong without damaging his argument or invalidating the conceptual tools that he has produced.

Paradoxically, the milieu of scarcity that can serve to create, first, antagonistically competitive relationships between people can, second, also serve to bring them together in a co-operative effort. Regarding the first, Sartre explains that,

> The negative unity of scarcity, which is interiorised in the reification of reciprocity, is re-exteriorised for us all in the unity of the world as the common locus of our antagonisms; and we will re-interiorise this unity in turn, in a new negative unity. We are united by the fact that we all live in a world which is determined by scarcity.[64]

Scarcity unites people at one level. Therefore, praxis to overcome scarcity unites people at one level, that is, everyone is engaged in such praxis. From this comes the argument that 'Scarcity ... is the basis of the possibility of human history.'[65] That history has been viewed in terms of antagonistic competition which in some way, at some time, involves everyone. However, there is an alternative. Thus regarding the second, Thomas Baldwin notes that because scarcity ensures that human beings cannot afford to neglect each other, 'it implies that they must co-exist either as competitors or as co-operators'.[66] In other words, given

---

[63] Aronson, 1973, p. 73.
[64] CDR I, p. 136.
[65] Ibid., p. 125.
[66] Thomas Baldwin, 1993, p. 211.

that there is scarcity which affects everyone, something must be done. We could compete but then again we could co-operate. If competition looks too much like a Hobbesian state of nature then co-operation would seem to be the rationally self-interested option. In any event, for one reason or another, praxis will realise certain dispositions, to be co-operative or to be competitive.

Praxis does not only realise certain dispositions it also has a consciousness-shaping effect. Indeed, only praxis is constitutive of social consciousness. It might be thought that in arguing that the development of social consciousness is possible only on the basis of praxis, Sartre is following Marx's view that, 'It is not the consciousness of men that determines their being, but, on the contrary, their social being that determines their consciousness.'[67] However, the dialectical nature of praxis means that Sartre's argument develops in a way that is significantly different from that of Marx. The social consciousness that arises from the social being, that is, the praxis of man, in turn informs that praxis. This observation is underpinned by two important points. First, there is, as we have seen, an epistemic dimension to praxis. Praxis is 'the measure of man and the foundation of truth'.[68] This dimension involves learning by doing or by being engaged.[69] The understanding is a doing. This is certainly Sartre's view since he argues that, '*Comprehension* is simply the translucidity of *praxis* to itself, whether it produces its own elucidation in constituting itself, or recognises itself in the *praxis* of another. In either case, the comprehension of the act is effected by the (produced or reproduced) act.'[70] An important point to note is that the understanding comes about through the process of praxis itself. Sartre notes that, 'Knowing is a moment of praxis.'[71] That, I suspect, is the real meaning of the eleventh of Marx's *Theses on Feuerbach*. The question is, when does that moment occur. Sartre argues that, '*Praxis* . . . is a passage from objective to objective through internalization.'[72] Pausing only to note that in her translation of *The Problem of Method* Barnes has translated 'intériorisation' as 'internalization', the significant point is that the understanding that accompanies praxis involves interiorisation and it is the interiorisation that produces a new social consciousness, hence a new praxis and so on. There is, therefore, a dialectical process which is circular in nature.

It might be assumed that the process of circularity affects praxis because praxis occurs in a milieu of scarcity. However, the point is that circularity is inherent in praxis itself. Circularity is inherent in praxis because praxis involves the interiorisation of the results of previous praxes, both of oneself and others.

---

67 Marx, Preface to *A Critique of Political Economy*, in McLellan, 1977, p. 389.
68 CDR I, p. 801.
69 Dominick La Capra says, 'Human praxis is itself a unifying, totalizing, dialectical movement of thought and action, which provides a basis for theoretical knowledge in the existential comprehension of lived, concrete experience'. (La Capra, 1979, p. 15)
70 CDR I, p. 74.
71 *The Problem of Method*, p. 92.
72 Ibid., p. 97.

This then leads to a re-exteriorisation. In this way, as has been said, praxis both interiorises and creates scarcity. This introduces the second important point which is that praxis has a social dimension. It affects and has already been affected by the praxis of others. The praxis of one individual connects with the praxis of others. Praxis inscribes itself on the material world and succeeding praxes then have to cope with the conditions created by the initial praxis. We create exteriority. Through praxis we interiorise that which is exterior to us and then we re-exteriorise it as our product.

It is through the process of interiorisation and re-exteriorisation that praxis produces a practico-inert field that fulfils its goals but imposes itself on further praxis as an exterior demand. Praxis stems from human need. Yet it can be hindered in its attempts to meet this need because it has to contend with the results of the past praxes both of oneself and of others. These previous praxes, in their attempts to satisfy needs, have left their mark on the practico-inert. For this reason, as Stack notes, 'man finds himself in a world which is already constituted – practically, socially, institutionally and historically – by the prior praxis of men'.[73] Moreover, in working on the practico-inert in whatever guise it encounters it, current praxis will produce the practico-inert in another guise, thus producing a potential hindrance to future praxis. Today's praxis creates new demands which set the terms of tomorrow's praxis. The new praxis has to take account of those material results. In these ways we are moulded by the very structures such as formal education, law, organised religion and the media, that we freely invent.

Aronson explains that, 'We are governed by matter to the extent that our praxis transforms it into worked matter – the practico-inert – to meet our needs.'[74] Therefore, starting with an original relationship with nature which, whatever else might be said about it, can be understood as praxis attempting to satisfy need, certain forms and certain terms of association arise. These forms and terms of association have an effect on subsequent praxes and are thus constitutive of identities. These subsequent praxes are themselves constitutive of forms and terms of association and so on, though, since praxis is free, not necessarily unchangingly. This means that, although we can be more specific about the process by which it happens, communities partly constitute individuals, just as communitarians claim. However, it also means that individuals partly constitute communities. The 'partly' acknowledges the existence of other constituting factors that affect individuals and communities such as, respectively, genetic make-up and climatic conditions. It will be seen that what is true of the individual is also, in this case, true of groups. Consequently, hindrances, which are imposed on praxis by the practico-inert field that it creates, involves a change in the group's praxis and, therefore, in the group itself. To a large extent the

---

[73] Stack, 1977, p. 66.
[74] Aronson, 1987, p. 187.

second volume of the *Critique* details this process in connection with the Bolshevik revolution, whereby the Bolsheviks were changed by the very changes that they themselves brought about in society. The point is that we interiorise the practices that we ourselves have generated. In turn these practices are re-exteriorised. In this way we shape our forms and terms of association and they also shape us. Thus we arrive at Sartre's argument which is that 'man is "mediated" by things to the same extent as things are "mediated" by man. This truth must be born in mind in its entirety if we are to develop all its consequences. This is what is called dialectical *circularity*'.[75] In chapter four it will become clear that there is another dimension to circularity. There it will be seen that the individual, on the basis of needs that are, at least in part, defined by the society in which that individual lives, identifies the resources, also in part defined by that society, that are required for satisfying those needs. These resources will in turn contribute to the definition of the individual by identifying him as an individual of a certain type with a certain place in society. Thus, for Sartre, the dialectic is the logic of praxis. What we have, says Aronson, is 'the specific praxis of specific individuals incarnating specific totalities in their action and being redefined by the specific results of their prior praxis'.[76] In fact there are two levels of the dialectical at work. In its immediacy, praxis is working towards an end. At this level of operation there is a dialectical process. It is this dialectical characteristic of praxis that provides the key to the understanding of the nature of associating and hence of forms and terms of association. At the level of reflection, as will be seen, Sartre will claim that the level of operation can be understood only dialectically.

It has to be said that Sartre's view of the nature and extent of freedom has changed considerably since the writing of *Being and Nothingness*. Sartre himself acknowledges as much when he says in an interview that, 'The other day, I re-read a prefatory note of mine to a collection of these plays – *Les Mouches*, *Huis Clos* and others – and was truly scandalized. I had written: "Whatever the circumstances, and wherever the site, a man is always free to be a traitor or not . . . ." When I read this, I said to myself: it's incredible, I actually believed that!'[77] The new element in Sartre's thinking is interiorisation. As Sartre explains, 'The individual interiorizes his social determinations: he interiorizes the relations of production, the family of his childhood, the historical past, the contemporary institutions, and he then re-exteriorizes these in acts and options which necessarily refer us back to them. None of this existed in L'Etre et Le Neant.'[78] 'Interiorise' and 're-exteriorise' are key ideas and enable Sartre to argue that the product of praxis does not only impose itself on further praxes, it

---

[75] CDR I, p. 79.
[76] Aronson, 1987, p. 226.
[77] Sartre, 'The Itinerary of a Thought', in *Beyond Existentialism and Marxism*, 1974, pp. 33–34. First published as an interview in *New Left Review*, no. 58, November–December, 1969.
[78] Ibid., p. 35.

is also interiorised by the individual, making him, as Sartre says, 'the product of his own product,'[79] and yet still retain the notion of a free, transcending, praxis. Sartre is clear that this is not a mechanical process. It does not deny the existence of individual freedom for in doing what he does the individual is making choices concerning how to do that thing.

During the course of this chapter it has emerged that praxis has a variety of characteristics or components. On the basis of these characteristics or components it is possible to posit a normative notion of praxis. David Crocker endorses this view of praxis and draws a distinction between descriptive and normative notions of praxis. He argues that Marx, for example, in holding that man is naturally a productive being and survives by producing, had a descriptive notion of praxis. Thus, 'This conception of *praxis* is a blend of Aristotle's notion of labour and making, for the stress is both on biological maintenance and on instrumental making of a separate product.'[80] For Aristotle himself the normative concept of praxis signifies the realm in which the good life is to be lived, namely the realm of political activity. However, in the *Critique* praxis also involves working directly on the non-human environment to produce the things that are needed and there is, therefore, a different sense in which it can be said that praxis is normative.

Sartre does not explicitly examine the normative nature of praxis. Nevertheless, in the *Critique* it can be seen that praxis makes certain recommendations. The normative notion of praxis, on Crocker's account, is one that views praxis as an activity that realises some human dispositions at the expense of others. It therefore involves an evaluation of which human dispositions are best and the realisation of those dispositions in activity.[81]

As has already been stipulated, praxis is free but it is constantly seeking that which is perceived to be of value. Ultimately, that which is perceived to be of value is human fulfilment itself. Again as has already been noted, if needs remain unsatisfied one is handicapped in pursuing one's vision of the good. Thus the satisfaction of needs is, according to Sartre, an aspect of human fulfilment. Therefore, praxis is normative because it is concerned with fulfilment and in particular with the acts and the qualities of being that are required if fulfilment is to be achieved. Sartre defines praxis as 'an organising project which transcends material conditions towards an end and inscribes itself, through labour, in organic matter as a rearrangement of the practical field and a reunification of means in the light of the end'.[82] It is the identification of the end and the nature of the movement towards that end that reveals that praxis is normative. In order to be satisfying of needs and thus transcending, praxis involves certain ways of acting which are selected on the basis of its own mode of comprehension or intelligibility which, in so far as it involves discerning the best means given existing circumstances and the end which is given in praxis, includes rationality.

---

[79] CDR I, p. 103.
[80] David Crocker, 1983, p. 52.
[81] Ibid., p. 57.

I have indicated that praxis also realises certain dispositions and, as will become clear, in its attempt to satisfy needs certain dispositions, which will themselves inform those acts, will emerge as being preferred dispositions. Thus praxis identifies certain preferred ways of being. Indeed, it is through praxis that one can make the connection between needs and moral agency.

In a demonstration of circularity in action, Sartre concludes Volume 2 of the *Critique* by returning to the very issue with which he began Book I of Volume 1, an investigation of need. At the end of the second volume of the *Critique* Sartre indicates that the basis of all practico-inert structures are human needs. Thus, 'neither the practico-inert, nor oppression, nor exploitation, nor this particular alienation would be possible if the huge, ponderous socio-economic machine were not sustained, conditioned and set in motion by needs'.[83] Sartre further indicates that the effects of the practico-inert and in particular the circularity of practico-inert and praxis might be controlled, at least to some extent, so that they can be used for the fulfilment of human needs, conceived of as a 'non-transcendable goal'[84] in that there is no further goal and that it is ultimately the aim of all praxis.

Thomas Anderson describes how the idea that the demands of the practico-inert appear as requirements because they arise from human needs is developed by Sartre in a lecture delivered by Sartre to the Instituto Gramsci in Rome on 23 May 1964.[85] Just as the demands of the practico-inert appear as such because they arise from human needs which insist on being satisfied, so too with moral norms which we experience as obligatory because of our needs. Anderson records that Sartre's argument is that, 'Needs *demanding* to be satisfied cause their goal, the fulfilled human organism, to be experienced as our *normative future*, the end that *has to be obtained*.'[86] For Sartre, every moral system possesses an unconditional normative character because it is grounded in the needs of human beings. Since Sartre's notion of human fulfilment is rooted in the satisfaction of needs and since it is through praxis that needs are satisfied then the normative notion of praxis, in providing an account of certain necessary actions and dispositions, requires us to be people of a certain kind, acting in a certain way, if human fulfilment is to be possible. It is in this sense that morality is the product of praxis. Of course, precisely the same can be said of immorality.[87]

It might be thought that an ethic based on need will inevitably be an ethic based on self-interest. This is a charge that is levelled at Hobbes's contract theory. There are four points to make by way of a reply. The first point is that, as has been seen, a normative notion of praxis enjoins us to be people of a

---

82   CDR I, p. 734 and Glossary of CDR II, p. 458.
83   CDR II, p. 388.
84   Ibid., p. 389.
85   This refers to a hand-written lecture recently made available to the Bibliotheque Nationale, Paris and entitled by the Bibliotheque Nationale, 'Conference a L'Institut Gramsci, Rome, 1964'.
86   Thomas Anderson, 1993, p. 120.
87   A Sartrean ethic is never going to be a deontological ethic.

certain sort, developing and practising the dispositions that are part of what human fulfilment means and which must be practised in order to pursue that goal. This will be examined in more detail in chapter six and then again in a different way in chapter seven. Second, self-interest is not to be confused with selfishness. There is no reason why the pursuit of the interests of the self has necessarily to preclude the interests of others. Moreover, the interests of others may be best served by first attending to the interests of the self. If someone is incapacitated then they must deal with that before they can be of assistance to anyone else. This leads to the third point which is that Sartre's focus on needs, going back to his *Notebooks*, emphasises the universality, or nonindividuality of needs. The door is open to the common pursuit of the satisfaction of needs that people have in common. In other words, the door is open to the development of a view of the kind of association that has in place those values and practices that make human fulfilment possible. This requires the outline of a normative theory of associations. In the context of this work such a theory must be based on a normative notion of praxis. This, in turn, leads to the fourth point which is that the common pursuit of the satisfaction of needs that people have in common can, in itself, be a source of satisfaction. As Malatesta explains, 'We hope that no one will want to ... start hair-splitting about egoism and altruism. We agree: we are all egoists, we all seek our own satisfaction. But the anarchist finds his greatest satisfaction in struggling for the good of all.'[88]

Praxis is, therefore, normative and dialectical in character. Sartre shows that social experience is dialectical. He argues that such experience can be understood only through a dialectical method of inquiry and through the application of dialectical reason and that, therefore, 'the dialectical method is indistinguishable from the dialectical movement'.[89] The method can, in fact, be derived from the movement. Sartre also argues that 'no one can discover the dialectic while remaining *external* to the object under consideration ... The dialectic reveals itself only to an observer situated in interiority, that is to say, to an investigator who lives his investigation'.[90] Sartre does supply empirical data but more than that he argues that it is experience itself that confirms the truth of the dialectic. Its evidence will be self-evidence. Therefore, 'The dialectic ... becomes a theoretical and practical method when action in the course of development begins to give an explanation of itself.'[91] His argument is largely successful. That it is not entirely successful is due to two, possibly related, reasons. The first reason is that he does not derive his dialectical method entirely from the dialectical movement of praxis alone. The method is derived in part from the distinction that Sartre draws between his own dialectic and that of Hegel, Marx and Marxists and which draws on the work of other theorists. It is

---

[88] Malatesta, in Vernon Richards, 1965, p. 23.
[89] CDR I, p. 36.
[90] Ibid., p. 38.
[91] Ibid.

also derived from the comparison between dialectical and analytical reason which, not unreasonably, turns the analytical into a moment of the dialectical but which, in so doing, leaves praxis behind due to Sartre's own view by which the analytical approach locates the investigator in exteriority. The distinction and the comparison made by Sartre are important. However, they should serve to demonstrate how the dialectical movement of praxis is indistinguishable from the dialectical method. The fact that they don't undermines the claim that the method can be derived from the movement. The second reason is that Volume 2 of the *Critique* is unfinished. This means that although there is a thorough portrayal of the dialectical movement of praxis the same cannot be said of the method. The result is that, on the basis of what Sartre has actually presented, we cannot be absolutely certain of what his dialectical method involves or how it may be applied.

However, there can be no doubt that what Sartre does have to say about his dialectical method, albeit with the use of sources other than praxis alone, is illuminating. The dialectical movement of praxis can be thought of as a singularised universal. As Stack says, 'It is singular insofar as it is manifested in particular circumstances, under particular conditions, and in the singular course of individual lives. It is universal in the sense that its particular expressions give rise to principles and laws of intelligibility which can be applied to similar phenomena'.[92] In an even more obviously Hegelian mode Sartre talks also of the 'concrete universal'.[93] This, for Sartre, is not a new idea. In his *Notebooks for an Ethics* he reflects on the notion of a concrete universal, arguing that 'In truth we have to choose the concrete universal' and 'In truth, one has to create the concrete universal.'[94] In *Existentialism and Humanism*, in connection with the dilemma facing the student, Sartre is adamant that Kantianism and Christianity cannot, of themselves, offer a solution to a moral dilemma because both are abstract. This idea is also to be found in his *Notebooks for an Ethics* where he argues that, 'There is no abstract ethics. There is only an ethics in a situation and therefore it is concrete.'[95] He also refers to the notion of 'a concrete ethics' by which he means 'a synthesis of the universal and the historical,'[96] and maintains that 'the dialectic is an attempt to introduce ethics into the concrete'.[97] Whatever use one might make of any or all of these normative

---

[92] Stack, 1977, p. 79.
[93] CDR II, pp. 40, 48. The singularised universal can be thought of in Hegelian terms as the concrete universal. The concrete universal is a term used in Hegelian philosophy to convey Hegel's view that thinking must be universal but not abstractly universal. Hegel refers to Rousseau's concept of the general will in an attempt to make his meaning clear. The laws of the state are universal in so far as they arise from the general will but since this will is the will of a particular community it is also concrete.
[94] NE, p. 7.
[95] Ibid., p. 17.
[96] Ibid., p. 7.
[97] Ibid., p. 167.

systems would depend, finally, on the choice made by the individual who is in the concrete situation. In fact, the choice is a choice of a way of life. Despite the reservations that may be voiced about *Existentialism and Humanism*, not least by Sartre himself, the search for intelligibility within the context of the concrete remains a key theme in Sartre's work. It should be noted that there can be degrees of concreteness and that which appears to be concrete in relation to a more abstract or partial perspective will itself be abstract in the context of a greater whole or more comprehensive totality. It will be seen that the concrete has primacy in the sense that one can abstract only from the concrete.

The emphasis on the concrete is reminiscent of Bakunin's writing on the limitations of science which, on Bakunin's account, are due to the fact that science cannot go outside of the abstract. Consequently, science is incapable of dealing with real and living individuals. According to Bakunin, science, 'concerns itself with individuals in general, but not with Peter or James'.[98] However, history is made by Peter and James, 'not by abstract individuals, but by acting, living and passing individuals'.[99] Elsewhere Bakunin compares French and German revolutionaries and comes to the conclusion that the latter could not 'outdo' the former because of the 'abstract method' by which German revolutionaries approached revolution. German revolutionaries 'proceeded not from life to thought but from thought to life. But anyone who takes abstract thought as his starting point will never make it to life for there is no road leading from metaphysics to life'.[100]

In fact, Sartre does employ the abstract. In the *Critique*, Sartre begins by presenting praxis as individual praxis operating on inert matter. Abdelkader Aoudjit explains that, 'He starts a la Hegel by what seems the most concrete but is in fact the most abstract, the individual praxis, and moves to the truly concrete, man within his social context.'[101] He is aware of Marx's objection to the 'Robinsonades'.[102] He knows, as noted above, that individuals are constitutive of social wholes in which they find themselves entangled. Sartre's defence is that he has deliberately chosen to begin his analysis at the outer limits of abstraction and to move from the abstract to the concrete level of analysis, from the individual to groups and society. Individual praxis is a logical, not historical, starting point for explanations. Sartre recognises, therefore, that the intelligibility of the concrete is partly dependent on the use of the abstract although, as will be seen, he overwhelmingly stresses the truth of the converse.

Sartre's dialectical method of inquiry may be thought of as Sartre's version of the holistic approach that we will see is attributed to communitarians. Indeed, Baldwin observes that in order to obtain the understandings that he seeks, 'Sartre

---

[98] Bakunin, 'On Science and Authority', in Arthur Lehning (ed.), 1974, pp. 160–65.
[99] Ibid.
[100] Bakunin, 1990, pp. 132–33.
[101] Abdelkader Aoudjit, 1987, pp. 88–89.
[102] Marx, *Capital*, in McLellan, 1977, pp. 439–41.

has ... to introduce the theme of holism.'[103] Manser offers a definition of a 'whole', 'A whole consists of a set of parts which are internally related in the sense that the parts take their character from the whole of the thing of which they are parts.'[104] Sartre's dialectic can be regarded as the study of such wholes. For Sartre, what happens at any moment can be made intelligible only by looking at the whole, the interplay between man and the practico-inert. The explanation of a particular event can be given only in terms of the dialectical relations it has with the milieu. To give an account of the forms that praxis takes at any time we have to use the method of the dialectic. The explanation will be circular because there is no necessary starting point for it.

The dialectical method of inquiry, being circular, is sensitive to paradoxical assertions. Sartre, like the Marxists, assumes that there are contradictions in society. It is not that acts are in themselves contradictory. It is the consequences of the act that produces a contradiction. For example, the employer keeps the wages of the workers low in order to maximise profits. Yet if all employers do the same the result will be a shortage of consumers. Each individual employer must, therefore, hope that none of the other employers will do the same. However, as has already been noted, Sartre opposes his own dialectic to the dialectic of contemporary Marxism. Sartre is attempting to free Marxism from what in his introduction to the first volume of the *Critique* Sartre calls the dogmatic dialectic that unfolds independently of human will and which appears as 'a divine law ... a metaphysical fate'.[105] Therein lies the importance of free praxis. Therefore, as has been said, man is not merely a passive victim of a dialectical process over which he has no control.

Sartre wants to move beyond the use of the dialectical method of inquiry and establish the existence of dialectical reason. In order to establish the existence of dialectical reason certain conditions must be met. Stack observes that, 'The condition for the possibility of dialectical reason, then, is the dialectical nature of man's critical or self-conscious social experience.'[106] Therefore, as with the dialectical method of inquiry, the existence of dialectical reason can be demonstrated only by engaging in it. It cannot be validated from anywhere outside of that engagement. More than that, 'if a dialectical interpretation of individual or group *praxis* (and of the original dependent relationship of man upon the material world) is plausible, and if it is possible to grasp the complex reciprocity of social relationships and show their intelligibility, then dialectical reason is possible'.[107] However, despite stipulating the condition for the possibility of dialectical reason Stack goes on to say that one can admit that there may be dialectical agents, a dialectical relationship between need and the

---

[103] Baldwin, 1993, p. 211.
[104] Manser, 'Praxis and Dialectic in Sartre's Critique', in Warnock (ed.), 1971, p. 343.
[105] CDR I, p. 36.
[106] Stack, 1977, p. 81.
[107] Ibid.

material-social world or a social dialectic manifested in the formation of groups without having to assume that there is something called dialectical reason which alone is capable of understanding such processes.[108] Nevertheless, Sartre, despite his own doubts, does seek to establish the existence of dialectical reason.

Sartre makes the possibility of the intelligibility of dialectical reason the grounds for the proof of the existence of the dialectic. For this intelligibility Sartre turns to the notion of totalisation. Totalisation can be grasped only by the dialectical method of inquiry. Analytical reason is unable to grasp the living inter-relatedness of the totalising process since its knowledge is derived from fragmenting its object of inquiry. Sartre, therefore, goes on to supply a condition for the existence of dialectical reason. He argues that,

> the basic intelligibility of dialectical Reason, if it exists, is that of a totalisation. In other words ... a dialectic exists if, in at least one ontological region, a totalisation is in progress which is immediately accessible to a thought which unceasingly totalises itself in its very comprehension of the totalisation from which it emanates and which makes itself its object.[109]

The region that Sartre has in mind is history. As Andrew Dobson says, the totalisation that occurs is not simply that A is followed by B and then C but that B contains A and C contains both B and A within them, that is in interiority.[110] The idea that each successive action contains or preserves the previous actions is part of what is meant by the indistinction of immanence and transcendence. As will become clear, immanence and transcendence are also motivationally connected and that too is part of their indistinction.

With history in mind, Sartre attempts to show how dialectical reason, if it exists, operates on the basis of a dialectical methodology and thus also on the dialectical movement of totalising praxis. However, Sartre appears to move off at a tangent by introducing additional complexities to support his original argument. Moving beyond praxis itself and using the structuralist terminology of Claude Lévi-Strauss, Sartre explains that his methodology is both synchronic and diachronic. The synchronic perspective studies the nature of a thing at a particular time. The diachronic perspective studies the nature of a thing as it develops over time. Joel Peterson observes that 'it is the diachronic perspective which encompasses the synchronic perspective, and ... the totality which is revealed in a diachronic perspective is always more concrete than a totality which is revealed in a synchronic perspective'.[111] Furthermore, using the work of Henri Lefebvre, Sartre announces in *The Problem of Method* his use of 'The Progressive-Regressive Method'. For Sartre, the regressive method is a moment in dialectical understanding. Sartre's use of the regressive method also draws

---
[108] Ibid., pp. 83–84.
[109] CDR I, p. 44.
[110] Andrew Dobson, 1993, pp. 64–65.
[111] Joel Peterson, 1981, p. 11.

upon Freud's claim that in order to understand a person's life one must regress to incidents in that individual's childhood. The Freudian-Lefebvrean cocktail enables Sartre to do two things. First, he is able to supplement Freudian psychoanalytical theory with an account of the influence upon a person of social, cultural, political and historical factors. Second, he is able to provide a response to his own criticism of Marxism which is that Marxism appears to assume that individuals come into society as fully-formed workers. The aim of the regressive method is to reach the component parts of the totality or totalisation that is being examined. I hope to demonstrate not only that the states of immanence and transcendence consist of component parts but also that the nature of those component parts can be revealed by praxis itself. Volume 1 of the *Critique* is a synchronic-regressive study and it was Sartre's intention that Volume 2 of the *Critique* should be a diachronic-progressive study. Volume two would be a study of social wholes, a reconstruction of history on the basis of the understandings acquired in Volume 1. According to Peter Caws, the progressive-regressive method 'provides the only adequate means of dealing with history because it makes the explanatory-causal chain (which is not, however, deterministic) pass *through* human agents'.[112] Sartre says of Volume 2 that it,

> will retrace the stages of the critical progression: it will attempt to establish that there is *one* human history, with *one* truth and *one* intelligibility – not by considering the material content of this history, but by demonstrating that a practical multiplicity, whatever it may be, must unceasingly totalise itself through interiorising its multiplicity at all levels.[113]

Of course, it is this volume that is incomplete and because of that, in so far as the progressive aspect of the methodology is incomplete, there is the possibility of an incomplete view of the dialectical method. Moreover, the possibility of the incompleteness of the view of methodology aside, it is apparent that although Sartre is presenting a dialectical methodology and a dialectical reason these are no longer based solely on the dialectical movement of praxis.

As I have said, part of the intention of this work is to show that a dialectical methodology can be based solely on the dialectical movement of praxis and that will be achieved, in part by showing that praxis can reveal the components of the states of immanence and transcendence. It is important, nevertheless, to understand what Sartre is attempting. According to Mikel Dufrenne, 'The *Critique* is, in a Kantian way, the search for the conditions of intelligibility within the social.'[114] Although that is certainly true there is more to be said. Richard Bernstein argues that Sartre sensed that something had gone wrong with the main tradition of Western philosophy, 'Philosophers have lost sight of,

---

[112] Peter Caws, 1984, p. 157.
[113] CDR I, p. 69.
[114] Mikel Dufrenne, 'Sartre and Merleau-Ponty', trans. Hugh Silverman and Frederick Elliston, in Silverman and Elliston (eds), 1980, p. 214.

or smothered in misleading abstractions, the human individual who must choose and act, and who defines himself by his action.'[115] That something has gone wrong with the main tradition of Western philosophy is a key theme in the work of MacIntyre. However, whilst MacIntyre traces the fault to the abandonment of a notion of human telos and the virtues necessary for the achievement of and which are part of that telos, Sartre identifies the fault as being the neglect of the dialectic of praxis. Readers might, however, have already started to become aware that a connection can be made between a human telos, virtues and the dialectical notion of praxis. This connection will be developed in subsequent chapters.

What may be noted at this point is that it is possible to develop an understanding of moral relations by viewing particular sorts of association in the light of the process of normative praxis. In his interview with Sartre, Leo Fretz reports that, 'He [Sartre] agrees that the epistemological exposition of the regressive analysis in CDR can be considered the basis for a new ethic. He announces that he will formulate the first principles of this ethic in a new book Pouvoir et Liberte (power and freedom)'.[116] He explains that he is writing this book with Pierre Victor and that in it he,

> will try to show that morals and politics can only make sense from the moment when the concept of power and the reality of power are truly removed. A society without power starts to become an ethical society, because a new form of freedom is established, which is the freedom of reciprocal relations of persons in the form of a we.[117]

There is, in fact, enough in the two volumes of the *Critique* to make sense of Sartre's notion of reciprocity and hence his notion of an ethical society. However, since Sartre concentrates on the dialectical process of praxis there is work to be done in developing an outline of a normative theory of associations that would be of use to communitarians at least in so far as certain communitarians advocate putting into place the values and practices, such as certain distributive criteria, conceptions of equality and certain types of relationships, that will bring proper community life into being.[118]

---

115 Richard Bernstein, 1972, p. 159.
116 Fretz, 'An Interview with Jean-Paul Sartre' trans. George Berger, in Silverman and Elliston (eds), 1980, pp. 224–25.
117 Ibid., p. 233. Pierre Victor is the Benny Levy of note 25 above.
118 Frazer and Lacey, 1993, pp. 115–16.

CHAPTER THREE

The communitarian case for community

The theory of praxis presented in the previous chapter enables us to begin to strengthen communitarian criticisms of liberalism and remedy the deficiencies in the communitarian account of community.

Since the communitarians who are the focus of attention in this work make their case, to some extent, by denying what liberalism affirms, some sense of liberal theory is required. According to John Gray, liberalism is characterised by four features or perspectives. It assumes the moral primacy of the individual against any collectivity, confers the same moral status on all individuals, affirms the moral unity of the species, and asserts the open-ended improvability, by the use of reason, of human life.[1] According to Anthony Arblaster, on the liberal view, the individual comes before society in every sense, 'He is more real than society. In the quasi-historical theories of the social contract developed by Hobbes, Locke, Paine and others, he is seen as existing before society temporally as well. Finally, his rights and demands come morally before those of society.'[2] Arblaster points out that whatever else might be meant by the notion of the 'individual', in liberalism the concept leans towards seeing the single human being in isolation, with society treated as context, 'with the implication that separateness, autonomy, is the fundamental, metaphysical human condition'.[3] Judith Shklar claims that, 'Liberalism has only one overriding aim: to secure the political conditions that are necessary for the exercise of personal freedom.'[4] These observations are given by their authors as being true of liberalism in general.

As an aside it is interesting to note that Sartre too values freedom. Moreover, as we shall see when we come to consider elections in a representative democracy, he also believes that people are isolated from each other. This he sees as a function of liberalism. Thus, in what Poster calls a 'refutation of liberalism'[5] Sartre argues that 'there is no such thing as man; there are people, wholly defined by their society and by the historical movement which carries them along'.[6]

---

[1] John Gray, 1995, p. 86.
[2] Anthony Arblaster, 1984, p. 15.
[3] Ibid., p. 16.
[4] Judith Shklar, 'The Liberalism of Fear', in Nancy Rosenblum (ed.), 1989, p. 21.
[5] Poster, 1979, p. 39.
[6] CDR I, p. 36.

In fact, it is important to distinguish between different types of liberalism. Doppelt distinguishes between Kantian-Rawlsian liberalism and bourgeois liberalism and argues that at the heart of the latter tradition is the conviction that it is through capitalist market relations and distributions that people are free to affirm their individuality and character. Thus, 'Within the standpoint of this bourgeois moral identity, competitive professional and economic performances of various kinds mark the measure of full personhood and human worth.'[7] At the heart of Kantian-Rawlsian liberalism is self-determination, 'the real freedom to embody one's normative judgement and will in one's life'.[8] It is important to distinguish between these two forms of liberalism because different communitarians target different forms of liberalism in their efforts to convey their notion of community and an understanding of that notion requires an awareness of what it is that is being criticised. Also, as Doppelt goes on to argue, the two forms of liberalism can come into conflict. On the one hand, bourgeois liberalism reduces Kantian self-determination by making it, 'a hostage of scarce socio-economic circumstance and class position'.[9] On the other hand,

> the Kantian ideal informs human interests and conditions of life (modern democratic citizenship, the state, rule of law, the public sector, etc.) which works to limit, and in some respects undercut, the role of market relations, private property and economic power, the competition for scarce goods, etc. in constituting social life.[10]

It is possible, therefore, for certain criticisms of one sort of liberalism to be regarded as constituting support for the other sort of liberalism with the potential for confusion over the different grounds for the claim by different communitarians that liberal theory has neglected the significance of the community and consequently over the different grounds by which different communitarians do assert the significance of the community.

As we saw in the Introduction, Sandel is quite clear about the significance of the community. His major claim is that liberal political theory has neglected the significance of the community as constitutive of the identity of individuals. He argues that a community is constitutive of an individual's identity to the extent that it is within the community that the individual acquires or develops certain attachments, exercises certain attributes and becomes aware of and pursues certain ends. This argument emerges from his criticism of the Kantian-Rawlsian species of liberalism. In *Liberalism and the Limits of Justice* Sandel explains that,

---

[7] Gerald Doppelt, 'Beyond Liberalism and Communitarianism: Towards a Critical Theory of Social Justice', in David Rasmussen (ed.), 1990, pp. 54–55.
[8] Ibid., p. 56.
[9] Ibid.
[10] Ibid.

The liberalism with which I am concerned ... is indebted to Kant for much of its philosophical foundation. As an ethic that asserts the priority of the right over the good, and is typically defined in opposition to utilitarian conceptions, the liberalism that I have in mind might best be described as 'deontological liberalism'.[11]

This means that Sandel is not going to be concerned with the liberalism of J. S. Mill and not with bourgeois liberalism either. He is, instead, concerned with the liberalism of Rawls's *A Theory of Justice*. A characteristic of this form of liberalism is that it gives justice primacy among moral and political ideals which is summarised by the view that the right is prior to the good both in the sense that its claims take precedence and in the sense that its principles are independently derived.

Rawls believes that the superiority of the deontological approach over the teleological approach, which asserts the priority of the good and defines right as that which maximises the good, resides in the idea that it is the only approach that provides for the distinctiveness of people. As Sandel says, the 'core thesis'[12] of deontological liberalism is that because society is pluralistic in the sense that each individual has his own aims, interests and conceptions of the good it 'is best arranged when it is governed by principles that do not themselves presuppose any particular conception of the good'.[13] In other words, principles of justice must be derived independently of the good since they need to respect the existence of a plurality of competing conceptions of the good. These principles will be justified, therefore, not on the grounds that they maximise social welfare or otherwise promote the good but on the grounds that 'they conform to the concept of *right*, a moral category given prior to the good and independent of it'.[14]

Deontological liberalism also, and on Sandel's account relatedly, asserts that in two senses the self is prior to the ends it chooses.[15] The self is prior to

---

[11] Sandel, 1982, p. 1.
[12] Ibid.
[13] Ibid., p. 2.
[14] Ibid., p. 1. Rawls has subsequently argued that 'the right and the good are complementary, and the priority of right does not deny this'. (Rawls, 1988, p. 252)
[15] Sandel argues that Rawls's conception of justice presupposes a particular conception of the person. Rawls has argued that his conception of the person in the original position is a political conception of the person as a citizen. Thus,

> The description of the parties may seem to presuppose some metaphysical conception of the person, for example, that the essential nature of persons is independent of and prior to their contingent attributes, including their final ends and attachments, and indeed, their character as a whole. But this is an illusion caused by not seeing the original position as a device of representation'. (Rawls, 1985, p. 238; see also Rawls, 1993, p. 27)

> The difficulties attending the possibility of Sandel's misunderstanding of the nature and function of the original position and the difficulties attending both Rawls's explanation of that misunderstanding and his broader contention that 'justice as fairness is intended as a political conception of justice' (Rawls, 1985, p. 224) are difficulties that, as indicated in the introduction, go

the ends it chooses first in the moral sense whereby the priority of the self over its ends is required if the self is to be autonomous and, therefore, worthy of respect and the bearer of dignity. The self is prior to the ends it chooses, second, in the epistemological sense whereby the priority of the self is required if the self is to be independently identifiable.

Sandel demonstrates that for liberals to establish the moral primacy of justice and the priority of the self over its ends it is necessary for them to provide a derivation of the principles of justice that grounds them in something other than the range of contingent and supposedly potentially competing ends adopted by human beings. As Sandel has indicated, Immanuel Kant provides that ground. For Kant, the morally significant characteristic of human beings, that which ensures their worth and dignity, is their capacity for rationally autonomous behaviour. What matters is not the ends that are chosen but the capacity to choose, on which a choice of ends depends. Moreover, since that capacity must be given prior to any particular end that is, in fact, chosen, what really matters about the individual is given prior to his ends. So it is that the constitution of the self, its identity, cannot be the result of the ends it chooses, for its unity is established prior to its making any choice. This 'antecedently individuated'[16] self is not dependent upon any social or other circumstances. The individual's capacity to autonomously choose its ends is not one amongst many equally valuable capacities but it forms the essence of that person's identity and is, therefore, the most fundamental value, to be protected above all others. Thus there is an understanding of the importance of rights as protectors of that capacity. A society that was organised in accordance with suppositions concerning any particular conception of the good would fail to respect the human being's capacity for choice. It is this Kantian argument that provides the foundation for Rawls's contractarianism, the 'original position', a term employed by Rawls to depict a contemporary version of the state of nature; the starting point for people deliberating over the terms of a social contract.

In Rawls's view, as presented by Sandel, just as the priority of justice arose from the need to distinguish the standard of appraisal from the society being appraised, the priority of the self arises from the need to distinguish the subject from its situation. If all the self consisted of was a collection of various desires and ends, there would be no non-arbitrary way for anyone to identify these desires and ends as the desires of a particular subject. Rather than be of the subject, they would be the subject. The distance between the situation and the subject would be collapsed so that 'just *any* change in my situation, however slight, would change the person that I am'.[17] Since my situation is always changing, it would mean that my identity would merge indistinguishably into

---

beyond the scope of this work. What is significant for this work are the implications for Sandel's communitarianism of the notion of a self that is prior to its ends.

[16] Sandel, 1982, p. 55.
[17] Ibid., p. 20.

my situation. In Sandel's words, one would become a *'radically situated subject'*.[18] However, the opposite position suggested by the Kantian perspective, whereby the self is totally detached not only from its ends but also, on Sandel's understanding of Rawls's original position, from its attributes and attachments, would seem no more than an abstract consciousness, presumably unaffected by that of which it is conscious. Thus a radically situated subject becomes a 'radically disembodied one'.[19] Rawls's conception of a self detached from its empirically given features is inadequate. A radically disembodied self is an abstraction, abstracted from the characteristics that people have and from their concrete circumstances. Following MacIntyre, Chadran Kukathas and Philip Pettit point out that, 'Such a subject would be incapable of rational choice. Shorn of all experience, it would lack motivation and have no capacity for deliberation. The price of such complete detachment is arbitrariness'.[20] In other words, such a self would be unable to exercise in any meaningful way the capacity that constitutes the essence of its identity.

Sandel argues that any account of the self must tell us two things. First, how the self is distinguished from its ends. Second, how the self is connected to its ends. Without the first we have a radically situated subject and without the second a radically disembodied subject. Sandel recognises that there must be some degree of detachment between the self and the attributes of the self otherwise we would be left with a radically situated subject. However, a self so totally detached from its empirically given features would seem no more than an abstract consciousness, a radically situated subject gives way to a radically disembodied one. Sandel concludes, rather vaguely, that there must be some distance, but not too much.

Sandel regards Rawls's conception of the self as problematic for three reasons. First, on Rawls's conception of a person a person's ends are always things to which he chooses to become attached and from which he may, presumably, choose to become unattached. However, this voluntaristic view is not the only way of characterising the relation between the person and his ends. For example, instead of an act of will the relationship could be regarded as an act of understanding, a process of self-reflection whereby the commitment to an end is a manifestation of some deep understanding about the good life. Thus the relation between the person and his ends becomes an act of discovery rather than act of choice. Second, if the self is antecedently individuated then no matter how closely it identifies with a given end that end can never become part of the self's identity. Thus, 'No commitment could grip me so deeply that I could not understand myself without it.'[21] Sandel argues that people cannot regard themselves as independent of certain loyalties because their 'moral force consists

---

[18] Ibid., p. 21.
[19] Ibid.
[20] Chadran Kukathas and Philip Pettit, 1990, p. 98.
[21] Sandel, 1982, p. 62.

partly in the fact that living by them is inseparable from understanding ourselves as the particular people we are'.[22] A self so thoroughly independent rules out any possibility of attachments that affect our identities and also the possibility of a public life in which the identity as well as the interests of the participants could be at stake. Third, it therefore follows that Rawls's conception of the self commits him to an impoverished understanding of community. A view of the self as antecedently individuated excludes any conception of community other than that it is a co-operative arrangement for the pursuit of personal advantage. An alternative view of the self, one that is constituted at least in part by its situation in the community, requires society to be a community in the 'strong sense', 'a society of a certain kind, ordered in a certain way, such that community describes its basic structure and not merely the dispositions of persons within the structure. [Such a] community must be constitutive of the shared self-understandings of the participants and embodied in their institutional arrangements'.[23] According to Sandel, liberals cannot admit that our personal identities are partly defined by our communal attachments. He argues that, 'On Rawls' view, a sense of community describes a possible aim of antecedently individuated selves, not an ingredient or constituent of their identity as such. This guarantees its subordinate status.'[24] Thus Rawls's view of the primacy of justice among moral and political ideals renders community one virtue amongst others within the framework for thinking about the relationship between the individual and society that is defined by justice, as opposed to being a rival to that framework.[25]

In contrast to Rawls, Sandel argues that the self is not prior to but rather is, at least in part, constituted by its ends. There are ends that we do not always choose but discover by virtue of being situated in a shared communal context. Therefore, not all that we do has to be the result of reflective choice. On many occasions we simply do what has to be done in a particular situation. One's social world provides an unchosen, though not necessarily coercive, framework which defines the shape of lives worth leading. So it is that Sandel argues that communitarian virtues such as benevolence and fraternity are not just affirmed by the members of the community, but contribute to the definition of their identity.[26]

At this point we should take stock of what Sandel is doing. Although he recognises the problem of the radically situated self, his real purpose is to condemn what he understands to be Rawls's conception of the self; one that is antecedently individuated and hence radically disembodied. Apparently ignoring his own location in a hinterland between two radical perspectives, Sandel goes

---

22 Ibid., p. 179. See also Sandel, 1984a, p. 90.
23 Sandel, 1982, p. 173.
24 Ibid., p. 64.
25 Ibid.
26 Ibid., p. 34.

on to expose the either-or of the voluntaristic view of the relation between the person and his ends as opposed to the view whereby the relation between a person and his ends is one of discovery and the either-or of a self whose ends forms no part of its identity as opposed to a self whose identity is, in part at least, constituted by its ends. On the back of these two either-or perspectives Sandel has the confidence to draw attention to the contrast between a sense of community that is a possible aim of the individual as opposed to a sense of community that is an ingredient of the identity of the individual.

This is interesting stuff and appropriate to the tradition within which Sandel is working. However, a different tradition offers an alternative view. An understanding of the nature of praxis provides the communitarians with a further argument to support the case that selves are not antecedently individuated. The identification of the self with needs and praxis shows, in another way, that the individual's attachment to his ends is, in fact, never voluntaristic through and through. Whilst it may be possible to choose either whether or how or in some cases both whether and how to satisfy one's needs, it is, in an important sense, not possible to choose whether or not to have them. Of course, we may, as a result of our own inventiveness or development, create or develop new needs. However, once they exist they are, as with all needs, manifested as negations demanding to be negated. It is in the sense of negations demanding to be negated that needs and, therefore, ends are non-voluntaristic. Whether or how the process of negating the negation occurs is another issue. At issue at the moment is the nature of needs as they are felt or realised by the needy. Furthermore, for Sartre the end is the organising project itself, or the organism thought of as free praxis. Praxis is the expression of the end which is man making himself as he transcends himself. There is, in short, no antecedently individuated self who is prior to and has a voluntaristic attachment to his ends.

The view of the self derived from praxis avoids, as Sandel desires, the notion of a radically disembodied self since it is a self that has needs and ends which are expressions of needs. It also avoids the notion of the radically situated self. Although there is an identification of the self with its needs and ends, it is through praxis, which is free, that the connection is made between needs and ends and therein lies the possibility of free choice regarding the satisfaction of needs and the means to achieve the end. On the basis of an understanding of praxis it is possible, therefore, to conceive of the self as neither radically situated nor radically disembodied.

This perspective also acknowledges the significance of one's social world. Current praxis has to contend with the results of previous praxes which have left their mark on the practico-inert. In doing so current praxis also impacts upon the practico-inert. So it is that, as we have already seen, communities partly constitute individuals and individuals partly constitute communities.

Part of the identity of the individual will be the individual's talents. However, to who or to what does the talent of the individual belong? According to Sandel, the difference principle from Rawls represents an agreement to regard the distribution of natural talents as a common asset and an agreement to share in the benefits of this distribution.[27] Thus the difference principle acknowledges the arbitrariness of fortune by asserting that the individual is not really the owner of his talents but merely their guardian and as such has no special claim on the advantages that the exercise of those talents might bring; 'no one deserves his place in the distribution of native endowments'[28] and 'such endowments are arbitrary from a moral point of view'.[29] Typically it is assumed that a person deserves what he achieves through his own effort. However, Rawls's argument is that even the willingness to make such an effort might be affected by family circumstances or other factors not directly of the individual's own making. Sandel argues that, 'On Rawls' conception, no one can properly be said to deserve anything because no one can properly be said to possess anything, at least not in the strong, constitutive sense of possession necessary to the notion of desert.'[30] For Rawls it follows that talents are a common asset rather than an individual possession, 'a social asset to be used for the common advantage'.[31] Since it is in the general interest that the individual cultivates and exercises the talents that he possesses, so that society as a whole may benefit from the results of that cultivation and exercise, society is typically arranged so that the individual is provided with incentives and resources for their cultivation. Rawls is happy to say that the individual is entitled to his share of the resulting benefits when he has qualified for them under the terms specified. However, according to the merit conception of distributory justice, these claims are legitimate expectations created by institutions designed to elicit his efforts, not rights. These legitimate expectations presuppose the existence of a co-operative scheme and can have no validity independent of those institutions.

According to Sandel, it is easy to see how the Rawlsian view of natural assets as failing to provide the basis of desert emerges seamlessly from a theory committed to a conception of the person as antecedently individuated. According to that conception the individual's specific talents are contingently given and wholly inessential attributes of the individual. They are inessential to the individual being that particular individual. However, as Sandel points out, to show that individuals as individuals do not possess or deserve their assets is not necessarily to show that society as a whole does. If they cannot be said to belong to the individual why automatically assume that they belong to the community? For the community to deserve the natural assets in its province, and the benefits that flow from them, it is necessary to assume that the community has a status that, until granted by an institution, individuals lack.

---

[27] Ibid., p. 70.
[28] Rawls, 1971, p. 104.
[29] Ibid., p. 312.
[30] Sandel, 1982, pp. 85–86.
[31] Rawls, 1971, p. 107.

Only in this way could the community be said to possess its assets in the strong, constitutive sense of possession necessary for desert.[32] This view would run counter to Rawls's individualistic assumptions and particularly his denial, acknowledged by Sandel, 'that society is an organic whole'.[33] Of course, the separation of the subject from his attributes means that the subject can never be used as a means to an other's end or to social ends for it is not the person but only his attributes that are being so used. This, however, invokes the notion of the disembodied subject.

Sandel argues that the only way in which Rawls might justify his assumption that assets not possessed or deserved by individuals are possessed and deserved by society is by making use of a completely different conception of the individual subject. Instead of claiming that the difference principle is justified because my assets rather than my person are thereby utilised for others, Rawls might question the sense in which those who share in 'my' assets are properly called 'others'. If Rawls allowed that the relevant description of the self might occasionally involve more than an empirically individuated human being, he could then argue that those assets are common because they belong to a common subject of possession, the community.[34] So it is that if the individual's identity is partly constituted by membership of a community then Rawls could use the argument just described. That talk would also facilitate the notion of intersubjective or common ends. Sandel's claim is that treating assets in this way can be justified only by invoking an intersubjective conception of the self and a constitutive conception of community, both of which Rawls is committed to rejecting for fear of invoking a radically situated subject. The theory that Rawls defends ends up relying not on the notion of the self as independently identifiable and prior to its ends but on an intersubjective conception of the self. Communal ownership is not a conclusion that is reached in the original position. There it is taken for granted. Therefore, Rawls has to rely on a wider subject of possession than the individual and this presupposes the existence of a community of a certain sort, one in which people are happy to share their assets and the benefits that they bring.

On turning to the nature of justice itself, Sandel claims that Rawls makes certain crucial, decisive, assumptions about how the parties to the original position view themselves when they deliberate about the terms of the contract. One such assumption involves the imposition of constraints upon their knowledge dictated by the veil of ignorance whereby, hypothetically, people contracting to start a society are ignorant of where in that society they will be in terms of socio-economic status, in terms of which period of history they will occupy and in terms of their skills or talents. This ignorance will prevent people from devising a contract that would serve their interests at the expense of others.

---

[32] Sandel, 1982, p. 101.
[33] Rawls, 1971, p. 264.
[34] Sandel, 1982, p. 80.

This is a device, therefore, to ensure impartiality. This is a form of contractarianism which emphasises the importance of impartiality as the defining characteristic of the moral point of view. The usual analogy is that the person slicing the cake into pieces does so in the knowledge that everyone else will be allowed to choose their piece of cake before he does. Immediately, however, this raises a problem. Robert Sugden notes that to derive a moral rule from a position of impartiality means that one has injected morality into one's initial position.[35] Therefore, the morality that one derives from that position is precisely the morality that informed it in the first place.[36]

Other assumptions are held to emerge in connection with the circumstances of justice which Rawls derives from Hume. Rawls argues that these 'circumstances of justice obtain whenever mutually disinterested persons put forward conflicting claims to the division of social advantages under conditions of moderate scarcity'.[37] Thus for Hume justice is a remedial virtue. It is necessary when both resources and human benevolence are scarce. Rawls notes that people in the original position know that these circumstances of justice obtain. Sandel argues that since Rawls's theory is based on Kant, Rawls has a problem. This is because,

> For Kant, the deontologically-given notion of right which Rawls seeks to recapture derives its force from a moral metaphysic that rules out precisely the appeal to contingent human circumstances on which Hume's account of the virtue of justice is based.[38]

According to Sandel, Kant does not have an account of the circumstances of justice that situates the virtue of justice in circumstances characteristic of human society. In fact, for Kant to provide one would be to contradict the essential point of Kantian ethics which is that man acts morally in so far as he is able to rise above the influences and determinations of his social and natural conditions and act according to a principle given by pure practical reason. Sandel argues that the Humean circumstances of justice contradict the Rawlsian claim that justice is the first social virtue. Since for Hume justice is a remedial virtue then on Sandel's account the Kantian and Humean elements in Rawls create an unresolvable tension.

Sandel is well aware that Rawls is not claiming that mutual disinterest is a characteristic of real people.[39] They are assumptions built into a 'device of representation'.[40] According to Sandel, however, an assumption of mutual

---

[35] Robert Sugden, 'Rationality and impartiality: Is the contractarian enterprise possible?', in David Gauthier and Robert Sugden (eds), 1993, p. 158.
[36] There are, in any case, a number of objections to the idea that impartiality is the sole defining characteristic of the moral point of view. See Lawrence Blum, 1980, chpt. III.
[37] Rawls, 1971, p. 128.
[38] Sandel, 1982, p. 36.
[39] Ibid., p. 42.
[40] Rawls, 1985, pp. 236–38; 1993, p. 27.

benevolence would have been no more problematic or contentious than that of mutual disinterest. Rawls assumes mutual disinterest because it follows from his conception of the self and the relation of the self to its ends. This introduces an individualistic bias to Rawls's theory and rules out or devalues such motives as benevolence, altruism or other community oriented sentiments.

The dialectical relationship between scarcity and forms and terms of association casts Sandel's criticism of Rawls's assumption of mutual disinterest in a different and more substantial light. Whatever the force of Sandel's argument, given that Rawls was not writing about people as they are, it is an argument that recommends replacing one assumption about people with another. However, the grounds for doing so are by no means clear. In order to establish such grounds it is necessary to attend to the conditions under which associating might occur. Similarly, a key communitarian claim is that communities are constitutive of the identities of individuals. Yet communitarians fail to show how that might be so. This is partly because they ignore the internal dynamics of associations. Those dynamics will be described in subsequent chapters. It is also, however, again partly because they neglect to provide an account of the possible conditions under which associating might occur and fail to acknowledge that these conditions both arise from and have an effect on particular forms and terms of association.

Scarcity is one such condition of which, with regard to just one sort of scarcity, Sartre says, 'The fact is that after thousands of years of History, three quarters of the world's population are undernourished. Thus, in spite of its contingency, scarcity is a very basic human relation, both to Nature and to men.'[41] People find themselves in a world that is constituted by the prior praxis of men. The role of praxis in interiorising and exteriorising scarcity illustrates how people can find themselves in a world that not only sustains a milieu of scarcity but which can also be sustained by that milieu in so far as it is a milieu that is interiorised by praxis. It will be seen that since praxis is free this process does not have to continue in that form into perpetuity. Nevertheless, the dialectical notion that the possible conditions under which associating might occur both arise from and have an effect on particular forms and terms of association becomes intelligible in view of the dialectical nature of praxis in constituting social wholes.

Where the conditions under which associating occur are characterised by scarcity, or by a milieu of scarcity, certain sorts of which arise from and can sustain particular forms and terms of association, then, as has been seen, certain things can follow regarding the identity of the individual members of that community. They could be competitors but then they could co-operate. What actually does follow will depend upon whether scarcity or the milieu of scarcity is allowed to prevail or whether some conception of the good life, which has as

---

[41] CDR I, p.123.

its source dissatisfaction with the status quo, determines a change in the nature of the association. Thus we arrive at the idea, to be developed further in subsequent chapters, that people can be conceived of as being either mutually disinterested or benevolent or as being competitors or co-operators and, more significantly, we are given a grounding in terms of praxis for making either identification. Furthermore, the condition of scarcity also provides a grounding for the development of a conception and pursuit of the good life as one in which human fulfilment for all the members of the community is best secured when the effects of scarcity are overcome. This means that it becomes reasonable to cite certain practices as practices that everyone can endorse as the basis for the politics of the good. The ways in which this can happen will be examined during the course of this work.

In fact, Sandel provides examples of forms of association where the virtues of benevolence and fraternity prevail. Sandel talks of the ideal family situation and relations between two close friends in these terms.[42] In those circumstances to act out of a sense of justice may not merely be superfluous but might lead to a reorientation of prevailing beneficent and fraternal understandings and motivations. The primacy of justice is predicated on the assumption that society is beset by discord.[43] It is in this sense that Sandel, following Hume, regards justice as a remedial virtue. Where a form of association has as its terms benevolence and fraternity then, on Sandel's account, there is no remedial work to be done.

Sandel closes his argument with the thought that liberalism, 'forgets the possibility that when politics goes well, we can know a good in common that we cannot know alone'.[44] John Wallach reflects that 'Sandel seems to be drawing on Aristotle's point that in political deliberation the judgment of citizens acting collectively is better than their judgments taken individually.'[45] Sandel's closing thought may also be taken to indicate that successful political processes can produce shared meanings. In fact Sandel does not think that at the moment the political process is successful. He has argued, with respect to the current state of America, that,

> Except for extraordinary moments, such as war, the nation proved too vast a scale across which to cultivate the shared self-understandings necessary to community in the formative, or constitutive sense. And so the gradual shift, in our practices and institutions, from a public philosophy of common purposes to one of fair procedures, from a politics of good to a politics of right, from the national republic to the procedural republic.[46]

---

[42] Sandel, 1982, p. 33.
[43] Ibid., p. 31.
[44] Sandel, 1982, p. 183.
[45] John Wallach, 1987, p. 595.
[46] Sandel, 1984a, p. 93.

In common with MacIntyre, Walzer and other communitarians, Sandel is an advocate of communities that are of a size to enable the effective participation in the affairs of the community by its members.

In summary, Sandel objects to the individualistic bias that he identifies in *A Theory of Justice* on the grounds that such a bias excludes or at least devalues motives such as benevolence, altruism and other community oriented sentiments. Therein lies the limits of justice. As Kukathas and Pettit say, what Sandel is attacking is Rawls's contention 'that community is the product of association by independent individuals, and that the worth of community is to be estimated by the justice of the terms upon which those individuals associate'.[47] Sandel and other communitarians want to maintain that it makes no sense to think of a community in this way because the very existence of individuals capable of agreeing to form associations, or assenting to particular forms and terms of association presupposes the existence of a community which is in part constitutive of the identities of those individuals and which is the arena for the exercise of 'co-operative virtues'.[48] How, therefore, are those co-operative virtues to be cultivated? This is a question that leads us into the work of MacIntyre.

Although MacIntyre does address some of his arguments specifically to Rawls, he criticises liberalism in general. As with Sandel, he argues that liberalism fails to understand the importance of communal life for the integrity and identity of the individual and he also believes that liberalism is by no means as neutral as it claims regarding various conceptions of the good life for human beings. However, MacIntyre's main criticism of liberalism is that it is a symptom of emotivism. The liberal self is an emotivist self. In ethics, emotivism is the view that moral discourse is simply an attempt on the part of one individual or group to change the views of another individual or group. The emphasis is on making the attempt which means that emotivism has no need to respect persons as rational beings capable of making their own independent judgement except in so far as according that respect might be a device that makes the attempt successful. The liberal self, thus construed, cannot be identified with any of the judgements that it makes. Since it is an unattached self and, therefore, on MacIntyre's account has no rationally held criteria, it believes that everything is open to criticism. However, any moral position adopted by the self will be an expression of an ultimately arbitrary personal preference. The relation of such a self to its ends is voluntaristic. Such a person cannot be said to have a history. It is not possible to tell an intelligible story of that person's moral development. There is no narrative continuity to tell of the development of that person's self-understanding. Moral agency involves standing back from one's situation and judging it from an abstract and universal viewpoint quite removed from any concrete communal particularity. In other words, the capacity to be a moral

---

[47] Kukathas and Pettit, 1990, p. 104.
[48] Sandel, 1982, p. 12.

agent is situated in the self and not in any of the social roles or practices with which the self is engaged. The resources for moral agency are to be found in the detached self and nowhere else outside of that self.

A previous, Homeric, age espoused a view of human telos. Enlightenment philosophers dispensed with that view. However, on MacIntyre's account, a view of human telos is important because it permits the transition from 'is' to 'ought'. An understanding of the final state of human nature enables us to distinguish between dispositions and behaviours that do and those that do not contribute to the development and realisation of that telos. Thus the reintroduction of the concept of a telos will be vital in any attempt to conceive of morality as an aspect of human life that can be said to be rational and objective in its content.

Herein lies the significance of the virtues, used by MacIntyre as a term to denote those excellences of character that permit a person to carry out the duties incumbent upon him and which are manifested by him when he does. Succeeding the Homeric conception of the virtues associated with specific social roles is the Aristotelian conception. Aristotle divorces the concept of virtues from specific roles but not from the shared role of being human. Human beings are understood as having a specific nature which sets them certain goals. The virtues are those excellences of character that allow them to move towards that distinctively human telos and which must be exercised in the course of so doing in order to live a complete human life.

The virtues cannot be exercised outside of the community. Their development and implementation in a complete human life requires that such a life be lived out with others all engaged in a common project of attempting to live the good life. Only the material and cultural resources of the community allow this to happen. Virtues such as courage, fidelity, empathy, loyalty and friendship constitute the framework conditions by which a community maintains itself and they are an essential part of the form of life at which the community is aiming.[49]

MacIntyre has a conception of community that acknowledges that they have histories and that they can take a variety of forms. In fact, MacIntyre is an enthusiast for small, geographically localised communities. However, one form of community that he identifies and which illustrates the significance of the virtues is the community of those who are engaged in the same 'practice'. In *After Virtue* MacIntyre offers a definition of what he calls a 'practice'. Thus,

> By a 'practice' I am going to mean any coherent and complex form of socially established cooperative human activity through which goods internal to that form of activity are realised in the course of trying to achieve those standards of excellence which are appropriate to, and partially definitive of, that form of activity, with the result that human powers to

---
[49] Stephen Mulhall and Adam Swift, 1992, p. 81.

achieve excellence, and human conceptions of the ends and goods involved, are systematically extended.[50]

According to MacIntyre, on that definition, throwing a football is not a practice but the game of football is. Farming is a practice but planting turnips is not. Chess is another practice. Scientific and historical inquiry, engagement in artistic and political activity and the making and sustaining of family life are all practices.

There are, in fact, two kinds of goods to be gained by engaging in a practice. On the one hand, there are the goods externally and contingently attached to goalkeeping, or whatever, such as prestige and money. These are external goods in that although they may result from being a good goalkeeper they are not inherently part of what it means to be a goalkeeper. Although these goods may arise out of excellence in a particular practice they are external to the practice in that they could, given similar success in another practice, have arisen out of that. External goods are always someone's property and possession. Usually the nature of such goods is such that the more one person has of them, the less there is for everyone else. Thus the holding of these goods by one person makes them scarce.

On the other hand, as the quotation above indicates, there are the goods that are internal to the practice in the sense that they can be obtained only by engaging in that practice and in no other way, and which can be specified as goods only in terms of that practice. Internal goods are of two kinds. There is the excellence of the practice itself, both the performance of the practitioner and the product of the practice. There is also the internal good of living out at least part of one's life as one engaged in a particular practice. Internal goods are such that their achievement is a good for the whole community who participate in the practice. Thus the skilled footballer may well win fame and fortune but whether he does or not his skilled performance will nevertheless benefit his own team and indeed footballers everywhere, by raising the standard of the game and, because practices are not fixed or static, by introducing new techniques, new tactics and so on. In other words, the communal nature of practices means that the practitioners will be involved in a particular kind of relationship with each other. This relationship will not only be with present but also with past practitioners and it is one which, at the very least, will involve the sharing of the aims and the procedures that are the characteristics of the practice.

However, the idea of relationships between practitioners gives rise to a further element of practices, which is that they involve virtues. If the individual submits himself to the demands of a practice with the intention of achieving internal goods in particular, he must submit himself to the standards of that practice, accept the authority of those standards, and judge himself accordingly. Part of this will involve submission to the authority of other practitioners and this in turn will involve a willingness to trust the judgements of those whose

---

[50] Alasdair MacIntyre, 1981, p. 175.

achievements have made them authorities. These judgements must in turn be both fair and honest. Moreover, since engagement in a practice involves extending one's skills and endeavouring to improve, the practitioner must be courageous enough to take risks and even risk being wrong, or a failure. In short, practices require the possession and exercise of certain virtues. MacIntyre points out that this is not to say that no great practitioners are ever mean or cruel. However, the mean and the cruel rely on the virtues of others for the practices in which they engage to flourish.[51]

Thus the individual's practice defines, to some extent, his moral responsibilities. To judge that someone is a good goalkeeper means that he has done those things that goalkeepers ought to do. He has fulfilled his obligations as a goalkeeper. This is not to say that the person who is a goalkeeper has discharged in total his moral responsibilities by virtue of being a good goalkeeper. It simply means that being a good goalkeeper involves certain responsibilities, including certain moral responsibilities, which are necessarily involved in good goalkeeping. MacIntyre does point out that he is not claiming that virtues are exercised only by engaging in a practice.[52]

So it is that involvement in a practice demands acceptance of the authority of certain criteria and rules associated with that practice and the exercise of certain qualities in order to engage in the practice. This is where the virtues are important. Thus, *'A virtue is an acquired human quality the possession and exercise of which tends to enable us to achieve those goods which are internal to practices and the lack of which effectively prevents us from achieving any such goods.'*[53] In fact MacIntyre argues that without the virtues the only goods that would be available would be external goods. He goes on to say that in any society that recognised only external goods, competitiveness would be the major feature. He argues that such a society would resemble Hobbes's state of nature.[54]

MacIntyre talks about the relationship between institutions and practices. No practice can survive for long without the support of an institution. However, practices should not be confused with institutions. He argues that, 'Institutions are characteristically and necessarily concerned with what I have called external goods.'[55] This means that they are characterised by their concern to acquire material goods such as money, by their structure which can be understood in terms of power and status and by the fact that they distribute money, power and status as rewards. These characteristics are necessary if the institution is to sustain both itself and the practices that it bears.

However, MacIntyre also recognises that practices are threatened by the acquisitiveness and competitiveness of the very group that is meant to sustain

---

[51] Ibid., p. 180.
[52] Ibid., p. 187.
[53] Ibid., p. 178.
[54] Ibid., p. 183.
[55] Ibid., p. 181.

them and they are under threat because the first priority of the group is itself.[56] For MacIntyre, the best defence against institutions are the virtues since, 'Without them, without justice, courage and truthfulness practices could not resist the corrupting power of institutions.'[57] In other words, in so far as the proper exercise of practices requires certain virtues, such as justice, courage and truthfulness, and these virtues will protect the practice, then it is the proper exercise of practices that provides for those practices the best defence against institutions. However, MacIntyre goes on to say, 'Yet if institutions do have corrupting power, the making and sustaining of forms of human community – and therefore of institutions – itself has all the characteristics of a practice.'[58] The potential conflict of interest revealed by this observation will be spelt out in more detail later in this work.

A view of praxis which understands it to be both dialectical and normative serves to further illuminate MacIntyre's notion of practices. The intention here is to understand practices as a species of praxis. The claim is not that all praxis can be regarded as a practice in MacIntyre's sense but that all practices are types of praxis. Like praxis, practices have a social dimension, realise certain ends and involve particular understandings. It is certainly the case that not all praxis is co-operative or aspire to standards of excellence. Nor is all praxis sustained by institutions. However, as will be seen in chapter six, some types of praxis have all of those characteristics and at that point further illumination of practices will be possible. The illumination that is possible at this point involves the idea that practices require and give rise to certain virtues. The dialectical nature of praxis explains how and to what extent this is so. On the dialectical view, people are determined by their practices to the extent that they engage in those practices. People become the product of their product. This means that the more that one engages in a practice, the more that one will be defined as such and such a person, successful or otherwise, both by other practitioners and by other people in the community. In this way, therefore, not only one's ends but also one's attributes are constitutive of one's identity.

Judgements within practices cannot be regarded as completely subjective or completely arbitrary, they are not a matter for individual preference and they cannot be subject to an emotivist analysis. They have to be in accordance with the criteria that define the practice. Whilst there is room for disagreement about the precise nature and importance of different criteria, nevertheless the practice itself provides the context for adjudicating between conflicting views. Shared notions of relevant criteria enable practitioners to arrive at objective judgements concerning the practice and thus overcome personal whims or fancies.

However, most people engage in a number of practices and may, therefore, be pulled by a number of different and possibly competing criteria. Consequently,

---
56 Ibid.
57 Ibid.
58 Ibid.

arbitrariness with regard to judgements concerning the pursuit of the good life can still occur. In order to prevent that, MacIntyre invokes the notion of a narrative unity of human life. This concerns our intentions and our views of what we are doing, and their value, in the context of our lives as a whole understood as the pursuit of the good life. Hence the virtues are not simply associated with the sustaining of and with the achievement of the goods internal to practices. They can also be understood, as has already been seen, as dispositions that will sustain and strengthen people as they search for the good for human beings. The virtues that MacIntyre has in mind are those that are required to sustain the kinds of communities, familial and political, in which people can, collaboratively, search for the good.[59]

The nature of this quest for the good is not the same for all people in all places and at all times. As MacIntyre says, 'What the good life is for a fifth century Athenian general will not be the same as what it was for a medieval nun or a seventeenth century farmer.'[60] Moreover, not only do individuals live in different social circumstances, they approach those circumstances as bearers of a particular social identity, as a son, a citizen of a particular State, a goalkeeper. This means that no one can seek for the good or exercise the virtues simply as an individual. These roles provide the individual with a notion of the good. They constitute the given of the life of the individual, the moral starting point for the individual and contribute to giving the life of the individual its own specific moral significance.

So it is that one has a social inheritance and one part of this social inheritance will be what MacIntyre calls a tradition which returns us to practices, albeit within a wider context. A tradition is constituted by a set of practices and is a way of understanding their worth. It is the way in which practices are shaped and transmitted across the generations. Such traditions, in MacIntyre's sense, can be, for example, religious, political, aesthetic or, if they are centred on a particular locality, geographical. The communal understanding of a tradition will be the subject of continuous debate. Therefore, when an institution such as a university or a football club is the bearer of a tradition its common life will be constituted in part by a continuous appraisal of what being a good football club or university means. The appraisal will be constrained by the tradition's best understanding of itself but that still leaves room for change and development. The fact that the individual acquires his moral identity from the communities to which he belongs does not mean that he is bound to be confined by the moral vision espoused by those communities. However, those communities do provide a basis from which to embark on the search for the good.

MacIntyre points out that this is quite a different stance from that of modern individualism which, as was seen earlier, he characterises as a position in which the self is detached from its social and historical roles. Thus the possession of a

---

[59] Ibid., p. 204.
[60] Ibid.

historical identity and the possession of a social identity coincide. One can rebel against that identity but in order to do so one must acknowledge it first. In fact, MacIntyre's ideal political agents are thoroughly social. He points out that in Aristotelian, Thomist and Humean practical reasoning it is the individual as the bearer of a social role who reasons, for example, 'the individual *qua* citizen'. However, 'in the practical reasoning of liberal modernity it is the individual *qua* individual who reasons'.[61]

MacIntyre argues that modern moral philosophy has made the mistake of believing that there is a coherent and intelligible system of universal moral principles which may be discerned through the exercise of pure reason. This has led moral philosophy away from reflection about the nature and purpose of the moral life as an expression of human well-being. Thus the most important questions of moral life have to be understood in terms of a teleological conception of human good and not in terms of an understanding of duty derived through the exercise of pure reason or in terms of the 'moral fiction'[62] that is human rights. As Stephen Mulhall and Adam Swift point out, taking MacIntyre's view, the very possibility of sustaining rationality and objectivity in the realm of moral and political evaluation depends upon locating individuals and their arguments with other individuals within an 'overarching and nested set of inherently social matrices'.[63]

Part of MacIntyre's argument involves a criticism of Rawls and Robert Nozick for their treatment of desert.[64] He maintains that the notion of desert is at home only in the context of a community. From MacIntyre's perspective it is only by working to establish and maintain the sort of shared understandings of the good that Rawls explicitly excludes from our deliberations about justice that we can confer any rationality upon the course of those deliberations. For it is only by introducing a conception of desert in relation to the common tasks of the community in pursuing shared goods that we can provide the basis for rational judgements about social virtues and social justice. Within the community that MacIntyre espouses the primary bond is a shared understanding both of the good for man and of the good of that community. Individuals identify their primary interests with reference to those goods. Just desert is, therefore, based on those shared understandings. Rawls, however, as has been seen, makes an explicit presupposition that we must expect to disagree with others about what the good life for man involves. We must, therefore, exclude any understanding of what the good life for man involves when formulating principles of justice.[65] MacIntyre disagrees and writes not only of a community of practitioners but also of the importance of communities with particular characteristics. He argues

---

[61] MacIntyre, 1988, p. 339.
[62] MacIntyre, 1981, p. 67.
[63] Mulhall and Swift, 1992, p. 93.
[64] MacIntyre, 1981, p. 232.
[65] Ibid., p. 233.

that, 'What matters at this stage is the construction of local forms of community within which civility and the intellectual and moral life can be sustained through the new dark ages which are already upon us.'[66]

As Wallach points out, MacIntyre's view of community is derived from ancient Greece and medieval Christendom. According to Wallach, 'These communities provided a collective understanding of the good for man, which the Greeks understood as *eudaimonia* – human flourishing – and how to achieve it, that is, how to be virtuous. Consequently, the good existed as a common end, a *telos*, for human beings and their community as a whole.'[67] H. N. Hirsch observes that, 'In MacIntyre's work, then, the longing for community is explicit and central to the argument, and the purpose of community is clear. Only a community can educate modern man in the tradition of the virtues.'[68] Galston shows that MacIntyre advances a tripartite theory of the virtues. They furnish internal goods by sustaining the co-operative practices that engender those goods. They sustain the narrative unity that gives individual lives meaning. They enrich tradition which provides individual identity and striving as its necessary point of departure.[69]

In summary, MacIntyre insists on the necessity of a telos embedded in the community and nurtured by virtues to enable us to make judgements about who we are and who we should be prior to any choices that we might make and which would, therefore, provide a basis for making those choices. John Horton and Susan Mendus note that on MacIntyre's account, 'Only social context can give substance to a person's life; and social context is not something a person chooses.'[70] Thus, according to MacIntyre, man's moral nature and his moral behaviour are connected with his participation in practices, his membership of a tradition, in short, his communality as opposed to his autonomous individuality. MacIntyre's communitarianism embraces the idea that there are different sorts of communities to which people belong, for example, different sorts of practices in which people engage, and that these communities have histories and can change.

Communitarianism is not really a unified theory but a family of tendencies within both moral and political philosophy. Lawrence Blum has attempted to trace the relationships within this family. He writes of identity, virtue and social communitarianism. Identity communitarianism is concerned with the significance of the particular group identities that make people into people of a certain kind. Thus, 'Identity communitarians claim that certain strands of liberalism contain a faulty notion of the person because they give insufficient place to these particularistic group identities.'[71] This is the communitarianism

---

[66] Ibid., p. 245.
[67] Wallach, 1987, p. 593.
[68] H. N. Hirsch, 1986, p. 430.
[69] Galston, 1991, p. 70.
[70] John Horton and Susan Mendus, 1994, p. 10.
[71] Blum, 1994, pp. 8–9.

of Sandel. By contrast, '*Virtue communitarianism*, identified most prominently with Alasdair MacIntyre's work, especially *After Virtue*, claims that moral and other virtues must be understood primarily in the context of communities.'[72] This means that virtues are nourished, supported and are partly defined by communities. Finally, social communitarianism advocates that a society should encourage the promotion of certain goods such as 'solidarity, family stability, mutual commitment, civic participation, and the like'.[73] These are viewed as specifically communitarian goods. They are, according to Blum, narrower in kind than the whole range of virtues associated with virtue communitarianism.

In fact, Blum's categorisation of communitarianism, whilst helpful in certain respects, is, in a crucial respect, unhelpful. It is unhelpful with regard to social communitarianism which is not sufficiently differentiated from with virtue communitarianism. Social communitarianism, as it has been described by Blum, is akin to what Elizabeth Frazer and Nicola Lacey call value communitarianism. Frazer and Lacey identify two strands within communitarian thought, social constructionism and value communitarianism. These two strands do not logically entail one another but typically run together. Social constructionism argues that conceptions of selfhood and actual persons are socially produced. Persons develop their identities in a social context, and in the context of prevailing communal values which look remarkably like the goods of social communitarianism. Thus communal values such as reciprocity, solidarity and community are values which can be realised only in the context of a communal life in which members share a recognition of both each other's moral claims and intersubjectivity. Value communitarianism places an emphasis on collective or public goods. Public goods refers both to particular practices such as democratic debate, and is in that way akin to Blum's social communitarianism, and to particular facilities such as schools and hospitals. These goods are institutional and the link between them and communal values is that a commitment to those kinds of framework values would typically engender a political practice which realised a range of public goods in the sense of facilities and practices designed to help members of the community to develop their common and hence their private lives. A commitment to these goods can be made without espousing a social constructionist stand, although such a commitment can be explained by social constructionism.[74]

The definition of public goods supplied by Frazer and Lacey broadens the notion of social communitarianism as depicted by Blum, distinguishes it more clearly from virtue communitarianism and invokes the communitarianism of Walzer. Walzer is primarily concerned with the meaning of public or social goods and with the just distribution of those goods and as such he is critical of certain aspects of laissez-faire liberalism. In *Spheres of Justice* Walzer says

---

[72] Ibid., p. 9.
[73] Ibid.
[74] Elizabeth Frazer and Nicola Lacey, 1993, pp. 102, 107–12.

that, 'My purpose in this book is to describe a society where no social good serves or can serve as a means of domination. I won't try to describe how we might go about creating such a society.'[75] Thus although Walzer does address certain of Rawls's ideas he is not primarily concerned with criticising the Rawlsian conception of the person, as is Sandel. Nor will he be relying overmuch on arguments involving notions of human rights. Rights arguments such as those to do with life and liberty can be useful with regard to certain issues such as war but they are, says Walzer, of only limited help in thinking about distributive justice. There are, in any case, no universal rights. Thus,

> To say of whatever we think people ought to have that they have a right to have it is not to say very much. Men and women do indeed have rights beyond life and liberty, but these do not follow from our common humanity; they follow from shared conceptions of social goods; they are local and particular in character.[76]

Nor is Walzer presenting a historical account of Western culture from which criticisms of liberalism may be derived, as MacIntyre does. However, he is concerned with equality in society and argues that such a society is, here and now, a practical possibility. It is already latent in our shared understanding of social goods. As Walzer says, 'It fits a certain conception of how human beings relate to one another and how they use the things they make to shape their relations.'[77] Walzer concentrates, therefore, on how we should understand the goods for which a theory of justice seeks to articulate distributive principles.

According to Walzer, human society is a distributive community. That is not all that it is, but that is an important part of it. People come together to share, divide and exchange. People also come together to make the things that are shared, divided and exchanged; but that very making, work itself, is distributed amongst people in a division of labour. Moreover, although human society is also a productive community that raises issues to do with the ownership of the means of production which is in itself a question of distribution. As Walzer says, 'Distribution is what social conflict is all about. Marx's heavy emphasis on productive processes should not conceal from us the simple truth that the struggle for control of the means of production is a distributive struggle.'[78] The key issue is the identification of the criteria by which goods may be justly distributed.

Walzer argues that people will be motivated by ideas and values that stem from the self-understandings and the lived experiences of the society in which they find themselves. He points out that,

---

[75] Michael Walzer, 1983, p. xiv.
[76] Ibid., p. xv.
[77] Ibid., p. xiv.
[78] Ibid., p. 11.

> Even if they are committed to impartiality, the question most likely to arise in the minds of the members of a political community is not, What would rational individuals choose under universalizing conditions of such and such a sort? But rather, What would individuals like us choose, who are situated as we are, who share a culture and are determined to go on sharing it?[79]

According to Walzer, that question is easily translated into a question about the choices that members of a community have already made and so into a question about the understandings that the members of a community already share. It is on the basis of those shared understandings that decisions may be made about the just distribution of social goods.

Each community seeks its own social goods and the meaning of each social good determines its own criteria of just distribution. For Walzer, the meaning of a good and an understanding of how it should be distributed go together and so the latter is as inherently social as the former. He argues that,

> it is the meaning of goods that determines their movement. Distributive criteria and arrangements are intrinsic not to the good-in-itself but to the social good. If we understand what it is, what it means to those for whom it is a good, we understand how, by whom, and for what reasons it ought to be distributed. All distributions are just or unjust relative to the social meanings of the goods at stake.[80]

So it is that Walzer argues that principles of justice are pluralistic in form in the sense that different social goods should be distributed for different reasons, in different ways, by different people and that all of these differences are due to the understandings that particular communities have of those social goods. In fact, as Miller notes, Walzer's theory is pluralistic in two senses. First, it is pluralistic with regard to justice, 'we see justice as the creation of a particular political community at a particular time, and the account we give must be given from within such a community'.[81] Second, it is pluralistic with regard to there being many kinds of social goods whose distribution is a matter of justice, with each good having its own particular criterion of just distribution.

Following from the idea that the meaning of each social good determines its own criterion of just distribution, Walzer is clear that no social good should be dominated by and hence distributed on account of the possession of any other unconnected good. Therefore,

> The critique of dominance and domination points toward an open-ended distributive principle. *No social good x should be distributed to men and women who possess some other good y merely because they possess y and without regard to the meaning of x.*[82]

---
[79] Ibid., p. 5.
[80] Ibid., pp. 8–9.
[81] Miller, 'Introduction' to Miller and Walzer (eds), 1995, p. 2.
[82] Walzer, 1983, p. 20.

Thus the use of, say, wealth to gain access to other goods which have no inherent connection with money itself is a tyrannical use of money. It constitutes an invasion from one sphere into another. The most obvious examples of such invasions would be the use of wealth to gain access to health care or better educational opportunities for one's children.

The way to achieve justice is to prevent conversions between goods whose meanings and hence principles of just distribution are distinct. What is unjust about contemporary capitalist society is not so much the unequal distribution of goods such as money as the fact that money is able to bring its possessor goods such as health care or education that properly belong to different distributive spheres. Thus money is a dominant good that exercises a tyranny over other goods. Walzer's argument is not that the dominant good, for example, money, should be redistributed more equally. Simple equality, the redistribution of money so that everyone has an equal amount, is not sustainable. Within a short space of time new inequalities with regard to wealth will inevitably occur. Therefore, rather than simple equality, Walzer advocates complex equality. Complex equality will prevent the invasion described and will protect different distributive spheres from other sorts of invasion as well. With complex equality unequal possessions are permitted but the possession of one type of good, no matter in how great a quantity, will not provide the possessor privileged access to other kinds of goods. In other words, no specific good is generally convertible into a good of another kind. Thus although one person may be superior to another by virtue of the office that he holds, that particular superiority cannot be translated into superiority with regard to any other good, such as superior health care or better access to schools for his children. Access to those other goods would be determined not by superior office but by the meanings that those other goods have for the community as a whole.

In any case, every citizen should be an 'office holder'.[83] What makes the holding of an office so important is that so much else is distributed along with it, including status, power and security. The rewards of office should be derived from the social understanding of the office itself. This would include an understanding of the nature of the office so as to appreciate the internal rewards of performing the office. Miller explains that 'Complex equality obtains when different people get ahead in each of the various spheres of distribution, but because they are unable to convert their advantages from one sphere to another, none is able to dominate the rest.'[84]

Walzer identifies need as a distributive principle. However, he points out that the principle, 'To each according to his needs' does not work for all goods, including, for example, the distribution of political power, sail boats, rare books and so on. Of course, these are not things that anyone, strictly speaking, needs. However, even if we understand 'need' to mean 'want' we are no better off.

---
[83] Ibid., pp. 132–33.
[84] Miller, 'Introduction' to Miller and Walzer (eds), 1995, p. 2.

Walzer points out that things like political power, sail boats and rare books cannot be distributed equally to those with equal wants 'because some of them are generally, and some of them are necessarily, scarce, and some of them can't be possessed at all unless other people, for reasons of their own, agree on who is to possess them'.[85] Therefore, although need fits the general rule concerning x and y above, that is, it is not having y but only lacking x that is relevant, there are other distributive criteria. He explains by pointing out that all States are, in principle at least, welfare States. The distribution of goods should take place in accordance with three principles which are that 'every political community must attend to the needs of its members as they collectively understand those needs; that the goods that are distributed must be distributed in proportion to need; and that the distribution must recognize and uphold the underlying equality of membership'.[86] Walzer maintains that these three principles can be summed up in a revised version of Marx's maxim, 'From each according to his ability (or his resources); to each according to his socially recognized needs. This, I think, is the deepest meaning of the social contract.'[87]

Walzer's communitarianism resides in the idea that although individuals may contribute to the meaning of social goods, individual choice with regard to access to those goods will always be over-ridden by the social meanings of those goods and where there is a conflict between individual choice and the social meaning of those goods, those goods would be distributed according to their social meaning. This implies a priority of the community over the individual. Thus Walzer denies what, according to Gray and Arblaster, liberalism affirms which is the primacy of the person against any community. The problem is that within any particular community there might be genuine disagreement or conflict about the meaning of specific goods. Walzer concedes that when there are such conflicts the community must acknowledge their existence, provide the means for their expression, the means for adjudication and alternative distributions.

According to Walzer, the methodological abstraction that generates Rawls's principles of justice makes those principles unworkable with regard to the distribution of specific social goods, such as health care, in the context of any particular society. Walzer acknowledges that rational people making choices from behind the veil of ignorance would probably opt for Rawls's formula. However, he goes on to argue that Rawls's formula is not very helpful in determining what choices people would or should make once the veil of ignorance has been lifted. Thus,

> In a world of particular cultures, competing conceptions of the good, scarce resources, elusive and expansive needs, there isn't going to be a single,

---

[85] Walzer, 1983, p. 25.
[86] Ibid., p. 84.
[87] Ibid., p. 91.

universally approved path that carries us from a notion like, say, 'fair shares' to a comprehensive list of the goods to which that notion applies. Fair shares of what?[88]

Distributions according to abstract principles are appropriate for people abstracted from their qualities and for goods abstracted from their meanings but it is doubtful, says Walzer, that such distributions can do justice to people constituted as they are, searching for goods as they understand them.

Moreover, the universal standpoint of Rawls does not attach any importance to the values and practices of particular communities. A theory of justice must be true to the understandings of a particular community. This indicates the importance, morally speaking, of the real people that make up that community. According to Walzer, 'A given society is just if its substantive life is lived in a certain way – that is, in a way faithful to the shared understandings of the members.'[89] Thus justice is rooted in the distinct understandings of place, honours, work of all kinds that together make a shared way of life. Walzer says that, 'To override those understandings is (always) to act unjustly.'[90] The problem with Rawls's approach, therefore, is its lack of attention to different kinds of particularity. The abstraction and universalism that Rawls's theory invokes involves, for Walzer, a lack of attention to the choices that people have already made and that are embodied in their culture's own particular understandings of the goods that are to be distributed. Goods do not 'appear', as it were, with meanings and values somehow attached to them. Neither do goods which are to be distributed within the community acquire meaning and value simply or only because of the interpretations of a particular individual. Such goods acquire meaning and value because of the understanding that the community has of those goods. If the meaning of those goods is necessarily social, they will have different meanings in different societies. It also follows that Walzer must reject Rawls's conception of primary goods. First, Rawls's attempt to come up with a list of goods that can be applied universally fails to respect cultural differences and abstracts from the meaning of those goods. Second, the situating of different goods in a single list neglects the fact that different goods should be distributed for different reasons.

When Walzer talks about a community's understanding of a social good he is talking about a complex process and, as will become clear, one that cannot be effectively engaged in by just any old community, not least because of the milieu of scarcity. However, it is the relationship between praxis and the meaning of social goods that is at issue here. Unfortunately, there is a problem with Walzer's notion of a shared understanding of a social good. Fortunately, the dialectic of praxis yields a response to that problem. The problem is to imagine

---

[88] Ibid., p. 79.
[89] Ibid., p. 313.
[90] Ibid., p. 314.

how a community can arrive at an understanding of a social good until a particular good has been identified as such and how a good can be identified as a social good until it has been understood. The response to the problem is that it is on the basis of need that praxis, as the negation of a negation, identifies a certain good as an end and in the identification lies the understanding. However, for there to be a common understanding the need must be perceived as a common need requiring a common praxis which could amount to a combination of complimentary praxes in the case of certain forms of association. The process by which this occurs will be examined in chapter six. However, for now it should be noted that neither praxis nor the social goods as ends identified and understood as such by praxis simply arise in some mysterious fashion. Since it is through praxis that needs are satisfied and praxis involves its own form of knowing, then when the satisfaction of needs requires a social good whatever else might establish the meaning of that good, praxis always will. Praxis and the social goods identified by praxis arise as the result of the interiorisation of the results of previous praxes. Moreover, the meaning of the product of the current praxis, the particular social good, will be interiorised by the community for whom that product is a social good thus making that community, in part, a product of that social good and, indeed, of that praxis. Thus the identification and understanding of social goods affects the community to the extent that the community has identified and understood social goods.

The argument that the identification and understanding of social goods affects the community to the extent that the community has identified and understood social goods can be developed further. The conditions under which people associate will of themselves be part of the meaning that people will bestow on those goods and that meaning will be an expression of the conditions under which people associate. Thus part of a definition of a good may, under certain conditions, be that it is a scarce good. However, defining that good as one that is scarce is also a way of defining certain conditions under which people associate.

The dialectical relationship that exists between a condition such as scarcity and forms and terms of association presents a particular difficulty for Walzer's view that it is the shared meaning of a social good that should determine the criteria for the just distribution of that good. If scarcity is a reflection of certain forms and terms of association then, on Walzer's account, where part of the definition of a good referred to its scarcity it could mean that, with regard to that particular good, no distribution at all could count as just, or, at least, as not unjust. In other words, since certain forms and terms of association both give rise to and can be sustained by certain sorts of scarcity, nothing need ever be done about the distribution of scarce goods and no injustice will ever have occurred. Therefore, for there to be a just distribution of a social good, scarce or otherwise, the community has to be a community of a certain sort.

Although according to Walzer, every political community must attend to the socially recognised needs of its members, the goods must be distributed in proportion to need and the distribution must recognise and uphold equality of membership,[91] Buchanan has pointed out that where resources are scarce there will be a problem with attempting to distribute those resources according to need.[92] However, serious though that is, the problem is not simply that there might not be sufficient goods to satisfy needs. It is also the case that a milieu of scarcity can in itself impact upon the process of the social recognition of need. Although the nature of the impact may vary according to circumstances, the fact that there can be an impact may be established by remembering that forms and terms of association can be sustained by a milieu of scarcity. Thus where needs are defined by society they can be regarded as part of the terms of that association and in so far as the association is sustained by a milieu of scarcity that milieu can impact upon the recognition of need. When there is a shortage of water we suddenly realise that we no longer need water for our baths. Moreover, the stipulation concerning equality of membership may do nothing to resolve the problem. One would want to know, with respect to any particular association, what entitlements that stipulation carried with it, or more precisely, which were excluded.

Walzer pursues the theme of separate spheres in his article, 'Liberalism and the Art of Separation'. There Walzer argues that liberal theorists practised the art of separation and that each division so created initiated a new liberty and this he regards as a liberal achievement. Thus the division between church and State created a sphere of worship into which politicians and bureaucrats may not intrude. Similarly, the separation of civil society and political community created the sphere of economic competition and free enterprise in which the sellers and the purchasers of goods are free to make deals and strike bargains without the interference of state officials. The separation of public and private life creates the sphere of individual and familial freedom so that, 'Our homes are our castles, and there we are free from official surveillance.'[93]

However, as Walzer says, the art of separation has never been highly regarded by Marxism, where the emphasis has been on both the interdependence of different social spheres and the influences on society of economic arrangements. For Marxists the liberal art of separation is, in some senses at least, a pretence and an exercise in hypocrisy. Thus the prevailing religious creeds suit the ideological demands of a capitalist society, universities provide the upper echelons of the capitalist work force, the market position of giant corporations is subsidised and guaranteed by the capitalist State and the freedom that people enjoy in their own homes is exercised largely in connection with the consumption of a variety of consumer goods.

Yet, as Walzer points out, Marx also believed that the liberal art of separation had, in a sense, been all too successful. It had created, as Marx wrote in *On the*

---

[91] Ibid., p. 84.
[92] Buchanan, 1982, p. 157.
[93] Walzer, 1984, p. 317.

Jewish Question, 'an individual withdrawn behind his private interests and whims and separated from the community'.[94] This condition was itself a social product, required by the relations of production and reproduced in all spheres of social activity. In this way society remained an organised whole even if its individual members had lost their sense of community. The goal of Marxism was to restore that sense, bring people to a new understanding of their interconnectedness as a means of giving them power over their common life. Thus, 'For Marx, separation, insofar as it was real, was something to be overcome.'[95]

The sort of separation that Walzer has in mind is not the separation of individuals from each other, or from their communities. Such separation is in any case, according to Walzer, impossible. He argues that,

> The goal that liberalism sets for the art of separation – every person within his or her own circle is literally unattainable. The individual who stands wholly outside institutions and relationships only when he or she chooses and as he or she chooses: This individual does not exist and cannot exist in any conceivable social world.[96]

The kind of separation that Walzer has in mind concerns institutions, practices, relationships of different sorts. He argues that we should aim not at the freedom of the solitary individual but at what can be called institutional integrity, the integrity of practices, and so on. Individuals should be free but that does not come from separating them from their fellows, or indeed from the various social and institutional contexts in which they are bound to operate. Thus, 'Freedom is additive; it consists of rights within settings, and we must understand the settings, one by one, if we are to guarantee the rights.'[97] The role of the State should be as an agent and defender of the separation of various institutions from tyrannical interference. The members of the institutions also, of course, protect themselves as best they can, but their ultimate resort when they are threatened is an appeal to the State. This is so even when the threat comes from the State itself. Then they appeal from one group of officials or one branch of government to another, or they appeal against the government as a whole to the body of citizens. In this way, 'Liberalism passes definitively into democratic socialism when the map of society is socially determined.'[98]

Is Walzer open to the charge of relativism? Is there no means whereby we can criticise the understandings both of our own society and the societies of others? Walzer believes that there is and pursues his argument on the rooted nature of understandings in *The Company of Critics* by arguing,

---

[94] Marx, *On The Jewish Question*, in David McLellan, 1977, p. 54.
[95] Walzer, 1984, p. 318.
[96] Ibid., p. 324.
[97] Ibid., p. 326.
[98] Ibid., p. 328.

against the claim that moral principles are necessarily external to the world of everyday experience, waiting *out there* to be discovered by detached and dispassionate philosophers. In fact, it seems to me, the everyday world is a moral world, and we would do better to study its internal rules, maxims, conventions and ideals, rather than to detach ourselves from it in search of a universal and transcendent standpoint.[99]

Thus, on the task of the social critic, Walzer points out that, 'Though he starts with himself, he speaks in the first person plural. This is what we value and want, he says, and don't yet have. This is how we mean to live and don't yet live.'[100] Sartre argues that social experience can be understood only through a dialectical method of inquiry and that this method requires that the investigator lives his investigation. In a similar vein Walzer justifies his view of the role and the stance of the critic by arguing that, 'It is a mistake, in social criticism as in moral philosophy, to suppose that we must escape our situation in order to describe it accurately.'[101] As Daniel Bell notes, this is criticism in the name of the community itself against those aspects of the community which are unfaithful to its own self image. Cultural standards are drawn from the shared meanings of a particular group of people rather than from an external viewpoint. Thus interpretation of shared meanings should be thought of 'as a sort of expertise in the understanding of the moral consciousness of the community, not dependent on the approval of the community at the time in which the interpretation has been formulated'.[102] The critic concedes that many citizens might well misunderstand the meaning of their own morality and it is the articulation of that meaning that the critic seeks to undertake.

Walzer develops the theme of connectedness in a particular way. Taking Albert Camus as one example, Walzer recalls what Camus said to a group of students in Stockholm in 1957 when he received the Nobel Prize, which was, 'I believe in justice, but I will defend my mother before justice.'[103] Walzer reports that,

> He repeated it later on, it is said, only because of the stir it created and the attacks from opponents on the left – who wrote as if they didn't have mothers or wouldn't think of defending them ... One might well ask, however, whether a solution to the problems of Algeria that ignored Camus's mother or the interests of the *pied noir* community generally could possibly be just. [104]

In fact, as Walzer indicates, this position was not a momentary aberration on Camus's part. In an essay included in the collection entitled *Resistance, Rebellion, and Death* Camus wrote, 'if anyone still thinks heroically that one's

---

[99] Walzer, 1989, p. ix.
[100] Ibid., p. 230.
[101] Ibid., p. 231.
[102] Daniel Bell, 1993, p. 65.
[103] Herbert Lottman, 1981, p. 618.
[104] Walzer, 1989, p. 145.

brother must die rather than one's principles, I shall go no further than to admire him from a distance. I am not of his stamp'.[105] Walzer explains Camus's stance by pointing out that, 'Camus's anti-absolutist politics depends not on critical distance but on critical connection.'[106] To be sure, Camus clearly rejected the role of the judge whose judgements are always determinedly impersonal, arguing that, 'My choice, if you think that I am making one, would at least be never to sit on a judge's bench, or beneath it, like so many of our philosophers.'[107] Walzer's point, illustrated by the example of Camus, is that radical social criticism is possible if understood in a particular sort of way. It has to be internal and connected, or perhaps concrete and specific, rather than abstract and universal.

In summary, Walzer emphasises the particularity of different communities, especially the particularities of the understandings and purposes that different communities might have with respect to the distribution of social goods. The understandings and the purposes that a community has, and criticism of those understandings and purposes must come from within the community itself. It follows, therefore, that the rights that people have are generated largely by the communities that those people inhabit. Like MacIntyre and Sandel, Walzer also admires small communities. However, whereas Sandel sees the vastness of America as the cause of procedural republicanism and MacIntyre admires small communities for their capacity to educate in the virtues, Walzer admires them for their capacity to generate shared meanings and hence for their capacity to insure a just distribution of goods. Indeed, for Walzer, identifying one of the communal values to be found in the social constructionism of Frazer and Lacey, the community itself is a good that is to be distributed. As Walzer suggests, 'The central issue for political theory is not the constitution of the self but the connection of constituted selves, the pattern of social relationships'.[108] Walzer concludes by saying that 'insofar as liberalism tends toward instability and dissociation, it requires periodic communitarian correction'[109] and the communitarian correction that he has in mind with regard to liberalism is to 'reinforce its internal associative capacities'. [110]

The issue of relationships is important. Walzer is talking about the distribution of goods between individuals. Yet such talk is most appropriate only with respect to certain goods within a certain sort of society and within the context of a particular understanding of what social justice involves. A view of society as a collection of atomistic individuals permits an understanding of social justice as simply the distribution of material goods among those individuals. Yet Walzer himself has a broader view of social goods, one that,

---

[105] Albert Camus, 'Preface to Algerian Reports', in Camus, 1961, p. 113.
[106] Walzer, 1989, p. 149.
[107] Camus, 1955, p. 165.
[108] Walzer, 1990, p. 21.
[109] Ibid.
[110] Ibid., p. 22.

for example, includes opportunities and a different view of society, one that, for example, is conducive to the generation of shared meanings. Given these broader and different perspectives, talk simply of distribution seems inadequate. As Iris Marion Young points out in *Justice and the Politics of Difference*, 'In the distributive logic ... there is little room for conceiving a person's enablement or constraint as a function of their relations to one another.'[111]

The communitarians have been engaged in two complementary yet distinct activities. The first activity has been a critique of existing society as they perceive it to be. In the pursuit of that activity they have produced a number of important criticisms of different sorts of liberal theory and associated practices. These criticisms will be developed further as this work proceeds since they partly inform the second activity. The second activity has been the development of an alternative vision not only of what community is and does but also of what it should be and should do. It is because this work is concerned with the relationship between praxis and associations and because of the prescriptive aspect of the vision of communitarianism that a normative notion of praxis is required. In the pursuit of that critique and that alternative vision communitarians have made certain assertions about the nature of community. Certain problems arise out of those assertions and it is appropriate now to note what these are. These problems can be thought of as deficiencies and can be divided into those things that the communitarians do say about the community but don't say very well and into those things concerning the community about which communitarians have little or nothing to say on their own account.

The main things that the communitarians say about the community but don't say particularly well arise, in fact, from their major claims which are that communities have a fundamental part to play in the lives of individuals because they are constitutive of our identities, a source for the conception and pursuit of the good life and a forum for the generation of shared meanings concerning social goods and their just distribution. However, it is not clear how communities of the sort espoused by communitarians do these things. We are not told how communities are constitutive of identities. We are told that people have attachments, ends and attributes. What is not clear is how, or in what way, these things are constitutive of identities. Accompanying that deficiency is the lack of detail regarding the source of a person's conception of the good life for human beings, except that it arises somehow out of a small community, or even of what that good might be. Apart from a hint as to its size, we are told neither what characteristics a community must have if it is to be capable of generating shared meanings, nor how a community that has the necessary characteristics would generate such meanings. Furthermore, if need is a distributive principle then how is need to be understood? The lack of attention to shared meanings is remarkable in the light of the fact that for some communitarians such meanings

---

[111] Iris Marion Young, 1990, p. 27.

are the essence of community. Amitai Etzioni, for example, argues that, 'Communities are webs of social relations that encompass shared meanings and above all shared values.'[112]

Communitarians claim that communities are good for people. However, there is, as Buchanan points out, an ambiguity about the nature of that claim. The claim that community is good for people may be understood as a psychological claim, which should be supported by evidence, that people desire community, or find it satisfying when they have it, or at least find it damaging when they do not. This is a claim advanced by, for example, Bell. He argues that we are indeed able to examine some attachments but there are others so fundamental to our identity, for example, the attachment to the family that raised me and which serves as a constitutive feature of my identity, that they cannot be set aside and that the attempt to do so would result in psychological damage. For most of us, our identities are bound up with some 'constitutive communities' however free and rational we might otherwise be.[113] The claim that community is good for people can also be regarded as a normative claim; community is an important objective good for people. This claim requires a theory of objective value, says Buchanan.[114] He adds that, 'Communitarians are often unclear as to whether they are advancing the psychological thesis, the normative thesis, or both.'[115]

If the nature of the communitarian claim that community is good for people is unclear then so too must be the claim that relationships, sociality and sharing are good. Furthermore, even without that lack of clarity, claims as to the necessary goodness of relationships, sociality and sharing are challenged by critics of communitarianism. Kymlicka comments on the communitarian regard for relationships and argues that, 'We do indeed find ourselves in various relationships, but we do not always like what we find.'[116] Nancy Rosenblum endorses that view, observing that belonging is not always positive; some people yearn to escape. Not all relationships are 'good', some are damaging, that is, people can be damaged by their constitutive attachments. Indeed, some relationships can be alienating in that they prevent people from living their lives as fully or as humanly as is possible. Rosenblum goes on to say that communitarians do not appear to have addressed the issue of alienation, 'alienation is absent from the communitarian vocabulary precisely because it means falling off from some original or possible unity'.[117] Alienation is, therefore, one of those things about which communitarians have little or nothing to say on their own account. Stephen Holmes argues that when communitarians

---

112 Amitai Etzioni, 'Old Chestnuts and New Spurs', in Etzioni (ed.), 1995a, p. 24.
113 Bell, 1993, pp. 90ff.
114 Allen Buchanan, 1989, p. 857.
115 Ibid.
116 Will Kymlicka, 1990, p. 213.
117 Nancy Rosenblum, 'Pluralism and Self-Defense', in Rosenblum (ed.), 1989, p. 216

use the word 'social' it is often meant to imply 'good'. But social is a descriptive term and can refer to bad as well as good practices, for example, ethnic cleansing. Similarly, argues Holmes, just because something is 'shared', even if that thing is a meaning, it does not necessarily follow that it is admirable.[118]

Kymlicka points out that, 'Communitarians believe that there are certain communal practices that everyone can endorse as the basis for a politics of the common good. But what are these practices?'[119] If communitarians wish to claim that such practices include sociality, sharing and developing and sustaining relationships then they will have to take into account criticisms which suggest that these things are not necessarily good. In fact one would also have to question the extent to which such practices were constitutive of the identities of individuals not only because there is a lack of clarity as to how that might be so but also because, as Kymlicka says, 'No matter how deeply implicated we find ourselves in a social practice, we feel capable of questioning whether the practice is a valuable one.'[120]

In addition to alienation, a key issue about which communitarians have little to say on their own account is that of rights. In the case of MacIntyre this is understandable since he regards rights as a moral fiction. Sandel is more concerned with the conception of rights to be found in deontological liberalism. Walzer would rather not talk about them at all except to say that they are located within particular settings. Etzioni thinks that talk of rights distracts people from thinking about their responsibilities, that there are too many rights and that, 'We should, for a transition period of, say, the next decade, put a tight lid on the manufacturing of new rights'[121] on the grounds that the proliferation of new rights devalues them as moral claims.

However, Gutmann points out certain weaknesses in the communitarian position, particularly that of Sandel. Commenting on the civic, as opposed to procedural, republicanism of which Sandel writes in 'Morality and the Liberal Ideal',[122] she argues that,

> We have little reason to doubt that a liberal politics of rights is morally better than that kind of republicanism. But if Sandel is arguing that when members of a society have settled roots and established traditions, they will tolerate the speech, religion, sexual, and associational preferences of minorities, then history simply does not support his optimism. A great deal of intolerance has come from societies so 'confidently situated' that they were sure repression would serve a higher cause.[123]

---

[118] Stephen Holmes, 'The Permanent Structure of Antiliberal Thought', in Rosenblum (ed.), 1989, pp. 231–33.
[119] Kymlicka, 1990, p. 226
[120] Ibid., p. 213.
[121] Etzioni, 1995b, p. 5
[122] Sandel, 1984b, pp. 15–17.
[123] Amy Gutmann, 1985, p. 319.

Gutmann continues by arguing that it is not the absence of an established community but the enforcement of liberal rights that stands between the moral majority and the contemporary equivalent of witch hunting.[124] Liberal individual rights in themselves provide valuable protections for the flourishing of community. As Buchanan says, freedom of association, expression and religion 'have provided a strong bulwark against attempts to destroy or dominate various communities within nation-states. They allow individuals to partake of the alleged essential good of community by protecting existing communities from interference from without and by giving individuals the freedom to unite with like-minded others to create new communities'.[125] Kymlicka also examines the issue of rights from the standpoint of the protection of subordinate groups within society. He argues that,

> If we look at the history of our society, surely liberal neutrality has the great advantage of its potential inclusiveness, its denial that marginalized and subordinate groups must fit into the historical practices, the 'way of life,' which have been defined by the dominant groups. Forcing subordinate groups to defend their ways of life, under threat or promise of coercive power, is inherently exclusive. Communitarians simply ignore this danger and the cultural history which makes it so difficult to avoid.[126]

Moreover, to claim as Sandel does that in an ideal family situation where benevolence reigns people may waive their rights is not the same as saying that they do not have them or will not need them. Rights can inform the nature of benevolence. Indeed, Caney makes a similar point regarding justice itself by pointing out that Sandel is mistaken in arguing that justice is required only in circumstances of limited benevolence because 'it can be required when there is extensive benevolence but disagreement about the best way to be benevolent'.[127] There is, therefore, the issue of how communitarians view rights.

Another omission in the communitarian account of community is a communitarian theory of commitment. Sandel points out that the liberalism of Rawls conceives of the self as being given prior to its ends. According to Sandel, on this view the self is incapable of commitment and incapable of community. The life of an autonomous chooser of ends undermines commitment. One does not enter into commitments with others, nor can one rely on the commitments of others to oneself. However, what is required is a communitarian theory of commitment which explains how commitments are made and sustained.

Communitarians seem unaware of the fact that the individuals who constitute communities are located somewhere and will have a relationship with the environment which will inevitably affect the relationship that they have with other people. What is significant about this omission is that it means

---

[124] Ibid.
[125] Buchanan, 1989, p. 858.
[126] Kymlicka, 1989, p. 902.

that the communitarians have nothing to say about the issue of scarcity which, together with the issue of how people relate to each other, informs Rawls's circumstances of justice. Indeed, Nicholas Xenos argues that for Rawls, scarcity serves as a justification for liberal institutions.[128] Walzer does refer to need as a distributive principle. However, as has been said, Buchanan points out that the principle of distribution according to needs is not a principle that prescribes the appropriate way to cope with competing claims to scarce goods and in any case it is not clear that scarcity, in all its forms, can ever be overcome entirely.[129]

At the heart of all the deficiencies that have been mentioned is the fact that communitarians do not have a fully-fledged political theory that is identifiably their own. The absence of a fully-fledged theory is pursued by Susan Moller Okin who writes that, 'The central debate in Anglo-American political theory during the 1980's has been between defenders of liberalism and its communitarian critics. There is a ghostly element to this debate, since communitarians have so far failed to come up with even the outlines of a theory of their own.'[130] The absence of a political theory of their own perhaps explains why communitarians fail to address issues to do with the nature of leadership and the causes and resolution of conflict. One of the distinctivenesses of the Marxist view is an understanding of the power relations embedded in social practices. MacIntyre, for example, largely ignores a range of power relations, such as those that exist between individuals engaged in the same practice, those between a particular group of practitioners and another group of practitioners engaged in the same practice but from within another tradition, those between practices and the institutions that support them, between different practices competing for the same resource such as a grant, and between any particular practice and the State. What is true of practitioners is also true of local communities. As Hirsch points out, MacIntyre does not tell us 'what relation such local communities will have to the nation-State, or how conflicts between locality and nation will be solved or how conflicts among these localised communities will be settled'.[131] Walzer acknowledges that there can be conflict over the meaning of a social good but it can be negotiated away and Sandel wishes it away by invoking the notion of the ideal family.

The lack of political theory is observed by Charles Larmore who, in fact, deliberately draws attention to Sandel's 'fantasy that society as a whole once was or might become a family or a club of friends'.[132] This raises the issue, identified by Hirsch, of how community is to be created and hence, further, the

---

[127] Caney, 1991, p. 512.
[128] Nicholas Xenos, 1987, p. 239.
[129] Buchanan, 1982, p. 157.
[130] Susan Moller Okin, 1989, p. 42. See also 'Humanist Liberalism', in Rosenblum (ed.), 1989, p. 46.
[131] Hirsch, 1986, p. 433.
[132] Charles Larmore, 1987, p. 126. See Sandel, 1982, pp. 32ff, 180ff. See also MacIntyre, 1981, p. 147.

issue of how, once it has been created, it is to be sustained.[133] Wallach agrees that the absence of a theory of their own is a problem for communitarians and argues that, 'Perhaps "justice as fairness" is flawed for supporting a theory of the unencumbered self, but its communitarian critics are at least equally at fault for providing theories of disembodied politics'.[134] For communitarians generally there is an avoidance of key questions in political theory, identified by Wallach as, 'how to relate the individual to the community, the private to the public, how to structure a society's politics, and how to shape the power that results from human associations in a way that serves the well-being of the collectivity as a whole'.[135] So it is that attention must be paid to the nature of associating itself.

What these criticisms indicate is that communitarians have failed to convey fully an understanding of their own position. However, if attention is paid to the major claims of the communitarians, a way of beginning to address these issues may be discerned. Taken together, the views of Sandel, MacIntyre and Walzer provide an overview of the significance of the communities in which people find themselves; find themselves both in the sense of being aware of their situation and of being aware of themselves. As has been shown, according to communitarianism, the two senses are connected.

Sandel celebrates such motives as benevolence, altruism and other community oriented sentiments. He insists that our identities are constituted by our ends, our attributes and our attachments and the extent to which these are realised through our situation in the community is the extent to which the community is constitutive of our identity. MacIntyre is also alert to the idea that communities are constitutive of identities, but argues that identities are derived from communities in that communities define and support the virtues that are necessary for members of the community to achieve their telos and which are part of that telos and that it is ultimately in connection with that telos and those virtues that an individual's identity is to be found. Like MacIntyre, Walzer is aware of there being different sorts of communities. Walzer emphasises the particularity of different communities, especially the particularities of the understandings and purposes that different communities might have with respect to the meaning and distribution of social goods.

These arguments can be developed further. Developing Walzer's argument, it can be seen that what a particular community does with respect to a specific social good is determined by its understanding of that good. This, as has been seen, begs all kinds of questions concerning the origins of those understandings, how they come to be shared and so on. One explanation would suggest that part of the meaning of a social good is determined by the use that the community makes of that good. However, what motivates the use of anything? One

---
133 Hirsch, 1986, pp. 434–40.
134 Wallach, 1987, p. 582.
135 Ibid., p. 601.

explanation suggests that it is through praxis that the meaning of a social good can be established. This explanation points to the relationship between understanding and action as something dynamic. The explanation is supported by MacIntyre's view of practices. It is, for example, by engaging in a practice that one acquires competence in that practice and hence the virtues that are inherent in that practice and which are required by that practice. The idea that people become the product of their own product explains how one's ends and one's attributes are constitutive of one's identity. Indeed, following MacIntyre, different forms of community will have different views of the good and will, therefore, produce people of different sorts. This would also seem to be Sandel's position in that it is through involvement in a community that we become the people that we are. However, this is only part of the story because communities partly constitute individuals and individuals partly constitute communities in so far as praxis has to cope with the practico-inert and thereby leaves its mark on the practico-inert. Furthermore, we have noted the importance of attending to the conditions under which associating might occur in that those conditions will have an effect on forms and terms of association and that particular forms and terms of association give rise to certain conditions.

The explanation offered above indicates that understandings and action are dialectically related and that is why communitarians require a theory of action and understanding, or, more specifically, of praxis. By examining the origins of praxis and seeking to make the connection between praxis and associating the nature of the relationship between the individual and the community have begun to emerge and the causes for concern that have been identified have thus begun to be addressed. In other words, an examination of praxis is a way of examining the nature of associating itself and, as has been said, it is the absence of such an examination by communitarians that has led to the deficiencies in the communitarian account of community. An examination of the nature of associating will reveal that associations have a variety of forms, each of which is accompanied by its own terms and that both forms and terms of association can be understood as arising from praxis.

At this stage it can also be said that the dialectical method of inquiry based on praxis should be of interest to communitarians for four main reasons. First, it is a method of inquiry that will serve to strengthen communitarian criticisms of laissez-faire liberalism by exposing what Sartre regards as contradictions in the terms of that form of association. Second, it provides the communitarian critic with a justification for refusing to accept the desirability of thinking about forms and terms of association from some hypothetical position outside of the community. Third, it is a method that focuses on the concrete individual and because it also concentrates on praxis it makes relationships between individuals and the interplay between the individual and the community intelligible in ways that are not available to the analytical method of inquiry. Fourth, as a result of the previous three, it is a method that can, when combined with the normative notion of praxis, provide an account of the sorts of relationships that might be considered to be the basis for an ethical society of the sort that might be advocated by communitarians. In other words, as has been said, when the dialectical nature of praxis is combined with the normative notion of praxis it opens up the possibility of constructing not only a method of inquiry but also a normative theory of associations. Each of these four points will be examined in more detail in the following chapters.

However, a further explanatory note is required. Holmes has noted a peculiarity in the communitarian critique of liberalism. It consists of what is apparently a contradiction. On the one hand, liberal theory, so communitarians argue, is wrong to suggest that individuals are pre-existent atomic units, and that all social relations are as instrumental as voluntary contracts struck in the market, because individuals are socially constituted, wholes are prior to parts and social relations do exist. On the other hand, communitarians argue, modern society has become atomised, social bonds have broken, instrumental relations are universal and group membership has become optional, that is, derivative from human wills and subservient to private interests. In other words, liberalism is, unfortunately, correct.[136]

What Holmes draws attention to is the distinction that may be made between criticisms of liberal theory and criticisms of liberal practice and to the confusion that can arise if that distinction is blurred. Frazer and Lacey are observing a distinction of this sort when they argue that, at the level of theory, liberalism is wrong to deny that people are socially constructed and are embedded in networks of relationships and that, at the level of practice, what people must do is put into place the values and practices that will bring proper community life into being.[137]

The distinction that has been attributed to Frazer and Lacey has also been commented on by Patrick Neal and David Paris. They point out that on the one hand, the practices of liberal societies have produced an atomistic society wherein the emphasis on rights has 'destroyed' public discourse[138] and where a sense of community is lacking. In short, liberal societies are societies in which there is not enough community. On the other hand, liberal theories do advance a notion of community but it is a community of the wrong type in that it is understood by its members to be simply the framework within which individuals voluntarily choose their ends and attachments. Neal and Paris argue that it is important to be aware of the distinction between the two types of criticism. However, they also warn that in so far as arguments about the philosophy of liberalism are meant to have practical implications 'we should ... avoid fully detaching contemporary political philosophy from its political and practical dimensions'.[139]

---

[136] Holmes, 1989, p. 234.
[137] Frazer and Lacey, 1993, pp. 115–16.
[138] Patrick Neal and David Paris, 1990, p. 420.
[139] Ibid., p. 439.

Maureen Bick also draws a distinction between levels of criticism although for her it is a distinction between political theory and the philosophy of politics. Political theory is understood as the systematic, critical way of thinking about practical politics, that is, for example, thinking about obligation, authority, rights, justice and civil disobedience. In other words, it is often concerned with relations between rulers and ruled, citizens and the State, individuals and the laws and institutions which stand over them. The philosophy of politics asks questions about the assumptions of a political theory, questions about the central concepts of a political theory and the methodology used to construct a political theory. Bick contends that at the level of the philosophy of politics the methodology adopted by the communitarians is that of holism. The communitarian argument is that social phenomena cannot be understood or described solely in terms of the actions of individuals because these occur within the context of a culture, or a set of rule-governed institutions or practices. Holism, therefore, in this case, is an understanding of political reality through the examination of the social structures, institutions or practices to which people belong or in which they are engaged. Bick contrasts holism with atomism understood as a methodology whose theories 'distort our understanding of reality because they isolate discrete actions, bits of knowledge or causes, which only make sense against some complex, social background'.[140]

In so far as communitarians can be said to have a philosophical methodology, albeit in the absence of a political theory that is identifiable as their own, it is a methodology that is not to be found within the analytical liberal tradition of which they are so critical. It is, however, to be found within the context of another tradition. That would be a tradition that acknowledges the dialectical movement of praxis but which avoids the passivity of the Marxist dialectic. Furthermore, if we invoke the notion of praxis then, as we have seen, the distinction between theory and practice can be broken down.

In fact, in what is to follow, distinctions will be made between theory and practice and between wholes and their parts. However, it will also become apparent that the maintenance of distinctions requires for its intelligibility an appreciation of the relationship that exists between theory and practice and between wholes and their parts. Indeed, it is the appreciation of the tension between distinctiveness and sameness at a variety of levels of inquiry that provides the basis for an understanding of the nature of associating. That appreciation, therefore, informs the argument of much of what is to come.

---

[140] Maureen Bick, 1987, p. 137.

CHAPTER FOUR

Associations and the natural environment

It has been seen that it is through labour that man converts nature into things that are useful to him in that they satisfy needs. These needs are indicators of certain values. However, the values that are indicated by needs do not arise simply from within the individual. They arise as a consequence of the individual interacting with the environment, that is, through praxis. Indeed, whatever other relationships people might have they are bound to have a relationship with the environment. In other words, all forms of association are constituted by people who interact with the environment. In this chapter this interaction will be seen to have important implications for an understanding of the nature of associating and hence an understanding of forms and terms of association. It should, therefore, be a factor in communitarian thinking.

In this chapter the intention is to develop the idea that the conditions under which associating occurs both arise from and affect forms and terms of association. The focus for this development will be the non-human or natural environment. The key argument will be that in order to understand the way that people relate together in communities it is necessary to understand the way that they relate to the natural environment. Although Sartre does not dwell on this point or explore it in any detail, initially, a particular condition, that of scarcity, was 'the contingent but fundamental relation of man to Nature' and it 'remains the context of the whole investigation'.[1] From this original relationship came certain forms and terms of association and now those forms and terms of association can both perpetuate and be sustained by the condition generated by the original relationship. In order to understand this fully and in a demonstration of the two-way movement of the dialectic of praxis it will be argued that the way that individually and collectively people relate to the natural environment affects the way that people relate to each other as members of a community and the way that people relate to each other as members of a community affects the way that individually and collectively people relate to the natural environment. This is the application of the formal law of praxis, that matter mediates people to the extent that people mediate matter, to the relationship between people and their environment. In short, an understanding of the activity of praxis on the natural environment will reveal something of the relationship between praxis and associations. The purpose of the argument will be to provide an understanding of the nature of associating with a degree of concreteness. This means that, with regard to the communitarian argument, the individuals who

---

[1] CDR I, p. 260.

both partly constitute and are partly constituted by communities will be located somewhere and will have a relationship with something tangible with which to satisfy needs, acquire an identity and arrive at certain shared understandings, including an understanding of the good life for human beings. The communitarian neglect of the environment constitutes an important limitation on what communitarians can say about these matters. In this chapter there will also be the beginnings of a comparison between the ideas of Sartre and those of Rousseau, again for the purposes of illuminating Sartre's ideas.

An acknowledgement of the significance of the natural environment on human relationships is a new departure for Sartre. This departure is commented upon by Manser who points out that whereas traditional philosophers tended to talk about human relations as if they were between disembodied spirits, Sartre, in *Being and Nothingness*, discusses human relations between creatures who have desires that depend on their possessing bodies. In the *Critique* there is a further development since, 'In *Critique de la raison dialectique* the material world itself is seen to be a central element in the relationship of man to man; both in itself and as modified by human action it is an essential part of our "world".'[2] In fact the embodiment that was characteristic of *Being and Nothingness* persists in the *Critique*. Manser does not mean to suggest otherwise. It is seen particularly in connection with need and with work to satisfy that need. Both embodiment and materiality have key roles to play in considering the relationship between the individual and the community.

In order to understand the dialectical nature of the relationship between human beings and their environments and, indeed, the dialectical nature of praxis it is necessary to understand what Sartre has to say about history. He argues that history has two principles.

> One is human activity, simultaneously all and nothing, which without the inertia of things would at once evaporate like a volatile spirit. The other is inert matter, within the agents themselves and outside them which supports and deviates the whole practical edifice at the same time as having stimulated its construction (inasmuch as it was already a synthetic and passive deviation of the previous praxis). Thus every action of the group upon inanimate matter (by which I mean a collective as much as a lump of coal) has as its necessary consequence the interiorization, within the group itself and in a form defined by its previous structures, of the very inertia in which its praxis is objectified.[3]

The main points that emerge from that lengthy quotation concern the significance of human agency, inert matter and interiorisation. Human activity requires inert matter and activity on that matter produces the interiorisation of that inertia. These principles apply both to individual and to group praxis, both affecting relationships and being affected by them. We shall see that man, who is a material

---
 2   Manser, 1967, p. 209.
 3   CDR II, pp. 135–36; *Critique de la raison dialectique*, Tome II (1985), p. 147.

being of a certain sort, can become inorganic materiality in order to work on the material world and master it. Where materialism can go wrong is in reducing man to the status of the very objects he has learned to master. Sartre is careful neither to submerge man in a world in which he is indistinguishable from other existents nor to make him a wholly non-material being. Therefore, man is neither radically situated nor radically disembodied but is, due to praxis, both immanent and transcendent. Sartre is able to maintain that his own philosophy, unlike Hegelianism or Marxism, gives due weight to both matter and consciousness. This, therefore, is a way in which Sartre's dialectic is more open than that of Hegel and a further way in which it is more open than that of Marx.

Sartre's juxtaposition of human activity with inert matter might cause a confusion if the implication is that human agency is dialectically prior to worked matter. There is an issue of what is meant by inert matter and whether or not it is different from inanimate matter. 'La matière inerte' and 'la matière inanimée' can both mean 'lifeless matter'. However, 'inerte' is most usually used to mean 'passive'. The importance of these observations resides in the status of the agent with regard to the matter that is being acted upon, bearing in mind that for Sartre matter includes the various manifestations of the practico-inert. Remember, there are different sorts of matter and not all matter is the in-itself. No matter is absolutely inert or absolutely passive, not even inanimate matter. Matter may be passive in relation to the agent who is working on it but still active in its own way. Yet despite the passivity of matter relative to the human agent it cannot be said that human activity is first in the order of the dialectical movement since, although it is human agency that works matter that is otherwise unable to work itself, for all its relative passivity, inert matter sets the conditions for the nature of that activity. The point of this is that despite the fact that praxis is a manifestation of human agency, in terms of process itself, the dialectical process of praxis accords no privileged status, by way of any kind of exemption from circularity, to the human agent. Thus people really are mediated by things to the extent that things are mediated by people. We have seen and will continue to see that the nature of associating is illuminated by this formal law. Later in this chapter it will become apparent that, through the dialectical process of praxis, inert matter has an effect on the normative nature of praxis.

In the two-way movement of the dialectic of praxis, nature impinges upon human freedom to the extent that human freedom impinges upon nature in order to satisfy needs. As H. W. Wardman says, 'nature exercises a constraint on society which is interpreted so that it appears as a scourge to be combated. Man's exigencies in relation to matter are constantly changed into demands which matter makes on man'.[4] Although human praxes are at work on the natural environment, the nature of that environment is such that by its 'passive activity'[5] the environment works on man and can produce a counter-finality.

---

4   H.W. Wardman, 1992, p. 281.
5   CDR I, p. 169.

Sartre illustrates the idea of counter-finality with the example of Chinese peasants engaged in deforestation as the means to obtain farm land. The peasants are competing to grow more crops in a response to need in a milieu of scarcity which includes scarcity of arable land. The praxis of individual peasants, working on their own and in ignorance of other individuals, in cutting down trees for more land is joined with the praxis of other individual peasants so creating the condition of deforestation. Sartre explains that although China's present leaders are aware of the seriousness of deforestation, those who lived in previous centuries could not perceive it since their aim was 'conquest of the soil,'[6] an attempt at domination. Deforestation, for those who lived in earlier centuries, was the elimination of an obstacle. Negatively, the elimination of an obstacle becomes lack of protection resulting in floods. Here we have an example of counter-finality or of praxis being deviated. Counter-finality is inscribed in the products that man produces as an off-shoot of his encounter with scarcity in nature. As Sartre says in 'The Itinerary of a Thought', 'The counter-finality of these peasants is cultural, but it concerns above all the relationship of a multiplicity of individuals with nature.'[7] All these individual praxes are united in the material world. So it is through their relationship with the natural environment that people are actually unified. As Sartre says,

> Through the unity of this counter-finality, deforestation negatively unites the enormous masses who people the great plain of China: it creates universal solidarity in the face of a single danger ... deforestation remains a *threat to be eliminated*, in the form of a common task whose success will give benefits to all.[8]

By his praxis, which is united with every other's praxis, the individual unites the material world around him and maintains that unity. Matter, through the unity that it receives from man, can serve to unite men in reciprocal relationships.

In the context of dialectical methodology each cutting down of a tree has a particular meaning but the particular meaning is only partial. It is the unification of the multiple cutting down of trees that produces dialectical intelligibility, deforestation. Each peasant is cutting down trees to gain more land, competing to grow more crops. Taken together, the peasants are destroying their own land. Thus dialectical intelligibility reveals the dialectic of praxis at the level of operation. The extent to which each individual action is united with all the other individual actions is the extent to which deforestation is produced and hence the extent to which the peasants become obliged to work together to deal with the floods that ensue. Thus action on the environment directly affects relationships between people. Given the argument that praxis stems from need, alternative ways of relating to the environment in order to satisfy at least certain

---

6 Ibid., p. 162.
7 Sartre, 'The Itinerary of a Thought', in *Between Existentialism and Marxism*, 1974, p. 52.
8 CDR I, p. 164.

needs, and certainly the need for survival, which, as has been said, is regarded by Sartre as being the most basic, could result in the elimination of at least some competition, namely, that competition which results from scarcities in the environment itself. In other words, changing man's relationship with the environment could achieve a change in men's relationships with each other. This notion has relevance with regard to Sartre's view of liberalism.

It is the existence of certain sorts of scarcity or at least the milieu of scarcity and the process of praxis within that milieu that provides the context for Sartre's criticism of the bourgeois liberal conception of the relationship between the individual and society. For Sartre, it will be recalled, scarcity was no longer a fact of the natural world. Scarcity is prevalent in human history only because human beings have decided to totalise the social field as one in which there is not enough. That decision arises from and in turn informs certain forms and terms of association so that a dialectical relationship exists between forms and terms of association and scarcity.

Sartre describes the conflict between the Chinese peasants and the nomads on the Chinese frontiers during the T'ang dynasty. The nomads always remain on the edge of the desert while the peasants gradually claim more arable land from the unproductive desert. The peasants regard the nomads as robbers 'capable only of stealing the fruit of the labour of others' and the nomads regard the peasants as 'pure colonialists, gradually driving them into an uninhabitable desert'.[9] Indeed, as Desan points out, the act of the peasants, the 'conquest of the soil', the act of domination, was also an act of colonisation over the natural environment, a 'conquest against Nature'.[10] This relationship with the land is the precursor of the relationship between the people. Each group views themselves and the other in the light of how they view the land. So it is that conflict between people can be given an explanation. Sartre points out that the origin of the struggle is always some form of scarcity. He argues that struggles are never accidents of human history, 'They precisely represent the manner in which men live scarcity in their perpetual movement to transcend it.'[11] Regarding Sartre's view of scarcity, Robert Birt points out that, 'It is a source of conflict in human relations in so far as these relations are mediated by materiality.'[12] Sartre argues that all relationships of men are mediated through materiality, pointing out that, 'Hegel... ignored matter as a mediation between individuals.'[13] Communitarians, in addition to ignoring scarcity, also ignore matter as a mediation between individuals. In doing so they fail to provide themselves with a full account of social goods.

---

[9] Ibid., p. 135.
[10] Desan, 1965, p. 103. See also Wardman, 1992, p. 280.
[11] CDR II, p. 13.
[12] Robert Birt, 1984, p. 22.
[13] CDR I, p. 113.

In Walzer's terms, the land is a social good. We can begin to see how the meaning of that good will affect its distribution, justly or not as the case may be. As far as the peasants are concerned, usable land is scarce and hard to obtain. The land that is usable has become usable through an act of conquest. Thus the praxis of the peasants totalises the land as a scarce and valuable resource that belongs to them. In other words, the meaning of that good arises from that praxis; there is no justice to be found in distributing the land amongst the nomads. Of course, the different praxis of the nomads invests the land with a different meaning and one that does not permit them to understand the justice of the peasants' distribution. The different praxis of the nomads requires a different distribution. In this example it is the praxis of each group as an expression of each group's relationship with the natural environment that establishes the meaning of that particular social good. Different praxes, different meanings and, again, whatever else might achieve this result, praxis will always establish the meaning of the social good in question. In other words, as was seen in the previous chapter, the shared meaning of a social good is rooted not simply in the community but, more precisely, it will be found in the praxis of the community. The praxis of a community can, of course, consist of a combination of differentiated yet complimentary praxes. Ultimately, since these meanings are contained within praxis and praxis stems from need, for these meanings to be shared those needs have to be perceived as common needs.

Interestingly, each group has engaged in the identification of practices that everyone in the group can endorse as a basis for the politics of the good as identified by praxis. To say, conversely, that it is a conception of the good that gives rise to praxis is a mystification. From where does the notion of the good come? There is need and praxis, responding to need and thus revealing the end, reveals the good. This can lead to group formations. The idea that different praxes produce different notions of the good comes from chapter two where it was argued that praxis pursues certain ends, which are given in praxis, and ultimately pursues human fulfilment which can be regarded, in part, as freedom from need. So what we see are different notions of the good also arising from these different praxes. What is good for the peasants simply cannot be good for the nomads and vice-versa. It might, of course, be said that the peasants and the nomads do have a common telos, namely, freedom from scarcity and the satisfaction of need. However, whatever the original praxis might have been, freedom from scarcity and the satisfaction of need can now have different meanings. For the peasants it means ownership and for the nomads it means the opposite. Thus the praxis relationship that each group has with the natural environment will imbue the telos of each group with different meanings. Therefore, it could not be said of the peasants and the nomads that they have a shared telos. Moreover, bearing in mind that praxis realises certain dispositions in pursuit of the good and that those dispositions are part of the good then given the different meanings of the good for each group that arises from the distinctive praxis of each group, it follows that the virtues required to achieve that good could also be very different. In this way both the telos of a group and the virtues required for its attainment can be rooted in the praxis relationship between the group and the natural environment. Thus talk of what is good for individuals and their communities, and how to obtain that good, must take into account the relationship that those individuals and communities have with their natural environments, and that relationship can be understood in terms of praxis.

Similarly, it becomes possible to understand the dynamics of a tradition. Given that a tradition is a set of practices, a way of understanding their worth and a way in which practices are shaped and transmitted across generations it can be seen that traditions must help practices to change if those practices are to survive. Engaging in the practice of being a peasant farmer includes, amongst other things, the cutting down of trees. This is part of what being a peasant involves. Peasants must have land to farm. However, as time progresses, it becomes apparent that deforestation is harmful to the practice of peasant farming since in the long-term land is being lost. In the context of the tradition as a whole the practice of peasant farming has to change. Again, in the context of the tradition as a whole the virtues associated with the practice of peasant farming will also change. Thus at all levels of discourse from practices and the virtues associated with those practices, through to traditions and on to telos and the virtues the common denominator, as it were, is praxis at work on the natural environment.

The Chinese peasants and the nomads illustrate a relationship with a scarce resource which causes a conflictual relationship between people. This is precisely the problem with laissez-faire liberalism which formalises the relationship under the banner of rights. It is the exercise of the rights of the individual, notably property rights, together with freedom of contract and market incentives, that is seen as leading to the concentration of ownership of capital and a system of power relations that negates the liberal goal of free, autonomous development for each individual. Thus liberal practices undermine liberal principles. Liberal ideas were born in and depended upon there being sufficient areas of unworked land. Once that land is used or owned, that is, once it becomes scarce, the gap between rich and poor is bound to intensify and the prospect of distributive justice and a more egalitarian society becomes more remote. In short, scarcity of at least certain sorts arises from and can sustain a particular form of association.

The vagueness of Sartre's position over the elimination of scarcity has already been noted. At times he appears to subscribe to Marx's view in which Marx identifies a realm of necessity in which man must struggle against nature and must do so in all social formations.[14] At other times Sartre argues that certain forms of association will eliminate scarcity. Again as has been noted, what is certain is that the effects of certain sorts of scarcity may be overcome,

---

14   Marx, *Capital*, in McLellan, 1977, pp. 496–97.

given the praxis that is productive of certain forms of association. The effect of a water shortage is a hosepipe ban. Neighbours can overcome that by sharing the water in their barrels. Thus, as distinct from Marx, for Sartre the condition of the possibility of overcoming the effects of certain sorts of scarcity, in so far as it exists at all, is to be found within the nature of the associations characteristic of particular groups. The nature of laissez-faire liberalism is not conducive to overcoming scarcity or its effects since it is a form of association that sustains scarcity thus affecting the distribution of scarce goods.

A contemporary example of scarcity of a natural resource intensifying the gap between the rich and the poor and hence an example of the dialectical relationship between scarcity and forms and terms of association is provided by Donella Meadows, Dennis Meadows and Jorgen Randers in *Beyond The Limits*. They report that the fishing industry around the world enjoys fairly free and vigorous markets and in recent years it has seen huge technological developments. For example, refrigerated processing ships allow fleets to stay at distant fishing grounds without having to return home promptly with the catch. Radar, sonar and satellite spotting bring boats to the fish with increasing efficiency. Drift nets 30 miles long allow economic large-scale fishing. Meadows et al comment that, 'The technology being called forth is not that which enhances fish stocks, but that which seeks to find and catch every last fish'.[15] The consequences of this for relations between people are described by Meadows et al. If scarcity of, for example, tuna has the result in the market place of increasing the cost of fish, the wealthiest people will still be prepared to pay that price. Meadows et al. observe that, 'the market does not allocate the fish to those who most need it for food, because the hungry have no power in the markets'.[16] The high price does not induce conservation. Indeed, it encourages even more fishing of tuna.

Here we have a combination of forces. High technology tools combined with, or in the service of, a particular kind of relationship with the environment, a free market approach which insists that the resource exists for the use of those who can afford it and which depends upon the tools to maintain supplies, has in fact produced a scarcity. This scarcity has caused prices to rise which means that only the relatively wealthy can afford fish. Rising prices encourage further fishing, further scarcity, higher prices and so on. They have in turn exacerbated divisions between people which already existed, due to previous scarcities.

One should not imagine that the technology used is somehow neutral. Sartre writes of the primitiveness of the techniques used until recently by rural workers in China. He concludes that, 'The extraordinary separation of rural workers in China, which the commune system has only recently caused to disappear, is obviously linked with the primitiveness and stagnation of techniques. These facts condition and express a definite system of social relations and a definite form of property.'[17] In this case technology is not neutral because it both arises

---

[15] Donella Meadows, Dennis Meadows and Jorgan Randers, 1992, p. 186.
[16] Ibid., p. 187.

from a social milieu and has social implications. As Andre Gorz observes, technical choices are in fact political choices. In other words a society, or a group within society, selects the technology that is appropriate to the logic of that society and that technology then imposes itself upon the structure and institutions of that society. Therefore, nuclear power is first chosen as a by-product of nuclear weaponry, which imposes a centralised, hierarchical, secrecy-dominated society.[18]

The criticism of laissez-faire liberalism that arises from understanding the dialectical relationship that exists between scarcity and a particular form of association has a Rousseauesque dimension. According to Rousseau man is corrupted not by nature but by the ownership of property and the forming of civil society itself. Whereas Locke saw the ownership of property as the basis of a just and equal civil society, Rousseau claimed it was a source of evil and inequality. Locke argued that men gave up the natural freedoms of the state of nature to gain collective security for property, including life and liberty. Civil society was a move to perfect relations among men. It was a product of man's rationality and desire for improvement. Rousseau, however, sees the formation of civil society as the product of man's greed and consequently of a kind of scarcity, since from the moment it appeared an advantage for one man to possess enough goods for two equality vanished. In *Discourse on the Origin and Foundations of Inequality Among Men* he famously argues that the real founder of civil society was the man who after enclosing a piece of ground got it into his head to claim it as his own and found people simple enough to believe him. Thus, contrary to Locke's formulation of a civil society as an agreement between equals, Rousseau construes civil society to be the work of the more powerful and wealthy. In an unequal society the rich found it necessary to preserve order, to control attempts to usurp them, and to legitimise the exploitation of the poor. It was therefore the rich who conceived of civil society and it was conceived to protect their own interests. As Carole Pateman says,

> The argument of Rousseau's conjectural history is that the liberal contract has no basis in 'nature'; it is a result of a particular form of social development, and far from securing all individuals' natural rights merely stabilizes inequality and gives an appearance of legitimacy to the dominance of some over others.[19]

However, the further point is that the particular form of social development is in itself an expression of the relationship that people have with the natural environment. Both Sartre and Rousseau can be understood as arguing that this relationship is paradigmatic of liberal societies. It is a relationship that both creates and sustains scarcity.

---

[17] CDR I, p. 164n.
[18] Andre Gorz, 1980, pp. 99–102.
[19] Carole Pateman, 1979, p. 148.

Laissez-faire liberal society can, therefore, be conceived of as an expression of a certain kind of relationship between man and the natural environment. In this case the relationship is one of domination coupled with ownership. Domination by itself is not peculiar to liberalism since it can also be seen in Marxist thinking. However, it is within the context of the ownership-domination relationship that the logic of the liberal society's relations between people becomes clear and hence also the validity of the communitarian criticism of that form of community. Moreover, it does not matter at all if the key argument proceeds from the opposite direction so that the ownership-domination relationship with the natural environment is said to be the expression of liberal conceptions of relationships between people. The two moves in the key argument are mutually reinforcing. The way that men work on the environment affects the way that men relate to each other and the way that men relate to each other affects the way that men work on the environment. Moreover, it must be said that the claim by one sort of liberalism to an indeterminacy of relationships between people, that is, that liberalism presupposes no particular form of social arrangement, is put in doubt by the nature of the relationship that, from within the context of another sort of liberalism, is perceived to exist with the natural environment.

That doubt arises because the results of the transformation of the natural environment, or at least some of them, are not only social in that they affect groups but they are also personal in the sense that the relationship that individuals have with their environment can be at least partly constitutive of their identity and of their relationship with each other. In another example, which provides an understanding of inequalities between men as arising from the way that men relate to the environment, Sartre describes how, from the window of his hotel room, he looks down and sees a road-mender on the road and a gardener working in a garden. Neither can see the other because between them there is a wall with bits of broken glass on top protecting the 'bourgeois property' where the gardener is working. Nevertheless, there is a relationship between the two men which is mediated by the watching individual, the 'petty bourgeois intellectual,' relaxing in the hotel. The work of the gardener and the road-mender on their material environment actually defines their relationship to each other in so far as they are both manual workers. Furthermore, that same work also defines the watching holiday maker as an intellectual and consequently his relationship with them. The manual workers have a relationship with each other through their relationship with the world which is their praxis ('weeding', 'digging') which the intellectual cannot share. The relationship between each of these two men themselves and their relationship to the watching intellectual becomes clear. The intellectual is not one of those men and he cannot do the work that they are doing. Sartre points out that he is not one 'man' confronted by the other 'men' because 'the concept of man is an abstraction which never occurs in concrete intuition'.[20] Sartre is a holiday maker whilst the others are a gardener and a road-mender. The relationship between them is defined by the work that they do, that is, by their relationship with the environment.

Man lives in a material world which he needs to change in order to survive and to continue to develop. It is in his act of changing the material world that he becomes himself, as a gardener, a road-mender, an intellectual, and this in turn establishes his relation of reciprocity with others engaged in their way of working on the material world. It is in this way that people are defined by what they do. Desan's conclusion, following Sartre, is that 'each individual relation is conditioned by the other through the environing materiality'.[21] In other words, as Warnock puts it, 'Work itself has a double sense; it is a direct link between men and the world of things, and it is also a primary relation between men and one another.'[22] Of course, the tools that people use to work the environment are also part of that identity and that relationship. It matters whether people use spades to dig holes in the ground or pens to write about digging holes in the ground. Fretz demonstrates that this scenario has a symbolic value in terms of the vertical division of labour (the intellectual looking down), the horizontal division of labour (the workers separated by the wall) and the institution of bourgeois private ownership (the garden which is separated from the street by the wall). It is, therefore, a symbol for 'our capitalist society, in which, as consequence of a rigid division of labour, interhuman relations are of a strongly atomistic structure'.[23] Therefore, as an example of a conflict between Kantian-Rawlsian and laissez-faire liberalism, under the latter people are not known or valued on the basis of some abstract generic capacity such as rational autonomy but on the basis of what they do, including what they own and the way in which they work the natural environment.

However, it is important to understand what work means because that will reveal further components of the key argument and reveal further understandings of inequality. According to Sartre, work means that the human being who, as has already been said, is a material being of a certain sort, is 'reduced to an inorganic materiality in order to act materially on matter'.[24] In other words, irrespective of any tools that are used, the individual himself becomes a tool. As Hayim says, 'to act upon the environment a part of the person must return to the level of *inertia*. The person becomes an instrument, a tool, and *recognizes* himself as such'.[25] Warnock points out that 'if men could not become tool-like in making changes in their environment they could do nothing; there would be no such thing as praxis'.[26] So it is that praxis creates a negativity and then

---

20 CDR I, p. 101.
21 Desan, 1965, p. 121.
22 Warnock, 1965, p. 153.
23 Fretz, 'Individuality in Sartre's Philosophy', in Christine Howells (ed.), 1992, pp. 93–94.
24 CDR I, p. 178.
25 Hayim, 1980, p. 69.
26 Warnock, 1965, p. 166. See also Ian Craib, 1976, p. 109; Stack, 1977, p. 74.

negates it in order to satisfy needs. The organic becomes inorganic and the inorganic is then negated to make the organism whole again. It is in the act of becoming that man shows himself to be a material being of a different order to the material world that is being worked on.

At this point, Sartre's argument adds extra weight to the communitarian criticism of deontological liberalism. It follows that in terms of the individual's relationship with the natural environment there can be no antecedently individuated selves. It is, as it were, by losing the self in inorganic materiality that one becomes the self that one is. This is as true of the intellectual as it is of the gardener and the road-mender. It is in that time of 'losing' that one's identity is defined and hence one's relationships with other people. Moreover, that time of 'losing' is a moment of praxis. What emerges is an individual with an identity based upon the individual's relationship with the environment, that is, based on praxis. Therefore, not only is there no antecedently individuated self who is prior to and has a voluntaristic attachment to his ends but it is also the case that the pursuit of those ends is partly constitutive of the individual's identity. This is one way in which the community is partly constitutive of the individual's identity. The community defines the meaning of the relationship that the individual has with the environment as a gardener, road-mender and intellectual. Thus the relationship that one has with the environment is provided by the community with a particular meaning which in turn defines relationships between people by identifying the individual as an individual of a certain sort. People are, therefore, defined by the community both by their ends and by their actions in pursuing those ends. Of course, as an example of the dialectic, the definition that is provided by the community is also a way of defining the community.

However, the identity that emerges is not given or fixed in any Kantian way. In a passage which is both a criticism of Kant and an explanation for alienation Sartre argues that man is a material being and he exists in a material world. He has to change the world in order not simply to survive but to change himself, to achieve a different status,

> to define himself as *the Other whom he will become*. Thus he constantly makes himself the instrument, the means, of this future statute which will realise him as other; and it is impossible for him to treat his own present as an end... in so far as my project is a transcendence of the present towards the future, and of myself towards the world, I always treat myself as a means and cannot treat the Other as an end.[27]

Notice that to say that people can be defined by their ends is not the same as saying that they are ends. Referring to Sartre's observation of the gardener and the road-mender, Warnock writes,

---

27 CDR I, p. 112.

From this simple scene he draws a specifically anti-Kantian moral. There is no such thing as a kingdom of ends; and it is wrong to speak of treating *humanity* as an end. Nothing can be an end for itself except for an idea, he says ... humanity is concrete, not a mere idea. We must recognize that, as with the workmen on either side of the wall, each man has his own end. So far from treating himself and others as ends in themselves, each man treats himself as an instrument of change, as a means of becoming what he is not. Kant believed in a static, permanent, single end – humanity. Sartre (and Marx) substitute a changing and developing end.[28]

Man becomes an instrument or means in his present state in order to achieve a future state. Since by their work people become instruments of their own change they cannot treat themselves as final ends and since this applies to everyone no one can treat anyone as a final end. Everyone, therefore, is a means united by praxis. The nature of reciprocity in the concrete world is contingent upon praxis. Treating people as ends, isolating them, makes them atomistic individuals.

The idea that a moral community can be based on people as ends-in-themselves, without reference to what they actually do is unintelligible to Sartre. Thus reciprocity cannot be based on universal and abstract principles, such as those to be found in Christian or Kantian ethics. Instead, 'It is the individual's *praxis*, as the realisation of his project, which determines his bonds of reciprocity with everyone.'[29] Reciprocity can be positive or negative but in each case people become means both for themselves and for others. With positive reciprocity, each person becomes a means for the other either to pursue their individual goals, as with the exchange or provision of services, or to pursue a single shared goal, as with communal undertakings. With negative reciprocity each refuses to serve anyone else's ends and uses everyone else, making them 'an instrument of his own ends in spite of themselves'.[30]

The idea that man objectifying himself has implications for reciprocity is developed by Sartre who views the objectification of man as the origin of alienation. Despite their differences over the mediating role of matter, Sartre shares with Hegel the affirmation that all objectification involves alienation and that alienation describes a moment in dialectical movement. However, for Hegel, it is the externalisation of ideas that results in the objectification of the world. In other words, the mind externalises material products and institutions yet fails to grasp that these things are its own externalisations and, therefore, treats them as things that are separate from itself. Alienation results from externalisation. Alienation for Hegel can also be seen as an activity of a surrendering or a repudiating of oneself as separate from that from which one is not essentially different, that is, a surrendering of oneself as alienated in the first sense. Alienation in this latter sense is necessary for overcoming alienation

---

[28] Warnock, 1965, pp. 164–65.
[29] CDR I, p. 110.
[30] Ibid., p. 113.

in the former sense and has an affinity with the social contract theory of, amongst others, Hobbes and Rousseau.[31] Sartre does not employ alienation to denote the activity of externalisation, nor does he use it to denote the activity of surrendering oneself in Hegel's sense. As has been seen, objectification, for Sartre, involves man becoming an object in order to work, which could be regarded as a surrendering of oneself to materiality in order to become whole again. So we have the inevitability of a kind of alienation, that which is based on the inevitability of objectification. Man working on matter must become an object in order to become a fulfilled, non-alienated subject. The paradox is that praxis and therefore human existence unavoidably alienates itself through the very activity in which it actualises itself.

However, Sartre writes of alienation in a further way, this time in the context of scarcity. In this second sense of alienation the ontological form acquires a social and historical dimension. The identification of scarcity as a contingent though ever present fact, as occasioning the milieu in which praxis must work, opens the way for the identification of alienation in terms of man's relationship with nature and, simultaneously and because of that, his relationships with other men. For Marx, man becomes alienated through his work in so far as such work maintains private property. Klaus Hartmann comments that, 'In Sartre's theory, on the other hand, alienation is traced back to praxis as affected by a universal contingency. Further, alienation is reduced to a pre-economic reason: I alienate myself in *matter* under conditions of scarcity.'[32] Ontological alienation makes possible a certain type of social alienation. Sartre argues that the worker becomes a commodity, 'his labour power is treated as an inert commodity; but, although it does in fact become a commodity in social terms, it represents in the worker the perpetual need to turn himself into an inorganic means to an end which has nothing to do with him, rather than an exterior materiality in which he might objectify himself'.[33] In doing so he is in competition for work in a milieu of scarcity with others who have to objectify themselves and this is another type of social alienation. Workers became '*mere inert things* who relate to other workers through competitive antagonism and to *themselves* through the "free" possibility of selling that other thing, their labour power'.[34] Thus the process of objectification which is alienating at one level becomes the processes of commodification and then competition which are alienating at another level. Hartmann notes that in the *Critique* 'alienation is explained by reference to interrelated principles – praxis, scarcity, matter – and not introduced unexplained as an object of criticism the way that it is in Marx's theory'.[35]

---

31 Richard Schacht, 1972, p. 47; Theodore Denise, 'The Concept of Alienation: Some Critical Notices', in Frank Johnson (ed.), 1973, p. 152.
32 Klaus Hartmann, 1970, p. 50.
33 CDR I, p. 208.
34 Ibid., p. 156.
35 Hartmann, 1970, p. 50.

Thus, for Sartre, alienation in the social sense exists because of ontological alienation and because praxis occurs in the milieu of sustained scarcity. Sartre reports that at the time of the Industrial Revolution 'a new kind of men came into being, "iron and coal men", produced by mining and by new smelting techniques, the industrial proletarians (and of course, industrialists and technicians, etc.) All this is well known'.[36] This is because mankind literally unearthed a source of energy through mining. However, mines are not inexhaustible and they may be exploited to the full in order to maximise gains for the owners, in just the same way as happens with tuna. As Sartre explains,

> All exploitive activities come to be based on the mode of exploitation of the mines, they are constituted in the perspective of rapid, brutal gains before the raw material is exhausted . . . And within the complex of materials and instruments, there had to be a division of labour: mines and factories created their capitalists, their technicians and their workers.[37]

Yet there is no obvious reason why the capitalist mode of production should have resulted in alienation. For example, it is not clear from Marx why the discovery of a new source of wealth, namely iron and coal, should produce more unpleasant conditions of poverty for certain sections of the community. Regardless of the means of production as such, everyone's condition should have become more pleasant. That this did not happen was due to the prior existence of the milieu of scarcity. It is the milieu of scarcity rather than the inevitable cruelty of individual capitalists that, ultimately, accounts for oppression. Indeed, at a local level individual employers may have been concerned for the well-being of their workers, albeit often for self-interested reasons.

Similarly, the division of labour in itself need not produce the class antagonism that in *Anti-Duhring* Engels claimed that it did produce. Sartre agrees that there was a division of labour but it was not the one that Engels mentions. The division of labour that Sartre has in mind is where, 'The peasant asks the noble to undertake the labour of war, that is to say, to defend him with violence against violence *in the milieu of scarcity.*'[38] Sartre asks, 'Why should the social division of labour, which is a positive differentiation, be transformed into class struggle, that is, into a *negative* differentiation?'[39] Sartre responds to his own question by arguing that,

> The only possible answer . . . is that negation be given *in the first instance* in the original indifferentiation, whether this is an agricultural commune or a nomadic horde. And this negation . . . is the interiorised negation of a number of men by scarcity, that is to say, the necessity for society to choose

---
36 CDR I, p. 154.
37 Ibid.
38 Ibid., p. 145.
39 Ibid., p. 146.

its dead and its underfed. In other words, it is the existence of a practical dimension of non-humanity in the man of scarcity.[40]

In other words, class as a negative differentiation arises from the relationship between the group and the environment in a milieu of scarcity.

In fact, the original indifferentiation mentioned by Sartre refers to two different ways of relating to the environment, that is, two different praxes attempting to satisfy need and hence two different meanings to the notion of freedom from scarcity. The meaning which prevails for the commune and the horde will constitute part of the terms of a particular form of association. So it is that we are unable to escape from the dialectical relationship that exists between scarcity and associations or, more basically, between praxis and associations. Society is fuelled and driven by a dynamic of its own making. However, this is not to say that it cannot change. Indeed, it must change if there is to be any equality of membership of a community. Equality of membership is a notion that has now acquired some substance with the reference to the dead and the underfed. With that reference in mind it becomes apparent that equality of membership is not possible in a community that gives rise to and is sustained by scarcity of certain sorts. Change is possible because praxis is, within the limits that are about to be described, free.

Of course man relates to the non-human world in a variety of ways and not just through labour. However, as the passage from Manser quoted earlier in this chapter indicates, it is through labour that Sartre analyses this relationship and it is through labour that we can see that man's relationship with the environment affects his relationship with men. Early in the first volume of the *Critique* Sartre indicates the nature of the relationship that exists between man and the environment. Man has a relationship with the environment by virtue of the fact that, first, he has certain needs and second, it is because of these needs that man works on matter and, in an illustration of the relationship between interiorisation and transcendence, this in turn makes him what he becomes because he is 'forced to re-interiorise the exteriority of his product'.[41] Thus, in the dialectic of praxis, man becomes the product of his own product, that is, a man of a certain sort. This has implications for the normative notion of praxis. The prescriptions for ways of acting and being that are revealed by praxis cannot emerge from praxis alone. They emerge from the dialectical relationship that exists between praxis and that upon which praxis is at work. This relationship is what makes praxis into a praxis of a certain sort. Thus the normative nature of praxis emerges from praxis working within a particular context. That relationship should not be misunderstood. This is not to say that praxis is determined by that upon which it works. Simply, that upon which it works has to be taken into account by praxis. No stronger claim can be made since for praxis to work at all it must be capable of transcending the material conditions

---

[40] Ibid., p. 147.

upon which it works. That capacity resides in the fact that praxis is free albeit constantly searching for that which is deemed to be valuable in the course of which it invokes the dialectical circularity which is contained within itself.

There is, for Sartre, nothing deterministic about the process of becoming the product of one's own product. Monika Langer, in her commentary on Merleau-Ponty's *Phenomenology of Perception* points out that although Sartre agrees with the determinists' view that every act must have a motive, he does not agree that it is the motive that causes the act. Sartre argues that the end effects the emergence of a cause. A cause is simply the apprehension of the world's objective structure, as it is disclosed in the light of the end, as the means for attaining the end. Or, the end reveals the cause of the action in the light of what the world is like. The cause does not determine the action since it is only because of praxis that it appears at all. The same is true of the motive. As Langer notes, 'Sartre . . . concludes that cause, motive and end are inseverable terms of a project which is itself a particular way of being-in-the-world – in short, a freedom.'[42]

Thus praxis is free but responds to the exigencies that it recognises. These exigencies, once recognised, are an example of the given limits to freedom mentioned in the previous chapter and referred to earlier in this. Sartre tells of how the poor performance of trains on even the gentlest of slopes meant that railway lines had to follow valleys. He argues that these material factors present men with certain exigencies. However, it is by men and through men that these exigencies appear and they would disappear if men did. Sartre concludes that,

> the example of the locomotive shows that the exigency of matter ends up by being extended to matter itself through men. Thus the very *praxis* of individuals or groups is altered in so far as it ceases to be the free organisation of the practical field and becomes the re-organisation of one sector of inert materiality in accordance with the exigencies of another sector of materiality.[43]

The passage just quoted illustrates the nature of the relationship between man and the environment very well in that it illustrates the relationship between freedom and facticity.

For Sartre, the relationship between freedom and facticity was always one of interdependence. In *Being and Nothingness* the mountain is hard to climb because someone has chosen to climb it. Someone can only choose to climb the mountain because there is a mountain to climb and his free choice reveals that it is a hard mountain to climb. Thus, 'Without facticity freedom would not exist – as a power of nihilation and of choice – and without freedom facticity would not be discovered and would have no meaning'.[44] Similarly, without

---
41 Ibid., p. 71.
42 Monika Langer, 1989, p. 136.
43 CDR I, p. 191.
44 *Being and Nothingness*, pp. 495–96.

need there would be no praxis and it is praxis that reveals obstacles in the form of the practico-inert.

The analysis of alienation conducted earlier can be applied directly to MacIntyre's notion of practices in order to emphasise its complexity. This application relies on the distinction between ontological and social alienation and will do something to temper the tone of the latter. In the previous chapter it was argued that practices are a species of praxis. It immediately becomes apparent that all practices are ontologically alienating. It is also apparent that many practices may also be alienating at a social level, particularly given the milieu of scarcity. Moreover, the virtues associated with practices can do nothing at all to relieve ontological alienation. Indeed, the degree of ontological alienation and the frequency with which it is experienced will increase in proportion to the exercise of those virtues. Fortunately, the same need not apply to social alienation, or at least to a certain type of that alienation in which the individual is viewed as a commodity. In the case of practices, the more that the exercise of virtues in connection with practices produces alienation at the ontological level the more that same exercise will actualise the individual due to the realisation of internal goods. Thus the increase in internal goods can bring relief from the status of a commodity at the level of a certain type of social alienation. This difference is due to the incorporation of virtues into the discussion. Since some forms of praxis are also practices then some forms of praxis may also avoid certain sorts of social alienation.

The fact that practices are ontologically alienating means that even communities that are not geographically located, that is, having a relationship with a particular place in the natural environment as a community, cannot ignore the relationship that they have with the natural environment. In other words, a community of practitioners, geographically dispersed, will, on an individual level, be related to the environment. This is a relationship that will affect the practice to the extent that the practice affects the environment.

So far, the emphasis in the key argument has been largely on that part which claims that the way in which people relate to the environment affects the way that they relate to each other. As Catalano observes, 'Sartre is particularly careful to show that class being and class praxis are the result of how we have worked the environment and how this worked matter then affects our future.'[45] Catalano's observation is, however, only part of the key argument. Certainly different forms and terms of association can be understood as arising from the relationship that man has with the natural environment. However, in the two-way movement of the dialectic of praxis, relationships between people affect their relationship with the environment. The importance of this two-way movement resides in the fact that each movement is reinforcing of the other. Thus a particular relationship with the environment begets a form of association

---

[45] Catalano, 1986, p. 248.

that is characterised by classes and a form of association that is characterised by classes begets a certain relationship with the environment. Thus although, so far, the emphasis in the key argument has been largely on the part that claims that the way in which people relate to the environment affects the way that they relate to each other, this has not been entirely the case because it is impossible to ignore the other part of the argument which says that the way in which people relate to each other in communities affects the way in which they relate to the environment and that there is a dialectical relationship between the two parts of the key argument which must be understood if the nature of associating is to be understood. We have already seen that, for example, choices concerning energy are political choices made within the context of a society at a particular stage of development.

In fact, Sartre's discussion of pollution can be used to illustrate the second part of the key argument. Sartre provides examples of two types of pollution. With reference to air pollution, specifically that caused by coal fumes during the industrial revolution, Sartre points out that the means for at least lessening the pollution were always available. It was, after all, caused by incompletely consumed carbon. He argues that,

> the failure to see this human and technical exigency, or to see it and take it seriously, is *precisely* what characterises the *praxis* of the bourgeoisie at this time ... They were constituted as a class (in this particular respect) by a refusal to see the effects of air pollution *on the other class* as a counter-finality.[46]

Here, membership of a particular class manifests itself in a particular way of relating to the environment, polluting it. Moreover, it has an effect on others, it causes ill-health. Therefore, a class relationship finds expression in a particular relationship with the environment, which in turn, it should be noticed, leads to a particular relationship with others. Sartre complements the example of air pollution with the example of the noise generated by steam machines and concludes that

> noise, like the black smoke which rose from the factory chimneys, demanded to be maintained as a material affirmation of new-found human power, that is the power of a new class produced in the context of a changing mode of production, and therefore, *in opposition* both to landowners and to workers.[47]

Pollution, therefore, was the visible and audible mark of the power of a certain class in relation to other classes. Furthermore, it becomes part of the meaning of industrialisation for that section of the community who cannot afford to live anywhere other than by the polluting factories and who have to suffer the pollution. It also becomes part of the meaning of industrialisation for the owners

---
[46] CDR I, p. 195.
[47] Ibid., p. 196.

of the factories but since they can escape the pollution it does not have the same meaning.

Bringing the two parts of the key argument together it may be apparent that fishermen, people who can afford to buy fish and those who cannot, Chinese peasants, nomads, intellectuals, road-menders and gardeners all occupy a world that is already constituted by past praxis. With regard to Sartre's intellectual, gardener and road-mender, they occupy a world in which intellectuals take holidays and in which gardeners and road-menders are employed because there are gardens to be tended and roads to be mended. It is a world, moreover, in which those who do the tending and the mending occupy a particular social position. It has been seen that Sartre's scenario with the intellectual, the gardener and the road-mender symbolises the vertical and horizontal division of labour and the institution of private property. However, the scenario is more than a symbol for capitalist society. The capitalist society, as a type of relationship between people, has produced real environmental barriers, a wall with bits of broken glass on top, people working in the open air and being watched by someone from behind a window, which enforce the separation of man from man and which are aspects of the process of interiorising that separation.

Both elements of the key argument are brought together in Sartre's example of industrialisation in revolutionary Russia. Industrialisation involved a changed relationship with the non-human environment and that affected relationships between men. Industrialisation also affected relationships between men and that affected their relationship with the environment. The second volume of the *Critique* describes how, in the case of Russia under Stalin, there was a demand for increased productivity. Increased productivity demanded, among other things, an increase in machines and consequently an increase in workers and these workers could be drawn only from the peasantry. Thus large numbers of rural workers were moved from the land and into the cities. There was, therefore, a change in the relationship with the natural environment. This brought about a change in the relationship between people. The increased number of factory workers had to be fed which meant that the agricultural workers, now fewer in number, had to work harder to produce the food that was required. At the same time, since heavy industry has a slow turnover and thus, initially at least, produces little wealth, the factory workers have little purchasing power and consequently cannot afford to pay for food. The demand for the agricultural workers to increase their productivity and hence change their methods of farming which had traditionally been by working small-holdings, was met with resistance in the form of a peasant movement led by capitalistic kulaks. In 1928 the peasant movement confronted Stalin with a 'grain strike'. There was, as Sartre says, 'a *real indeterminacy* of relations between the sovereign and the agricultural masses'.[48] The peasantry, united amongst themselves, does not become

---

[48] CDR II, p. 170.

integrated into the sweep of the sovereign's unifying praxis but becomes 'the fleeting disunity that placed unity in danger'.[49] The factory workers unite against the countryside in which every peasant was viewed as a possible kulak, hoarding grain for private profit while workers were starving. In the light of the relationships that now existed between people new methods of farming were forced upon the agricultural workers. Increased agricultural productivity required the mechanisation of farming which in turn made sense only if farming was to be carried out on a large scale through collectivisation. There was, therefore, a new way of relating to the environment. The plan was that the larger yields from the collectivities would encourage other peasants working on small-holdings to join the collectivities. Moreover, mechanisation would give the peasant and the factory worker a common culture. Although it adds nothing to the argument, it is interesting to note the similarities between Sartre's description of the relationship between the peasants and the city workers and that of Bakunin in 'Letters to a Frenchman on the Present Crisis'.[50]

The collective in Russia becomes another way of relating to the environment, different from that of the Chinese peasants who worked initially on their own. The Chinese peasants worked as individuals, in ignorance of each other. The multiplicity of those individual praxes brought about the threat of the loss of their land. The Russian peasants were organised into collectivities and mechanised. This resulted in increased agricultural production. However, it should be noted that the formal law of praxis remained unchanged. The form of association that obtained between people affected their relationship with the land and their relationship with the land affected their form of association.

Sartre's example of industrialisation in Russia also provides an insight into what the idea of the meanings of social goods might involve in terms of relationships. The social goods at issue here include farms and factories. What becomes apparent is that these goods can take on different meanings for different groups within the community and this can be a source of conflict between those groups. Factories will mean one thing for the Bolshevik elite and another thing for the peasants forced to work in them. The same applies to farming, either on a small-holding or on a collective farm. The values associated with either form of farming will be different according to whether one is a kulak or a factory worker. Moreover, even when a particular social good does have the same meaning, that meaning can in itself be the occasion for conflict. A collective farm, it might have been agreed, would mean giving up one way of life and embracing another. Some peasants might have been happy to do this whilst others, such as the kulaks, would not. Thus even when there is no disagreement over the meaning of a social good such as a type of farm, when everyone agrees that such farms are expressive of a certain way of life and identity, the different

---

[49] Ibid., p. 172.
[50] Bakunin, 'Letters to a Frenchman on the Present Crisis', in Sam Dolgoff (ed.), 1973, p. 201.

values associated with that meaning can be the cause of conflict within the community. The response to this could be that if a particular good, such as a farm, evokes different values then it cannot be said to have the same meaning. The different values invest the farm with different meanings. Unfortunately, this move does not resolve the problem of arriving at the shared meaning of social goods. It simply makes such shared meanings harder to obtain by tightening the criteria for what constitutes a shared meaning. Moreover, as will become clear in the next chapter, agreements and even the holding of the same meanings may not be synonymous with shared meanings.

The clue to the meaning of Sartre's example of industrialisation in Russia is the dialectical circularity that is inherent in praxis. In other words, it is the operation of praxis itself and the interiorisation of the results that produces the conditions that have been described and consequently, just as the social consciousness that arises from praxis also informs praxis, it makes no sense to ask if the process begins with man's relationship with nature or with man's relationship with other men. Sartre is not attempting to establish a point of departure for understanding any specific element of that relationship. It is true that he believes that praxis stems from need. One might wish to point to that as the origin of the dialectical nature of praxis. However, Sartre takes the argument a step further by relating needs and the resources to meet those needs to society as a whole. He argues that, 'it is the organism and its needs that define the resources ... which – determined by technology – recondition the latter, and pass with all their inertia (in the form of raw matter and worked matter) into the primary social structuration'.[51] This means that when the organism defines the resources that it needs, the resources that are in fact produced redefine needs, in accordance with the formal law of praxis, thus indicating a movement into the future. This is because, as David Pepper indicates, when man works on nature to produce objects he is not merely attempting to satisfy basic physical needs. Man transforms nature in order to meet needs, which he does because, 'In the main nature does not offer ready-made subsistence to man, neither does man take direct possession of nature's resources. He has to transform them.'[52] However, as man transforms nature he learns more of how it works. This knowledge enables man to satisfy more needs and more sophisticated needs. In other words, his needs will change. As the needs change so too do the resources to meet those needs. If resources are thought of as things in nature that can be

---

51 CDR II, p. 277. Agnes Heller makes a similar point. According to Heller,

'Man's need and the object of the need are correlated: the need is always related to some concrete object or to an objective activity. The objects 'bring about' the needs and the needs bring about the objects. The need and its object are 'moments', 'sides' of one and the same complex'. (Heller, 1976, p. 41)

However, this does not obviously contain the suggestion of movement into the future that is conveyed by Sartre's notion of 'recondition'.

52 David Pepper, 1989, p. 162.

useful to men then they can be defined only in the context of a particular society's stage of technological development. Thus oil is a resource that is becoming increasingly scarce in the developed world. For certain hunter-gatherer groups in the Amazon basin it is not a resource at all. Moreover, where oil is a resource it can create new needs. If needs can be acquired then they are not purely biological. They can have a social or a cultural dimension. This is the point that Sartre makes. In transforming nature man comes to transform himself and his praxis and consequently his relations with other people. Conversely, and with equal justification, social changes can produce changes in needs which require a different transformation of nature and so the cycle continues. Therefore, a way of relating to the environment is simultaneously a way of relating to each other and any way of relating to each other at the level of society will impact upon the environment.

In the previous chapter it was noted that the liberal view of the individual places the individual before society. In other words, according to this view, the individual is more real than society, the individual existed before society was formed, and the rights and demands of the individual are morally precedent to those of society. The communitarian response argued, on the one hand, that at the level of theory this view is wrong because it suggests that individuals are pre-existent atomic units and that social relations are voluntary and, on the other hand, that at the level of practice liberalism was wrong because modern society has become atomised, social bonds have broken and group membership has become optional and that these are states of affairs to be regretted and remedied. Relating the community to the environment yields some perspectives that support the communitarian view of the individual by showing that the individual is more embedded and attached than liberalism acknowledges.

An examination of the nature of the relationship between the individual, the community and the natural environment reveals that it would be an error for any theory to claim that, with regard to the natural environment, individuals are pre-existent atomic units who have a voluntary relationship with the natural environment. The individual does not come before the natural environment in the sense of being more real. Indeed, the reality of the individual requires the reality of the natural environment. Consequently, the individual does not come before the natural environment temporally either. In fact, the individual is a relative newcomer. The issue of the primacy, morally speaking, of the individual's rights invokes deliberations concerning moral considerability and status and concerning judgements of instrumental and intrinsic value which, in relation to the natural environment, are beyond the scope of this work. What may be said is that it is not obviously the case that all human rights come before all the rights attributed to the natural environment or to elements within it except in the very limited sense that it is humans that make the attribution. Neither can it be said that individuals are atomistic units if by that it is meant that individuals are isolated and separated from the natural environment. People are in and of the world and every attempt that they may make to distance themselves from the world in, for example, their choice of clothing, food and man-made environments, requires the natural environment and in any case reveals a relationship. In that sense it follows that the individual does not have a voluntary relationship with the natural environment. Individuals and groups may choose to do all kinds of things to the environment but the one thing that people cannot choose is to refuse to relate to the environment entirely. Living or dead the individual has an ineliminable relationship with the environment. It is, moreover, a relationship with social consequences.

The key argument has provided a degree of concreteness to an understanding of the nature of associating that is otherwise lacking in the work of the communitarians. With an understanding of man's relationship with the environment comes some understanding of the nature of men's relationships with each other. This chapter has begun the process of examining men's relationships with each other. That examination will be continued in the next chapter.

CHAPTER FIVE

Forms and terms of association: series

We can now be confident that forms and terms of association give rise to certain conditions and those conditions will have an effect on forms and terms of association. The nature of that dialectical relationship was illustrated by the argument which said that the way that people, individually and collectively, relate to the natural environment will affect the way that they relate to each other as members of a community and, in a demonstration of the two-way dialectic of praxis, the way that people relate to each other as members of a community affects the way that individually and collectively they relate to the natural environment. So it is that people are defined at least in part by what they do, and what they do to satisfy needs in a milieu of scarcity inevitably impacts upon others. With that in mind it has been argued that the nature of reciprocity in the concrete world is contingent upon man's praxis.

It will now be argued that an understanding of the nature of associating requires an understanding of the different forms and terms of association that are characteristic of different ways of associating. This will help to strengthen communitarian claims regarding the benefits of community since they are claims that can stand only with regard to communities of certain sorts, distinguishable by particular forms and terms of association. In so far as Sartre provides a developed view of different sorts of associations and in so far as the communitarians do not, the account of associations that is offered in this and the following chapter will follow Sartre's classification of associations. The forms of association identified by Sartre are the series, the group-in-fusion, the pledged group, organisation and institution. These are located within society as a whole and function under the aegis of the State. These forms of association will be seen to be accompanied by particular terms of association and that the one is supportive of the other. From this it will be seen that the dialectical relationship between forms and terms of association, which is rooted in the dialectical and normative nature of praxis, can not only give rise to notions of the good but can also be the product of such notions. Following the argument of the previous two chapters, it will become clear that where the meanings of social goods are rooted in praxis those meanings will affect the nature of associations even whilst being the product of an association. Moreover, the manner by which not only the form and related terms of a particular type of association are constitutive of the identity of individuals but also the manner by which the form and related terms of an association are themselves constituted by individuals, first discussed in chapter two, will be examined further. The Sartrean analysis of the constituting and constituted nature of associations will begin to illustrate the nature of the relationship between the individual and the community. It will be seen that it is the dialectical relationship between forms and terms of association that enables us to understand what associating involves and how associations can be sustained.

The form of association that is to be examined in this chapter, the one that Sartre examines first, is the series. This is the form of association where individuals are collectivised by objects and structures yet remain other to and separate from other collectivised individuals. Although this is Sartre's starting point, he is at pains to point out that, 'It is no part of our project to determine whether series precede groups or vice versa, either originally or in a particular moment of history'[1] and 'Who could claim that collectives come before groups?'[2] Thus 'on account of dialectical circularity – any form can emerge either before or after any other'.[3] Hartmann explains that,

> It would be a mistake to surmise that Sartre meant to depict the making of social formations in any empirical and historical sense ... Rather he seeks to rationalize those *intelligible* practical relationships between individuals which can be adduced to explain social formations. What we have is a systematic theory of various ensembles with no implication that what comes early in the theory also comes early in history or vice versa.[4]

Clearly the formation of a group implies that prior to that formation the members of the group, or at least some of them, had a different kind of relationship with each other. However, this does not mean that seriality cannot follow immediately upon the first formation of the group or indeed upon any other subsequent group formation. It is also the case that the series can co-exist, in the life of any individual, with a variety of other group formations.[5] Moreover, seriality can be a characteristic of society as a whole within which certain groups might operate. Thus Sartre is not describing a historical sequence of events. Having established what he does not intend, Sartre goes on to explain what it is that he does. According to Sartre, 'the *only* thing which matters to us is to display the transition from series to groups and from groups to series as constant incarnations of our practical multiplicity, and to test the dialectical intelligibility of these reversible processes'.[6] Of course, it is important not to forget that the transitions of which Sartre speaks will occur within the context of what in the previous chapter emerged as the interweaving relationship between needs,

---

1 CDR I, p. 65.
2 Ibid., p. 348.
3 Ibid., p. 583.
4 Hartmann, 'Sartre's Theory of Ensembles', in Schilpp (ed.), 1981, p. 634.
5 However, Sartre also says that groups 'can arise only on the foundation of the collective' (CDR I, p. 253–54) which would seem to indicate an order of succession.
6 CDR I, p. 65.

resources and technology which, as mediated by praxis, both produces and is the product of particular forms and terms of association extending through time.

The examination of the series will expand upon and give weight to communitarian criticisms of liberal political and economic structures as being unfriendly to the fostering of communal attachments. Communitarians criticise the atomisation, isolation and detachedness that they regard as features of liberal society. Sandel argues that these features arise from a conception of the self as antecedently individuated. MacIntyre argues that these features arise from the liberal failure to recognise the significance of the community as a source for the conception and pursuit of the good life for human beings. Sartre's argument differs from those of Sandel and MacIntyre even whilst resonating with themes that may be discerned in both.

Sartre describes serial relationships as atomistic, they are 'a plurality of isolations'[7] and because of that 'seriality is a measure of my impotence'.[8] According to Barnes, 'The series is characterized by impotence, isolation, and alienation. Each one is other to all the others.'[9] As Jacques Salvan puts it, 'A series is an inorganic social entity. Each one in the series feels that he is just another person, and feels the solitude of his otherness.'[10] Sartre's view of seriality, therefore, contains elements of the communitarian view of both deontological and laissez-faire liberalism and which, with regard to the former, Sartre is giving a concrete setting. In the isolation and impotence that is characteristic of seriality people are vulnerable to control. Anderson points out that, 'The masses of consumers may, in fact, be so conditioned by the propaganda of advertising and public opinion that, while remaining an impotent series, they believe that they are part of an effective organisation simply because they buy the same, vote the same, and think the same as others.'[11] Aronson argues that, 'The serial individual acts by himself, but as *others* would want him to. Standing alongside each other, we only appear to act together: each of us is dominated and radically isolated.'[12] Sartre provides a number of examples of seriality in order to draw attention to its isolating and dominating characteristics.

Perhaps the most well known example of seriality provided by Sartre is the queue of people waiting for a bus at the Place Saint-Germaine. The isolation of each individual in the queue is quite deliberate. In an indication that seriality is not an all or nothing condition, Sartre explains that it is their way of coping with their movement from one group, their homes and families, to another group, their offices and their colleagues. Their way of coping requires that they

---

[7] Ibid., p. 256.
[8] Ibid., p. 273.
[9] Barnes, 1974, p. 121. See also Hayim, 'Seriality is common to all unorganized and marginal human groups. It stands for feelings of isolation, powerlessness and alienation'. (Hayim, 1980, p. 83)
[10] Jacques Salvan, 1967, p. 168.
[11] Anderson, 1993, p. 97.
[12] Aronson, 1980, p. 251.

'do not care about or speak to each other and, in general, they do not look at one another; they exist side by side alongside a bus stop'.[13] To the extent that each individual is the other to all the other individuals in the queue they are the same. Their sameness resides in their mutual otherness. Additionally, in their otherness they have what at first glance appears to be the same interest in wanting to catch the same bus. According to Sartre, 'these individuals form a group to the extent that they have a *common interest*'.[14] At this level each individual is interchangeable with any other. As Ingbert Knecht observes, 'In his individuality, he is unessential. Everyone could stand in his place.'[15]

The queue and the bus journey are both manifestations of an established order. Thus the queue is neither a random gathering nor is it disorganised. It contains a structure and this structure is provided by the ticket machine attached to the bus stop. In other words, the individual in the queue has a serial reality which is brought about by the ticket machine dispensing numbered tickets. That procedure is described by Sartre as 'an inert practice, endowed by instrumentality, whose meaning is that it integrates him into an ordered multiplicity by assigning him a place in a prefabricated society'.[16] The bus travels at a specific time, along a specific route. As Knecht says, 'Everything is rigidly ordered. One must insert oneself into the given order or else choose another means of transportation.'[17] The practico-inert presents a pre-given order but it is an order that has been created by individuals.

Sartre observes that interdependence can be suffered in serial alterity, 'everyone depends on the others in so far as they are Others'.[18] The queue at the bus stop can be a queue only because of this interdependence. Knecht describes this as 'a diversity of relations of reciprocal dependence [which] arises within a plurality of isolated individuals'.[19] This interdependence in no way affects their serial condition for once again reciprocity is rooted in the concrete, material world with its persistent overtone of scarcity. There may not be enough seats. The people in front may take the last seats. It is a concern that everyone has in common. Therefore, in a queue the only significance that an individual has is as a queuer. For the purpose of the queue nothing else is required. Of course, it would be better for each individual in this queue if every other queuer was to go elsewhere.

The bus stop is described as being in front of the church. Yet the church as a symbol for the judgement of individual dispositions, qualities or virtues and for the assignment of appropriate rewards is an irrelevance. It is impossible to

---

13   CDR I, p. 256.
14   Ibid., p. 258.
15   Ingbert Knecht, 'Seriality: A Ground for Social Alienation' trans. James Bernauer and Hugh Silverman, in Silverman and Elliston (eds.), 1980, p. 195.
16   CDR I, p. 265.
17   Op. cit.
18   CDR I, p. 472.
19   Op. cit., p. 196.

differentiate between the members of the queue on the basis of any judgement of any individual's inherent qualities. The ticket machine is far more important. The ticket machine is the common or collective object that defines the individuals at that bus stop as members of a series. Each individual has a ticket which indicates their place in the queue. The individual's place in the queue does not depend on any distinctive characteristic that the individual might have but instead depends on the actions of that individual in arriving early or late in relation to the arrival of each of the others. Consequently, the relationship that the individuals in the queue have with each other is in all important respects the same as the relationship that each individual has with the ticket machine. The 'inert rule of alterity'[20] imposed by the ticket machine affects the way that people view themselves as individuals, it affects the way that individuals view their relationships with other individuals and as a consequence affects everyone's behaviour. Customs are part of the practico-inert. Isolation consists in the fact that people do not know each other and, following custom, they therefore do not speak to each other. Thus seriality establishes ways of thinking about oneself as an individual and ways of thinking about other people from which social practices are devised and developed which are themselves perfectly rational given that seriality is their basis. The form of association, the nature of the relationship between individuals, is that each is isolated. The terms accompanying that form include the custom of keeping oneself to oneself. This is an example of the dialectical relationship between forms and terms of association. So it is that according to Sartre, 'There are serial behaviour, serial feelings and serial thoughts; in other words *a series is a mode of being for individuals.*'[21] Sartre calls this way of thinking, feeling and behaving 'the formula of the series'[22] in what could be taken to be a direct reference to Kant's categorical imperative.

McBride points out that there are certain difficulties with Sartre's example of the bus queue. Were the bus service to be discontinued there is a strong possibility that people would organise to protest. They would, therefore, says McBride, be protesting to retain that series.[23] Yet this is not entirely true. The people would really be protesting in order to have the bus service reinstated. They would not be protesting in order to bring back the queue. Bus queues as manifestations of seriality are simply a consequence of operating a bus service which has designated places for getting on and off the bus. Moreover, if people do organise to protest then they have in any case overcome seriality. The people will have organised themselves, in response to a need, identified as a common need, into a new form of association and if the protest is successful that organisation might persist at least until some of the protesters obtained jobs elsewhere or new people joined the queue. McBride's second difficulty is more compelling. Part of the reason for that protest might be that for some people

---

[20] CDR I, p. 266.
[21] Ibid.
[22] Ibid.

queuing regularly at the bus stop and catching the same bus was not a serial experience at all; relationships might well be formed in such circumstances. McBride argues that, 'The public transport vehicle, unlike the private automobile, has about it some of the communal aspects of the market places of ancient cities.'[24] Here McBride is expressing a doubt as to the appropriateness of the bus queue as an example of seriality, although, of course, the force of the example resides in the manner by which the queue is constructed. Nevertheless, this doubt serves to warn against treating seriality as an all or nothing state. For any given manifestation of seriality, what might be isolating for some will not be so for others. This should serve to temper some communitarian criticism of liberalism.

In another example Sartre tells of listeners to a radio programme. Here, unlike the example of the bus queue, seriality does not depend upon the presence of all the other individuals. One could be listening to the radio programme alone. Yet the experience of impotence would remain. For example, one could stop listening to the programme as a protest. However, this would in itself do nothing to stop the broadcast. As Sartre says, 'I will merely have rushed into the ineffective, abstract isolation of private life . . . I will not have negated the voice; I will have negated myself as an individual member of the gathering.'[25] Furthermore, as Sartre points out, the listener has no possibility of communicating directly with all the other listeners.

Yet another example reported by Sartre as a result of a visit to America is that of the 'top ten' records. These records supposedly reflect the taste of music lovers across the nation. Through these records serial individuals feel a kind of unity. Everyone is buying the same thing. Sartre makes the point that the individual who listens to the 'top ten' on the radio every Saturday and who buys the number one record every week will find that he has accumulated the record collection of the other, that is the record collection of no one in particular. The emphasis in the example is on the custom of buying the number one record simply because it is the number one record and regardless of whatever it may sound like. Thus, 'Ultimately, the record collection which is no one's becomes indistinguishable from everyone's collection – though without ceasing to be no one's.'[26] The 'top ten' does not reflect the taste of the record buying public since the function of the 'top ten' is in any case to sell records. More than that it reflects the marketing policy of a small number of record company executives.

Of course, it could be objected that listening to the radio and hearing of the 'top ten' records are examples of shared experiences and a source of meaning. However, the force of Sartre's examples is clarified by the observation made by Haim and Rivca Gordon that being a member of a series involves absorbing

---

23 McBride, 1991, p. 138.
24 Ibid.
25 CDR I, p. 272.
26 Ibid., pp. 650–51. The example of the 'top ten' records is one that had occurred to Sartre when he was engaged with his *Notebooks for an Ethics*, see pp. 86–87.

'the objects, facts, values, ideas, and thoughts that the external world and society provide; it means stifling one's spontaneity and only rarely initiating or acting in a manner unique to one's individuality; it means determining oneself as an Other'.[27] In seriality the individual abandons responsibility and at the same time acquires a kind of safety. One can abandon responsibility because 'it will be the Other, always the Other, only the Other, who is responsible for what is happening in society or in the world'.[28] Similarly safety resides in looking to the other person to define, for example, good taste in music, or to articulate what is currently being thought. However, it is a peculiar kind of safety in that it relies upon others and is in that way potentially unstable. From the idea of looking to others Gordon and Gordon point out that serial existence is 'terribly mediocre'.[29] This is a mediocrity generated by the isolation and impotence of individuals.

Sartre has presented seriality in the context of various manifestations of the practico-inert which he calls collectives. The collective is a particular object or structure within the practico-inert which is itself an expression of a society's stage of social, cultural and technological development. It is the mediation of these objects or structures within the practico-inert that confers upon the individual the manifestations of seriality such as isolation and impotence even whilst being the product of individuals. When millions of people listen to the same radio programme or buy the same record they are in the presence of a collective. The collectivity of listeners and buyers are not present to each other but to the same collective object. The ticket machine is a collective object. Sartre argues that the series is a kind of pseudo or false reciprocity in so far as the series represents the use of otherness as a bond between individuals under the 'passive action of an object'.[30] The object, whilst apparently uniting them, can actually keep people apart.

Young applies the concept of seriality to gender.[31] The application of the concept of seriality to gender enables Young to argue that it is possible to talk of 'women' as a collectivity without, at the same time, implying that 'women' are a group with a set of common essential attributes and a determined identity. Just as people at a bus stop can have different goals, histories and experiences, so too can women. Young points out that the attempt to specify the essential attributes of 'women' has one of two consequences, 'Either it empties the category *women* of social meaning by reducing it to the attributes of biological female, or in the effort to locate essential social attributes, it founders on the variability and diversity of women's actual lives.'[32] Regarding individual

---

27 Haim Gordon and Rivca Gordon, 1995, p. 146.
28 Ibid., p. 147.
29 Ibid., pp. 147, 149.
30 CDR I, p. 266.
31 Young, 'Gender as Seriality', in Young, 1997.
32 Ibid., p. 32.

identity, Young argues that there is no way to distinguish the gender part of the person from the race part or the class part. Consequently, on the argument presented, Young is able to say that, 'No individual woman's identity, then, will escape the markings of gender, but how gender marks her life is her own.'[33] The practico-inert realities that construct gender include the sexual division of labour. Here the relevant collectives include work stations, locker rooms and uniforms. On Young's account, therefore, 'women' is a term for a serial collectivity that is defined neither by a common identity nor by a common set of attributes that are shared by all the individuals in the series. Instead it 'names a set of structural constraints and relations to practico-inert objects that condition action and its meaning'.[34]

The application of the concept of seriality to gender is just one example of the many applications that are possible. Thus seriality can also be a general characteristic of society an explanation for whose origins may found in Rousseau's conjectural history. The market is another collective which constitutes and which is constituted by the isolation and hence powerlessness of the serial individual. A nation is a collective according to Barnes[35] and so too is a social class so long as its members remain a series. In fact, Chiodi observes that, 'class, insofar as it is the product of capitalist exploitation, does not possess the unity of a group but it is the statute of serial dispersion and passivity'.[36] As Thomas Busch points out,

> Class being is seriality writ large. Individuals driven by need and in a condition of scarcity employ means to survive which define their lives and relationships. Their very number puts them in competition for jobs and scarce commodities. The machines they work at, the division of labor, the working hours of the modern industrial workers, isolate them from one another.[37]

The circularity inherent in praxis means that it is the isolated individual who has to compete in order to 'get on' yet in competing the individual becomes more isolated. Thus the form of association which is characterised by isolation is accompanied by certain terms, individuals must compete, and these terms in turn become the form in that competition describes a form of relationship in which people are isolated. The series is a form of association that is marked by a reciprocity of isolation. The reciprocity indicates that this isolation does not just happen, it has to be achieved. The achievement is a reflection of those competitive terms, the various manifestations of which are to be examined later in this chapter.

---

33 Ibid., p. 33.
34 Ibid., p. 36.
35 Barnes, 1974, p. 121.
36 Chiodi, 1978, p. 70.
37 Busch, 1990, p. 74.

Forms of association exist in a dialectical relationship with terms of association in that either can be understood with reference to the other. In the second volume of the *Critique* Sartre shows how seriality becomes a way of ruling. Through the use of propaganda the Soviet leaders created the illusion that the workers constituted a group. It was only an illusion because at the same time the leaders wanted to keep the workers in 'serialities of impotence' so that they could not organise themselves. Thus the 'mass became an apparatus you could operate like a lever, provided only that you knew how to use the passive forces of seriality'.[38] Sartre observes that 'what was involved was actually an operation directed by the sovereign against the masses; and one that consequently maintained them in the separation of alterity, the better to make use of them'.[39] He goes on to describe the creation of 'Soviet man'.[40] The means that kept the workers in a state of seriality, namely oppression, become interiorised to produce a certain kind of toughness. In this way the means of praxis were also its ends.[41] This toughness manifested itself not only in self-discipline in order to maintain the rate of production but also in the criticism of neighbours who were perceived to be letting people down with their 'slackness'. The toughness and the criticism are connected by the passivity that is the consequence of the seriality quite deliberately produced by the sovereign praxis. So it is that the form of association gives rise to certain terms of association and can be regarded as the manifestation of those terms. The dialectical relationship between forms and terms of association is the result of praxis. In the case of Soviet man, the praxis that produces a particular form of association is interiorised to produce a particular kind of person and re-exteriorised as terms of association which in turn support that form of association. That this happens is due to the fact that praxis contains its own mode of comprehension which informs and is informed by the process of interiorisation and re-exteriorisation. Oppression interiorised becomes toughness. Toughness is re-exteriorised as terms which condemn slackness. This is not an unconscious process and it does not just happen. Moreover, Stalin's Russia is just one example. Another example would be Thatcher's Britain where freedom was interiorised as greed and re-exteriorised as competition.

It has been seen that forms and terms of association are the result of individual praxis and in turn have an effect on individual praxis. Praxis affects and has already been affected by the praxis of others. It has to cope with the mark on the practico-inert made by past praxes and in doing so it makes its own mark on the practico-inert. People are, therefore, moulded by the social structures that are their products. In this way communities partly constitute individuals but also individuals partly constitute communities and do so as a result of praxis.

---

38 CDR II, p. 148.
39 Ibid., p. 149.
40 Ibid., p. 160.
41 Ibid., pp. 161–62.

In a milieu of scarcity, which can be regarded as a product of praxis both in its original recognition by praxis and in the fact of its interiorisation and re-exteriorisation by praxis, praxis produces certain sorts of associations. Some are marked by co-operation and some are marked by competitive antagonism and both sorts will have an effect on future praxis.

The dialectical movement of praxis explains why it is in seriality that the milieu of scarcity is most virulent and, dialectically, it is that form of association that has characteristically been the product of that milieu. The one feeds off the other. In a milieu of scarcity, seriality becomes characterised by competitive self-interest. There is a competition for scarce resources which can have disastrous effects as the deforestation carried out by the Chinese peasants demonstrates. According to Sartre, scarcity 'transforms separation into antagonism'.[42] Violence, as 'interiorised scarcity', becomes the basic structure of human relations.[43] This is not necessarily direct or explicit physical violence. More usually it is a structured violence in which a society, by the way it structures human relations according to, for example, social class, chooses, as was seen in the previous chapter, 'its dead and its underfed'.[44] It is a structure that originally arises from certain sorts of scarcity but which then comes to sustain that scarcity and which can also be sustained by that scarcity. Therefore, exploitation, Sartre remarks, takes place not by violence but in violence,[45] meaning that violence, direct or structured, is inherent in all human relationships conducted in seriality in a milieu of scarcity. Thus 'the process of exploitation is a practice of alienated and serialised oppression'.[46] More usually still, it must be said, antagonism is not even structured violence of this sort either. More usually antagonism is due to the fact that the buses don't have enough seats.

However, it is important not to be too dismissive of Sartre's notion of structured violence since an examination of that notion reveals further the relationship between forms and terms of association. This can be illustrated with reference to laissez-faire liberal forms and terms of association. Sartre maintains that individual freedom is of paramount importance yet, as Richard Maundrell notes, 'he remains a staunch opponent of liberalism'.[47] Sartre does not suggest that serialisation is a condition unique to liberalism. He does suggest that it is the structural precondition for the isolation and impotence that is definitive of liberal societies. In fact, as Maundrell says, 'Sartre's condemnation of liberalism seems, to a large extent, to be directed toward the exploitation which serialised relations make possible rather than with liberalism itself'.[48]

---

[42] CDR I, p. 221.
[43] Ibid., p. 815.
[44] Ibid., p. 147.
[45] Ibid., p. 153.
[46] Ibid., p. 743.
[47] Richard Maundrell, 1992, p. 61.
[48] Ibid., p. 198.

In other words, it is directed towards a kind of praxis that this particular form of association makes possible which is a praxis that is a manifestation of that form's terms. So exploitation is not inevitable even in a liberal society. It is just that when seriality is a feature of society then that produces the isolation and impotence that makes exploitation possible.

Bakunin is less subtle. He writes about what he calls the 'bourgeois principle' which he says can be summarised in a single word, '*individualism*'. He explains that by individualism he means a tendency to consider all members of society as mutually unconcerned rivals and competitors, a tendency, 'which impels the individual to gain and erect his own well-being, prosperity, and good fortune to the disadvantage of everyone else, despite them and on their backs'.[49]

An important part of Sartre's criticism of liberalism is directed at the liberal view of rights and in particular at the political ideal of negative liberty that is espoused by liberalism. These rights can be regarded as the terms of association that accompany a particular form of association. Maundrell notes that for Sartre, liberalism in practice 'is a serialised social order which serves the same end as the colony. A population atomised in powerlessness according to a set of strictly negative rights is serialised in a way which serves the bourgeois interests of appropriation and exploitation.'[50] Thus, to construct a society on the basis of negative rights is to construct a serialised social order. Broadly speaking, Sartre follows what Jeremy Waldron (who regards rights as a kind of safety net for individuals in the event of a breakdown in harmonious relationships) calls the 'vulgar Marxist line' on human rights.[51] This line argues that in their traditional formulations, doctrines of rights represent the preoccupations of the bourgeois capitalist individual as though they were universal and compelling principles of human nature. The right to liberty, to property, to personal security, to resist any government that interferes with bourgeois activity, are all rights whose fundamental orientation is towards the selfish desires of the acquisitive individual. Bourgeois ideology permeates even the form of rights which is individualistic. It presupposes that the potential for conflict within society will always be so great that each person requires some coercively maintained guarantee that the acts of others will not imperil the pursuit and fulfilment of the individual's interests. These rights, therefore, express a particular understanding of association and serve to sustain a particular form of association. Sartre's particular view of liberal rights has been succinctly summarised by Steven De Lue who writes that,

> liberal democracies which foster competition between the various groups for certain economic goals merely create a condition where one segment of

---

[49] Bakunin, 'Three Lectures to Swiss Members of the International', in Robert M. Cutler (ed.), 1985, p. 57.
[50] Richard Maundrell, 1992, p. 197.
[51] Jeremy Waldron, ' Introduction' to chpt. 5 in, J. Waldron (ed.), 1987, p. 126.

society will be able to outstrip the other segments for the available privileges and benefits. This situation is always, for Sartre, justified in the name of the 'rights' of individuals to pursue their own interests in accordance with the 'equal rights' granted to all men.[52]

In *On the Jewish Question*, Marx distinguishes between human rights, the rights of man and the rights of the citizen. Human rights is the most general category and includes the other two as sub-categories. The rights of the citizen are rights of political participation and in particular the right to vote. Rights of man include freedom of thought, expression and belief, equality before the law, private property, security of life and limb and liberty. These rights, it should be remembered, are the terms of association that accompany a particular form of association. In other words they are required because of the nature of praxis in a bourgeois society. Therefore, 'we notice the fact that the so-called rights of man, the rights of man as different from the rights of the citizen are nothing but the rights of the member of civil society, i.e. egoistic man, man separated from other men and the community'.[53] Thus, in the language of forms and terms of association and praxis, for Marx civil society is capitalism with a praxis organised towards private ownership of the means of production, a market for commodities and competition for scarce goods. This praxis can work only in a society that protects itself with certain terms of association, that is, with certain rights. Rights, thus considered, are the terms that protect and enable that capitalist praxis. That praxis, competitive, egoistic and so on, gives rise to, because it requires, certain terms of association. Conversely, terms of association will affect man's praxis. In other words, these terms serve to encourage or promote further praxes which are in accordance with those terms.

Regarding property rights, Buchanan makes the observation that,

> If the existence of private property does lead persons to view each other at best as mere means and at worst as lethal threats, and if private property rights are needed to secure oneself against intrusions by others then it makes sense to describe the right to private property as a right which is valuable for man in so far as man is an isolated, egoistic monad. And *if* individuals would not so view each other but for the existence of private property, then it is plausible to say that the right to private property is valuable *only* for egoistic monadic man.[54]

He goes on to argue that, on the basis of the analysis above, the right to private property can be said to separate the individual from the community in that it protects him from interference from others and also relieves him of any responsibility for their welfare. As De Lue says, 'Sartre believes that Western democracies foster unhealthy competition to the degree that individuals are

---

[52] Steven De Lue, 1971, p. 25.
[53] Marx, *On the Jewish Question*, in McLellan, 1977, p. 52.
[54] Buchanan, 1982, p. 63.

forced to think of society only in terms of one's own private interest. The Western individual never learns how to become part of a community where he would be able to give his entire life's activity to the maintenance of the common good of the whole community.'[55] Thus the right to private property can be thought of as something that both illustrates and at the same time encourages a state of affairs in which there are conflicts of interests between people. It is an example of how a particular kind of relationship with the environment affects relationships between people and vice versa. The secure possession of property in a milieu of scarcity is intended to guarantee the satisfaction of needs but in doing so, as has been seen, it contributes to the creation and maintenance of that milieu. Thus if the answer to the question, 'What does one need to do in order to satisfy needs in a milieu of scarcity?' is 'Have private property', then it is an answer that generates the condition that prompted the question. As Sartre says, 'What the bourgeoisie was defending was not even capitalist property; it was liberalism.'[56] Moreover, for Sartre, liberal rights allegedly prohibit violence and thus serve to legitimate and secure the status quo and the previous violence on which the status quo is based. As Sartre had already observed in his *Notebooks for an Ethics*, 'The right of liberalism is therefore mystification in its most pure form.'[57]

Communitarian criticisms of rights echo much of what Sartre has to say. Mary Ann Glendon, for example, argues that,

> Our rights talk, in its absoluteness, promotes unrealistic expectations, heightens social conflict, and inhibits dialogue that might lead toward consensus, accommodation, or at least the discovery of common ground ... In its relentless individualism, it fosters a climate that is inhospitable to society's losers, and that systematically disadvantages caretakers and dependents, young and old.[58]

Therefore, if a person conceives of himself as a bearer of rights, he conceives of himself as having a legitimate claim or entitlement to something. He thinks of himself as being able to demand that to which he has a right, to stand up for that to which he is due. On the communitarian view to stand up for one's due is to view oneself as a potential party to conflicts in which standing up for one's due becomes necessary. However, communitarians argue, there would be no need for rights if there was no potential for conflict between individual interests or between an individual's interests and the social good. Rights are required only if there is a possibility that individuals will come into conflict. Thus Sandel claims that in a family, where a spirit of generosity prevails, appeals to rights are not required. The need for rights would disappear in a harmonious egalitarian society. The view of rights espoused by Glendon and other communitarians is

---

55 De Lue, 1971, pp. 231–32.
56 CDR I, pp. 764–65.
57 NE, p. 145.
58 Mary Ann Glendon, 1991, p. 14.

a view of rights in a liberal context. However, whilst Sartre's view of rights in that context is broadly similar, being critical of certain sorts of rights and of their function within a liberal form of association, he shows, as we will see, that in other forms of association certain rights can perform a different and more valuable function.

It is not simply rights as an aspect of liberal terms of association that exercise Sartre. He also examines a further issue of concern to Sandel. This issue concerns the viability of the Rawlsian contract. Sandel argues that we may assess the justice of a contract from two points of view according to whether the contract was entered into freely and according to whether the terms of the contract were fair. While we might assume that a contract freely agreed to would also most probably be fair and that fair terms might suggest a free, as opposed to coerced, contract, there is no necessary connection either way. Any contract, however free, can also always be assessed for fairness because what makes a contract fair is not simply that it was agreed to freely. Similarly, any contract, however fair, can always be assessed for its freedom. Being treated fairly neither necessarily make us free nor requires us to be so. The morality of contract, therefore, consists of two distinguishable ideals, says Sandel. The first is autonomy, an act of will, whose morality consists in the voluntary character of the transaction. The second is reciprocity in which the contract is an instrument of mutual benefit whose morality depends on the underlying fairness of the exchange. Each ideal suggests a different basis for contractual obligation. With autonomy, a contract's moral force derives from the fact of its voluntary agreement. Therefore, when a person freely enters into an agreement he is bound by its terms whatever they may be, fair or not. He has brought those terms upon himself and the fact that they are self-imposed provides one reason for his obligation to fulfil them. Reciprocity derives contractual obligation from the mutual benefits of co-operative arrangements. Thus, 'Where autonomy points to the contract itself as a source of obligation, reciprocity points through the contract to an antecedent moral requirement to abide by fair arrangements.'[59] In other words, unlike obligations voluntarily incurred, obligations arising under the ideal of reciprocity must presuppose some communally agreed criterion of fairness independent of the contract, some way in which the objective fairness of an exchange may be assessed. Such obligations are thus not contractual in the sense that the contract creates the obligation, but rather in the sense that the contract helps to identify or clarify an obligation that already exists. It follows that the carrying out of a contract is not essential to the existence of the obligation. In principle at least, there may be ways of identifying such obligations without recourse to contract. As Michael Lessnoff indicates, if the contract is determined by what is morally obligatory, independently of the contract itself, then that contract would seem to be redundant.[60]

---
[59] Sandel, 1982, p. 107.
[60] Michael Lessnoff, 'Introduction: Social Contract', in Lessnoff (ed.), 1990, p. 15.

The Rawlsian contract cannot be said to be unfair since the veil of ignorance ensures that there can be no advantage to any particular party on the basis of an awareness of differences of knowledge or power. Here, impartiality is the defining characteristic of the moral perspective. However, there is the issue of whether the Rawlsian contract is free. Setting aside the point made by Kukathas and Pettit to the effect that the Rawlsian person does not make choices because it is incapable of deliberation, Sandel's point is that if the original position is constructed so as to guarantee that any agreement reached in it is fair, then there is no scope for the exercise of choice by people in the original position. Moreover, neither could any discussion take place between people all of whom are presumed to reason in the same way, with no distinctive perceptions or concerns and all of whom are bound to draw the same conclusion. As Rawls says,

> the acceptance of these principles is not conjectured as a psychological law or probability. Ideally anyway, I should like to show that their acknowledgement is the only choice consistent with the full description of the original position. The argument aims eventually to be strictly deductive.[61]

So, although they are, in principle, free to choose any principle they wish, the contractors' situation is such that they can, rationally, choose only those principles upon which they can, rationally, agree.

The strictly deductive stipulation ensures that no bargaining can be said to go on in the original position because bargaining occurs in the face of differences in the interests, knowledge and power of the bargainers. The veil of ignorance removes all awareness of such differences. If bargaining and discussion are not possible then neither is agreement in any strictly contractual sense. The strictly deductive stipulation ensures that every person in the original position is bound to reach the same conclusion as everyone else. Jean Hampton argues that 'we get a very peculiar selection environment where there are no conflicting interests that need to be mediated, where everyone prefers the same two principles and where the agreement on these principles is unanimous'.[62] There is no bargaining, discussion or agreement behind the veil of ignorance because the plurality of people which that notion presupposes is missing. The Rawlsian notion involves a contract between people with no distinguishing characteristics whatsoever. Deprived of all individuality, the contracting parties are, in a vital sense, all the same thus making this a contract with oneself. Sandel argues that what goes on in the original position is not a contract after all but the self-discovery not of many persons but of one subject, of an intersubjective being of the kind formally denied by Rawls.[63]

Whilst Sandel scrutinises the contract to be found in the deontological liberalism of Rawls for fairness and freedom, Sartre conducts that same scrutiny

---

61 Rawls, 1971, p. 121.
62 Jean Hampton, 1980, p. 315.
63 Sandel, 1982, pp. 24–28.

in respect of the contract to be found in bourgeois liberalism. According to Sartre, bourgeois liberalism proclaims a concept of humanity in which everyone exists as free individuals. However, reciprocity is not a freely chosen relationship. It is rooted in the individual's historical situation. What Sartre calls the 'swindle of capitalist exploitation,'[64] which is based on contract, is to pretend not to notice this. The contract is one device for setting out the terms of association connected with the series and part of its function is to preserve that form of association. The pretence is that the worker freely enters into a contract with the employer whereas the reality is that the worker 'is forced by the constraint of needs to sell himself as a material object'.[65] The liberal appeal to negative liberty suits the employer's ends since he can, if he chooses, ignore the fact that the worker is not free in relation to his property, that is, himself. Sartre observes that, 'Absolute respect for the freedom of the propertyless is the best way of leaving him at the mercy of material constraints, at the moment of the contract.'[66] Sartre's point is that equal rights to freedom of contract ignores the background of inequality. The rights do nothing to remove the inequality. They simply sanction the contract and through the contract the original inequality. As Buchanan observes, 'Mere recognition of an individual as a being with the right to engage in exchange ... is an abstract and superficial conception of respect for persons, but it plays a very foundational role in a system which treats persons as mere things.'[67] Of course, the clear conscience of the employer rests upon the moment at which the contract is agreed which, at that moment, appears to be an act of freedom on the part of the worker. At that moment the employer is not coercing the worker into accepting the contract. All the employer has done is fix the rate for the job which means that he can turn away those who ask for more. However, 'the constraint of needs,'[68] the possibility or threat of unemployment which is a constraint on freedom experienced by the worker requires him to moderate his demands for fear of losing the contract to another worker. Thus the relationship between the workers themselves is also one of conflict but that, allegedly, is not the fault of the employer. At the moment of agreeing the contract the worker is free.

In fact, in accepting the contract the worker reveals himself as less than fully free, that is, as less than fully human. Sartre identifies in this a contradiction which is 'both to recognise that the worker is free and to introduce him by compulsion into a system in which it is *also* recognised that he will be reduced to a sub-human level'.[69] The worker 'becomes a *thing* for the Other'.[70] At the

---

64 CDR I, p. 110.
65 Ibid.
66 Ibid.
67 Buchanan, 1982, p. 80.
68 CDR I, p. 110.
69 Ibid., p. 740.
70 Ibid., p. 110.

moment of making the contract the worker is raised to the level of a fully free individual. He can reject the contract. Yet at the next moment the individual worker loses that freedom and his humanity, 'In this abstract, fleeting instant, the worker is integrated into humanism: the bourgeois defines him as his fellow by the very act of transforming him into a commodity.'[71] Therefore, the labourer's situation is not only one of ontological alienation which is a characteristic of all labour but also his labour power has become a commodity and thus he can experience, as we have seen, a form of social alienation. It is not the worker that the employer requires, but his work. By becoming a 'material object'[72] the worker is able to enter freely into the contract. By renouncing his freedom the worker fleetingly regains it, only to lose it immediately. This is illustrated in the second volume of the *Critique* with Sartre's example of the boxers. The boxers are attempting to escape the exploitation of bourgeois society by allowing themselves, through their contracts with managers, promoters and so on, to be exploited by bourgeois society. As Aronson observes, the boxing match reveals 'the structure of the bourgeois competitive market – as a highly profitable organized conflict between two individuals'.[73]

The process of producing the boxer, the training, the development of personal traits and so on, leads to the contractual moment when the boxer turns 'his violence into a commodity in order to leave his class'.[74] In other words, in order to achieve a fully human status, the boxer is dehumanised. The anger and the violence that once belonged to the boxer now belong to the spectators. By purchasing the violence 'the bourgeoisie recuperates and transforms it. Alienated, the aggression of the oppressed individual is changed into a competitive antagonism: commodities clash as if they were men and each seeks to force up its price by destroying or forcing down the other.'[75] Thus the bourgeois public imposes its own meaning on the event and that too is a further manifestation of violence in society. Even 'the common violence of the oppressed'[76] is transformed into a profitable competition. It becomes another market activity, revealing to the audience the bourgeois value of individualism carried out in seriality by serialised individuals who are attempting to escape by means characteristic of seriality the serial conditions established by the bourgeois class. As Sartre ironically notes, it is an activity '*stimulated by the exploiting class which even provides it with its rules*'.[77]

The less than fully human deserve to be treated as such. The freedom of the worker to enter into a contractual arrangement with the employer is important

---

71 Ibid., p. 753.
72 Ibid., p. 110.
73 Aronson, 1985, pp. 166–67.
74 CDR II, p. 37.
75 Ibid., p. 44.
76 Ibid., p. 47.
77 Ibid.

for the employer because it justifies the employer's subsequent treatment of the worker. At one level the employer is able to say, 'This is what you have freely agreed to and given that free agreement you can now have no legitimate grounds for complaint.' If the worker is less than fully human it is because that is what the worker has 'freely' chosen to be. Since he is free, it is the worker's own fault that he is a worker, and not himself an employer. However, even as less than fully human, labour can exercise freedom and this is dangerous from the employer's point of view. From the employer's point of view there were good grounds for regarding the proletariat as the enemy. Therefore, at another level, it allows the employer to use repressive measures in case the worker 'abuses' his freedom.

Yet, in a further contradiction, the attempt to objectify the other person is, in one sense, doomed to fail. In order to treat the other person as an object one must first recognise him as a subject and as requiring objectification. In the *Critique*, treating people inhumanely requires a recognition of their humanity. Sartre makes this clear in writing about the relationship between slaves and their masters in seventeenth century America. The slave owners refused to raise the children of slaves in the Christian faith in order to justify their treatment of them as sub-human. However, that refusal contained the implicit recognition of their humanity. They differed from the owners only in as much as they lacked the religious beliefs of the owners and the care that the owners took to keep them from acquiring those beliefs was a recognition of their capacity to do so. Sartre concludes that, 'This is the contradiction of racism, colonialism and all forms of tyranny: in order *to treat a man like a dog*, one must first recognise him as man.'[78] The contradiction to which Sartre refers becomes even more apparent if the labour in question is a type of praxis such as farming, which is also a practice. In the previous chapter it was argued that practices will be alienating at the ontological level and that the exercise of the virtues associated with practices can do nothing to alleviate that. However, it is the exercise of those virtues that brings about the realisation of internal goods and it is those internal goods that prevent the practitioner from becoming a commodity. The contradiction that emerges in the case of the worker being engaged in a practice is, therefore, that the more diligent and skilful the practitioner becomes, the more commodity-like he appears to be, but due to increasingly realising internal goods the less commodity-like he is in reality. Moreover, the extent to which the employer wants the practitioner to be diligent and skilful is precisely the extent to which he does not really want the worker to be a commodity. Thus the swindle of liberalism consists on the one hand of proclaiming the importance of freedom whilst at the same time, in the name of freedom, giving rise to and supporting a form of association, serialisation, which renders certain people powerless in the pursuit of the satisfaction of needs and on the other hand in treating people as commodities whilst at the same time benefiting from the fact that they are not.

---

[78] CDR I, p. 111.

So it is that equal negative liberty offers the individual the right to freedom from interference and constraint without at the same time granting him the enabling conditions which would allow him to act on that freedom. For Sartre, the inadequacy of negative liberty is that non-interference allows for and indeed supports inequality in the distribution and acquisition of material goods, that is, private property. Thus non-interference guarantees that one may dispose of one's property as one wills. Yet this offers no protection for those whose only property is that which resides in their own being.

Sandel is clear that the justice of a contract may be assessed according to whether the process of bargaining and the outcome of that process was free and fair. However, that requires a background of moral agreements concerning some communally agreed criteria of fairness and that in turn requires certain forms and terms of association. Sartre has shown that, at the very least, laissez-faire liberalism's forms and terms of association will not necessarily provide that background.

Sartre's analysis of relationships in the series provides further insight into the way that communities are constitutive of the identities of individuals. Communities are constitutive of the identities of individuals to the extent that the dialectical relationship between forms and terms of association favours certain relationships and practices and discourages others. In the series in a milieu of scarcity, where the form of association is characterised by isolation and the terms of association are competitive which in turn is also a characteristic of the form of association, the individual is constituted as isolated and competitive and as such he is constitutive of that form of association with its particular terms. This explains still further how forms and terms of association give rise to certain conditions which will themselves have an effect on those forms and terms of association. The mediating link at all levels is human praxis at work on the results of previous praxes which have been interiorised and which create the conditions for future praxes.

Although examples or instances of types of seriality can occur in socialist societies, it is a form of association which in such a society involves a contradiction. The administrators of the 'Plan' in Russia had to create a general interest in raising production whilst at the same time keeping consumption down and the workers atomised. This they did through the reintroduction of 'competitive and antagonistic practices'.[79] Everyone would be given the opportunity to live better, in competition with everyone else. Sartre points out that the contradiction of 'socialism in one country'[80] led to the contradiction of keeping the working class in a state of impotent seriality in order to create a socialist community. This in turn led to the conflict between workers and bureaucracy.

---

[79] CDR II, p. 132
[80] Ibid., p. 98.

However, whatever other contradictions occur in capitalist societies and free market economies, there will be no contradiction of the sort seen in Russia under Stalin. Seriality is the logic of capitalism. Sartre notes that in such a society, with such an economy, 'The price imposes itself on me, as a buyer, because it imposes itself on my neighbour; it imposes itself on him because it imposes itself on his neighbour, and so on. But conversely, I am not unaware that I help to establish it and that it imposes itself on my neighbours because it imposes itself on me; in general, it imposes itself on everyone as a stable collective reality only in so far as it is the totalisation of a series.'[81] As Desan observes, 'What we are seeing here is that the collective object, the market, is characterized not by consensus, an organized unity, but by a flight, a disunity. I, who am a powerless member of the series gathered around the market, nevertheless help to constitute it, by virtue of my isolation from the others.'[82] According to Gordon and Gordon,

> Seriality allows capitalism to flourish, with its widespread oppression and rapacious exploitation. Capitalists do not want to deal with persons but with workers or with consumers, that is, with members of a series, or, in other words, with the human being devoid of his or her ability to express freedom and singularity. In short, capitalists, and especially corporate capitalists, relate to human beings through the Other and as the Other.[83]

That relationship describes a particular form of association which exists dialectically with the terms of capitalism.

The series is not a form of association which has the terms that are conducive to either the generation of shared meanings or the establishment of equality of membership. In seriality the meanings come from elsewhere, from the radio or the ticket machine, and the serialised individual passively accepts them. Of course, the radio, the ticket machine, the work station and the locker room do not mysteriously emanate meanings all on their own. The meanings are there but they are put there by the praxis of others who may themselves be serialised and these meanings are realised by the praxis of those who listen to the radio and queue for buses. These serialised individuals may accept the same meanings as each other but they need not be shared meanings. Two people might agree that such and such a thing means this or that at a particular level of significance. Thus for both of those people, if the bus has no vacant seats it means that they will be late for their appointments. At that level of significance being unable to board the bus has the same meaning. However, since for one person being late is an excuse not to keep an unwanted appointment and since for the other person being late will result in a lost opportunity, not catching the bus has different levels of significance. There is, therefore, no shared meaning in respect of a

---

[81] CDR I, p. 288.
[82] Desan, 1965, p. 124.
[83] Gordon and Gordon, 1995, p. 145.

bus with no vacant seats and ultimately, of course, given the different levels of significance, not boarding the bus does not even mean the same thing, through and through. Thus whatever else is included in the notion of a shared meaning one thing that must be part of that notion is a common level of significance.

One way of establishing a common level of significance is through engaging in a shared or common praxis towards shared or common objectives which are contained within praxis. However, the praxis and the objectives must be shared and not apparently, at one level, simply the same. In the series people can have the same objectives and, therefore, engage in the same praxis but neither the objectives nor the praxis need be shared. The people in the bus queue have the same objective, or, as we have seen Sartre call it, a '*common interest*',[84] namely, to obtain a seat on the bus. However, there is a possibility for confusion here. Although this is a common interest, this cannot be a shared objective. It is simply an interest that they all happen to have. However, they happen to have it individually. In the queue there is no common praxis attempting to satisfy a common need. Indeed, the fact that each of the queuers has the same objective in that each wants the same thing means that the objective cannot be shared since there is a scarcity of seats. It is, therefore, the fact that the individuals in the bus queue are engaged in the same praxis that prevents that praxis from being shared. As the next chapter will show, it is from a common or shared praxis addressing a need that is felt to be common or shared that shared meanings can arise. A common praxis and a common need is to be distinguished from the same praxis and the same need. As we shall see, a common or shared praxis makes people, in a sense, the same. Yet even so, they will not be identical. Regarding shared meanings, in the absence of a shared praxis then whatever else might give rise to shared meanings it will not be praxis. Moreover, it becomes clear that in the absence of a shared praxis there can be no shared meanings with regard to that area of understanding and action.

Sartre makes the same point concerning praxis and meaning in connection with the notion of an agreement. He argues that,

> Agreement presupposes, in effect, that different individuals or groups, with different horizons, and characters and habits of totally different kinds realise a contractual agreement in reciprocity *on a minimum basis*. Idealist optimism may then claim that this minimum will rise to a higher minimum, this minimum to another, so that, finally, agreement will reign in the whole of human knowledge or activity.[85]

Sartre argues that this is what appears to happen but that what is really involved is a 'resurrection of unity through seriality and the creation of groups in the serial milieu *without the dissolution of alterity*'. Such 'induced unity' is described

---

[84] CDR I, p. 258.
[85] Ibid., p. 531.

as a 'degraded product'.[86] Sartre's claim is that it is wrong to assume that the truth can be the same for individuals divided by class, influence, income and so on. Sartre illustrates this idea with the example of the welder and the owner of the ship yard. Both may be convinced of the truth of Archimedes' principle but this kind of agreement is unimportant and even lacking in 'concrete reality' due to the different praxes, different needs and different ends of the welder and the owner.[87]

On examining the content of the bourgeois capitalists' definition of themselves, the first thing to note about capitalists is that they compete. This is a capitalist's terms of association. As a class, remembering that in seriality a class is not a group, they compete with the workers in certain ways and this competitive praxis is a feature of the normative definition of capitalism. It is this praxis that gives capitalism its meaning. That said, it must also be admitted that at a local level, as has been seen, the individual capitalist may not be the oppressor of the workers but may, indeed, engage in genuine negotiations with them about the issues of production. However, even where this occurs the individual capitalist will be in competition with other capitalists. Thus capitalists compete because that is the basis of capitalist self-awareness. It is competition that precludes the possibility of shared meanings with regard to the occasion for the competition. Thus, for example, competition over a social good such as scarce land cannot produce a shared meaning with regard to that land. Furthermore, even though there may be a shared understanding concerning the fact that there is a competition, the meaning of the competition cannot be a shared meaning because the praxes of the competitors pursue different objectives. Each wants to win and neither wants that for the other.

The argument concerning competition and shared meanings can usefully be developed. The milieu of alterity which allows, requires and encourages competition, exploitation and oppression is, as has been seen, sustained by an ideology of laissez-faire liberalism, that is, certain terms of association. In other words, these are the terms of association that have been produced by the praxis of the dominant class. This evokes the notion of a dominant ideology whereby, according to Anthony Giddens, a dominant class seeks to stabilise its position by presenting 'a legitimating ideology, which "rationalises" its position of economic and political domination and "explains" to the subordinate class why it should accept its subordination'.[88] This is reminiscent of Rousseau's argument in his *Discourse on the Origin and Foundations of Inequality Among Men*. The argument there is that the poor became tired of struggling against the rich and tacitly accepted their authority. This led the rich to believe that their authority over the poor was legitimate since it was based on the consent of the poor. This de facto power of the rich became a de jure right to authority thus sustaining

---
[86] Ibid.
[87] Ibid., p. 532.
[88] Anthony Giddens, 1973, p. 29.

and perpetuating inequality. Marx provides an explanation for this phenomenon and Sartre provides an example. In *The German Ideology* we read that:

> The ideas of the ruling class are in every epoch the ruling ideas, i.e., the class which is the ruling material force of society, is at the same time its ruling intellectual force. The class which has the means of material production at its disposal, has control at the same time over the means of mental production, so that thereby, generally speaking, the ideas of those who lack the means of mental production are subject to it.[89]

According to Sartre, it is the praxis of bourgeois democracy that defines the anti-repressive actions of the workers. Thus,

> If the working class is able to respond, its response is anti-repressive, organised violence: strikes are violent . . . in that they present themselves as a breach of contract. Of course, strikes are violence against violence, but in the context of bourgeois democracy, even when they are legal, they appear as *the first violence*.[90]

We have already seen that praxis gives rise to certain meanings. Here is a particular example of a particular praxis acquiring a particular meaning. It is, moreover, a meaning that is acquired on the basis of the praxis of the dominant class which is a praxis of domination. Thus the praxis of domination ascribes a meaning to the praxis of the dominated. Therefore, it is in seriality that a 'way of life' can be defined by a dominant class, if not actually a dominant group, in the manner that in chapter three we saw Kymlicka pointing to as something that communitarians ignore. What this means is that it is hard to understand how there can be any notion of a shared meaning derived from praxis between all the members of a series divided by class. The idea that the terms of association that accompany seriality can be derived from the praxis of the dominant class is relevant not only to the notion of shared meanings but also to the distribution of social goods and to the notion of communities being partly constitutive of an individual's identities.

The meaning of a social good can be the result of the praxis of the dominant class and that is why, in some places, fish are scarce. We have already seen that where part of a definition of a good referred to its scarcity and where that definition is an expression of certain terms of association then that could have a bearing on the nature or even the possibility of its distribution. For there to be a just distribution of a social good, the community has to be a community of a certain sort. If the community is the sort in which a good is defined as scarce, as a result of the praxis of the dominant class, then a just distribution of that good is unlikely. In this case the meaning generated by the praxis of the dominant class is another example of how relationships with the environment affect

---

[89] Marx, *The German Ideology*, in McLellan, 1977, p. 176.
[90] CDR I, p. 790.

relationships between people and vice-versa. Moreover, as we will see, even if there is an agreement regarding the scarcity of fish it cannot be assumed that the meaning of that scarcity is shared.

For shared meanings to be derived from praxis then, as has been said, that praxis must be a common praxis which stems from common needs and has common objectives. Therefore, not any old community can produce shared meanings derived from praxis. Since societies which are clearly dominated by a particular class are unlikely to be capable of generating shared meanings derived from praxis they are, on Walzer's account, for that reason and to the extent that the dominant praxis prevails, unlikely to be just. Lyle Downing and Robert Thigpen argue that 'societies in which there is more participation in the development of shared meanings should be considered to be more just than societies in which there is less'.[91] To the suggestion that what matters is not the manner by which shared meanings originate but only the quality of the present sharing, they point out that if current understandings perpetuate a way of life that was institutionalised through domination then the distinction disappears. In oppressive regimes, shared meanings reflect the existing allocation of power. From that Downing and Thigpen argue that 'respect for a community's shared values should depend in part on the way in which the values are generated and shared'.[92]

With regard to the series, community values, such as they are, can be understood as being the terms of association that are derived from the praxis of the dominant group, in so far as there is one. Thus in the series people are not only defined as gardeners, road-menders or intellectuals by virtue of their praxis and not only does the community ascribe a meaning to those praxes but it is also the case that part of that meaning will reflect the values of the dominant class. Part of that meaning will reflect particular terms of association. This means, therefore, that in the series people will be defined partly in terms of their competitiveness, that is, in terms of success or failure in being, in some way, dominant. So it is that we have an explanation for the point made by Doppelt and noted in chapter three to the effect that the bourgeois conception of moral identity measures full personhood according to competitive performance. Therefore, to say that a community's values are in part constitutive of a person's identity is not to say very much. What is important is to know how any community comes to have values and to what sort of a community the individual belongs.

It is also the case that meanings can define associations and reflect the identity of individuals. In chapter two it was seen that part of the definition of a social good may, under certain conditions, be that it is a scarce good. It was argued that defining that good as scarce is also a way of defining the conditions under which people associate. The mechanics of how a definition of a good can

---

[91] Lyle Downing and Robert Thigpen, 1986, p. 457.
[92] Ibid., p. 463.

also be a way of defining the form of a community and its terms of association now becomes clear. In an elaboration of the argument in chapter two to the effect that a community was the product of its social goods, in the series in a milieu of scarcity the praxis of the wealthiest in buying the fish does nothing to make fish less scarce but everything to make fish less affordable. In this way the praxis of the wealthiest not only contributes to the meaning of fish it also defines certain forms and terms of association. If fish are understood to be goods that may be afforded by only some then that immediately defines a certain form of relationship between people. In short, the meaning of a social good is neither neutral nor passive with regard to the forms and terms of association from whence they emanate and which they can maintain. Moreover, in seriality, that which applies to Archimedes' principle applies to fish. If an agreement about fish was to be possible, such an agreement should not be taken to indicate that there is a shared meaning with respect to fish. Indeed, an agreement about the scarcity and price of fish is likely to produce quite different meanings depending on whether one can or cannot afford fish. Here, the meaning attributed by an individual to a particular good is an aspect of the identity of that individual.

Precisely the same arguments can be employed with regard to the notion of the common good or the good for human beings. Different praxes produce different notions of the good for human beings. As was seen in chapter four, what is good for the peasants cannot be good for the nomads and vice versa. In the series there will either be no common view of the good for human beings, or if there is such a view it will be what Sartre has already called a 'degraded product'[93] derived from the praxis of the dominant group. Certainly, in seriality, people cannot have a conception of the good life for human beings devised along the lines which, in connection with the significance of the community, are described by MacIntyre.

As has been seen, part of Sandel's criticism of liberalism is directed at the Kantian argument that the morally significant characteristic of human beings is their capacity for rationally autonomous behaviour. This means that what is important about the individual is not the ends that the individual chooses but the capacity for choice itself, on which a choice of ends depends. Sandel argues that this 'antecedently individuated' self is not dependent upon social, political, economic or indeed any other circumstances. As Sandel points out, the Kantian argument is used to support Rawls's view of the self as being separate from its situation for the purpose of establishing principles of justice. Sandel argues that this provides us with a radically disembodied subject, devoid of community oriented sentiments, or any particular attachments. The view of the self as antecedently individuated is held to exclude any conception of community other than that of being a co-operative arrangement for the pursuit of private advantage and that this is in itself but one option to be found within the framework defined

---

[93] CDR I, p. 531.

by justice. Community can never be regarded as providing an alternative framework.

Sartre's identification of seriality as a form of association provides Sandel's argument with an additional dimension. The condition of seriality contains features that are to be found in Rawls's circumstances of justice, namely, mutual disinterest and scarcity. The additional dimension is that the terms of association to be found in liberalism, conceived of as seriality, are precisely the terms that sustain those circumstances. Of significance, therefore, is the framing of the problem. Thus, for Sandel, if the conditions such as mutual disinterest and scarcity that arise from liberalism-seriality is the problem that principles of justice are meant to address then it seems odd to address it using the terms of association identified by Sandel since they are terms that are derived from and can sustain the source of the problem.

It is not difficult to see parallels between Sartre's notion of seriality in the milieu of scarcity and Hobbes's state of nature. In fact Marjorie Grene calls Sartre a Hobbesian.[94] As Warnock says, 'It is not, I think, unduly fanciful to see the dreaded state of seriality as the counterpart of the war of all against all in the state of nature.'[95] McBride agrees. He comments that, 'It is interesting to consider, by way of contrast, the case of Thomas Hobbes, to whose observations on the condition of human beings in his imagined "state of nature" some of Sartre's statements about underlying violence, especially in the *Critique of Dialectical Reason* may usefully, though with a number of important qualifications, be analogized.'[96] In the state of nature man has the right of nature, namely, 'the Liberty each man hath, to use his own power, as he will himselfe, for the preservation of his own Nature; that is to say, of his own Life; and consequently, of doing any thing, which is in his own Judgement and Reason, he shall conceive to be the aptest means thereunto'.[97] Hobbes also argues that, 'if any two men desire the same thing, which nevertheless they cannot both enjoy, they become enemies; and in the way to their End, (which is principally their owne conservation, and sometims their delectation only,) endeavour to destroy, or subdue one an other'.[98] Without a common power to keep individuals in awe 'they are in that condition which is called Warre; and such a warre, as is of every man against every man'.[99] As has been seen, the condition of war involves not only violence but also the propensity for violence and the fear that accompanies that propensity.

Of particular importance in understanding human motivation in Hobbes is the desire for glory and for self-preservation with the latter being particularly

---

[94] Marjorie Grene, 1973, p. 248.
[95] Warnock, 1965, p. 173.
[96] McBride, 1991, p. 21.
[97] *Leviathan*, chpt. 14, p. 73.
[98] Ibid., chpt. 13, p. 70.
[99] Ibid., chpt. 13, p. 71.

important. According to Hampton in *Hobbes and the Social Contract Tradition*, a close inspection of self-preservation reveals that what is particularly important is pleasure. The key to Hobbes's theory of motivation is the concept of felicity understood as the smooth and orderly achievement of the many desires that one has in a lifetime. It is a continuous process involving continual success. Sitting on one's laurels is not an option. As Hobbes says,

> Continual successe in obtaining those things which a man from time to time desireth, that is to say, continuall prospering, is that men call FELICITY; I mean the Felicity of this life. For there is no such thing as perpetuall Tranquility of mind, while we live here; because Life itself is but Motion, and can never be without Desire.[100]

This is similar to Sartre's notion of needs as the origin of praxis. In so far as people have needs, praxis will occur. In Hobbes's view, people largely differ in what they desire and even when they desire the same thing they will differ over how they are to set about achieving what they desire. Even so, this achievement is likely to involve antagonistic relationships of the kind that can occur between serialised individuals in a milieu of scarcity. In general, the goal of felicity requires one to obtain an advantage and keep it. As Tom Sorell explains,

> One way of doing this is by disabling other people. And the most effective way of disabling other people is to kill them. So long as it is common knowledge that people will try to get or increase an advantage over others, perhaps by disabling others, no-one can be sure that he is not on someone else's hit list. So survival becomes a thing one has consciously to struggle for.[101]

Sorell agrees that struggling for survival is far removed from felicity but points out that the demands of pursuing felicity threaten to reduce one to struggling for survival because the goal of felicity requires one to obtain an advantage and keep it.[102] For Hobbes considerations of security are overwhelming. Life without security other 'than what their own strength, and their own invention shall furnish them' is a life of 'continuall feare, and danger of violent death; And the life of man, solitary, poore, nasty, brutish and short'.[103]

Hobbes's description of life without security is, therefore, very similar to Sartre's description of life in a milieu of scarcity and intensified by seriality. There are, however, three important distinctions to be made between Sartre's notion of seriality in a milieu of scarcity and Hobbes's state of nature. The first distinction comes from Hampton's observation that, 'Throughout *Leviathan*, Hobbes's discussion of human beings assumes that minds never meet, that ideas

---

[100] Ibid., chpt. 6, p. 33.
[101] Tom Sorell, 1986, p. 101.
[102] Ibid..
[103] *Leviathan*, chpt. 13, p. 71.

are never really shared among human beings, and that each of us is always and finally isolated from every other individual.'[104] On Sartre's account groups can and do co-exist with seriality so that seriality is not an all or nothing affair. Seriality does not exclude the possibility that one can have mutually satisfying relationships. Sartre's gardener, road-mender and intellectual could be very close friends. Even in seriality people queue for buses.

The second distinction is that, unlike the state of nature, seriality and the current milieu of scarcity are both human constructs. In referring to a praxis of oppression, Sartre, as was seen in the previous chapter, both agrees and disagrees with Engels. He agrees with Engels's criticism of Duhring when Engels argued that class oppression is not the result of the cruelty of individual capitalists. At a local level there is no reason to suppose that individual capitalists would be cruel or oppressive or that there would inevitably be a division of classes on the basis of oppressors and oppressed. In other words, it should be understood that the dominating class does not refer to a group of individuals who have freely united to oppress another group. However, Sartre disagrees with Engels's attribution of class struggle to the means of production, economic laws and, as has been seen, with the division of labour. This new praxis of oppression came from a condition which allowed it to be possible, the milieu of scarcity. Thus Sartre's answer to the question of the origin of oppression is to locate praxis in the context of scarcity. The real origins of classes and class struggle lies in what gives rise to certain means of production and rigid economic laws, namely the milieu of scarcity. In fact, as Busch notes, 'While Sartre is indeed insisting on the connection between mode of production and class, he is not interested in providing a genetic account of class in the usual Marxist manner. His interest bears upon class as a particular type of structured existence.'[105] Thus, as has been seen, class struggle as a negative differentiation arises from an original relationship with the environment which is interiorised and hence produces certain forms and terms of association, namely, those that are now characteristic of seriality. Now it is the case that in the two-way movement of the dialectic of praxis, seriality allows only some to afford the fish and when only some can afford the fish that allows seriality.

The third distinction is that Sartre's description of seriality in a milieu of scarcity performs a different function in Sartre's theory to that performed by the description of the state of nature in Hobbes's theory. Hobbes wishes to legitimate a social contract and a particular form of political association. Sartre is describing a form of association which he finds disturbing and although he describes other forms of association his description of seriality in a milieu of scarcity will not lead him to propose a legitimating basis for a particular kind of State.

Anarchism makes two key charges against the State. First, it has no right to exist. Second, it is the cause of a host of social ills. Regarding the first charge,

---

[104] Hampton, 1986, p. 9.
[105] Busch, 1990, p. 68.

it is argued that States are simply taken for granted. There is very little serious work on justifying the State. However, if pushed, defenders of States will point to social contract theories and argue that States perform important functions, particularly in providing public goods. However, many anarchists will have nothing to do with social contract theory and there is a serious question mark against just how effective States are at providing these goods. Furthermore, even if States were to provide such goods, this is not to say that those goods could not be provided in other ways, less intrusive of individual freedom and more responsive to local needs.

The question mark against the effectiveness of States at providing public goods heralds the second charge against the State. States are the cause of a host of social ills. They are environmentally unfriendly, not least due to their support of a range of big businesses, including the dangerous nuclear and chemical industries. They are devices for the protection of wealth and privilege. Far from managing extensive scarcity many States are the causes of scarcity. Even relatively wealthy States preside over gross inequalities in the provision of for example, health care and educational opportunities. A counter to this argument is that without States things would be even worse. The implicit assumption here is that people are selfish. However, even if we concede the truth of that observation we do not have to concede that they are naturally so. If they are selfish then that could be due to the State itself. Even if we accept the idea of certain social contract theories as an argument for the existence of the State, we would not have to accept it as an argument for the kind of State that exists today. Rousseau's contract, for example, does not point to an over-mighty and all pervasive governing body. Moreover, far from rescuing people from a brutal state of nature, the State is itself the cause of much brutality often visited upon its own citizens who are pressed into serving the State's expansionist or defensive interests. If we aren't pressed, the intrusive State ensures that we are registered, taxed, licensed, numbered and assessed, usually without consultation or permission.

If States are desirable at all it is because they undermine the conditions that make alternatives to the State possible. It does this by assuming many of the functions once performed by local communities and thus undermines those communities. Many of the powers of local government have been centralised as has the provision of a range of public goods, albeit, partly as a result of that centralisation, not particularly effectively. This centralisation, of course, contributes to the growing power of the State. Unsurprisingly, there are, therefore, demands for the reduction of the State. Yet such demands are often met with responses that do not go far enough and proceed in the wrong way. For example, the State typically continues to support big businesses by enacting legislation that is favourable to big business, such as imposing conditions on the withdrawal of labour, whilst also, having centralised the local provision of public goods, it proceeds by reducing or privatising the provision of a range of social safety nets.

For Sartre the notion of a liberal State reeks of class divisions and thus of seriality and that to argue, as Locke does, for a legitimate State is an absurdity. Sartre argues that,

> what is known as the State can never be regarded as the product or expression of the totality of social individuals or even of the majority of them, since the majority is serial anyway, and could not express its needs and demands without liquidating itself as a series, so as to become a large group.[106]

In seriality no one has sworn any kind of allegiance to the State. Yet in seriality no one proclaims the State to be illegitimate. Modern societies consist of a complex mixture of groups and serial collectives of all kinds. The result is that the modern State can never be an expression of all or even of most of the members of society. However, the State, whilst lacking the legitimacy of the kind of group portrayed by Sartre and described in the next chapter, except in the sense of it being an expression of the will of the relatively small number in the ruling group that constitutes the inner circle of government and which is in any case regularly changing, cannot be said to be illegitimate either. Some sort of acceptance of the State does prevail amongst people, largely due to passivity born of impotence. Thus for Sartre the question of the legitimacy or otherwise of the State admits of no particular answer. The State is obeyed not because it is regarded by the majority of citizens as legitimate but because, given their serial impotence, they cannot do otherwise; hence the 'pseudo-legitimacy'[107] of the sovereign State.

Representative government is thought to be an instance of serial alienation. In *Hope Now* Sartre argues that liberal democracies are not really democracies at all, that there is no government by the people because there is no 'people'. People's lives are 'entirely individuated'.[108] It would follow, therefore, that the relationship of the individual to the State could not be one of obligation. Sartre argues that, 'All kinds of electoral systems constitute the set of electors as a passive material for other-direction; and the election results no more represent *the will* of the country, than the top ten records represent *the taste* of the customers.'[109] In his article, 'Elections: A Trap for Fools', Sartre argues that people have been given the vote 'for the purpose of atomizing them and keeping them from forming groups', that is, for the purpose of keeping them powerless.[110] Sartre does not think that 'the fact that every five or six or seven years they perform one very specific act, which is to take a piece of paper with some names on it and drop it in a ballot box'[111] is any sign of people power. He argues that,

---

[106] CDR I, pp. 635–36.
[107] Ibid., p. 637.
[108] *Hope Now*, p. 83.
[109] CDR I, p. 654n.
[110] Sartre, 'Elections: A Trap for Fools', in *Sartre in the Seventies*, 1978, p. 203. Originally published in *Les Temps modernes*, no. 318, January, 1973.
[111] *Hope Now*, p. 84.

'Voting is a fragmentary act that has no connection with one's work or with the totality of one's personal concerns'.[112] Thus, as Brian Seitz notes, 'the subject represented in liberal politics is a serial identity'. He argues that, 'Sartre's outrageous attack on voting and elections is a powerful philosophical attack on beliefs axiomatic for modern liberal thought, which continues to equate general elections and the practice of representation with democracy'.[113]

The notion that there is an entity known as the people is attacked in the writing of both Proudhon and Bakunin. Proudhon writes of how, 'The people imagine themselves, in their obscure manner, as a huge and mysterious entity, and their language serves to reinforce this notion of indivisible unity. They call themselves the People, the Nation.'[114] According to Bakunin, 'In a republic, a fictitious people, the "legal nation" supposedly represented by the state, smothers the real, live people.'[115]

Social anarchists in general have a pretty dim view of the electoral process and of representative democracy as the result of that process. Voting is seen as a way of colluding with the State by endorsing the decision-making procedure of the State and, moreover, of allowing the State to bestow upon those decisions, irrespective of what they might be, a moral authority by virtue of the process itself. Bakunin's view of 'so-called *representative democracy*' is that it is 'based on the pseudo-sovereignty of a sham popular will, supposedly expressed by pseudo-representatives of the people in sham popular assemblies'.[116] Elsewhere he argues that, 'The whole system of representative government is an immense fraud resting on this fiction: that the executive and legislative bodies elected by universal suffrage of the people must or even can possibly represent the will of the people.'[117]

Kropotkin also argues that representative democracy is defective and that, 'these defects are not merely accidental, but inherent in the system itself'. Parliament has shown itself to be incapable of attending to all the affairs of the community and incapable of reconciling varied and often opposing interests. Moreover, 'Elections proved unable to find out the men who might represent a nation, and manage, otherwise than in a party spirit, the affairs they are compelled to legislate upon'. He comments that these defects are so striking that they put in doubt the justice of the principles of the representative system.[118]

Proudhon takes the argument a step further. He argues that, 'An elector's vote is of no real value ... against authority unless it represents a real force and

---

[112] Ibid.
[113] Brian Seitz, 1991, p. 365.
[114] Proudhon, 1979, pp. 57–58.
[115] Bakunin, 1990, p. 23.
[116] Ibid., p. 13.
[117] Bakunin, 'Representative Government and Universal Suffrage', in Sam Dolgoff (ed.), 1973, pp. 220–21.
[118] Kropotkin, 1913, p. 6.

property is that force.'[119] The questions to ask, therefore, are, 'To which section of the population do political parties tend to pitch their policies?' 'Who do they seek to attract?' 'To what extent does the answer to these questions affect the formulation of policy?' The idea that voting in itself bestows upon a decision a kind of moral authority becomes particularly disturbing when what is being voted for reflects the agenda of a sovereign body that seeks to attract the most powerful or influential, since it means that, ultimately, it is the interests of the most powerful or influential that are granted a kind of moral authority.

At this point the distinction between analytical reason and the dialectical method of inquiry becomes important. Having argued that analytical thought operates by fragmenting its object of inquiry and that only the dialectical method can grasp the inter-relatedness of the totalising process which is revealed to an observer situated in interiority, Sartre now argues that there are differences between the bourgeoisie and the proletariat with regard to their adherence to, respectively, analytical and dialectical reason. Thus,

> The bourgeois class conceals the operation of the dialectic under the atomising rationality of positivism, whereas a theorist of the proletariat will demand explanations in the name of the dialectic itself. Thus, at one level of abstraction, class conflict expresses itself as a *conflict of rationalities*.[120]

This indicates a way in which forms and terms of association give rise to and are sustained by forms of meaning. Sartre argues that analytical reason and an analytical understanding of history are approaches that are well suited to and which are, therefore, used by the bourgeoisie. There is as a consequence a criticism of the rationality underpinning the laissez-faire tradition of liberalism. Analytical reason is a bourgeois weapon, an 'oppressive *praxis*'.[121] Analytical reason is an oppressive praxis in that it produces an atomistic view of social experience which severs the connections between people and the connections between events. Sartre says of analytical reason that 'it gave service to liberalism, and it provided a doctrine for procedures that attempted to realize the "atomization of the Proletariat"'.[122] As Dobson argues, 'competition comes about in a competitive society and to the extent that analytical reason splits things apart rather than recognising their interior bonds, the analytic provides a philosophy tailor-made for competing individuals rather than co-operative groups'.[123] Poster points out that the bourgeoisie must employ analytical reason because 'analytical reason obscures the contradictions, reducing them to quantifiable differences'.[124] An analytical account of seriality reveals the

---

[119] Proudhon, 'Theory of Property', in Stewart Edwards (ed.), 1970, p. 139.
[120] CDR I, p. 802.
[121] Ibid., p. 804.
[122] *The Problem of Method*, p. 5.
[123] Dobson, 1993, p. 67.
[124] Poster, 1979, p. 108.

moment by moment freedom of people to enter into contracts and buy whatever fish they can afford to buy. The dialectical account locates these moments in a milieu of scarcity and thereby reveals the constraints upon, for example, the propertyless. Analytical reason reveals that at the moment of voting, just as at the moment of signing a contract, the people are free. However, as we have already seen and as De Lue notes,

> The rights of free speech and the vote are for Sartre only palliatives which keep the workers atomized, fragmented and impotent as a body. Democratic liberalism tends to propel the citizens most in need of assistance into an abstract individualism . . . thus making impossible the resurgence of a political community of activists.[125]

The dialectical method of inquiry reveals that the process of voting perpetuates an already established decision-making procedure whereby the electorate are merely doing more of the same, in this case, alienating their decision-making power to someone else.[126]

Whereas, for Sartre, analytical reason fails to convey reality accurately, you will recall that for Bakunin it is science. Since science cannot deal with real people, only with abstraction, it should not be allowed to rule, 'Since its own nature forces it to ignore the existence of Peter and James, it must never be permitted, nor must anybody be permitted in its name, to govern Peter and James.' What Bakunin demands, he says, is not to destroy science, 'that would be high treason to humanity', but to revolt against the government of science.[127]

Dialectical reason, or at least the dialectical method, is 'the *praxis* of the oppressed'[128] and can be used to wrest from the bourgeoisie their hold on truth. Dobson observes that, 'Sartre's vision is that of a co-operative society, and he sees the founding of the historical dialectic as fundamentally instrumental in achieving that end.'[129] The dialectical approach therefore becomes a critical tool that can usefully be used by communitarians. If we are to understand history as a struggle against scarcity then dialectical reason, if it exists, is the only sort that enables the process to be made intelligible as a whole. The positive thing about analytical reason is that it can be a moment of dialectical reason. However, essentially, as Grene says, 'Analytical reason atomizes, dialectical reason totalizes.'[130]

As an example of a totalisation groups can form and group praxis can, at least for a time, overcome seriality and alterity, at least at a local level. These groups may not be long-lasting but they do raise in their members an awareness

---

[125] De Lue, 1971, p. 310.
[126] See Pateman, 1979, pp. 17–20.
[127] Bakunin, 'On Science and Authority', in Arthur Lehning (ed.), 1974, pp. 160–65.
[128] CDR I, p. 804.
[129] Dobson, 1993, p. 67.
[130] Grene, 1973, p. 203.

of the problem of seriality. Sartre points out that this is what Marx meant when he spoke of the sociality of the worker. Sartre goes on to say that 'this sociality appears on the *joint* negation of the reciprocal aspects of the practical field: a negation of the common object as destiny and a connected negation of multiplicity as seriality'.[131] In other words, it is necessary to overcome the rule of things like the 'top ten' and the market which influence the course of the individual's life and overcome the related condition which is epitomised by standing in a bus queue. However, in accordance with his dialectical sensitivities, Sartre anticipates the circularity of serial and group life. He uses as his example the struggle of a labour union which will 'dissolve into seriality when the workers – victorious or defeated – resume work' and which will be re-formed when the workers, having learnt from that experience of seriality, become active again.[132]

In 'Gender as Seriality', Young provides an example of a movement from seriality to local group. The example is taken from the novel *Rivington Street* by Meredith Tax. This novel portrays the lives of Russian Jewish immigrant women on the Lower East Side of Manhattan at the start of the twentieth century. At one point some of the women find out that a local merchant has rigged the chicken market in order to make more profits on the chickens he sells in that area. The women are angered by this discovery and they organise a boycott. Young notes that, 'The chicken boycott arises from the serialized condition of these women defined by the sexual division of labor as purchasers and preparers of food.'[133] The women, normally serialised as shoppers, come to understand themselves, on the basis of a particular shared experience, as a group with the power of collective action. When the boycott succeeds the women revert to the passive unity of the series.

The point of the movement from seriality to group to seriality again is that Sartre does not see forms and terms of association as static or fixed and immutable. As MacIntyre noted, communities can and do change. Kropotkin, too, writes of 'ever changing, ever modified associations which carry in themselves the elements of their durability and constantly assume new forms which answer best to the multiple aspirations of all'.[134] The ways in which groups do what Kropotkin says that they do will be examined in the next chapter. For now it is important to note that no one can say of the group, 'This is the group, now and forever.' The group changes. New individuals might join. Goals might be re-specified. However, the sense of this is available only to a dialectical method of inquiring into the nature of associations.

Two questions arise. First, how can the individual move from the collective State of seriality into the communal State of the group, or, how does individual

---

[131] CDR I, p. 310.
[132] Ibid., p. 687.
[133] Young, 'Gender as Seriality' in Young, 1997, pp. 34–35.
[134] Kropotkin, 'Anarchism: Its Philosophy and Ideal', in Roger N. Baldwin (ed.), 1968, pp. 123–24.

praxis become group praxis? This problem is akin to that noted by Hampton in connection with Hobbes. She writes that, 'Hobbes's account of conflict seems to generate sufficient strife to make the institution of the sovereign necessary, but too much strife to make that institution possible.'[135] A similar problem confronted Rousseau, as the next chapter will show. It will be seen that Sartre is able to make the move and that in doing so he supplies an answer to the second question. The second question is, given that some people might wish to avoid responsibility, power and close relationships and might crave for isolation, why should the individual want to make this move? An answer to this question is also to be found in the next chapter.

---

[135] Hampton, 1986, p. 136.

CHAPTER SIX

Forms and terms of association: groups

In order to support the communitarian case against liberalism this chapter will develop further Sartre's criticisms of the liberal conception of community. The main aim of this chapter, however, is to provide something that is missing from communitarianism, namely, a view of why and how communities are formed and sustained and in particular a view of how they can be formed if, as communitarians charge, the overly individualistic liberal view of society militates against the formation of communal attachments. Two questions emerge. How can the individual move from the collective state of seriality into the communal state of the group? Why might he wish to do so? In addition to the answers to those questions what is also required is a more sensitive account of communities than that provided by the communitarians, who acknowledge that there are indeed various communities, but fail to differentiate between them in terms of their various forms and terms of association. As a consequence, communitarians have provided an account of community that is deficient in many respects. One way of providing answers to the two questions and of remedying deficiencies in the communitarian account of community is by examining the constituting activity of praxis. This constituting activity will not only be dialectical, it must also be normative and in that way it will provide the basis for a normative theory of associations. The provision of that basis will mark the limits of this work's aspirations with regard to such a theory.

Sartre's groups, like those of Sandel, MacIntyre and Walzer, are small; certainly they are small enough to sustain the kinds of relationships that Sartre describes. It is significant that Sartre is concerned with different types of real groups, which he regards as being examples of communities.[1] This is because not only is it possible to derive from that concern an explanation for why and how these forms of association exist at all and with why and how they might change in the course of time, it is also possible to derive an explanation for the work that is done by communities.

The answer to the second question posed in the opening paragraph arises from the answer to the first. Part of the answer to the first question is that even in a liberal society no one is completely serialised. People do have group memberships of various sorts and can belong to different sorts of groups at the same time. For example, each serial individual can also be a member of a family and have colleagues at work, both of which Sartre says are true of the people in

---

[1] See CDR I, pp. 350, 419, 485, 591, 612; CDR II, p. 72.

the bus queue. However, being a member of a family, for example, does not eliminate the seriality of the market. Rather such membership exists side by side with and is affected by seriality. Moreover, not only may certain groups or communities exist within the seriality of a liberal society's political and economic structure but also, in some cases, they exist because of that structure. Seriality, on a national scale or otherwise, acts as a source of energy for the group in that the group 'is still engulfed in it *by the other serial relations of its members*'.[2] The presence of seriality serves as a reminder to the members of the group of the importance of group membership. Sartre, in fact, distinguishes clearly between groups and the 'national community'[3] which, whether serially structured or not, will inevitably contain examples of both groups and serialities. After all, people all over the world listen to the radio and catch buses. Therefore, individuals in groups might well have had an experience of some form of seriality. The success of a communitarian community might, in fact, require a background of seriality.

Given that in a serial society groups will exist, it is still necessary to understand why and how groups as such can come into being. An understanding of why and how groups are formed will also provide us with an understanding of four aspects of community life which communitarians have neglected. First, we will obtain an understanding of the source of community values. Second, the sense in which and the means by which communities can be constituting of the identities of individuals will be furthered clarified. Third, the conditions by which shared meanings are possible will become apparent as will the idea that not only do communities generate shared meanings but when meanings are perceived as being shared they can generate communities. Fourth, the first steps in understanding the nature of leadership will be taken.

The Group-in-fusion

When the anarchists to which I have been referring talk of ways of forming a community, their talk usually invokes the notion of spontaneity. The spontaneous formation of communities is held to be preferable to their formation on the basis of either elections or the work of a revolutionary vanguard. Thus none talk of a community being formed on the basis of elections whereby a mechanism of the State is used to dissolve the State. Those that do refer to the work of a revolutionary vanguard do so in the most cautious of terms. Bakunin, for example, argues that,

> revolutions are never made by individuals or even by secret societies. They come about of themselves, produced by the force of things, the tide of

---

[2] CDR I, p. 687.
[3] Ibid., p. 385.

events and facts. They ferment for a long time in the depths of the instinctive unconscious of the popular masses – then they explode, often triggered by apparently trivial causes.[4]

Bakunin talks of a 'spontaneous socialist revolution'[5] which is not led or created by a secret society. Even where there is a secret society its task is to 'organise spontaneous popular forces'.[6] So,

> Contrary to the authoritarian communist type of thinking – in my opinion completely erroneous – that a Social Revolution can be decreed and organised, whether by a dictatorship or whether by a constituted assembly resulting from some political revolution, our friends, the socialists of Paris, thought that it could not be made or brought to its full development except by the spontaneous and continuous action of the masses, the groups and the associations of the people.[7]

Should there be any doubt, Bakunin confirms that 'collectivism can come about only through the pressure of circumstances, not by imposition from above but by a free spontaneous movement from below'.[8]

However, we still need to know how we can characterise that free spontaneous movement. The key part of the answer to the question of how can the individual move the collective state of seriality to the communal state of the group has already been alluded to in previous chapters. It is that the transition from serial to group life occurs through praxis itself. Sartre's argument is that it is the awareness by the individual of his needs and of his isolation and impotence in the face of some threat that motivates the formation of groups. In the state of seriality and under some threat to the continuing satisfaction of needs, the individual realises that it is impossible to remain in a condition of isolation and impotence. It is seriality itself which, by keeping people isolated and impotent, makes people aware of their isolation and impotence. That awareness is the basis of a choice. Without the possibility of that choice serial individuals would remain impotent. The choice is exercised through praxis finding the most effective way to satisfy needs. A group forms when individual praxis encounters the same praxes of others attempting to satisfy common needs and instead of competing chooses to co-operate so that the same praxes, acquiring the necessary level of significance, become a common or shared praxis. Thus praxis identifies a certain preferred way of acting and being. This normative notion of praxis will go some way towards the development of a normative theory of associations.

---

[4] Bakunin, 'Four Anarchist Programmes', in Arthur Lehning (ed.), 1974, p. 172.
[5] Bakunin, 'Revolutionary Organisation and Secret Society', in Arthur Lehning (ed.), 1974, p. 182.
[6] Ibid.
[7] Bakunin, 'The Paris Commune and the Idea of the State', in Arthur Lehning (ed.), 1974, p. 204. The 'authoritarian communist type of thinking' is a reference to Marx.
[8] Bakunin, 'Letters to a Frenchman on the Present Crisis' in Sam Dolgoff (ed.), 1973, p. 200.

A community forms, therefore, on the basis of praxis 'feeling individual need as common need, and by projecting itself, in the internal unification of a common integration, towards objectives which it produces as common'.[9] Thus as Hayim recognises, 'The realisation that the Other shares my need as I do his, produces a state of enthusiasm; in other words, the universal character of deprivation leads to the discovery of one's Self in the Other.'[10] This was the point of Sartre's observation concerning the nonindividuality of needs[11] and the fact that everyone gets hungry,[12] noted in chapter two of this work. Although other things may give rise to common objectives, whatever those other things might be, common objectives can always arise from common needs. This means that it is not simply the case that socially defined needs are the product of the community. It is also the case that the community can be the product of needs that are perceived to be common.

The awareness of the existence of common needs indicates the importance of dispositions such as empathy. The awareness of a shared need confirms the existence of the dispositional component of praxis. Praxis both gives rise to and exercises certain dispositions. In this case empathy can be regarded as an aspect of the 'being' dimension of praxis in that individuals within the group discover a fellow feeling through the recognition of a shared predicament. So it is that mutual disinterest is replaced by mutual benevolence. This idea is associated with Sartre's notion of human fulfilment. Human fulfilment requires the development and exercise of certain dispositions. As was noted in chapter two, human fulfilment requires us to be people of a certain kind. To paraphrase MacIntyre, these dispositions allow the movement towards human fulfilment and are exercised in the course of so doing because dispositions are rooted in praxis itself, considered normatively. Human fulfilment, conceived of as a goal, is also given in praxis. Therefore, dispositions can be regarded as those excellences of character that allow people to pursue their goals and which are part of those goals by virtue of being a component of praxis. To put it another way, dispositions and fulfilment come together in that the former leads to the attainment of and is part of the meaning of the latter. Praxis is an explanation for how that is so. Dispositions can arise from the community in the sense that they are a component of the praxis that constitutes, sustains and sometimes seeks to change the community. The acknowledgement of feeling provides a dimension to the notion of association that is absent from Rawls's contractarianism. This is a point that Mary Midgley makes in arguing that it is strange to focus on one single virtue, justice, whilst ignoring the background of 'general morality' which determines the shape and meaning of justice. Included

---

[9] CDR I, p. 350. Interdependence of fate is a significant factor in group formation. See Jacob Rabbie and Murray Horwitz, 1969, pp. 269–77.
[10] Hayim, 1980, p. 90.
[11] NE, p. 66.
[12] Ibid., p. 71.

in this background are 'awkward and non-contractual' virtues such as compassion and 'humanity'. Midgley argues that such a focus, 'isolates the duties which people owe to each other *merely as thinkers* from those deeper and more general ones which they owe each other as beings who feel'.[13]

The question of how the individual can move from a serial existence to a group existence is asked by Sartre himself with reference to the threat that led to the storming of the Bastille. Thus,

> After 12th July 1789 the people of Paris were in a state of revolt. Their anger had deep causes, but as yet these had affected the people only in their common impotence. (Cold, hunger etc. were all suffered either in resignation – or in unorganised outbursts, riots etc.). On the basis of what exterior circumstances were groups to be constituted?[14]

Sartre's answer is that in Paris serial action became fused action in response to government edicts, military violence in the Tuilleries and the threat of a massacre in the Quartier Saint-Antoine. Therefore, Sartre's answer to his own question is that groups are constituted on the basis of common or shared needs such as the need for security in the face of danger, or the need for survival. Under certain conditions, as when being faced by a threat, serial individuals can form into a 'group-in-fusion'. This happens when individual praxis is recognised by other individuals as also being praxis for them. In this way individual praxis becomes common praxis and groups arise from the practico-inert. It is possible, therefore, for competitive praxis to become co-operative praxis once it becomes clear that co-operation is a more efficient means to achieve the same end. The dissolution of seriality does not immediately produce a stable and organised group. It is simply that within the group seriality is liquidated.[15]

It is important to be clear as to the nature of this coming together. The common sense view might be that previously serialised individuals come together to confront the danger. Sartre insists, however, that 'this kind of rationalism is not dialectical, and, though Marxists sometimes make use of it, its analytical, utilitarian origins are quite apparent'.[16] Sartre's idea is that at a certain point, such as in the face of danger, everyone becomes aware that the danger faced by him is the same danger being faced by everyone. In the example of Paris in 1789, the praxis of the group came about through the individual act of arming oneself. That particular act was spontaneously recognised as the common praxis of everyone ('Oh, I see that you're getting a gun as well'). This was, therefore, a series of self-interested actions stemming from the need to

---

13 Mary Midgley, 'Duties Concerning Islands', in Robert Elliot (ed.) 1995, p. 93. Reprinted from R. Elliot and A. Gore (eds), *Environmental Philosophy*, St. Lucia: University of Queensland Press, 1983, pp. 166–81.
14 CDR I, p. 351.
15 'Liquidates' is Sartre's word. CDR I, p. 612.
16 CDR I, p. 351.

survive rather than an example of 'an organised common action'.[17] Instead of an organised common action the individual engages in an individual praxis in order to satisfy his own need for safety. He arms himself as quickly as possible because given a scarcity of weapons 'everyone's attempt to get a rifle became for the others the risk of remaining unarmed'.[18] In acting to protect himself, the individual realises that he is protecting other people and other people are protecting him. That particular praxis was recognised by others as also being their praxis. Recognising a common or shared praxis based on common or shared needs, the fusing of the group occurred. Thus mutual benevolence can be an expression of rational self-interest. This, therefore, is an example of where self-interest does not preclude a concern for the interests of others. In this case the two sets of interests coincide and are mutually reinforcing.

Sartre's emphasis on praxis can be regarded as an echo of Kropotkin's 'The Spirit of Revolt'. There it is action itself that awakens a revolutionary movement. Thus, 'it is through *action* that minorities succeed in awakening the feeling of independence and that spirit of audacity without which no revolution can come to a head'.[19] In this context, 'the act is one with the idea'[20] and they are actions which '*embody the thought it represents*', the '*it*' here referring to a revolutionary party with its aspirations, theories and programmes.[21]

Although the outside group does exert an influence on the unification of the group-in-fusion, the beginning of the new group cannot be provoked by an external agency if the need is not, as has been said, actually felt by individual members. As Desan says, 'the unification which is definitely not wanted by the outside group is produced from the *inside* of the *groupe en fusion*'.[22] The integration of individual praxes must be needed by the individual constituents. Individuals interiorise the multiplicity of praxes as an act of consent, thus forming a group. In this chapter it will become clear that Sartre has a view on consent as a device for establishing and maintaining associations.

Here we have the first moves in providing an answer to the question of the source of shared community values. Further moves will involve a consideration of the other types of group described below. Shared community values can be understood as arising out of individual praxis responding to need in so far as needs are indicators of values and in so far as individual praxis becomes common praxis. That praxis is the meaning of the group. The meaning is comprehensible because it is to be found in the praxis of each individual which is in turn integrated into the common praxis. Common praxis is not of a different order from individual praxis; it is subject to the same type of analysis as individual praxis.

---

17 Ibid., p. 354.
18 Ibid.
19 Kropotkin, 'The Spirit of Revolt', in Roger N. Baldwin (ed.), 1968, p. 39.
20 Ibid.
21 Ibid., p. 42.
22 Desan, 1965, p. 137.

This is because the group can be thought of as a constituted praxis, constituted, that is, by the constituting praxis of the individual. Thus the suppression by the group of seriality is a constituted praxis. Only individual praxis can be constituting. As Sartre frequently and explicitly explains, groups are not hyperorganisms with ends of their own.[23] Groups do not have ends of their own. The goals of a group are the goals of the individuals constituting the group. Therefore, groups are constituting the identities of individuals because of the constituting activities of the individual members of the group. The manner by which this happens will be described later in this chapter. So it is that the group is defined by its common praxis which is the source of the values of the community and which reveals those values. The common praxis reveals and is directed towards common ends and in that way the common praxis establishes and is an expression of certain terms of association, which are an expression of those ends. Those terms of association accompany a particular form of association and that too is established by common praxis. This is simply an elaboration of the idea that there is a dialectical relationship between forms and terms of association which is the result of praxis, as was noted in the previous chapter.

It now becomes possible to understand something not only of the conditions by which shared meanings are possible but also of the work that shared meanings can perform. We have seen that the meaning of a social good can arise from praxis. For example, the praxis of the peasants totalises the land as a scarce and valuable resource or the praxis of a particular section of the community creates a scarcity of fish so that fish are given a particular meaning. In other words the meaning of a social good is rooted not simply in the community but it will also be found in the praxis of the community, which is the praxis of its members and, as was seen in previous chapters, it is a way of defining the community. Ultimately, since praxis and the meanings contained in praxis arise from need, for those meanings to be shared those needs have to be perceived as common needs giving rise to a common praxis which has shared objectives. However, we may now see that not only can the community generate shared meanings in the sense described but an awareness arising from praxis that certain meanings are shared can generate communities. The group-in-fusion is an example of a form of association which is itself based on certain shared understandings in that individual praxis is recognised as common praxis. Therefore, as well as the community generating shared meanings, under certain conditions it is the awareness that a meaning is shared, such as a shared conception of the good and its pursuit ('This is what to do to be secure'), and including the shared meaning of a social good ('Oh, I see that you're getting a gun as well') that generates the community.

Of course, the dangers that produced the group do not need to be so momentous as those experienced in Paris in 1789. Neither need the praxis be as

---

[23] CDR I, pp. 506–507, 539.

dramatic as the storming of the Bastille. It could be that Chinese peasants would come together to avert the danger of a flood. The women on the Lower East Side of Manhattan might simply boycott the chicken. Perhaps the road-mender and the gardener, tired of working for long hours at a time, feel the need for a mid-morning break. They independently make their way to the conveniently located hotel and are seen doing so by other road-menders and gardeners who also feel the need for refreshment. In this way the custom of the mid-morning break is established for those workers in that area. 'If we are working in this area we take a break at this hotel.' Most obviously, groups can be formed to combat certain sorts of scarcity, or at least the effects of certain sorts of scarcity. Thus not only may certain forms of association give rise to and become sustained by scarcity but other forms may arise as a reaction to scarcity and be sustained by the fear of scarcity. Sartre admits that, 'The fact that the origin of the grouping was Terror is not actually very significant.'[24]

What is significant is the fact that the group exists only through individual praxis which becomes a common praxis. Unity in the group-in-fusion is not the product of a collective mind or consciousness. Unity is not achieved by a union of consciousness. Neither is it the product of a contract. It is achieved through spontaneous free praxis which becomes common praxis. In the group people view each other as free subjects united to achieve common ends. The only ends are those of the individual and they can be understood in terms of human fulfilment. The group-in-fusion is merely a means. It is not a hyperorganism with its own ends. Thus the unification of the group takes place on the basis of common objectives. In seriality, people have certain objectives but they are serial objectives. Even when people have the same objective, for example, to catch a bus, they remain individual objectives. It is no part of the objective of any serial individual who is waiting to catch the bus that any other serial individual should catch the bus. However, we still need to understand what the unification of free individuals involves.

What is required at this point, and what communitarianism neglects to provide, is an understanding of the relationship between the individual and the community. This is required in order to make sense of the idea that not only are communities, through their individual members, partly constitutive of individual identities but individuals are also partly constitutive of communities. In order to understand how the group can be constituted out of individual praxis that becomes common praxis and in order to understand further how groups can be constitutive of individual identities it is necessary to be clear about the kind of unification that members of groups possess. Sartre's notion of unification involves two key ideas, that of the 'third party' and that of 'the same'. The group and indeed any community does not simply consist of more people getting together. A group does not simply come into being by virtue of the fact that

---

[24] Ibid., p. 405.

there are more people around.[25] Sartre's use of the notion of the 'third party' and 'the same' reveals that the dialectic as a process inherent in praxis is the dynamic of the group. It is, to repeat, the absence in communitarianism of an explanation of the dynamic of the group, that is, with the nature of associating and hence forms and terms of association, that accounts for the communitarian neglect of community.

The notion of the third party provides us with the sense in which it can be said that communities are constituted in part by individuals and individual identities and attachments are constituted in part by communities conceived of as communities of individuals. The function of the third party is to bring about the unity of those with him in the group. In an interview with Fretz, Sartre describes the notion of the third party. He says,

> That is an arbitrary person in a group. Who is an outsider with respect to the reciprocity between two people. If there is a group of three persons, then there are two who stand in a relation of reciprocity . . . and the third, who is the relating element in this notion of reciprocity, and who consequently is indispensable because the relation of reciprocity is incomplete by itself.[26]

Thus the road-mender and the gardener could not totalise themselves as a group for themselves even if they could become aware of each other. It takes the watching intellectual to constitute them as a group, not by virtue of being an intellectual but by virtue of being the third party. Married couples conceive of themselves as being married to each other. They do not totalise themselves. In terms of the reality of the relationship itself, any acknowledgement of their attachment, indeed, the process of engaging in an acknowledgement, requires their ontological distinctiveness. In order for one of them to conceive of themselves as a unit as in 'a pair', 'a couple', or even 'an item', they have to acknowledge the distinctiveness of the other. The totalisation of a pair requires a third party. The third party totalises the other group members in a way that is not possible for a second party. Sartre argues that, 'A binary formation, as the immediate relation of man to man, is the necessary ground of any ternary relation; but conversely, a ternary relation, as the mediation of man amongst men, is the basis on which reciprocity becomes aware of itself as a reciprocal connection.'[27] This is because C can totalise A and B and can in turn be totalised by both A and B with regard to B and A and so there is a mediated reciprocity of totalisations, understood as both process and outcome, consisting of A and B, B and C, and A and C. The fact is that A cannot totalise both himself and B so that they become A-B and B cannot totalise both himself and A so that they

---

25 See the critical comments of Roger Garaudy, 1970, p. 91; Aronson, 1973, p. 83; 1980, p. 265.
26 Fretz, 'An Interview With Jean-Paul Sartre', trans. George Berger, in Silverman and Elliston (eds), 1980, p. 236.

become B-A. From the communitarian perspective, this process of totalisation provides a further sense in which attachments can be non-voluntaristic.

For totalising to occur the totalising praxis must be apart, or distinct from, that which is being totalised. This is because the process of totalisation which makes the group possible is not a process that can be undertaken by an individual who has, as it were, become one with the group. In short 'a totalising *praxis* cannot totalise itself as a totalised element'.[28] For this reason Sartre argues that,

> We willingly grant that the *group* never has and never can have the type of metaphysical existence which people try to give it. We repeat with Marxism: there are only men and real relations between men. From this point of view, the group is in one sense only a multiplicity of relations and of relations among those relations.[29]

Were the totalising praxis to be able to totalise itself it would simply disappear into what would become, in the context of group formation, a hyperorganism. The ontological distinctiveness of the individual would also, therefore, disappear. Instead, Sartre's use of the term 'third party' is intended to indicate that each member of the group 'totalises the reciprocities of others'[30] and the role of each third party is to make 'reciprocity visible to itself'.[31] Therefore, I can recognise that my actions are part of the totalisation whilst in that act of recognition I remain detotalised.

The third party is the one who sees his fellow group members as undertaking actions that are the same as each others' and his own. Since each person in the group is the third party in relation to all the others, each actualises the unity of the others and is in turn unified with others by every other group member as third party. Ian Craib describes the process thus,

> In my own individual praxis I freely create the group praxis (obtain arms, put up barricades etc.) and each other member of the group – who is also a Third – is doing the same. In such a situation, each of my actions is a command to the others and vice versa: my praxis becomes the group praxis and I make the group praxis mine.[32]

It is this process that gives the group its unity. Its unity lies only in the common praxis and the common purpose as interiorised by each of the members. Notice

---

27 CDR I, p. 109.
28 Ibid., p. 373.
29 *The Problem of Method*, p. 76. In developing the idea that there are only men and real relations between men, Sartre adds in parenthesis 'for Merleau-Ponty I add things also and animals, etc'. in a clear reference to an observation made by Merleau-Ponty who says in *Adventures of the Dialectic* that, 'Since men and things are face to face (let us forget animals, for which Sartre, as a good Cartesian, should not care very much), wills do not continue living a decadent or fertile life in the things they mark.' (1974, p. 147)
30 CDR I, p. 374.
31 Ibid., p. 116.
32 Craib, 1976, p. 175.

that the role of the third party is to unify actions not individuals. Again, this avoids the implication that a hyperorganism is being created. Alterity still exists yet as Flynn says, 'It is by the organic agent as Third that multiplicity is interiorized and alterity rendered harmless in view of a common object.'[33]

Sartre's notion of the third party provides us with an insight into something that the communitarians neglect to mention in connection with their communities, leadership. As a third party each individual becomes quasi-sovereign, that is, regulatory. In so far as each individual is a third party to all the others every individual's praxis is regulatory. Each third party accommodates his action to the actions of the other third parties as normative. Every individual action becomes a common action and consequently there is group praxis. The relationship of each quasi-sovereign, that is everyone, with the group is both transcendent and immanent. However, it is not transcendent in the sense of being other or apart from the group. It is transcendent because each quasi-sovereign unifies the group. It is immanent because seriality is liquidated only to the extent that this unity is interiorised by each group member. So it is that notions of immanence and transcendence, which are absent in communitarian thought, provide us with a particular way of understanding the nature of associating and with a view on how to relate the individual to the community. In the case of the group, the third party is a mediator. However, 'the mediator is not an object, but a *praxis*'.[34]

Communitarians are critical of the laissez-faire view of the individual pursuing his independent way. By understanding the individual as a mediating third party involved in a complex of mediated reciprocities, we can understand how there is dependency within the group but it is the dependency of free individuals. In a conversation with Benny Levy, Sartre maintains that 'I hadn't determined what I am trying to determine today: the dependence of each individual on all other individuals.'[35] The reciprocity of dependency means that everyone is a kind of leader or quasi-sovereign. Thus the presence of the third party does not constitute a hierarchy since every member of the group will be a third party to all the others and everyone can exercise a leadership role. True to the spirit of anarchism, Sartre is clear that the *Critique* is anti-hierarchical.

The dynamics are such that the individual retains his freedom but gains power. Sartre explains that 'the third party comes to the group which already possesses him, as a *constituent and constituted power*. That is, he receives the power he gives, and he sees the other third party approaching him as *his* power.'[36] It is through praxis that each individual gives to the group the power that he gets from the group. In other words, empowered by the group, the individual is

---

[33] Flynn, 'Mediated Reciprocity and the Genius of the Third', in Schilpp (ed.), 1981, p. 353.
[34] CDR I, p. 377.
[35] *Hope Now*, p. 72. It is the interest in the nature of that dependence that marked the development of Sartre's moral theory in 1980.
[36] CDR I, p. 376.

able to contribute that power to the group. The power that each one receives from the group is his own power multiplied by the members of the group and interiorised. Bakunin makes a similar point, arguing that, 'In order to be free, I need to see myself surrounded by free men and be recognised as such by them. I am free only when my individuality, reflected in the mirror of the equally free consciousness of every individual around me comes back to me strengthened by everyone's recognition.'[37] In the group-in-fusion, plurality is no longer considered negatively in terms of conflict but positively as a powerful union of individuals pursuing common goals for plurality consists of the abundance of those who are not other than but the same as the individual member. The particular meaning that Sartre gives to 'the same' will be examined shortly. Thus life in the group is quite different from life in the bus queue. In the queue, need reveals the impotence of the isolated individual. However, in the group, where the reciprocity of isolation is transformed into the reciprocity of dependency, need generates a response that has power. Although the bus queue itself is a manifestation of reciprocal dependence it is the dependence of isolated individuals none of whom needs or even wants anyone else to be part of the queue. It is, moreover, a dependence that is dictated by the ticket machine. The queue is quite unlike the group-in-fusion. The group can be regarded as an instrument for the praxis of every individual. However, the converse is not true. The individual is not an instrument of the group understood as a subject. He is, however, a means in reciprocity with other free praxes.

Communitarians such as Sandel, Etzioni and Glendon are critical not only of the laissez-faire view of the independent individual but also of the individual who, as a symptom of that independence, lacks responsibility. A reason offered to explain this lack of responsibility is that the liberal individual suffers from a surfeit of rights that support the individual's independence. It has been said that these rights insulate people from each other so that they do not develop a sense of community. However, the problem of the lack of responsibility (and the absence of a sense of community) is not to be solved by curtailing rights but by initiating particular forms of association. Rights are, as we have seen, an expression in part of particular terms of association. The work that they perform can vary according to the form of association. Indeed, as will become clear, in certain forms of association rights become inextricably linked with responsibilities. However, even in the group-in-fusion there is an ethical imperative on each third party as responsible for common praxis. As Hayim notes, 'The basic difference between the serial and the fused group is that the latter experiences co-essentiality and co-responsibility. The sense of power and sovereignty it experiences is shared by everyone.'[38] Flynn notes that 'the genesis of the group can be seen as "interiorization of responsibility" such that "my"

---

[37] Bakunin, 'Three Lectures to Swiss Members of the International', in Robert M. Cutler (ed.), 1985, p. 48.
[38] Hayim, 1980, p. 93.

responsibility becomes "ours"'.³⁹ As Flynn argues, the phenomenon of interiorising multiplicity is more than a psychological process. It should be thought of as the imperative, 'Accept responsibility for the whole.' Flynn regards this as Sartre's social imperative par excellence because it challenges particularist, self-centred consciousnesses to judge and act in terms of meanings larger than themselves, 'In Rousseau's sense, it turns men into citizens.'⁴⁰

Sartre has to account not just for the unity which the group achieves but for the specific unity of that specific group. He also has to avoid the claim that the group is a whole with characteristics independent of the sum of its individual parts. To do this he uses the notion of 'the same'. This is not an abstract idea as in the notion of a universal. Neither does it mean that every person is identical. The members of the group are concrete and they remain distinct individuals. However, they are not unconnected or separate as are members of a series. They are unified by virtue of their common praxis towards common goals. Here ends can be seen to be constitutive of identities. In the group-in-fusion the individual is empowered rather than impotent, active rather than passive, co-operative rather than antagonistic, empathic rather than disinterested and responsible rather than lacking in responsibility. All of this occurs as a result of and in the pursuit of the goal of dissolving seriality which is a goal that was already present in the praxis of the individual members. The third party perceives his actions as the same as those of the other group members and in that sense does not see himself as other than or separate from others as objects whose unity he actualises. Thus, 'the practical unity which my totalisation reveals and which negates the objectivity of the group thereby negates my own in relation to the group, since this practical unity is *the same* (not in me *and* it, but *in us*)'.⁴¹ In the group, the other third party is no longer an object. In the group-in-fusion the individual recognises in the other not an other but himself and sees in the other his own project of freedom. In this way seriality is liquidated.

Sartre's notion of 'the same' avoids the charge that group life requires conformity and loss of freedom. It is through the power of common praxis that the individual finds his freedom enhanced. Thus the concept of the group-in-fusion overcomes the objection that, for Sartre, freedom is radically individualistic and it overcomes the idea that only in liberal societies can people be truly free. In conforming to the group one is conforming to oneself. In obeying the regulations of the group one is obeying one's own regulations. In fact orders are not obeyed as such, 'It is simply the common *praxis* becoming . . . regulatory of itself.'⁴² Thus in relating the uprising in Paris, Sartre describes how the third

---

39 Flynn, 1984, pp. 118–19.
40 Ibid., p. 202.
41 CDR I, p. 373.
42 Ibid., p. 380. The existence of a common goal and agreement about the means for attaining it is one of the explanations for conformity. Another explanation concerns the social construction of reality. These social constructs act like mini-theories, guiding actions and helping us to interpret social events. However, it is important for us to have some way of verifying or testing our theories.

party gives the command to stop or to go ahead. These commands, or more accurately, re-orientations of the group's praxis, are not the products of the group. They come from an individual. However, in the act of understanding and of executing them, the individual, who did not give the order, recognises himself and his free choice confirms it. This is the act of consent. Consent in this case has dimensions of both immanence and transcendence. It occurs within the group yet in occurring it changes the group.

Our understanding of shared meanings, of the community as constituted in part by individuals and as in part constitutive of individual identity and our understanding of the relationship between the community and the good life for human beings can be furthered when cast in terms of immanence and transcendence. Shared meanings will occur within the group as a result of the transcending act of an individual third party attempting to satisfy needs which are perceived to be common. That act is interiorised and confirmed by the other members of the group. In other words, groups as such do not generate shared meanings. For a meaning to be shared it must be both transcendent and immanent. The transcending movement of praxis is also part of the process by which the individual's identity is constituted in the group-in-fusion. In other sorts of groups, as will become clear, there are other processes also at work and so other factors will also contribute to the constitution of the individual's identity. Inevitably, however, the individual's identity is constituted in part by the transcending praxis of the third party, recognised as being a praxis for the other members of the group. That praxis contains within it a particular end. This, therefore, becomes another way whereby, through praxis, ends become constitutive of identities. In addition, the individual so constituted is himself a third party and as such, through his transcending praxis, is a constituting member of the group and recognised as such by the others. The transcending praxis of both the individual and the other members of the group constitute the individual as a member of the group and it is through that constituting praxis that the individual can be identified by the ends that are pursued. Finally, it was that transcending praxis that defined the nature of the good and it was the commonality of that view that produced the group. As has been said, this is not an explanation that has been used by communitarians.

By way of illumination, some interesting comparisons between Sartre's analysis of the relationship between the individual and the group and that of Rousseau may be made. Certainly their starting points are familiar. McBride argues that Rousseau's claim, 'Man was born free, and he is everywhere in chains',[43] 'is *roughly* similar to Sartre's view of the human condition in the

---

Yet unlike more scientific theories, we usually do not have any objective means or agreed procedures for so doing. Therefore, we turn to other people for confirmation of our views. The validation function provided by social comparison means that people value 'sameness' in groups and will often behave so that it will be maintained. See Leon Festinger, 1950, pp. 271–82 cited in, Bertram Raven and Jeffrey Rubin, 1982, p. 569; Donelson Forsyth, 1987, p. 286.

[43] *The Social Contract*, Bk. 1, chpt. 1, p. 49.

domain of the practico-inert'.[44] For both Sartre and Rousseau the motivating force is that people must protect themselves not from the non-human environment, as was once the case, but from other people.

Sartre's theory of the group can be regarded as a development of Rousseau's attempt to reconcile modern individualism with the classical, that is, republican Roman and Spartan, view of the priority of the community. Both Sartre and Rousseau argue that the individual cannot be fully free and effective apart from involvement in some sort of community. Both believe that people have the capacity within themselves to create a form of association the terms of which will serve the common good and that these forms of association are the products of individuals acting together 'to shake off the yoke'.[45] The problem for both writers is to show how people can be free and effective whilst being part of a group. The task for both is to create a form of association the terms of which will preserve life whilst at the same time ensuring that the freedom of the individual remains intact. As Rousseau puts it, the individual must be able to merge his strength and liberty with that of others, 'without putting himself in peril and neglecting the care which he owes to himself'.[46]

Moreover, this form of association, designed to overcome impotence, must be created by individuals in a state of impotence. Rousseau's problem was that if the individual had known only a state of impotence and even if that impotence was somehow perceived as unjust and thus deserving of change, how could the individual know that it would be necessary to form an association, or what kind? This is similar to the problem identified in connection with Hobbes at the end of the previous chapter. Rousseau explains that he assumes,

> that men reach a point where the obstacles to their preservation in a state of nature prove greater than the strength that each man has to preserve himself in that state . . . the only way in which they can preserve themselves is by uniting their separate powers in a combination strong enough to overcome any resistance, uniting them so that their powers are directed by a single motive and act in concert.[47]

There is, therefore, for Rousseau as for Sartre, an existential moment of awareness followed by choice. For Rousseau, as for Sartre, the individual in the group assumes responsibility for attending to the common interests of the whole group. Rousseau argues that, 'this act of association creates an artificial and corporate body composed of as many members as there are voters in the assembly, and by this same act that body acquires its unity, its common *ego*, its life and its will'.[48]

---

[44] McBride, 1991, p. 126.
[45] *The Social Contract*, Bk. 1, chpt. 1, p. 50.
[46] Ibid., Bk. 1, chpt. 6, p. 60.
[47] Ibid., Bk.1, chpt. 6, pp. 59–60.
[48] Ibid., Bk. 1, chpt. 6, p. 61.

Of course, for Rousseau, the will in question is the general will. However, even here a parallel with Sartre may be noted. Flynn argues that,

> In his conception of the mediated reciprocity of the regulating Third, and especially in his analysis of the mot d'ordre as vehicle of sovereignty, Sartre is doubtless inspired by Rousseau's notion of the general will which confers freedom on the individual precisely because it involves obedience to a command he has given to himself.[49]

Here, presumably, Flynn has in mind Rousseau's desire to find a form of association whereby each individual 'while uniting himself with the others, obeys no one but himself, and remains as free as before'.[50] Flynn is no doubt correct in observing that Sartre was inspired by Rousseau's notion of the general will. However, that is not the same as claiming that the nature and function of the general will and the third party are identical. Indeed, it is not a claim that Flynn makes. Whilst it is useful to note the similarities between the two ideas, it is also instructive to be clear about the differences. John Noone Jr argues that,

> Sovereignty, law and general will are so interrelated that there are very few contexts where one is intelligible without the other two. Sovereignty pertains to a people insofar as they act in a certain way. The termination of this process is law, and law is said to be an expression of the general will. The general will, then, may be regarded as a kind of mediating link between sovereignty as a process and law as its termination.[51]

The third party may also be regarded as a mediating link which, as will become apparent, terminates in the pledge, a binding oath supported by sanctions. The purpose of the third party serves a similar purpose to that of the general will. Rousseau's ideal was that of classical cohesiveness now willed by individuals who were concerned with legitimisation by consent as a reason for obligations to the State. Sartre also wishes to argue for the value of certain sorts of groups and to legitimise those groups as the voluntary creations of free consenting individuals. However, in his case groups arise from the free praxis of individuals. Sartre's device for basing group life on free praxis is the third party. Unity arises out of the individual praxis of each third becoming common praxis. In other words, it is through praxis rather than will that unification is achieved. Sartre and Rousseau wish, therefore, to achieve similar goals. The goals are similar rather than the same because the primary purpose of the praxis of the third party is the satisfaction of need rather than the legitimisation of the State.

Further similarities and differences emerge on examining the nature of the general will itself. This is no easy task since, apart from defining it as a kind of mediating link, as Lester Crocker notes, commentators 'have sought in vain

---

[49] Flynn, 'Mediated Reciprocity and the Genius of the Third', in Schilpp (ed.), 1981, p. 357.
[50] *The Social Contract*, Bk. 1, chpt. 6, p. 60.
[51] John Noone Jr, 1980, p. 73.

some clear decisive definition. It is not surprising that they have not found it, or that Rousseau himself was never able to either.'[52] What may be said of the general will is that it is what remains when the self-interested private and particular wills of all the individuals in the putative community have cancelled each other out. Here another similarity between the general will and the third party may be noticed. Both involve people who are set in the context of known material conditions and who know about themselves. Both, therefore, differ from Rawls's notion of contracting parties in the original position. What remains after the cancelling out process is common to all. In that sense the general will is the will of the sovereign and the sovereign is the collective body that is formed out of the act of association whereby individuals agree to the social contract.

It will become apparent that Sartre is not engaged in developing a social contract theory and he also has a different view of sovereignty at least in so far as it exists within groups that are not relapsing back into seriality. Moreover, it is not the case that there is a process of cancelling every individual praxis against every other individual praxis until all that remains is a common praxis. Unity occurs through the multiplicity of individual praxes which are seen to be common. Rousseau has no notion of a third party. Therefore, while Rousseau is able to offer an explanation of the nature of the self-understandings of a community he is denied a particular opportunity for explaining how those understandings are to be mediated between the members of that community. To describe the general will as a 'mediating link' is to say nothing about the process by which the link is mediated. In the absence of a theory of mediation such as that provided by Sartre in the form of the praxis of the third party, Rousseau's notion of the general will appears as a mystification.

An understanding of why and how groups are formed reveals something of the ways in which a community operates. Without an understanding of how a community operates, communitarians are unable to say much about how individual identities are constituted by communities or about how shared meanings are both generated and, as communitarians fail to acknowledge, generating. Neither can they say much about the relationship between the individual and the community or about specific aspects of community life such as leadership. For Sandel and Walzer communities are somehow just there. A communitarian response to this criticism could be that communitarianism is concerned simply with the present, that is, with communities as they are now. However, a communitarian criticism of liberalism is that liberalism fails to recognise that the individual is tied to his family, his community and his history and that these ties cannot be accounted for by liberalism. According to Jean Bethke Elshtain, for example, these ties are not a matter of choice but rather constitute elements of a thick self. This self 'acknowledges that he or she has many debts and obligations and that one's history and the history of one's society

---

[52] Lester Crocker, 1968, p. 88.

frames one's own starting point'.[53] However, communitarians must also apply this argument to communities. An understanding of communities must necessarily involve an understanding of how they operate, of the constituting elements and how they are related. In other words, communitarians who insist that they are concerned with communities as they are can be accused of having, at best, a partial view of community not only by virtue of ignoring the environments in which communities are located, as was argued in chapter four but also, as a development of a particular aspect of that argument, by virtue of ignoring the praxis that constitutes associations. Therefore, an understanding of how things are now and in particular an understanding of community values and other shared meanings can be developed through an understanding of the role of praxis and an understanding of praxis requires an understanding of previous praxes.

The pledged-organised group

The community having been formed, the problem, ignored by communitarians, is how to ensure that it will be sustained. An examination of how a community sustains itself will reveal that it is individuals who do the sustaining. In order to do so a regulatory device for binding people together must be found. The members of the group must consent to being regulated by this device and it will become clear that regulation and consent are essential elements in sustaining communities. The act of consent provides the constituting activity of the members of the group on themselves and on each other, which is now the activity by which the group is sustained, with a particular content thus making the members of the group people of a particular sort. In sustaining the community through regulation and consent attachments become formalised and the way in which these attachments become constitutive of identities will become apparent. The community is sustained because it is viewed not only as an instrumental good but also as an end in itself. It is a source and an expression of the good life for human beings. Viewing the community as an end provides another way of thinking about communities as constitutive of identities. The process of sustaining a community reveals further why not all ends and attachments can be viewed in purely voluntaristic terms. It also reveals how and in what sense the legitimacy of the authority of the community can be established and the mechanism by which commitment to the community is engendered.

For both Sartre and Rousseau it is a threat of some sort that brings people together. So the particular problem facing both Sartre and Rousseau is how to sustain the community once the threat that brought people together has disappeared. For Sartre the solution to the problem is to be found in the pledge which, in its manner of operation, has certain similarities with the solution

---

53 Jean Bethke Elshtain, 'The Communitarian Individual', in Etzioni (ed.), 1995a, p. 105.

proposed by Rousseau albeit also with distinctly Hobbesian overtones. Thus once formed, the group may seek to maintain itself, prevent the return to seriality and protect itself from impotence and isolation and hence from scarcity or its effects by taking, in one form or another, an oath or 'pledge' by which each member of the group binds himself to every other member, thereby initiating the pledged group. Sartre argues that when people are no longer sufficiently afraid of the external threats posed by the enemy there is a danger of disintegrating. This new danger must be overcome, 'by the negation of the absence of fear'.[54] In other words fear must be re-created and it is this that gives the pledge its force. The pledged group replaces the fear of the enemy, which is fading with the passing of time, with its own fear. In less dramatic terms, in the absence of needs demanding immediate satisfaction, the group initiates a system of regulation.

The binding nature of the pledge, in the absence of an external threat, is achieved through the internal threat of violence which Sartre calls 'Fraternity-Terror,' that is, death.[55] In the pledged group individuals take an oath, the substance of which is that each individual promises not to engage in any action that would destroy the group and return its members to a state of seriality, thus rendering them more vulnerable to scarcity. The penalty of Fraternity-Terror, being part of the freely taken pledge, is agreed to freely by all the members of the group. Sartre draws a distinction between the unity of the fused and that of the pledged group thus, 'the unity of the fused group derived its materiality from the intolerable pressure of the enemy group; *it was* the interiorisation and inversion of this pressure (of this totalising destruction)'.[56] The unity of the pledged group comes from within the group itself. The pledge is, 'A free attempt to substitute the fear of all for the fear of oneself and of the other in and through everyone, in so far as it suddenly reactualises violence as the intelligible transcendence of individual alienation by common freedom: that is what pledges are.'[57] The pledge is the group's guarantee against mutual betrayal which is fear of others but also fear of oneself in so far as one might become a betrayer of the group.

For Sartre, the pledge as praxis is a further example of constituting activity, which although different in content is the same in form as the process described in connection with the group-in-fusion. Each individual takes the pledge and in taking it makes taking the pledge possible for everyone. Thus everyone can promise fidelity and protect themselves and everyone else from becoming betrayers of the group. The individual is engaging in an activity to determine the constitution of the group and the group is constituting the individual, in this case, not to be a traitor. More precisely, it is the other members of the group,

---

[54] CDR I, p. 430.
[55] Ibid., pp. 437ff.
[56] Ibid., p. 429.
[57] Ibid., p. 433.

and the individual himself, who are and who is doing the constituting and thereby defining themselves and each other as loyal members of the community. This again reinforces the idea that there is a dialectical relationship between forms and terms of association which is based on constituting praxis. Therefore, the pledged group is a form of association whose terms bring stability to attachments between people. In this way the communitarian idea that certain attachments cannot be set aside for they are constitutive features of our identities acquires further intelligibility. The basis for this intelligibility is to be found in the constituting praxis itself. In constituting the pledged group individuals are constituting themselves and each other. That constituting activity involves a relationship that is wrought by every individual as a third party each of whom is affected by every other third party. The constitution and maintenance of individual identities requires the establishment and maintenance of that relationship. This is quite different from the claim regarding the setting aside of attachments that is made by certain communitarians, which is that setting aside certain attachments which are constitutive of identities can cause psychological damage.[58] That claim does not explain how attachments might be constitutive of identities, only what might happen if they are set aside. Moreover, in so far as this constituting praxis has a normative dimension we can see a further development in a normative theory of associations. The best sort of association is the association that, among other things, inculcates a sense of loyalty.

Of course, one might have doubts concerning the nature of the means deployed by Sartre for inculcating loyalty. However, the draconian nature of Fraternity-Terror may be tempered by remembering that if the group was originally formed as a response to less drastic circumstances then less drastic penalties could be invoked to make the pledge binding. Sartre is, of course, talking about a pledge being taken under particular circumstances in Paris in 1789. It could simply be that the flood faced by the Chinese peasants has been averted, or some other need satisfied, thus permitting complacency and as a result a return to seriality and which, in view of the damage caused by the floods, the Chinese peasants pledge to avoid. As Sartre says,

> the intensity of the group's actions arises from the intensity of the external threats, that is to say, from danger; and if this intensity no longer manifests itself as a real pressure but the danger itself still exists, then it is replaced by the artificial substitute of Terror. Terror is a real *product* of men in groups, but it still depends, *in itself* and for its degree of intensity, on hostile violence.[59]

In fact, in *Hope Now*, Sartre admits that he was never quite clear as to 'the real relationship between violence and fraternity'.[60] He argues that 'violence is not

---

[58] Bell, 1993, pp. 90ff.
[59] CDR I, p. 439.
[60] *Hope Now*, p. 93.

going to speed up the pace of history and draw people together. Violence merely breaks up a certain state of enslavement that was making it impossible for people to become human beings.'[61] Thus terror is necessary to guarantee fraternity in a milieu of scarcity and betrayal, but violence of itself will never further the development of man. It is because there is a limit to the integration of any individual into the group that the pledge becomes necessary and has to be provided with some kind of force. The pledge is Sartre's way of using the power of the group in a way that serves the well-being of the group as a whole.

In explaining the transition from the group-in-fusion to the pledged group the pledge offers, as McBride notes, an explanation of the need for regulations and constitutions in even voluntary associations and establishes a connection between law and force and, since 'droit' means both law and right, between rights and force.[62] In the absence of an external threat which can serve to bind the community together one might hope that the community could be bound by ties of affection, mutual regard and a desire on the part of the members to work for the well-being of all. However, even where that proves to be the case, certain terms of association will be required and those terms will be, in part, regulatory. They will, for example, be an expression of what is meant by and required for the achievement of the well-being of all. In fact, the notion of the pledge contributes to our understanding of the relationship between forms and terms of association. As we have seen, the praxis of taking the pledge initiates a particular form of association with the pledge itself constituting the terms of that association.

The praxis of taking the pledge is consistent with and is, in fact, an explanation for the anarchist account of self-regulation. An alternative to State compulsion would be the emergence of communal norms where each person plays a part in ensuring that others maintain those norms. Anarchists generally believe that social life is to a large extent self-regulating and that when this self-regulation fails individuals can be punished, in the case of social anarchists, by the community itself. This is not thought to be a limitation on freedom since membership of the community is not compulsory. One is free to associate and equally one is free not to associate. If one agrees to associate then one agrees to a certain form of social life. Such an agreement is not a limitation on freedom. The fact that I have agreed to abide by a promise, or to co-operate with a particular individual or group, or meet my mate in a pub cannot mean that I have, by making an agreement, limited my freedom. Agreeing to meet a friend does not involve a limitation on freedom but instead involves its exercise. Moreover, it is precisely because the agreement has been freely made that some form of sanction for breaching the agreement is appropriate. Bakunin argues that voluntary agreements should not be violated and that, 'Persons who violate

---

[61] Ibid., p. 92.
[62] McBride, 1991, pp. 152–53.

voluntary agreements... will be penalized according to the laws of society'.[63] Taking a particular example, he insisted that those who wanted to belong to the International Workingmen's Association would have to pledge to do certain things and in particular to pledge solidarity and that, 'The least betrayal of this solidarity will be considered the greatest crime.'[64] What we have, therefore, is a form of association where talk of political obligation is appropriate but where the obligations that are owed by individuals are owed not to the State but to each other.

The nature of the dependency to be found in the pledged group is far more formal than that of the group-in-fusion. In the pledged group, the individual as a third party continues to regulate and continues to be regulated by all the other individuals as third parties. However, in this case the regulation is supported by enforcement. Unsurprisingly, both Hobbes and Rousseau also examine enforcement.[65] In something resembling Sartre's pledged group, Rousseau's social contract constitutes the members of the association as a sovereign body or as their own legislative assembly. The members enter into a reciprocal commitment with each other not just as individuals but also to constitute their new status as legislators. Law in this instance is not meant to deal with specific cases as statute law does. Instead it is meant to define the structure of general rights and duties that each man has to others in the community. The law facilitates the pursuit of one's private needs and organises one's relationships with others so that one is also upholding the common good. Therefore, the law ensures the maintenance of the community even when the immediate danger has passed. However, Sartre's pledged group clearly has a Hobbesian dimension. Warnock, comparing Sartre with Hobbes, argues that it is possible 'to see the oath backed by terror as the covenant supported by the sword'.[66] What Hobbes does is create an enforcer of covenants. For it to be reasonable to trust that the other person will keep the covenant then it must be known that not keeping the covenant would be dangerous for the other person. In *Leviathan*, each individual makes his power freely available for the maintenance of security on the condition that everyone does the same. Since the alternative is the continuation of war in the state of nature, everyone has a good reason for entering into this agreement. Having entered into the agreement, there is good reason for not reneging since the power of everyone is available to everyone and will be used against those who do renege. However, for Hobbes, this power is given up to a particular sovereign or assembly.[67] In Sartre's pledged group, everyone is pledged to be an enforcer. Thus the reciprocity of dependency acquires particular content as the reciprocity of enforcement.

---

[63] Bakunin, 'Revolutionary Catechism', in Sam Dolgoff (ed.), 1973, p. 81.
[64] Bakunin, 'The Policy of the International', in Sam Dolgoff (ed.), 1973, p. 162.
[65] *Leviathan*, chpt. 15, p. 82; *The Social Contract*, Bk. 2, chpt. 5, p. 79.
[66] Warnock, 1965, p. 173.
[67] *Leviathan*, chpt. 17, pp. 99–100.

It is important to emphasise that the pledge is freely taken with the intention of guaranteeing freedom. The pledge which grants the right to punish betrayal and which serves to defend people from themselves, as noted above, is the equivalent of Rousseau's forcing man to be free.[68] Rousseau's idea in *The Social Contract* is that it is not men, as in community, but man as an individual who can be forced to be free. In *The Social Contract* this idea refers to the individual who, as a result of being enslaved by his passions, disobeys the law, or the general will. The general will is something inside each man as well as in society as a whole, so that the man who is suffering the force of the community for a breach of the law is being brought back to an awareness of his own true will. In this way the law enlarges freedom. It is a view that is quite at odds with that of Hobbes, who thought that to be free was to be unopposed and unconstrained in doing what one wants to do. For Hobbes, the less the law forbids, the freer one is. This is the state of nature in which, according to Hobbes, men are free. Yet it is at best a partial understanding of freedom which is rooted in the absence of constraint.

The absence of constraint produces a condition in which one has to take measures to ensure one's security and the extent to which that is so is the extent to which one lacks the freedom. For Sartre, the fullest freedom is to be found within the group. Sartre's argument is that the claim on every member of the group is a guarantee of security and thus a guarantee of freedom continuing into the future. This security, it should be remembered, is a safeguard and a weapon against scarcity. The group combats scarcity, effectively satisfies needs, and in that lies freedom. Security can be regarded as a common good, meaning that it is good for A and at the same time good for B. If security is thought of as being a state of mind then it is not a common state of mind in the sense of there being a single state of mind but a state of mind that people happen to have in common. In fact, Sartre offers a further definition of the pledge, 'It should be defined as everyone's freedom guaranteeing the security of all so that this security can return to everyone as his *other-freedom* so as to ground his free, practical membership of the group as an untranscendable exigency.'[69]

Although the members of the group pledge loyalty and so impose inertia upon themselves, each acting as a regulator for all the others just as all the others are also regulators and although, as Hayim notes, 'Unity rather than praxis, becomes the aim',[70] it is an inertia that is freely chosen and imposed by the free praxis of making the pledge. Sartre's point is that the pledge is 'a free relation of free commitments'.[71] Every free choice involves the free acceptance of limitations, every free choice involves the elimination of a possibility. In choosing to do this one is limited to doing this rather than that. As Sartre says,

---

68 *The Social Contract*, Bk. 1, chpt. 7, p. 64.
69 CDR I, p. 428.
70 Hayim, 1980, p. 94.
71 CDR I, p. 433.

reinforcing a point made earlier, 'It would be absurd to suggest that an individual freedom could be limited by itself.'[72] In so far as unity can be regarded as an expression of a shared meaning it can be seen that the pledged group is an example of a form of association which is not simply the generator and sustainer of its shared meanings but which is also, as was noted earlier, generated by meanings that are perceived as being shared.

So it is that Sartre believes that it is in the relationship established within the pledged group that man finds the greatest possibility for the enhancement of his freedom. Here, therefore, the normative notion of praxis further develops the normative theory of associations. In the pledged group men possess the most effective means of overcoming all obstacles to freedom. It is also the case that, for Sartre, an individual's freedom requires the freedom of everyone since if everyone is not free then there are certain possibilities that cannot be realised by the individual.

A central claim in social anarchism is that far from one person's freedom being limited by the freedom of others, no one could be really free except in a community where each person works to promote the freedom of the rest. Bakunin, for example, argues that freedom is eminently social because it can be realised only in society through solidarity. He explains that freedom is eminently social because, 'It is the fullest development of all the faculties and powers of every human being, by education, by scientific training, and by material prosperity; things which can only be provided for every individual by the collective, material, intellectual, manual, and sedentary labor of society in general.'[73] So for Bakunin, the realisation of individual freedom requires the collective power of society.[74] Elsewhere he writes that, 'The freedom of individuals is by no means an individual matter. It is a collective matter, a collective product. No individual can be free outside of human society or without its cooperation.'[75] This is an idea which Bakunin develops by arguing that freedom requires not only solidarity but the freedom of all.[76] He argues that, 'the slavery of even one man violates humanity and negates the freedom of all'.[77] In another publication he argues that, 'it is the slavery of other men that sets up a barrier to my freedom, or what amounts to the same thing, it is their bestiality which is the negation of my humanity'.[78] Sartre too, despite his claim to have discovered dependency only recently in connection with the group-in-fusion, had quite early in his career argued that, 'in thus willing freedom, we

---

[72] Ibid., p. 424.
[73] Bakunin, 'God and The State', in Sam Dolgoff (ed.), 1973, p. 238.
[74] Ibid., pp. 236–37.
[75] Bakunin, 'Three Lectures to Swiss Members of the International', in Robert M. Cutler (ed.), 1985, p. 46.
[76] Bakunin, 1950, p. 17.
[77] 'Bakunin, Revolutionary Catechism', in Sam Dolgoff (ed.), 1973, p. 76. See also 'Principles and Organisation of the International Brotherhood', in Arthur Lehning (ed.), p. 65.
[78] Bakunin, 'God and the State', in Sam Dolgoff (ed.), 1973, p. 237.

discover that it depends entirely upon the freedom of others and that the freedom of others depends upon our own'.[79] He provides a different perspective on that thought in *Anti-Semite and Jew* when he writes that, 'Not one Frenchman can be free so long as the Jews do not enjoy the fullness of their rights. Not one Frenchman will be secure so long as a single Jew – in France or *in the world at large* – can fear for his life'.[80]

I think that from this collection of thoughts on freedom and solidarity four distinct ideas emerge. The first is that the realisation of individual freedom depends upon the resources of the community. Lack of education and ill-health, for example, impact upon the exercise of positive freedom. The second is that unless everyone is free there are certain possibilities that cannot be realised by the individual. The third is that the denial of the freedom of an individual is the denial of the humanity of the individual and the denial of the humanity of one individual amounts to the denial of the humanity of all individuals. The fourth is that if it is possible for the freedom of anyone to be at risk then it is possible for the freedom of everyone to be at risk.

Overcoming obstacles to freedom is Sartre's moral and political ideal.[81] Although the pledge brings obligations and limitations, they are freely chosen and they are of the sort that will make the group effective in promoting freedom in the long term. The freedom at stake, it will be recalled, is freedom to flourish and pursue fulfilment which as a minimum requires freedom from seriality and the accompanying milieu of scarcity, which also means freedom from need, or freedom to have needs satisfied.

Freedom from seriality and coping with scarcity can be related events because in seriality men compete. Whilst certain forms of scarcity or their effects may never be eliminated, other forms of scarcity and also the alienation that arises from the milieu of scarcity may be tackled through the construction of particular interpersonal relationships at a local level, that is, in the pledged group with its enhanced power. Anderson points out with a reference to scarcity that, 'insofar as the group enriches the power of the individuals within it, it increases their freedom. It increases this by being the most efficient way to deal with one root of hostility among men, and by enabling them to obtain goals they could never achieve alone.'[82] This sort of group, therefore, has a fundamental part to play in the good life for human beings because, as has been said, the individual's free presence in the group is a means to attain degrees of human

---

[79] *Existentialism and Humanism*, p. 51–52.

[80] *Anti-Semite and Jew*, p. 153.

[81] According to Annie Cohen-Solal, the principle political ideal of the Rassemblement Democratique Revolutionnaire, the political party that Sartre helped to found and which, according to Germaine Bree, he left in 'a characteristic mood of moral indignation and ill-concealed relief' (Bree, 1974, p. 179), fearing that it would turn into an anti-Communist front, was defined by Sartre as 'the integration of a free individual into a society conceived as the union of the free activities of the individual'. (Cohen-Solal, 1988, p. 304)

[82] Anderson, 1979, p. 103.

fulfilment that are otherwise unattainable. As Anderson observes in connection with individual human fulfilment, the group 'enables him to more effectively attain what he naturally seeks'.[83] Furthermore, as was seen in chapter four, by altering our terms of association we effect a change in our relationship to the environment which brings its own implications for scarcity as an original relation between man and the environment which has become a man-made relation. References to human fulfilment indicate that taking the pledge can be regarded as an example of a communal practice which, since they have taken it, everyone in the group can endorse as a basis for the politics of the good.

Hobbes focuses on the effect of viewing one's fellows as competitors. As Gauthier says, 'Little in Hobbes's argument suggests a more positive role for co-operation. We are aware of each other as competitors, and so we come to co-operate in order to avoid mutually destructive conflict, but we are less aware of each other as potential sources of mutual benefit.'[84] Sartre's depiction of the group is quite different. With the formation of the pledged group there is an awareness that in the state of seriality there is the potential for mutually destructive conflict, but also an awareness of each other as a source of mutual benefit. This awareness accompanied by action is, according to Proudhon, a mark of political capacity. He argues that, 'Having political capacity means being *conscious* of oneself as a member of a collectivity. It means affirming the resulting *idea* and working towards its *realization*. Any person who fulfils these three conditions is politically capable.'[85]

In taking the pledge there is something akin to the free surrendering of oneself as alienated in one sense for the sake of overcoming alienation in another sense. In a similar fashion Hobbes argues that under the pact by which men enter into civil society everyone makes a total alienation of his rights to a sovereign. For Rousseau the alienation was that of natural liberty and the right to take anything that attracts the individual to a sovereign body which included the individual. Both regarded their respective forms of alienation as an advantageous exchange because it is only through living in a society of a certain sort that men can experience respectively security and their fullest freedom. Thus Rousseau argues that in society what is surrendered are precarious rights based on the exercise of power for rights that are invincible since they are based on law. Therefore,

> What man loses by the social contract is his natural liberty and the absolute right to anything that tempts him and that he can take; what he gains by the social contract is civil liberty and the legal right of property in what he possesses.[86]

---

[83] Anderson, 1993, p. 117.
[84] Gauthier, 1986, p. 115.
[85] Proudhon, 'On the Political Capacity of the Working Class', in Stewart Edwards (ed.), 1970, p. 173.
[86] *The Social Contract*, Bk. 1, chpt. 8, p. 65.

In this way 'each man recovers the equivalent of everything he loses, and in the bargain he acquires more power to preserve what he has'.[87] In freely accepting limitations for the sake of the freedom and security of all a similar sort of exchange is made with the pledge. The difference between Sartre and Hobbes at this point is that the Hobbesian position still leaves people atomised, albeit uniformly coerced by a sovereign. The difference between Sartre and Rousseau at this point is that for Rousseau the exchange takes man away from what is natural whereas for Sartre it enables him to attain what he naturally seeks. The difference between Sartre and both Hobbes and Rousseau at this point is that Sartre is not attempting to lay the foundations for a particular kind of society.

Therefore, Sartre views the pledge as a source of strength and argues that it is indeed 'the origin of humanity'.[88] In a footnote Sartre explains that every association based on the pledge is always a victory of man's freedom over seriality. He writes that although this victory was already won by the group-in-fusion, 'it is through the pledge that the group posits itself for itself, no longer as the implicit means of a common *praxis*, both produced and absorbed by it, but as the means of attaining a more or less distant objective, and *therefore* as its own immediate objective'.[89] Later Sartre argues that the group defines and produces itself both as an instrument and as a mode of existence. He explains that,

> it posits itself for itself – in the strict determination of its transcendent task – as the free milieu of human relations; and on the basis of the pledge, it produces man as a free common individual, and confers new birth on the Other: thus the group is both the most effective *means* for controlling the surrounding materiality in the context of scarcity and *the absolute end* as pure freedom in liberating men from alterity.[90]

Thus the pledged group is both a means for the use of men and it is also an end. This is an important point and one that is endorsed by Blum. Blum argues that the distinctive values of community are lost if one treats communities only as a source of good or meaning for oneself. Blum's point is that communities are 'independent sources of value in their own right'. Treating communities simply as instrumental to one's own good is 'in a sense' to fail to 'treat them as communities'.[91] To treat communities in this way is to lose the point of the kinds of things that communities are. Blum goes on to say that as a result one derives less from community membership. By treating communities simply as a means one fails to derive the greater good that communities can actually

---

[87] Ibid., Bk. 1, chpt. 6, p. 61.
[88] CDR I, p. 436.
[89] Ibid., p. 430n.
[90] Ibid., p. 673.
[91] Blum, 'Vocation, Friendship and Community: Limitations of the Personal-Impersonal Framework', 1994, p. 119. Reprinted from O. Flanagan Jr. and A. Rorty (eds), *Identity, Character, and Morality: Essays in Moral Psychology*, Mass: MIT Press, 1990.

provide. Some sense of this can be obtained by the application of Sartre's argument. According to Sartre, it is the free praxis of taking the pledge that constitutes the community as a source of value in as much as values are revealed by praxis satisfying needs. Therefore, the pledged group has a fundamental part to play in the good life for human beings, not simply because it enables individuals to achieve ends but also because it is, as a result of praxis, an end. Constituted on the basis of the praxis of taking the pledge that is intended to guarantee such values as commitment and freedom, the community becomes an end in being the repository and manifestation of those values and is a value in itself.

We have already seen that ends are constitutive of the identities of individuals. The community as an end, therefore, becomes another way of thinking of communities as constitutive of identities. Of course, the process by which this constituting happens is precisely the same as before. Ends and therefore communities as ends are given in individual praxis which becomes common praxis. Praxis, it will be recalled, is an expression of the end which is man making himself as he transcends himself. Communities as ends constitute identities in the sense that individuals, through their praxis, constitute and sustain communities. The constituting and sustaining of communities requires people to be people of a certain sort. Furthermore, in the two-way movement of the dialectic of praxis, first described in chapter two as the process of interiorisation and re-exteriorisation, the community thus constituted becomes the basis of further praxis which is also constituting. In the case of the pledged group it can be seen that the pledge itself is taken on the basis of a particular view of the good life for human beings. In being constituted the pledged group becomes constituting through its members and the basis of praxes that are intended to sustain it as a source of value and as an expression and source of the good life.

In chapter three it was seen that on Rawls's conception of a person an individual's ends or goals are always things he chooses to attach himself to and from which he may, presumably, choose to become detached. Sartre's analysis of different forms of association reveals that not all ends, attachments to those ends, or communal attachments generally can be conceived of as arising from acts of will through and through. Instead our ends arise from needs. In chapter two it was argued that ends are non-voluntaristic in that they arise from needs understood as negativities demanding to be negated. Therefore, although the satisfaction of an end may be a matter for choice, the presentation of an end is not. It can now be argued that since it is praxis that reveals that certain needs are best satisfied by working co-operatively in groups it follows that the significance that we ascribe to certain of our communal attachments can be viewed as a result of discovery rather than an initial choice. The choice that is made is, as has been said, based on a prior awareness. Thus ends arising from the satisfaction of needs and certain communal attachments associated with the achievement of those ends cannot be viewed in purely voluntaristic terms but instead as the result of an awareness of what is required by a particular conception of human fulfilment.

By taking the pledge and putting communal attachments on a formal footing everyone remains the same. Reference to 'the same' might appear to be reminiscent of criticisms of the situation in Rawls's theory whereby the contracting parties are all the same, thus making Rawls's contract a contract with oneself. The Rawlsian contract is a way of embodying a certain conception of equality and a way of extracting the consequences of that conception for the regulation of social institutions. Sartre's pledge can, to a degree, be regarded in like manner. It is through the praxis of taking the pledge that equality of membership of a community is established. However, this is an equality that is manifested by mediated and co-operative reciprocity which is most fully developed in the pledged group. The parties to the pledge are not the same by virtue of being stripped of their identity as is the case with Rawls. This develops the point of difference between Sartre and Rawls, that is, it supplements the point above whereby for Sartre, and Rousseau, people know about themselves and their material conditions.

The pledged group can be thought of as a legitimate authority. The terms of association of the pledged group are such that each individual is the legitimating agent on behalf of all the other individuals who are also legitimating agents operating on behalf of, yet distinct from, the group as a whole. The praxis of taking the pledge can be regarded as an act of consent whereby each individual incurs certain obligations in return for directly related benefits. Thus Sartre provides a basis for understanding the nature of obligation which is significantly different from that to be found in liberal theory and which provides an additional dimension to the views of Sandel on that matter.

The liberal assumption is that people are both free and equal. However, in liberal theory there is a fundamental problem of why and in what ways any free and equal individual could legitimately be governed by anyone else at all. In order to address this problem liberals also invoke the notion of consent. The problem with consent in a liberal democracy is that it is hard to explain when and how the consent took place, who consented and to what. A response to these issues typically refers to the notion of tacit or hypothetical consent which is predicated upon the fact that individuals freely engage in certain activities such as, most obviously, the acceptance of certain social or State benefits, or activities such as the participation in liberal democratic institutions such as voting. J. P. Plamenatz uses the example of protection by the law which is said to create on the part of the person protected an obligation to obey the law.[92] To accept the protection of the law was equivalent to a tacit consent to the general governmental activities of the persons who enforced the law and that here was a case of an obligation to obey the government based ultimately on consent.

---

92   J. P. Plamenatz, 1968, pp. 24, 27.

The meaning that is ascribed to activities such as receiving benefits including the protection of the law, or voting, is that the individual thus engaged must have accepted the legitimacy of the source of those activities and it can, therefore, be inferred that the individual has consented to certain obligations with regard to that source. The consent is regarded as hypothetical in the sense that it is not explicitly given but implicitly assumed on the basis of freely chosen participation in certain activities.

There is, however, a problem with this notion of hypothetical consent. As Plamenatz notes, these were rather crude endeavours to maintain the contract theory through a distortion of the proper meaning of the word consent.[93] The problem is that the meaning of activities such as voting, or being protected by the law, or walking along a road is, for any individual, not necessarily the meaning that has been ascribed to it by those who are seeking to explain consent in a liberal democracy. The meaning thus ascribed is at best a hypothetical meaning or one that could or should be assumed. However, until in reality it is it cannot be the basis of consent. The person walking down the road is doing so for exercise, or to meet a friend, or to protest at the folly of a government that permits the building of so many roads. These activities as they are, and not some underlying or background understanding of what makes these activities possible, are expressions of the meaning of walking down the road. Therefore, just as hypothetical contracts are not contracts at all, so hypothetical consent, assumed on the basis of hypothetical meanings, is not consent at all.

Of course, fair play could suggest that the receipt of benefits can create obligations. In other words, if the benefit is obtained at the cost of the imposition of a burden on the other members of the community, for example, they have to pay taxes, then it might be thought obligatory for reasons of fairness to agree to the imposition of those burdens upon oneself. This is particularly the case where the benefit is of the kind that is actually wanted as opposed to benefits that arrive unbidden. Here the obligation would be the product of fairness. It would, however, imply that the community has already agreed to certain terms of association which included the notion of fairness and that certain measures were in place to deal with those who choose to act unfairly.

Obligations place a restriction on the individual's freedom and this is compatible with the idea that individuals are free and equal only if individuals place themselves in that relationship as a result of their own free decision. In other words it is a self-assumed obligation in the sense of taking on a commitment through an act of will. A promise or pledge is the most obvious example of a self-assumed obligation. As Pateman points out, promising is important to liberal contract theory because it brings into being a relationship that is simultaneously an expression of individual freedom and equality and an expression of obligation.[94] The political counterpart of the social practice of

---

[93] Ibid., p. 27.
[94] Pateman, 1979, p. 13.

promising would be the practice of voting. In the political sphere, voting is also the undertaking of a self-assumed obligation. In a liberal democracy, citizens vote for representatives whose task then is to make decisions for them. As Pateman says this is, therefore, like a particular kind of promising, namely, promising to obey. The essence of liberal theory is that individuals ought to promise to obey representatives to whom they have alienated their right to make political decisions. Promising also implies that individuals are capable of independent judgement and rational deliberation and of engaging in their own relationships and executing their own actions. However, promising to obey is to limit to some extent the individual's freedom and equality and their ability to exercise these qualities. It will be pointed out that citizens can vote their representatives out of office. Yet in doing that they are also choosing new decision-makers. Liberal democracy is, says Pateman, a series of renewals of the decision to obey. In other words, the only way for voters to modify what they have done is to perform the same action again and then only when given permission. As Pateman says, 'To promise to obey is to state that, in certain areas, the person making the promise is no longer free to exercise her capacities and decide upon her own actions, and is no longer equal, but subordinate.'[95]

Sartre's views on representative democracy and elections under that system were noted in chapter five. Nevertheless, in *Hope Now* Sartre is clear that democracy is a way of life. He argues that, 'One lives democratically, and in my view human beings today should live in that way and in no other.'[96] However, the democracy that Sartre has in mind is participatory. That system creates an obligation that is owed by each individual to every other individual. On Sartre's account and in tune with the anarchist thinking noted earlier in this chapter, the obligations that people have are to each other rather than to the State and it is that idea that Sartre attempts to capture with the notion of the pledge.

The pledge, in this context, is important because, of course, participation is, in itself, no guarantee of justice. The group could always be manipulated by the members of a particularly vociferous faction wishing to pursue their own interests. It is the pledge that can provide a safeguard against that happening. Only 'can', however, because, as we shall see, the opening of schisms and the return to seriality are also always possibilities and possibilities which can also be occasioned by the pledge. The pledge is a safeguard but it cannot accommodate all contingencies.

Sartre, Hobbes and Rousseau differ from advocates of representative democracy in that for Sartre, Hobbes and Rousseau everyone is an active participant within the group. Sartre differs from Hobbes and Rousseau and also from the advocates of the notion of hypothetical consent in that the pledge is a real event. Taking the pledge actually happens and consent is actually obtained. This is also, of course, a further point of difference between Sartre and Rawls.

---

[95] Ibid., p. 19.
[96] *Hope Now*, p. 83.

However, this is not to say that some people do not find themselves members of a pledged group without having, in the first instance, taken the pledge. Yet even where this is the case, a decision to continue to participate will ultimately be required. Sartre explains what he means with reference to baptism where he argues that,

> From birth onwards, the arrival of the child in the milieu of the pledge is the equivalent for him of making a pledge; anyone who arrives within a pledged group finds himself to be pledged – not as a passive object receiving his statute from outside, but as a free common agent who has been granted his freedom.[97]

In a footnote Sartre reflects on baptism and comes to the conclusion, which he confesses he found surprising, that baptism was a 'mortgage of future freedom'.[98] He argues that at one time he had thought that total indeterminacy was the true basis of choice. However, from the perspective of the group the opposite is true. Baptism not only provides the individual with an identity and a set of relationships but it is also the way in which the individual interiorises the common freedom and the shared meanings of the group so that when he comes to exercise his own freedom he is already operating at a higher level of ability, 'so that he can, with all his power and in complete knowledge, decide whether to remain in the group, whether to change his function . . . in it, or whether to withdraw'.[99] Parents will inevitably make choices for their children. However, the parent's choice for the child is a choice that 'can mark him only to the extent that he has freely interiorised it and it becomes a free self-limitation of his freedom rather than an inert limit assigned to him by his father'.[100] In short, the individual might find himself in a community in which shared meanings are already established and in which he has the freedom, as a constituted and constituting member, to choose to remain and participate, or leave. In this way Sartre confirms the view that the fact that the individual acquires his moral identity from the communities to which he belongs does not mean that he is bound to be confined by the moral vision espoused by those communities. However, those communities do provide a basis from which to embark on the search for the good.

Given the reason for taking the pledge, fear of seriality and scarcity, one has to ask if taking the pledge is not simply an exercise in self-interest which is associated by communitarians with laissez-faire liberalism. The self-interested motive certainly underpins social contract theory. Midgley points out that social contract theory retains the model, drawn from seventeenth century physics where the ultimate particles of matter were conceived as hard impenetrable, homogenous little billiard balls with no hooks or internal structure. She argues that, 'This

---

[97] CDR I, p. 485.
[98] Ibid., p. 485n.
[99] Ibid.

model shows human society as a spread of standard social atoms, originally distinct and independent, each of which combines with others only at its own choice and in its own private interest.'[101] Midgley goes on to endorse, without explicitly mentioning it, the communitarian sentiment whereby people are recognised not only as individuals but also 'as members of their groups, families, tribes, species, ecosystems, and biosphere, and have moral relations as parts to these wholes'.[102] However, the either-or of self-interest or moral relations does not stand up to scrutiny as the work of that obviously self-interested contractarian, Hobbes, shows.

Hobbes argues that the contract can itself provide no binding commitment to itself; it is fear that keeps people in subjection. Hobbes thought that people were basically selfish, out for themselves, naturally anti-social. As J.W. Gough explains, 'Hobbes' basic doctrine, in fact, was his view of human nature as essentially selfish and at the same time timorous . . . Their ruling motive is desire for protection – for the preservation of their lives.'[103] Whilst this amounts to self-interest, self-interest, as has already been said, is not to be confused with selfishness. One can have an interest in one's self-preservation but self-preservation, in the absence of other considerations, is not normally regarded as a sign of selfishness. Furthermore, the desire that one has to survive and pursue the goal of felicity does not exclude the possibility that one can desire that for other people as well. Indeed, as has already been noted, to pursue the felicity of the other can in itself be a source of satisfaction. Moreover, as Sorell says, on Hobbes's view, 'from a rational agent's point of view there is always more to be got out of discharging one's moral obligations than out of not doing so'.[104] This might seem to indicate that Hobbes has no notion of moral obligation at all since these obligations are only discharged in the furtherance of self-interest.

However, it is important to notice what is going on. Alan Goldman comments on the laws of nature thus,

> While these rules promote the good of the group, Hobbes also holds that they promote the good of each individual, since each benefits from peace and co-operation within the group. In promoting my security I must promote the security of others as well. It is this congruence that allows the reduction of rightness to prudence or egoistic rationality for Hobbes.[105]

This is rational self-interest rather than simply selfishness. The rational self-interest in this case concerns survival. However, the requirements of rational

---

[100] Ibid.
[101] Mary Midgley, 'Duties Concerning Islands', in Robert Elliot (ed.), 1995, p. 91. Reprinted from R. Elliot and A. Gore (eds), *Environmental Philosophy*, St. Lucia: University of Queensland Press, 1983, pp. 166–81.
[102] Ibid., p. 92.
[103] J. W. Gough, 1957, p. 111.
[104] Sorell, 1986, p. 109.
[105] Alan Goldman, 1990, p. 29.

self-interest do not necessarily preclude the possibility of morality. Hobbes, for example, identifies moral rules, virtues and obligations according, as Goldman says, to a normal understanding and then shows that they have a deeper prudential grounding. Moral obligations can arise from self-interested acts. People can enter into contracts for self-interested reasons. They might, for example, need to borrow some money. In that case the contract creates an obligation. So it is that one can have self-interested reasons for entering into contracts from which obligations arise. Moreover, one creates the contract by virtue of agreeing to it. In fact Gauthier thinks that we can 'find the emergence of a moral personality within a contractarian understanding of morality as rationally agreed constraint'.[106] Thus the rational agent recognises that it is necessary to be willing to agree to certain constraints on his initial freedom of action, provided others are willing as well, and then to commit himself to abide by the agreed constraints which, on Gauthier's view, makes the Hobbesian sovereign redundant. With a self-assumed obligation we create the obligation and then we are bound by it. Therefore, we are both above or superior to our obligations and at the same time subject to them. The nature of obligation is, therefore, like the nature of consent in that both have an immanent and a transcendent dimension. It is in this light that the taking of the pledge may be viewed as an act of a moral agent.

It is also the case that freedom from need is bound up with the very nature of the demand that people act morally in the interests of others. One cannot be a moral agent without the time and security to reflect on what one ought to do. For most people time and security require freedom from need. This security and freedom from need is what the pledge is designed to ensure. Therefore, self-interest in the satisfaction of needs can be an important aspect of moral agency and the taking of the pledge can again be regarded as an act of a moral agent.

An understanding of the nature of the pledge and the work that it performs provides us with a particular view of the nature of commitment. According to Sandel, the deontological liberal view of the self has to admit that the self is incapable of commitment. One does not enter into commitments oneself and neither is it expected that one could rely on others entering into or fulfilling commitments. Yet communitarians do not have a theory of commitment of their own. Sartre's notion of the third party shows that in the pledged group, commitment is more than a hypothetical social contract or a meeting of minds resulting in a rational agreement. As has been seen, it is self-interest that leads to the formation of the group-in-fusion and thence to the pledged group. However, initially, this did not involve an agreement but the self-interested praxis of the individual being recognised as common praxis. It was on that basis that the pledge, as another praxis, was taken and agreements established. The pledge creates self-assumed obligations or commitments. In Sartre's view,

---

[106] Gauthier, 'Between Hobbes and Rawls', in Gauthier and Sugden (eds), 1993, p. 37.

therefore, it is on the basis of praxis and with a view to attaining objectives that are perceived to be common that self-assumed obligations or commitments occur. It is the praxis of the third party that explains how the self is embedded in and partly constituting of and constituted by communal commitments in the pledged group. The individual who makes a commitment to the group makes it possible for everyone to make a commitment. If everyone does make a commitment, every commitment will reinforce and be reinforced by every other commitment.

Inherent in the praxis account of self-assumed obligations are certain dispositions such as loyalty and empathy. In other words, these dispositions are required by and sustained through that particular praxis and are sustaining of that praxis. It is, therefore, on the basis of that praxis and in order to sustain that praxis that the moral personality develops. So it is that the individual is defined in terms of what he does and in terms of the dispositions required and exercised by what he does. Of course, those who do not make the commitment will not be part of the group. One of the interesting features of Sartre's argument, therefore, is that it is able to accommodate on the one hand choice and private interest and on the other hand, moral relations. Indeed, the indistinction of immanence and transcendence reveals that this accommodation is not analytically one hand, and then the other hand but the continuous development of the individual as a constituting and constituted member of the community. The self-interested reason that created the obligation continues to inform the obligation and the moral relations that it involves. Sartre's notion of consent and commitment as praxis indicates the manner by which these moral relations arise and function. They arise out of need and function on the basis of mutual dependency. In this respect Sartre differs from social contract theorists as well as from communitarians.

Despite the references to Hobbes and Rousseau, which are intended to clarify Sartre's argument and provide it with a background, Sartre is clear that the pledge is not to be regarded as a type of social contract.[107] It is not to be regarded as the basis for a particular kind of society and although Sartre's theory of the group can be regarded as a development of Rousseau's attempt to reconcile modern individualism with the classical view of the priority of the community, the pledge does not even mark the movement from a state of individualism to a social organisation. Instead it is to be regarded as the step that is necessary for changing a group-in-fusion, which is impermanent, to a permanent, 'organised' group that can continue to afford its members protection from scarcity.[108] The pledge is a device, therefore, to facilitate that change.

In fact there is a tradition of opposition in anarchism to the idea of a social contract of the type proposed by Rousseau and others. Bakunin, for example writes of, 'that individualist, egoist, base, and fraudulent liberty extolled by the school of Jean Jacques Rousseau and every other school of bourgeois

---

[107] CDR I, p. 420. See Chiodi, 1978, p. 74; McBride, 1991, p. 153.
[108] CDR I, pp. 419–20.

liberalism'.[109] What particularly irks Bakunin is the idea of the hypothetical contract. He acknowledges that, 'The majority of jurists and modern writers, whether of the Kantian school or of other individualist and liberal schools ... take ... the *tacit contract* as their point of departure' and goes on to exclaim, 'A tacit contract! That is to say, a wordless and consequently a thoughtless and will-less contract: a revolting nonsense! An absurd fiction, and what is more, a wicked fiction!'[110] In *Marxism, Freedom and the State* he provides something of an argument by saying that, 'If we accept the fiction of a free State derived from a social contract, then discerning, just, prudent people ought not to have any need of government or of a State.'[111] In order to make a point about elections and electors Malatesta reverses the argument by saying that, 'if you consider these worthy electors as incapable of providing for their own interests, how can they ever be capable of themselves choosing directors to guide them wisely?'[112]

Proudhon also criticises the idea of the hypothetical contract and proposes an alternative. He too regards the social contract of Rousseau as 'a legal *fiction*' and he proposes another sort of social contract, one that is rooted in his federal system. He explains that,

> In the federal system, the social contract is more than a fiction; it is a positive and effective compact, which has actually been proposed, discussed, voted upon, and adopted, and which can properly be amended at the contracting parties' will. Between the federal contract and that of Rousseau and 1793 there is all the difference between a reality and a hypothesis.[113]

Elsewhere he explains that what he wants, therefore, is 'not an abstract sovereignty of the people as in the Constitution of 1793 and subsequent constitutions, or as in Rousseau's *Social Contract*, but an effective sovereignty of the working, reigning, governing masses' and this would require a real contract.[114] In yet another publication Proudhon draws a contrast between his social contract and the social contract which he dubs a contract with society. He argues that under a contract with society the contracting party loses some of his liberty and submits to a solidarity of a burdensome kind in the uncertain hope of some gain. His social contract, however, not only leaves the contracting parties free but it also increases their freedom. It not only leaves the contracting parties with all of their possessions but it also increases their property. It makes no stipulations with regard to the labour of the contracting parties; it is concerned

---

[109] Bakunin, 'The Paris Commune and the Idea of the State', in Sam Dolgoff (ed.), 1973, p. 261.
[110] Bakunin, 'Federalism, Socialism and Anti-Theologism', in G. P. Maximoff (ed.), 1953, pp. 136 and 165.
[111] Bakunin, 1950, p. 32.
[112] Malatesta, 1942, p. 35.
[113] Proudhon, 1979, pp. 38–39n.
[114] Proudhon, 'On the Political Capacity of the Working Classes', in Stewart Edwards (ed.), 1970, pp. 116–17.

only with exchange. On Proudhon's account none of these things is true of the contract with society; in fact, they are all completely contrary to the contract with society. Ultimately, says Proudhon, 'The notion of government is succeeded by that of Contract.'[115] As we have seen, Bakunin too endorses the idea of voluntary agreements that people make with each other.

Essentially, social anarchists conceive of contracts as not between that fictitious entity dubbed 'the people' but between specific individuals. In this way anarchism can accommodate pluralism. The liberal contract should in principle also be accommodating of pluralism. The problem is that the liberal contract is hypothetical. It is less obvious that communitarianism can accommodate pluralism given its emphasis on tradition within the communitarian community.

The pledged group is an abstraction, an analytical moment in the process of the dialectic. However, the pledge itself is real and, as will become apparent, achieves concrete form in the organisation with the allocation of roles or functions to individual group members. Since promising is a form of praxis, the transition from the group-in-fusion to the pledged group can be explained in terms of praxis itself. The pledge can be thought of, in part, as a moral claim about the nature of human relationships. It is a means for describing a certain sort of relationship, in this case, as has been said, mediated and co-operative reciprocity. Thus Sartre's view on consent illuminates the nature of relationships between people as determined ultimately by man's praxis. It does not provide a justification for the initiation of a particular kind of State. In fact it is, therefore, the crucial role of praxis, including the taking of the pledge, that clearly distinguishes Sartre's notion of consent as something quite different from an agreement devised according to a social contract.

Sartre's account of the origin of groups in the *Critique* illuminates the influence of material circumstances such as scarcity and of other sorts of pressures and threats combined with a small degree of deliberative decision-making in the formation of groups. On the one hand, although the contractarians' view of the origins of groups is similar, their view of individual rational decision makers deliberately agreeing (contracting) to build tidy constitutional structures is quite at odds with Sartre's view of human reciprocity. Human activity is often untidy, unstructured and spontaneous. Sartre's view accommodates this whilst the classical contractarians neglect such activity in favour of neat legal frameworks. On the other hand, the communitarians have no account of the origins of groups either and concentrate their efforts on producing neat moral frameworks.

For the group to achieve its goal of satisfying needs in a milieu of scarcity thus maximising the freedom of all, it clearly has to do something, which is to say that the members have to do something. They have to perform certain roles

---

[115] Proudhon, 'General Idea of Revolution in the 19th Century', in Stewart Edwards (ed.), 1970, p. 98.

or functions and these functions are allocated to the members of the group. In this way the pledged group takes concrete form as an organised group. At this point we can begin to understand what it is that the members of a community have to do in order to achieve their goals, which are the constituting goals of the community. When it is understood that people in a community will play different sorts of roles we then need to know how a community can continue and even thrive when people are differentiated in that way. In other words, we can develop further an understanding of the conditions whereby diversity or plurality cease to be a threat to the group and can work for the good of the group. An understanding of those conditions is precisely what is required if we are to identify the communal practices that everyone can endorse as a basis for the politics of the good. On the basis of those conditions further observations about the nature of leadership become possible. An identification of the kind of reciprocity that exists between individual identity, ends and forms and terms of association also becomes possible. The relationship between the individual and the community that is thereby revealed also provides an appreciation of the reciprocal nature of rights and duties and of the work that these can perform. Following from that the issue of the ownership of talents can be addressed and from that we can acquire an understanding of how conflict can occur within a community and what conflict might mean to a community. This alerts us to the fact that seriality will always be a threat to any community. The response that a community might make to the threat of seriality reveals something of the nature of the relationship between an institution and its practices.[116]

Reciprocity or interdependence is a key idea in social anarchism. It is an idea that forms the basis of the connection between the individual and the community. A recognition of reciprocity is a means by which individuals can work together to meet their common interests in an environment that fosters and maintains freedom and equality. As Malatesta argues,

> He [the anarchist] knows that the activity of the individual influences, directly or indirectly, the lives of every other being, and therefore recognises the great law of solidarity, which predominates in society as in nature. And since he wants freedom for everyone, he must desire that the operation of this essential solidarity instead of being imposed and undergone, unconsciously and involuntarily, instead of being left to chance, and

---

[116] On the basis of MacIntyre's work we can certainly see how seriality can threaten a community of practitioners. MacIntyre makes the point that the desire for only external goods can prevent us from achieving the goods that are internal to the practice thus rendering the practice pointless except as a device for achieving external goods. (MacIntyre, 1981, p. 178) He pursues this point by arguing that a society where the pursuit of external goods became dominant would not only, as has been noted, resemble Hobbes's state of nature but would also neglect the virtues and in that way such a society could threaten practices. (MacIntyre, 1981, p. 183) In so far as seriality is characterised by the pursuit of external goods it can threaten practices. One response to the threat of seriality is to transform the organised group into an institution. However, as we will see, that transformation itself can create problems for practices.

exploited for the advantage of a few to the detriment of the majority, should become conscious and voluntary, and be applied for the equal benefit of all.[117]

Indeed, according to Malatesta, the good of all cannot be really attained except by the conscious participation of everybody.[118]

Bakunin supplies a practical reason for acknowledging interdependency. He points out that the isolated labour of individuals would not be able to feed and clothe a small tribe let alone a great nation; 'a great nation becomes rich and survives only through collective labor, where the work of one person depends on that of the other'.[119] He goes on to say that since labour, which is the production of wealth, is collective the enjoyment of wealth should also be collective.

Malatesta extends the interdependence argument by noting that the individual 'would not exist as a human being but for the fact that he carries within him the sum total of the work of numberless generations'.[120] This is an idea that appears explicitly in the work of Kropotkin. In *The Conquest of Bread* he argues that, 'There is not even a thought, or an invention, which is not common property, born of the past and the present. Thousands of inventors, known and unknown, who have died in poverty, have co-operated in the invention of each of these machines which embody the genius of man.' He goes on to say that each discovery, each advance, owes its being to work of people both present and past.[121] Bakunin makes the point by asking rhetorically, 'Does isolated and solitary labor produce all the marvellous riches of which our age boasts, has it produced them?'[122] Kropotkin illustrates his argument with the example of a house. He points out that the value of a house results from the fact that the house is built in a town,

> that is in an agglomeration of thousands of other houses, possessing paved streets, bridges, quays and fine public buildings, well lighted, and affording to its inhabitants a thousand comforts and conveniences unknown in villages; a town in regular communication with other towns, and in itself a centre of industry, commerce, science and art; a town which the work of twenty or thirty generations has made habitable, healthy and beautiful.[123]

Thus the value of a house in Paris is the result of all that is Paris. From this he concludes that,

---

[117] Malatesta, in Vernon Richards (ed.), 1965, p. 23.
[118] Ibid., p. 22.
[119] Bakunin, 'Three Lectures to Swiss Members of the International', in Robert M. Cutler (ed.), 1985, p. 58.
[120] Malatesta, in Vernon Richards (ed.), 1965, p. 22.
[121] Kropotkin, 1995, pp. 15–16.
[122] Bakunin, 'Three Lectures to Swiss Members of the International', in Robert M. Cutler (ed.), 1985, p. 58.
[123] Kropotkin, 1995, pp. 75–76. See also Kropotkin, 1913, pp. 15–16.

> Individual appropriation is neither just nor serviceable. All belongs to all. All things for all men, since all men have need of them, since all men have worked in the measure of their strength to produce them, and since it is not possible to evaluate everyone's part in the production of the world's wealth.[124]

From an acknowledgement of interdependency comes an acknowledgement of the need for organisation. What if, for example, the community needs both beans and potatoes but everyone prefers to grow beans. If both beans and potatoes are needed, then someone is going to have to grow potatoes. Yet doesn't this raise the spectre of authoritarianism? Malatesta thinks not. He argues that it is a mistake to think that organisation is not possible without coercive authority.[125] He takes issue with the argument which says that an organisation presupposes an obligation to co-ordinate one's own activities with those of others and so it violates liberty and fetters initiative. His argument is that 'what really takes away liberty and makes initiative impossible is the isolation which renders one powerless. Freedom is not an abstract right but the possibility of acting.'[126] Consequently, for Malatesta, 'organisation, far from creating authority, is the only cure for it and the only means whereby each one of us will get used to taking an active and conscious part in collective work and cease being passive instruments in the hands of leaders'.[127] The idea is that in putting aside private interests and in voluntarily pursuing the common good, freedom is enhanced. Those who worry that a particular geographically located community might have all the beans and potatoes whilst another community has none should remember that we are talking here of groups forming on the basis of needs to be satisfied.

From social anarchism, therefore, comes the following ideas. For the good of each individual in the community, it is important that people work together. It is important to acknowledge that each is dependent upon and benefits from the contributions of others. These contributions require some sort of organisation. Yet organisation need not be an obstacle to freedom. Indeed, it can become a condition for its possibility. These ideas are all to be found in Sartre's description and discussion of the organised group.

It is within the organised group that the communitarian view of the community can be realised. It is here that the normative notion of praxis finally produces an outline of a theory of associations. The organisation is as far as this work will go in developing such a theory. For Sartre, 'The word "organisation" refers both to the internal action by which a group defines its structures and to the group itself as a structured activity in the practical field, either on worked matter or on other groups.'[128] In the organisation everyone is a participant,

---

[124] Ibid., p. 19.
[125] Malatesta, in Vernon Richards (ed.), 1965, p. 84.
[126] Ibid., pp. 86–87.
[127] Ibid., p. 86.
[128] CDRI, p. 446.

working to ensure the success of the group in achieving its ends. Sartre argues that, 'The aim of the parties to the pledge . . . was urgent but still vague . . . The unification of an organised group, in contrast, is always defined by its objective, which is *concrete*.'[129] In chapter five the work of Downing and Thigpen was cited to make the point that the more participation there is in the generation of shared meanings then the more justice will be found in the community. It will be seen that it is, indeed, in the organised group with its emphasis on participation and its particular view of rights and duties that justice is to be found.

Organised groups are based on the pledge whereby everyone pledges to remain the same. However, the pledge results in what Sartre calls a contradiction in that it becomes 'the basis of the heterogeneity of functions'.[130] Differentiation enters into the group as a way of ensuring the success of the group, preventing it from returning to seriality but also still denying it the status of a hyperorganism. The pledge creates the conditions of stability so that people can have different functions yet remain the same. Though the members of the group are and remain distinct individuals they are not unconnected. They are unified in performing their functions for common goals. Consequently, Sartre can claim that the practical unity of the group, which is based on individual praxis, is the absolute contradiction of ontological unity. It is the existence of differentiation that enables the group to operate at all. These differences amount to the reintroduction of 'otherness' or 'alterity' as a description of the relations between people, albeit in a different form from that to be found in seriality. As Sartre explains, 'As a member of a series, I do not understand why my neighbour is other; serial alteration reinforces accidental alterity (birth, organism) and renders it unintelligible.'[131] In the organisation, however, alterity is comprehensible. 'He is other because it is necessary . . . that this or that should be done.'[132] Thus relationships in the organised group occur within the context or framework of the common goal. As Sartre says, 'it is necessary for A to do what he does for the common *praxis* in order that B can do what he does, and conversely'.[133] The common praxis here refers to a combination of complementary yet differentiated individual praxes. It is on the basis of the performance of functions towards a common goal that reciprocity occurs.

Of course, the allocation of functions itself presupposes differentiation. As Sartre says, 'This first moment of differentiation . . . is, therefore, fundamentally an action of the group, upon itself.'[134] Essentially, therefore, the group acts upon itself in order to achieve its purposes. This is the result of the members of the group having a certain view of themselves and of their purposes. The group

---

[129] Ibid., p. 467.
[130] Ibid., p. 577.
[131] Ibid., p. 465.
[132] Ibid.
[133] Ibid., p. 474.
[134] Ibid., p. 447.

creates its own meaning and does so on the basis of a common goal, given in praxis, which ultimately is the satisfaction of needs. On the basis of the group's understanding of its purposes it creates roles for people to fill and then creates people to fill them.

In the organisation there is a reciprocity of participation whereas in the pledged group there was a reciprocity of enforcement and in the group-in-fusion a reciprocity of dependency. However, enforcement and dependency are kinds of participation and the process by which reciprocity works in the organisation is precisely the same as that in the pledged group and in the group-in-fusion in that it is a reciprocity of third parties. It is through this reciprocity that people come to value each other. It is perhaps ironic that a hint of this is supplied by Rawls. Gauthier recalls Rawls's example of the musicians in the orchestra who could have trained themselves to play every instrument to an acceptable standard but who have opted instead to perfect their skills on one so as to enhance the performance of all.[135] Gauthier argues that each person 'values both the shared activities and the sharing or participating' and that 'we may suppose that in valuing participation, a person comes to value her fellow participants'.[136] The reciprocal nature of participation is the basis for understanding the relationship between the individual and the organised group. It is also the case that, along with the taking of the pledge, that is, along with regulation by consent, the performance of one's function as a concrete form of the pledge becomes another of those communal practices that everyone can endorse as a basis for the politics of the good. Indeed, both the pledge and function invoke a particular sort of sociality which can also be endorsed as a communal practice which serves as a basis for the politics of the good.

It is the nature of functions that they impose limitations of a certain kind on the freedom of the individual. As Sartre says, 'The relations between concrete individuals must, therefore, be constantly created within the limits laid down by a concrete task and solely with a view to the successful completion of this task.'[137] Thus function, in the organised group, is the concrete form of the pledge. It is the pledge with positive content. Therefore, just as the pledge is the freely undertaken individual limit on freedom for the sake of greater overall freedom, so too is function.

However, the limits that are imposed by function concern the definition of role not the dictation of action. Sartre explains that,

> As functions, in fact, they are still the condition for the *praxis* (of the common individual and of the totalising group), but they are not the *praxis* itself; on the contrary, it is their inert instrumentality (on the limitation of their possibilities) which conditions everyone's efficacity.[138]

---
[135] Rawls, 1971, pp. 523–25n.
[136] Gauthier, 1986, p. 336.
[137] CDR I, p. 467.
[138] Ibid., p. 488.

Therefore, the role having been defined it is up to the individual occupant of that role to decide how the role is to be performed. Furthermore, definitions of functions make individual talent in performing the action possible. Sartre's example of the football team illustrates his meaning. He argues that 'the efficacity of a goalkeeper, as well as his personal possibility of being good, very good, or excellent, depend on the set of prescriptions and prohibitions which define his role'.[139] The good goalkeeper works in such a way that by surpassing the definition of his role he fulfils himself as a goalkeeper. The definition of his role does not dictate his concrete choices on the field. He is better than the goalkeeper on an opposing team not by going outside his assigned task but by the way the concrete choices he makes on the field go beyond the abstract definition of his role. Generally, the difference between winning and losing is the difference between the concrete choices the players make on the field. The point is that praxis, while regulated by function, is not reducible to it. Indeed, the proper practice of the function makes that impossible. Individual freedom is required to fulfil the potential of the function. In fact, it is what the individual members of the group do towards the achievement of the group's goal, that is, the fulfilment of individual functions, that defines the organised group rather than the list of functions themselves that are employed by the group. Thus the group is defined by the praxis of its members.

The sense in which the identity of the individual can be constituted in part by his attributes now becomes clear. Whilst the ascription of a function to an individual within the group amounts to the allocation of a role and whilst the function itself does not determine the actions that the role might require, it does make the individual's actions intelligible. The functions of each of the group's members can properly be understood only in the light of the goals of the group and in relation to the functions of the other members of the group. Thus the goal of the football team is to win, to be successful and thus to satisfy certain needs in a milieu of scarcity by scoring goals against the other team and preventing the other team from scoring goals. In this context the function of the goalkeeper makes sense. Since a team of goalkeepers would not be adequate to the task of the group, the function of the goalkeeper has to be understood against the functions of all the other members of the team. The understanding of a function within the context of other functions is part of a person's identity as is the talent with which the function is performed. Therefore, a sense of identity can be constituted in part by an individual's attributes. That man is a talented goalkeeper.

Actions are the concrete form of the function. (There are degrees of concreteness, remember.) In acting, once again, each individual exercises a kind of sovereignty, 'quasi-sovereignty'. This is simply a development of Sartre's view on leadership that was described earlier in connection with the group-infusion. In the context of the pledged group the role of the regulating third party

---

[139] Ibid.

is to ensure that every other member of the group maintains the pledge in such a way as to make every other member also a regulating third party. In the organised group each member becomes a regulating third party by virtue of the exercise of his function. In this case, the action of any individual in performing their function impacts upon the actions of others who are engaged in their own function. This can be understood by examining the manner by which each person in a group is a regulatory third. Thus footballer A performs a regulatory action in that it affects B's action in reaction to A. Both actions contribute to the common aim such as the football team attempting to win the game. Regulatory and regulated actions and hence power relations within the group are reciprocal in that A can regulate only because B has put himself into a position that is conducive to him being regulated. Therefore, when A decides to pass the ball he acts as a regulatory-third in that his action affects the actions of his team mates. In that sense A becomes a sovereign but it is, at this stage, a limited sovereignty in that the effects of A's action are limited by the other members of the team. A can pass the ball only if the positions of the other members of his team make passing the ball a sensible practical option. Moreover, in having passed the ball to B and so regulated B's action B now exercises limited sovereignty, he may return the pass or whatever. Each regulatory act is a totalisation of the group. Sovereignty involves organising the environment to suit one's purpose. This is what A does but it is also what B and all the other team members also do in due course. Consequently, every member of the team exercises a sovereignty that is limited by the reciprocal sovereignty of everyone else. Since it is limited by its reciprocity this sovereignty does not make each person transcendent to the group in the sense of organising or regulating it from a position outside of the group. Instead, everyone is sovereign, from which 'it should not be inferred that no one is'.[140] The relationship between the individual performing his function and the rest of the group is the same as that between the third party and the group-in-fusion. It is transcendent in totalising the group and immanent in that the totalisation is interiorised by the other group members and provides the basis for future praxis.

Part of the intelligibility of functions and the identity of the individual resides in the ascription of rights and duties. In fact, Sartre argues that where rights exist they exist as a consequence of the purposes of the group and are, therefore, the product of different forms of association and created or revealed by the terms of a particular association. In the absence of a communitarian theory of rights what Sartre has to say might be offered as a candidate. As was seen in chapter five, Sartre is critical of the view of rights espoused by laissez-faire liberalism. However, although Sartre is critical of liberal rights as an expression of the terms of a particular form of association he is not dismissive of rights per se. He argues that with certain forms of association rights perform a valuable service and one that is different from that performed by rights in a bourgeois liberal form of association.

---

[140] Ibid., p. 579.

It is within the context of the terms of association of the pledged organised group that Sartre sees rights as operating to serve the whole group. In creating itself the group also creates rights and duties due to the differentiation of functions. With the ascription of function to the individual comes not only the freedom to perform that function in the light of the meaning that the group gives to its own activity but also an understanding of the reciprocal nature of rights and duties. Thus,

> Function is both negative and positive: in the practical movement, *a prohibition* (do not do *anything else*) is perceived as a positive determination, as a *creative imperative*: *do precisely that*. But in the milieu of the pledge, doing that is the right of each over all, just as it is the right of all over each: the definition of *power*, in so far as a concrete function particularises it, is that for everyone it is the right to carry out his particular duty.[141]

In fact, in the organised group rights and duties are more than reciprocal, they are equivalent. The duty to be a good goalkeeper is the right to be trained properly, and the team's right to have a good player is its duty to provide training and equipment. The web of these rights and duties is in fact a source of strength for the group. The equivalence of rights and duties occurs as a result of the sense that the group has of its own purpose. If in the light of this purpose certain things have to be done then individuals have a duty to do these things, but equally the members of the group have a responsibility to ensure that these duties can in fact be performed. Similarly, the right that the individual has for the members of the group to ensure that he can fulfil his function is the equivalent of the right of the members of the group against the fulfilment of that function. In seriality, the usual distinction which makes the rights of others into the duties of the individual and the rights of the individual into the duties of others was valid. However, once the content of function has been defined, 'There is no ground for stating *a priori* that the diet involved in the training of a *particular* sportsman is either a right of the Other (of the other members of the team) or his own right.'[142] Whatever rights the individual has regarding the performance of his function, bearing in mind the origins of rights in the group's task, must, by virtue of the fact that this function is part of the group's totalising praxis, be rights that everyone else has. Similarly, the right that the individual has regarding the performance of his function is, at the same time, that individual's duty. In the context of the organised group rights and duties are simultaneously one and the same which third parties can hold over the individual and which the individual, as a third party, can hold over all the others.

So rights, where they exist at all, exist as a consequence of the purposes of the group; they arise from the community in the sense that they are created by the community and, furthermore, they exist to serve in the achievement of the

---

[141] Ibid., p. 450.
[142] Ibid.

purposes of the community, serial or otherwise. Thus as Gauthier says,

> The moral claims that each of us makes on others, and that are expressed in our rights, depend neither on our affections for each other nor on our rational or purposive capacities, as if these commanded inherent respect, but on our actual or potential partnership in activities that bring mutual benefit.[143]

Rights are, therefore, an expression of the terms by which we associate. In liberalism, the rights of the individual are paramount and by being understood in that way express certain terms of association. In Sartre's organised group, rights arise out of the community. This is quite different from the situation presented in chapter three where it was pointed out that rights can inform the nature of benevolence. There the context was that the rights of the individual informed everyone else. However, in the pledged group it is not the case that individuals hold rights as trumps against society as a whole because the right of the individual to perform his function is simultaneously the right of the community to have the function performed. Precisely the same holds true of duties.[144]

It also follows that the performance of functions involves certain moral obligations. There are clear obligations to the group as a whole. In fact the reciprocity of the members of the organised group is a significant development of the reciprocity to be found in both the group-in-fusion and the pledged group. In the organised group one has an obligation to fulfil one's function as part of the common praxis, working towards the common goal. The obligation to fulfil one's function has implications for the ways in which one relates to others. It

---

[143] Gauthier, 1986, p. 222.

[144] It is worth noting some intriguing problems that arise from the position just espoused. Normally, having a right implies that the individual has the liberty to exercise that right. It also, normally speaking, means that the individual has the liberty not to exercise the right. It would be odd to say of someone that they had the right to do something despite the fact they lack the liberty not to do so. Yet that is precisely what must happen in the group which makes rights, in that case at least, mandatory or inalienable. Yet if it is odd it is not impossible. A right can become inalienable by appealing to the rights of other individuals in the group. In the case of Sartre's organised group, of course, the proper performance of a function is underpinned by the freely taken and enforceable pledge.

There is a further problem to be found in deriving rights from goals. The goal of the football team is to win. Yet the players in the team have the right to play the game according to the rules, which is also presumably a duty. The players have the right not be coerced into committing professional fouls. They actually take the playing of football itself very seriously. Thus rights and goals appear to have different normative functions. A goal involves everyone in pursuing it as best they can whilst rights apply to particular individuals by way of either protection or licence. To derive a right from a goal it will, therefore, be necessary to have the goal impose constraints on its own pursuit. However, in adopting a goal the group will be committed to doing whatever is necessary to achieve it, in which case there is a justification for overriding any constraints. Goals appear to be incapable of generating any restrictions. Much, therefore, stands on the nature of the goals themselves, or rather, the purposes for which the group was formed. The significance of this lies in the idea that if the goals of the community change then so too might that community's moral sensibilities.

invokes the notions of rights and duties and also the ethical implications attached to the manner by which one performs one's function. This is the point that MacIntyre makes in connection with practices. Thus the individual's function defines, to some extent, his moral responsibilities. As a goalkeeper there are certain things that one is obliged to do. There are moral obligations that goalkeepers have to the rest of the team. As was noted in chapter three, this is not to say that the person who is a goalkeeper has discharged in total his moral responsibilities by virtue of being a good goalkeeper. It simply means that being a good goalkeeper involves certain moral responsibilities which are necessarily involved in good goalkeeping. This is an important point. MacIntyre's portrayal of Sartre's thought at a certain time, 'I speak now only of the Sartre of the thirties and forties,'[145] shows that Sartre has a view of the self as distinct from any particular social role that the self might happen to assume. To identify the self with its roles involves both bad faith and intellectual confusion. MacIntyre observes that, 'The self thus conceived, utterly distinct . . . from its social embodiments . . . may seem to have a certain abstract and ghostly character.'[146] MacIntyre goes on to argue that the separation of the self from the roles that the self plays means that 'the unity of a human life becomes invisible to us'[147] and that such a self 'cannot be conceived as a bearer of the Aristotelian virtues'.[148] This is because a self separated from its roles 'loses that arena of social relationships in which the Aristotelian virtues function if they function at all'.[149] In the *Critique* Sartre appears to have anticipated MacIntyre's criticism of his thought at a certain time. Sartre's view of the self has changed. It now involves an acknowledgement of social roles and, going a little further still, it is reasonable to include an acknowledgement of the virtues associated with the performance of those roles.

Sartre's view of rights and duties in the organised group contributes further to our understanding of the relationship between ends and the identity of the individual. In order to achieve its goals the community ascribes particular functions to the members of the community. These functions are partly constitutive of the identities of the individuals who perform them. Since these functions are designated on the basis of a common end there is a clear relationship between the identity of the individual and the goals of the community. We have already seen that group praxis involves certain dispositions. If the function is also a practice in MacIntyre's sense, such as football, then certain virtues are also involved. Moreover, since all functions in any case carry with them certain rights and duties which are also required for the achievement of the end then it follows that the common ends, already given in praxis, are partly constitutive

---

[145] MacIntyre, 1981, p. 30.
[146] Ibid., p. 31.
[147] Ibid., p. 190.
[148] Ibid., p. 191.
[149] Ibid.

of the identity of the individual not simply as a gardener or a goalkeeper but also as a moral agent. This is an extension of the idea that man is the product of his own product in that man is also the product of the manner by which he engages in production. In the dialectic that exists between consciousness and social being, the manner in question is the result of the relationship that exists between praxis (and the virtues involved in praxis) and the thing to be produced, which could be a form of association.

In locating the source of obligations and rights within the context of a particular form of association Sartre differs significantly from Hobbes. Hobbes presupposes mutual obligations and rights but fails to solve the problem of their origin. For Sartre, their origin is praxis attempting to satisfy need but the nature of that praxis will depend upon the form of association under consideration. In the organised group, which is itself the result of praxis, praxis is function and it is on the basis of that function and, therefore, in pursuit of common goals as an expression of the terms of association which in any case allocates functions, that the individual has rights and duties. Thus rights and duties could be expected to vary from one form of association to another. As was noted in chapter three, Walzer argues that freedom consists of rights within settings and if rights are to be guaranteed it is necessary to understand each particular setting. Thus the rights that accrue to the members of a football team would, to some extent at least, be different to the rights that accrued to, say, the members of a religious order and if the goalkeeper left the team to take up holy orders he would have no further entitlement to his footballer's rights. In other words, different forms of association require and are accompanied by different terms of association rooted in common goals as revealed by common praxis.

Sartre, whilst arguing that the views of Engels are too simplistic, acknowledges that 'exploitation, in its many historic forms, is basically a process which corresponds to a differentiation of functions, that is to say, ultimately, to the development of the mode of production'.[150] Here Sartre is referring to differentiation of function in a state of seriality affected by the milieu of scarcity. In the organised group, although there is a differentiation of function, exploitation does not appear. It is also the case that in the organised group there is the possibility of control over the mode of production such that man's relationship with the environment and thus his relation with other men might be changed. So it transpires that another aspect of the ethical dimension of functions concerns the mode or means of production. This is because, as was seen in chapter four, the way that we relate to the environment affects the way that we relate to each other. Therefore, the means (tools, machines) we use to work the environment affects relations between people. If we change the way that we relate to the environment, or if we change the meaning that is attributed to a particular way of relating to the environment, that affects the way that we relate to each other. What is required, therefore, and what the organised group makes possible, is a change in both the way of relating to the environment and the meaning that is accorded to different ways of so relating. Of course, the meaning that is attached to the manner by which the individual works on the environment, which is the meaning that is attached to the manner by which the group obtains certain of its social goods, is, as we saw in chapter four, part of the terms that define the identity of the association. Given certain terms, that is, given an association of a certain sort, the way that the road-mender and the gardener and the intellectual relate to the environment can have the same significance. The climate in the organised group is right for this to occur and it is because of that climate that exploitation does not appear.

The climate in the organised group is right because of the terms that accompany that particular form of association. As already noted above, in the organised group it is necessary for A to do what he does in order for B to do what he does, and conversely. As Hayim says, 'Each person (whether as a soldier, farmer, worker or intellectual) is my equal as long as his function helps me to carry out mine in the context of the group aim'.[151] This equality is particularly important to Bakunin. As he explains, 'Since freedom is the result and the clearest expression of solidarity, that is, the mutuality of interests, it can be realized only under conditions of equality. Political equality can be based only upon economic and social equality. And justice is precisely the realization of freedom through such equality.'[152] Certainly, gross economic inequality will undermine political equality. After all, in practical political terms, the poorest in society tend not to bother voting and those who are homeless can't vote and in practical political terms there are more votes to be gained by furthering the interests of those who have the most 'disposable income'. However, it is the issue of equal social and moral worth or status that I take to be most significant. It is through the performance of this function that equality of membership of a community, first established on the basis of the pledge, is maintained. This means that equality of membership of a community is not mysteriously established and maintained through the exercise of will but through praxis. In the organisation it is by doing gardening and road-mending that people enjoy equality of membership. The road-mender is needed only in so far as people need to use roads and the gardener who has to transport his lawn-mower is one such person. Thus the gardener needs the road-mender and he, in turn, needs the gardener. Both are needed by a community which values easy access to well-kept gardens. Therefore, the equality is based on reciprocity of participation and in this way every citizen becomes, in Walzer's terms, an office holder. Since, as we have seen, participation is, in itself, no guarantee of justice, it is equal status, rooted in the pledge, that can provide a safeguard against that vociferous faction, noted earlier, who wish to manipulate the group. Indeed, as

---

[150] CDR I, p. 738.
[151] Hayim, 1980, p. 105.
[152] Bakunin, 'The Programme of the Alliance of International Revolution', in G. P. Maximoff (ed.), 1953, pp. 156–57.

an extension of Bakunin's argument, equal moral status is not only part of what social justice means, it is also necessary for the achievement of social justice.

It is in the organisation, where the terms accompanying the organisation include reciprocal participation in pursuit of common objectives and equality of membership, that meanings can be generated that are truly shared. It is the reciprocal nature of the participation, along with the equivalence of rights and duties which are the terms intended to sustain this form of association, that establishes the justice of the organised group and underlines the idea that respect for a community's shared values should depend in part on the way in which the values are generated and shared.

One aspect of the relationship between the individual and the community as established by certain terms of association is the issue of the ownership of the talents of the individual agents. Do they belong to the individual or to the group? To whom do the rewards that attend the exercise of those talents belong? Sandel's argument was that the difference principle from Rawls represents an agreement to regard the distribution of natural talents as a common asset and an agreement to share in the benefits of this distribution. For Rawls, a conception of the person as antecedently individuated allows for the idea that the individual's talents are inessential attributes of that individual. From his conception of the person Rawls draws the conclusion that those talents are possessed and deserved by the community. However, as Sandel points out, to show that individuals do not deserve or possess their assets is not necessarily to show that the community does deserve or possess them. For the community to possess the talents of the individual and to deserve the benefits that flow from them it is necessary to assume that the community has an ontological status that both Rawls and Sartre are unwilling to concede to the community, for it is only with that status that the community could be said to possess its assets in the strong constitutive sense necessary for desert. Sandel argues that the only way that Rawls can justify his position regarding the community's claim to the ownership of talents and the deserts arising from that ownership is by making use of a very different conception of the individual subject. If Rawls allowed that the self was an intersubjective self, partly constituted by membership of a community, then it would be possible to talk of common talents being used for common goals. However, Rawls cannot make this move because to do so would invoke the notion of the radically situated self.

Sartre's position is different in that he has a conception of the person that is different from that of both Rawls and Sandel. Sartre's view of the subject is based on the idea that the individual has needs and that from needs stems praxis. The human being is thus a praxis being and as such and in order to satisfy needs can engage in a common praxis with other individuals. This avoids the individual-community dichotomy by allowing for both individual praxis and common goals. In the organised group individual praxes combine in pursuit of common goals. This gives rise to the equivalence of rights and duties. There is, for example, the possibility of training people or in some way providing them with the skills that the group requires in order to achieve its goals. This was the duty of the group and the right of the individual who having been trained and because of being trained finds that his right is also a duty which the group has the right to expect him to fulfil. In fact talents and the rewards arising from their exercise can be understood as being the property of both the individual and the community by virtue of the role of each individual praxis in achieving the group's goals.

At the heart of this issue is the essentiality of the individual. On the one hand it could be said that it is the function that is important to the group and the individual is dispensable, but on the other hand it is individual initiative in the performance of the function that is important. According to Sartre, 'everyone comes to everyone, through the community, as a bearer *of the same essentiality*'.[153] The issue that this raises concerns the status of the individual. Whilst nobody is indispensable, at the moment of action, as the ball hurtles towards the net, that goalkeeper is essential. Even if that goalkeeper could be replaced immediately it is that particular goalkeeper at that particular time who is essential and, as Sartre says, *'the essential moment –* is always that of the free, individual dialectic and of the sovereign organisation of the practical field'.[154] Therefore, at that moment, the individual becomes essential.

Sartre has turned the Kantian notion of respect for persons into something concrete. For Kant the duty to respect others is grounded in the value of their humanity, the significant feature of which is the capacity for rationally autonomous agency. For Sartre respect is not an abstract quality that is due to the individual by virtue of some abstract capacity, that of rationally autonomous behaviour, which is abstract in the sense that it is abstracted from the total, that is, whole person situated as they are on the basis of constituting dialectical praxis. Respect is due to concrete people in their concrete situation. In other words, respect is accorded to a person by virtue of the significant feature of the person as it emerges in a particular context. This significant feature need not be the capacity for rationally autonomous behaviour, or at least not that alone. Therefore, in the organised group, respect is attached to the proper performance of the individual's function. In the organised group different talents as exercised by different individuals contribute to the common objective and are part of the common praxis. In that sense individual talent and creativity are necessary. Therein lies mutual respect. Thus the proper performance of the individual's function which is due to obligations to the achievement of the group's goal gives rise to an understanding of the ways in which people who fulfil their obligations should be treated. So it is that in the organised group respect is occasioned by praxis.

At this point it is possible to make sense, in a particular way, of the claim that the community partly constitutes the identity of the individual. As was

---

[153] CDR I, p. 599.
[154] Ibid., p. 584.

seen in the previous chapter, it is from the dialectical relationship between the form and the accompanying terms of association that identities are constituted. The praxis view of associations shows that communities constitute identities in that individuals in pursuit of certain ends constitute communities and establish certain terms of association which are, in part, an expression of those ends. Some forms of association achieve unity through the mediating reciprocity of third parties. The mediating reciprocity that is characteristic of certain forms of association is also part of the terms of those associations and has the purpose of achieving the ends of the community by establishing certain sorts of attachments. Those attachments constitute, in part, the identity of the individual. Other forms of association, less communal in nature, lack those sorts of attachments. However, the lack of attachments is also a way of defining the identity of an individual and is also, in part, the terms that define that form of association. In order to pursue individual or communal ends the individual may perform some function. Part of the individual's identity will, therefore, be constituted by that function, by the attributes, including the moral attributes, that are realised by the performance of that function and by the meaning that is ascribed to that function, which is also an expression of the association's terms, and hence, in turn, defining of the community. Thus the individual is defined by the manner in which he pursues certain ends and by the meaning that is ascribed to that manner. Meanings as expressions of an association's terms are not only attached to functions, they are also attached to people who can and people who cannot afford fish. Of course, affording and not affording fish is also a manifestation of particular forms and terms of association as constituted by the constituting praxis of individuals. Ends and meanings as aspects of terms of association will vary according to the form of association. It is in that sense that identities are constituted, in part, from the dialectical relationship that exists between forms and terms of association.

Finally we arrive at the closest that this work will get to a normative theory of associations. It is a theory that recommends putting into place certain values and practices and which provides us with a view of a form of association that might effectively facilitate the pursuit of the good life for human beings and which might, in fact, be the result of that pursuit. Thus the recommended form of association is one that liquidates isolation and impotence by establishing, on the basis of common objectives, the conditions such as an acknowledgement of the importance of interdependency which are required for reciprocity of participation, the exercise of quasi-sovereignty and the development of the moral personality through the exercise of certain dispositions, including loyalty and empathy, and the equivalence of rights and duties. These are conditions that will effectively allow the individual to satisfy his needs in a milieu of scarcity, enhance his freedom and enable him to pursue the goal of human fulfilment, which is itself defined in terms of the satisfaction of needs, the exercise of freedom and the pursuit of social justice. Clearly the theory can be developed further. However, further development requires a dialectical method of inquiring into the nature of associations and it is to an articulation of that method that this work aspires. Nevertheless, enough has been said to provide communitarians with a foundation and a justification for a community of a certain sort.

However, even a communitarian community can experience conflict. Yet communitarianism takes little account of that fact beyond Walzer's acknowledgement of conflict over the meaning of a social good which can be settled by negotiation. Whilst conflict would be expected between serial individuals in a milieu of scarcity and between a ruling group residing over a seriality that is challenged by a group-in-fusion, it is less obviously clear that it can occur in a pledged-organised group.

The fact that even the pledged-organised group can experience conflict can be overlooked due to Sartre's portrayal of the organised group which is too neat to be realistic. He acknowledges the problem, arguing that,

> So far, we have always described organised groups as if they were composed of relatively homogeneous individuals or of ones who differed only in respect of some qualities whose very diversity correspond harmoniously to the differentiation of their function... In fact organisation takes place on the spot, with whatever means and men are available.[155]

So it is that Sartre, Rousseau and Hobbes, recognising the potential for conflict within communities, have devices for dealing with conflict. However, even these devices cannot guarantee an absence of conflict. As Sartre says, 'Terror does not inflexibly define the permanent limits of freedom for everyone ... it makes it *less probable* that one will abandon one's post, go over to the enemy, etc. Treason, as a new form of human action, is nevertheless always a concrete possibility for everyone.'[156] (This, of course, is not the same argument as the claim he had made in a prefatory note to a collection of plays and which he subsequently repudiated.) Acknowledging the constraints upon individual freedom, Sartre admits that its probability depends upon historical circumstances. Sartre goes on to say that the group is, among other things, the totalisation of its points of rupture, that there are certain thresholds above which the rupture will occur, that these thresholds are extremely variable and that although from one perspective differentiation within the group can be a source of strength, from another perspective the more differentiated the group is the more points of rupture there will be.

Thus whilst interdependence is in principle and in practice the route to Sartre's moral and political ideal and on the basis of his description and discussion of the organised group can be seen to be at the heart of social anarchism it is not, as Sartre demonstrates, the infallible solution to the problems which social anarchism seeks to address. Indeed, out of interdependence can come a quite particular problem associated with the especially essential individual.

---

[155] Ibid., p. 474.
[156] Ibid., p. 444.

In the organised group, in the moment that the individual becomes especially essential he suddenly stands out, in a sense, above the rest, other than the rest and consequently, in this context, in opposition to the group. Sartre observes that, 'The individual agent has not transcended or betrayed his pledge; he has executed his mission, performed his function; and yet, in a way, he has created a new isolation for himself, as beyond the pledge.'[157] The contradiction here is that in exercising his power in the execution of his function the especially essential individual becomes a threat to the group. As a threat to the group the individual risks exile and so, due to the performance of his function for the sake of the group, the individual may be compelled to leave the group. In this way the group can begin to dissolve itself. This also works the other way around. At the essential moment it is the group that is inessential: 'I am the goalkeeper and at this precise moment nobody else is necessary.' Indeed, the gifted goalkeeper could decide to move to another, more prestigious and wealthier, team thus rendering his former team inessential to him. In deciding to leave the team the goalkeeper exposes the team to the danger of dissolution. Sartre sums up the situation by pointing out that, 'What is feared now is dissolution *through excess*, and a pledge has no power against this new danger, since it arises precisely *from* pledged fidelity.'[158] In these two ways seriality is introduced into the group. Interestingly, although everyone agrees that they should recruit the best possible goalkeeper or the goalkeeper with the greatest potential, the better the goalkeeper is or becomes the more of a problem he can become for the group. In this case the agreement threatens the unity of the group.

Sartre takes the conflict argument a step further in volume two of the *Critique*. In order to pursue this task Sartre examines the case of two subgroups in conflict with each other within a pledged group. Sartre shows that when the pledged group is faced with a problem, different sub-groups, that is, the members of different sub-groups, may lay claim to a solution which they will advocate in the interests of the unity of the whole group but also to advance their own interests. Each sub-group seeks, 'to re-establish the compromised unity – but each attempts to re-establish it to his own advantage'.[159] Thus there is conflict within the group. Sartre intends to show how this conflict can be intelligible. He argues that each sub-group opposes the other in the name of the totalising praxis of the organised group. Therefore, 'In this sense, the conflict can never spring from differences (individual or collective) prior or external to the constitution of the group.'[160] Each sub-group sees its opponent as a traitor because the opposing sub-group threatens the unity of the whole group by deliberately usurping the other sub-group's functions. Thus, as Aronson notes, 'To have its function now claimed by another sub-group is to simultaneously

---

[157] Ibid., p. 584.
[158] Ibid., p. 585.
[159] CDR II, p. 65.
[160] Ibid., p. 52.

be challenged, in its very existence as a part of the group, as well as (in its own eyes) to threaten the very well-being of a group depending on it to carry out such-and-such a function.'[161] Thus the group's unity and goals are the occasion of the conflict. The two sub-groups are in conflict because each sees itself as the custodian of the whole group's best interests as a group and because both wish to maintain unity. The conflict is dominated by the goal of restoring the unity of the whole group. Indeed it is unity that makes the struggle possible. Sartre argues that, 'Not only does this unity represent the intimate bond between each side and the group, it also constitutes *the meaning* of the antagonistic relation itself. And the violence of the duality is just the unremitting effort to restore unity.'[162]

However, not all conflict is bad, or at least all conflict is not bad through and through since it can contribute to the understanding that the group has of itself. The communitarian failure to account for conflict constitutes a significant omission of the means by which shared meanings in general may be generated. On Sartre's analysis the conflict is in itself a process of sharing and although it may not lead to progress towards a common objective at least the process is intelligible and in its intelligibility to the group it contributes to the understandings of the group. Conflict can be a totalising activity. Sartre illustrates what this means by looking at two possible outcomes of conflict. One possible outcome of conflict is schism. Sartre provides the example of the schism between Eastern and Western Christians. Here the schism is the result of an inability to do away with the other sub-group. Thus, 'That which, for a third party, took place as a break-up was produced by each religious community as an *amputation*. Each recovered its unity purified by the expulsion of the other. Each defined itself as perpetuating the unity of the original church.'[163] The other possible outcome of conflict is the liquidation of one sub-group by the other. The danger to the whole group is overcome by one sub-group's victory over the other in the name of unity. The group's reunification casts new light on events, creating an orderly and structured sense of those events. Thus victory by liquidation is a means by which conflict is intelligible, 'For it is produced as the reunification of the dissociated unity, through the regrouping of organs and individuals according to new common perspectives.'[164]

The communitarians also fail to distinguish between the understandings that the group has of itself which are generated from within the group and the understandings that the group has of itself which are received from outside the group. The individual members have what is best described as an idea of the group which is something that the group itself creates. This idea or meaning is something that is shared by the members of the group as their view of themselves,

---

[161] Aronson, 1987, p. 82.
[162] CDR II, p. 67.
[163] Ibid., p. 72.
[164] Ibid., p. 80.

their purpose and their relation to the rest of the world. As a group idea it is often totally unknown to the outsider. Of course, the outsider can know certain things about being a member of Derby County football team. One can know that practices and training are held at such and such a time, that failure to attend training sessions will involve certain penalties and so on. These sorts of issues, to do with the structure and governance of the group are observable or at least readily communicable. Viewed from the outside, Derby County is a premier division club which, with its players of national standing, is bound to achieve success. However, a different view of what it means to be a player for Derby County football team is available to those who are players and are, therefore, aware of particular weaknesses, lapses of confidence, possible transfers and fears of relegation.

Nevertheless, the outside view of the group affects the inside view, and in turn affects the behaviour of those in the group. From the outside the group functions as an organised totality working to accomplish a common end. Sartre explains that 'the group is seen in its totalised unity by the ensemble of the others and that this pressure is so strong that even in its relations of pure interiority it interiorises this unity as its *being-from-behind (être-de-derrière)*'.[165] The view from the outside affects the shared meanings of the members of the group. In short, the group interiorises the ignorance of others. However, the group does not have the ontological unity that on the basis of its praxis it would appear to have. Indeed, as has been said, the practical unity of the group which is based on individual praxis is incompatible with ontological unity. Still, everyone is defined by this non-existent unity. The realisation that, in this sense, the unity of the group is non-existent leads to a feeling of uneasiness. The sense of unease brought about by the realisation that the group does not have the ontological status which, on the basis of its praxis it quite simply cannot have, can lead to the institutionalisation of the group. In fact, praxis can reveal the absence of even practical unity and thus intensify feelings of unease. For example, it has been seen that the exercise of individual talents gives rise to the threat of seriality. Whilst it is not inevitable, with competitive quasi-sovereignty there will always be a tendency for the group to dissolve into seriality. In order to combat this threat and also to create the unity assumed by outsiders, the organised group changes its praxis from organised praxis to institutional praxis.

The institution

Since it is the praxis of the group that will create unity and because the group requires ontological status in proportion to the threat of the dissolution of the group that is posed by the revival of seriality, everyone's reciprocal work consists

---

[165] CDR I, p. 582.

of projecting ontological unity on to practical unity. This praxis turns individuals into instruments or tools, 'inorganic instruments'.[166] There is thus a return to the practico-inert against which the group was formed in the first place. It should be made clear that the kinds of institution that Sartre is writing about in this way are what he calls 'degraded forms of community'[167] which, he claims, have unfortunately become the norm. In the organised group the individual becomes the common individual working for the common goal. Individual praxis requires initiative and freedom and is essential. Sartre observes that in the institution, however, 'the individual ... is constituted as inessential in relation to his function'.[168] In other words, as Salvan says, 'In an institution the individual becomes inessential and the function essential.'[169] This is because the first priority of the institution is itself. Individuals see themselves as the impotent other at the service of function. Yet again, the processes at work are precisely the same as in the other group formations in that the institution, its goals, its meaning and the constituting of individual identities are the products of the constituting work of praxis. That constituting praxis has produced new goals and meanings which are appropriate to the new form of association. This form of association is accompanied by its own terms which are in part a statement of goals and meanings. These terms cast MacIntyre's practices into a new light.

Whereas Sartre talks about the relationship between institutions and functions MacIntyre talks about the relationship between institutions and practices. MacIntyre's institutions are more akin to Sartre's organisations yet there are also similarities with Sartre's institutions. Thus in chapter three it was seen that for MacIntyre institutions are concerned with external goods such as money. Institutions are structured in terms of power and status, and they distribute money, power and status as rewards. They must do this in order to sustain both themselves and the practices of which they are the bearers. However, whilst no practices can survive for any length of time unsustained by institutions, the ideas and the creativity of the practice are always vulnerable to the acquisitiveness and competitiveness of the institution. In fact, practices are threatened by the very group that is meant to sustain them because the first priority of the group is maintaining itself.

It was seen that, for MacIntyre, the best defence against institutions is the proper exercise of the practices themselves and in particular the virtues associated with practices. On MacIntyre's account, the proper exercise of practices requires certain virtues, such as justice, courage and truthfulness and these virtues will protect the practice from the corrupting power of institutions. However, there is a problem because although institutions have the power to corrupt practices, the sustaining of institutions is itself a practice. If the

---

[166] Ibid., p. 599.
[167] Ibid., p. 591.
[168] Ibid., p. 600.
[169] Salvan, 1967, p. 171.

individual's function is to sustain the institution (he is perhaps a manager of some sort) and he becomes very good at this function, using initiative in the exercise of individual praxis, exercising quasi-sovereignty, then he too can become the agent of seriality. The consequence is that the very person whose practice is to sustain the institution as a sustainer of practices ends up producing a degraded institution which has become its own goal. Thus the manager has courageously, and possibly also truthfully and justly, institutionalised individual praxis including, presumably, his own.

Although, as Sartre says, this sort of consequence is unfortunately the norm the proper response might be to argue that where this does occur it occurs because the manager has misunderstood the nature of his function or misunderstood or failed to exercise the appropriate virtues. However, to argue that the manager has misunderstood his function is to argue that he is not very good at what he is supposed to do whereas Sartre's argument is that it is precisely those who are good at what they do that become a threat to the group. So it is that practices can threaten each other and even, in certain circumstances, themselves.

Practices can threaten each other and even themselves because, as both MacIntyre and Sartre acknowledge, success in a practice brings with it power. In some cases, power is not simply an external good as MacIntyre claims. For some practices, power is part of what the practice means. Power is part of the practice of managing the institution. It is a good that is internal to the practice and is exercised in the proper performance of that practice. In MacIntyre's work, power and the way that it is exercised is a much under-considered point. Sartre can be seen as adding a missing dimension to practices which is one that concerns the role of the institution and organisation and the power relations that exist between practices and institutions, between practices within institutions and within practices themselves. It is not simply the power of the manager that has to be acknowledged. The power accruing to practitioners and the power relations embedded in practices of all kinds will have an effect on those practices. Thus powerful practitioners can vie with each other, on behalf of that practice, or simply on behalf of themselves and against fellow practitioners, for institutional rewards. Exceptional practitioners can create schisms within a practice and one branch of a practice could liquidate another branch. Lighthouse keepers, for example, are now deemed to be unnecessary.

Desan points out that, the emergence of the institution involves two main transformations, 'the introduction of a certain desired inertia, and the appearance of authority'.[170] This means the appearance of one sovereign emerging from all who are quasi-sovereign. At the level of the organised group individuals have power and indeed a kind of authority by virtue of their function. However, Sartre argues that authority does not emerge in its full development except at the level of institutions. At this level the sovereign emerges to combat the return to seriality

---

[170] Desan, 1965, p. 187.

and it is at this level that there is a development in Sartre's view of that aspect of community life that is absent in communitarianism, namely, leadership.

The success of the institution in doing the very opposite of what it is designed to do is closely related to the function of the sovereign. For Hobbes there is a tension between preserving the liberty available in the state of nature and the fear of violence and war which is a feature of such a state. This leads to an individual relinquishing power to a sovereign. Just as Sartre warns against the group relapsing into seriality so Hobbes fears the state of nature and fears political society relapsing into such a state. Hobbes was clear that the purpose of the sovereign was '*the procuration of the safety of the people* . . . But by Safety here, is not meant a bare Preservation, but also all other Contentments of life, which every man by lawfull Industry, without danger, or hurt to the Common-wealth, shall acquire to himselfe.'[171] Men should, in their own self-interest, acknowledge full obligation to the sovereign which could take the form of either a single individual or an assembly. Leviathan is, therefore, the state in which all individuals are subjects except the individual, or assembly, on whom all have agreed to confer power. Once sovereignty is instituted its subjects are bound to obey. According to Hobbes, by the terms of the contract they have surrendered all their liberty to the sovereign. Whatever the sovereign does is done by virtue of the powers conferred upon the sovereign by the people.

For Hobbes, sovereignty derived its authority from the assent of the people. It was transferred from the people to the ruler as a result of the social contract, thus rendering the sovereign separate from the people. Rousseau held that no such transfer of sovereignty need, or should, take place. However, groups can degenerate and where that is the case Rousseau argues that, as a member of the group, the individual is subject both to the prevailing regulatory principles of the group and to a sovereign who can act in the name of the sovereign body and utilise the power and potential of the whole group. Hobbes argues that the sovereign is authorised by the people to do whatever he desires to do, though Sartre, like Rousseau, regards this as evidence of the degeneration of the group and the return to seriality. As B. Cannon says, 'the resort to sovereignty is an evasion of freedom and responsibility'.[172] Poster notes that,

> The failure of groups to preserve their unity is the condition under which authority comes to rest with the leader. When Hobbes writes that only a strong leader can guarantee social order he forgets that a social order which requires such a leader has already collapsed, that society had already lost the vital commitment of its members.[173]

---

[171] *Leviathan*, chpt. 30, p. 200.
[172] B. Cannon, 1991, p. 211.
[173] Poster, 1979, p. 97 Aoudjit observes that, 'Unlike Hobbes, who thought of the monarch as the guarantor of stability and cohesion . . . for Sartre the appearance of a powerful leader is a sign that the group has already collapsed and that there is not any cohesion anymore'. (Aoudjit, 1987, p. 142)

Sartre argues that the proper activity of the sovereign 'is to struggle against the invasion of the group by seriality, that is to say, against the very conditions which make his office legitimate and possible'.[174] However, it is the emergence of the sovereign that hastens that return to seriality. This is because 'the sovereign reigns through and over the impotence of all; their living practical union would make his function useless, and indeed impossible to perform'.[175] Thus, as Sartre says, 'in fact he emerges in the moment where these relations are on the decline. His instituted presence undoubtedly contributes to their decline'.[176] In other words the supposedly unifying action of the sovereign creates the very condition the signs of which led to sovereignty in the first place. The elevation of a particular individual to the position of sovereignty completes the process of reserialisation. In this way sovereignty perpetuates itself whereas, in fact, if it was 'successful' it would eliminate itself.

Bakunin questions not only the competence of rulers to rule, in his terms, justly but also the possibility of competence in that endeavour. To be ruled are a large number of people with different occupations, interests, aspirations and cultures. Of the sovereign body Bakunin writes that,

> even if were a thousand times elected by universal suffrage and controlled in its acts by popular institutions, unless it were endowed with the omniscience, omnipresence and the omnipotence which the theologians attribute to God, it is impossible that it could know and foresee the needs, or satisfy with an even justice the most legitimate and pressing interests in the world.[177]

Similarly Malatesta asks, 'Are the governors such very exceptionally gifted men as to enable them, with some show of reason, to represent the masses, and act in the interests of men better than all men would be able to do for themselves?'[178] Crucially, in social anarchism, there is a fundamental objection to top-down political authority so that no one has the right to issue directions which another has to obey. Of course, we might comply with the directions of an authority in a particular realm, where those directions concern that realm. So we might comply when our doctor tells us to take more exercise for the sake of our health because we trust the doctor's expertise in the realm of health and because we want to be healthy, or because we recognise that it is in our interests to be healthy. We might comply with someone's directions because there are moral reasons to do so. Here, however, we would be acting out of a recognition of those moral reasons, that is, on our own moral assessment of the situation. Social anarchists have no objections to compliance in these sorts of cases. Their objections concern the basis of the legitimacy of the exercise of political authority.

---

174 CDR I, p. 628.
175 Ibid.
176 Ibid., p. 623.
177 Bakunin, 1950, p. 31.
178 Malatesta, 1942, p. 5.

Regarding the legitimacy of sovereignty and in words reminiscent of his argument concerning the legitimacy of the State, Sartre argues that, 'If it were really necessary to find a foundation for sovereignty we could be searching for a long time: for there is no such thing'.[179] According to Sartre there is no such thing because there is no need for any such thing. Sovereignty resides in free individual praxis. What is created within institutions is a sovereign individual or body whose task is to maintain unity. Thus there is a single regulatory third party who must, if he is to be a sovereign at all, be accepted by the other members of the group. However, this acceptance need not and usually does not imply consent. Usually it is the outcome of passivity. The source of sovereignty is precisely the opposite of communal consent in that it arises from seriality and impotence. The consequence of sovereignty is the perpetuation of seriality and impotence. Therefore, 'Everyone obeys in seriality: not because he directly adopts an attitude of obedience, but because he is not sure whether his neighbour has undertaken to obey. This is far from preventing orders from being seen as *legitimate*: in fact it prevents the question of legitimacy from being raised.'[180] In order to avoid complete impotence and the return to seriality everyone agrees to obey the sovereign who appears to be the only one with both the capacity to understand the common praxis and the power to ensure its continuation. However, that common praxis has already disappeared and the agreement of everyone is born of passivity. As Aoudjit notes, 'For Sartre therefore there is no such thing as a legitimate leader since a leader comes to power as a result of the failure of all forms of contract and association.'[181] However, it is difficult to say whether in the relation between the sovereign and his people, he belongs to the people or the people belong to him. No a priori solution can be provided. The concrete circumstances of sovereign and people must reveal whether or not the sovereign incarnates the end and wishes of the people or whether they are merely his instrument.

Conclusion

The identification of different forms and terms of association permits a more sensitive account of certain communitarian themes than is provided by communitarians themselves. For example, Sartre's view of the transformation of the organisation into the institution indicates the precarious nature of Walzer's concept of complex equality. Although in the organised group A recognises the importance of what B does because it enables A to do what he does, and conversely, and although this means that everyone can acquire status by virtue of their function, there is always the danger that the exercise of individual talent

---

[179] Ibid., p. 610.
[180] Ibid., p. 630.
[181] Aoudjit, 1987, p. 142.

will give rise to the threat of seriality. This can produce the institution in which quasi-sovereignty is lost to a single sovereign. Whilst Sartre is clear that there is no inevitability about this it is at least always a possibility. Furthermore, it would appear that complex equality is a certainty only within the context of a particular form of association, the organised group, which can be supported by particular terms of association. Complex equality is less of a possibility in all forms of association because not all terms of association will be as supportive as the organisation. Seriality is not as supportive and neither is Sartre's institution. Thus, the precariousness of complex equality arises, first, from the fact that where it does exist it can be easily lost as a result of the transformation of that group, which can arise from the possibility of complex equality itself, that is, complex equality can contain within itself the seeds of its own destruction by creating the especially essential individual or the powerful practitioner. It arises, second, from the fact that it cannot readily exist in all forms of association.

The more sensitive account of certain communitarian themes can be developed further. As was noted earlier, communitarians have little to say about what it is that brings people together. According to Sartre people are drawn together in the attempt to satisfy needs in a milieu of scarcity and it is in this attempt that shared meanings including the shared meanings of social goods arises and this can in itself instigate a form of association. What is significant about Sartre's account is that it demonstrates that different forms of association will react to need in different sorts of ways. Therefore, even if a social good is the same for different sorts of communities, the means by which it is attained might vary. In order to understand this it is necessary to contrast the role of praxis in the group-in-fusion with the role of praxis in the pledged group. What is also significant is that different forms of association may in fact seek, to some extent at least, different sorts of goods because different needs have been identified. The group-in-fusion seeks to eliminate a threat. The pledged group has of itself become a good. This means that, on the basis of praxis attempting to satisfy needs and in as much as needs are indicators of values, different forms of association can have different values. In fact the analysis has to be turned around. It is not the case that the community as an entity identifies the goods that are required and then decides how to acquire those goods. It is praxis, individual or common, that defines the meaning of the goods that are being sought, the meaning of the manner by which they are to be obtained and thus both the forms and the terms of association which are in turn the basis of further praxis.

Variations can also occur with regard to the conception and pursuit of the good for human beings. As MacIntyre says, the nature of the quest for the good is not the same for all people in all places and at all times.[182] We have seen that different praxes produce different conceptions of the good. For example, what is good for the peasants cannot be good for the nomads and vice-versa. It is

---

[182] MacIntyre, 1981, p. 204.

also the case, therefore, that each form of association can have its own conception of the good and, indeed, can come into existence on the basis of a conception of the good that is perceived as being shared. Moreover, given the different meanings of the good for each group that can arise from the distinctive praxis of each group, it follows that the dispositions required to achieve the good and which are part of what the good means could also be very different.

It is instructive to view Sartre's view of forms and terms of association in the context of Blum's depiction of the forms of communitarianism as described in chapter three. It will be recalled that, according to Blum, there are three forms. One is social communitarianism whereby the community promotes certain social goods and virtues, such as, on the one hand, schools and hospitals and on the other hand, family stability, security and civic responsibility, solidarity and loyalty. Another is identity communitarianism which refers to the embedded self and emphasises the moral significance of the particular group identities that make us what we are. Finally there is virtue communitarianism for which moral and other virtues must be understood primarily in the context of communities on the grounds that communities nourish, support and partly define virtue.

Sartre's theory of groups does not marry precisely with Blum's taxonomy. Nevertheless, comparisons are informative. Thus the group-in-fusion, organisation and institution all contain elements of social communitarianism. That is to say, each group formation promotes security and solidarity. What is instructive is that, even though the dynamics of the constituting praxis remain the same, each group seeks to do so in a different way and this is because the good in question can acquire different meanings. The group-in-fusion seeks security and solidarity on the basis of individual praxis being spontaneously recognised as a common praxis. The organisation uses the device of the pledge as the basis upon which functions are allocated. The institution seeks to reintroduce inertia into the group. It becomes apparent, therefore, that whilst different forms of association may, up to a point, seek the same goods, they will do so in different ways according to their various terms of association. Equally, each form of association may, up to a point, seek different social goods and indeed may be constituted on the basis of attempting to achieve those goods. The group-in-fusion required weapons and the organisation requires and fosters skill in performing a function which is, of course, not simply a different social good but a different kind of social good. As has been said, in so far as social goods are identified on the basis of need and in so far as needs are indicators of values it follows that different forms of association will have different values. From this it emerges that in order to talk sensibly about the community and its social goods attention must be paid to the particular form of association and its related terms. Crucially, attention must be paid to the fact that different forms and terms of association require different sorts of praxis. Different groups are constituted on the basis of different praxes and once constituted will be known by their particular praxis.

The group-in-fusion, the organisation and the institution can all be regarded as manifestations of identity communitarianism albeit in quite different ways. In the group-in-fusion the isolated and dominated individual becomes connected and empowered. In the organisation, the individual's identity is associated with his function and with the moral sensitivities and dispositions that arise from and which are required for the exercise of that function. In relation to that function the individual is essential and active. In the institution, however, the function is identified and the individual is inessential and passive. His identity is reduced to being an inorganic tool. Although these are different manifestations of identity communitarianism, it should be noted that in each case the identity of the individual is constituted on the basis of ends that are given in praxis.

We have seen that different forms of association can have different views of the good for human beings. This means that, with regard to virtue communitarianism, whilst both the organisation and the institution provided the community context for the promotion of certain virtues, the virtues that each form of association promote are, on account of their terms which are established by and manifested in praxis, in many ways either different or, if the same, then prioritised differently. The organisation requires initiative and the exercise of individual talent which the institution finds problematic for all but the sovereign. For the institution, obedience would be a prime virtue. The identification of those virtues will require an understanding of different forms of association. Notice also that seeking different social goods or the same social good in different ways requires different virtues. In other words, different forms of association constitute and are constituted by different kinds of people. Certainly with regard to the development of those virtues, the means for their development will be informed by the prevailing forms and terms of association. They will, in short, be informed by the praxis of that group. Finally, as different associations may require different virtues, the virtues that are required can be a basis for judging that association.

From the analysis above it will also be apparent that each form of association embodies different types of communitarianism to different degrees. Thus the group-in-fusion is largely an embodiment of certain aspects of social communitarianism and partly an embodiment of identity communitarianism in so far as it illustrates how the individual can become embedded in a community and change his identity from that of serial to communal being with the identity of a third party. The virtue communitarianism that is to be found in the group-in-fusion is to be found in connection with the role of the third party. The organisation embodies all three types of communitarianism in pretty much equal measure. Finally, the institution embodies social and virtue communitarianism but contains little of identity communitarianism except in so far as it serves to make the individual malleable in pursuit of its own ends. Once again these distinctions between different forms of association reveal that to talk of the individual's identity being constituted at least in part by the community, or of the community being a source for the conception and pursuit of the good, or a forum for the generation of shared meanings requires an appreciation of the form of association to which these sorts of references are being made. Moreover, such talk is one-sided in the sense that individuals are constitutive of communities and so too can a notion of the good and other shared meanings be similarly constituting.

It is perhaps still not entirely clear why the liquidation of seriality is thought to be desirable. The answer is that forming a group, especially an organised group based on the pledge, enables individuals to increase their freedom since in the group they can more effectively control the practico-inert forces, including those of the non-human environment, that act upon them. With the liquidation of seriality other people are no longer alienated or alienating. This is because in the group it is more possible to alleviate the effects of certain sorts of scarcity, even if scarcity cannot actually be overcome in all of its forms. In other words, overcoming the isolation and impotence of seriality allows the individual to become more fully human in the sense of becoming more free, more effective in satisfying needs and hence better able to achieve his goals. This is what Sartre means by human fulfilment. Human fulfilment requires us to be people of a certain kind and other than the serial kind. The normative notion of praxis provides an account of certain necessary dispositions that lead to human fulfilment and which are part of what human fulfilment means. It also establishes the basis of a normative theory of associations which, incorporating that account of dispositions, provides us with a view of the kinds of associations in which human fulfilment may most effectively be pursued and which may themselves be the result of that pursuit. Of course, if people are not interested in human fulfilment, or not interested in human fulfilment in these terms, then they may not be interested in liquidating seriality either.

The exploration of the nature of associating has now reached the point where it becomes possible to address directly the criticisms of the communitarian account of community that were identified in chapter three. This will be the first aim of the next chapter. The next chapter will also examine deficiencies in the communitarian account of community from alternative perspectives. It will, however, become clear that these alternative perspectives can be illuminated by and yet also illuminate the Sartrean view of praxis. On the basis of that illuminating work a method for understanding the nature of community will be described.

CHAPTER SEVEN

Praxis, communitarianism and beyond

We are now in a position to review both the deficiencies in the communitarian account of community and the ways in which an interpretation of Sartre's theory of practical ensembles and his ideas on the intelligibility of history may be used to correct those deficiencies. Following this review, the deficiencies in the communitarian account of community will be re-examined from a different perspective, one that is concerned with the psychology of moral agency and in particular with the importance of the dispositions. The point of this re-examination is two-fold. On the one hand it will be seen that this perspective does, in certain ways, address some of the deficiencies in communitarianism that have been identified. On the other hand it will be seen that this perspective is not only provided with an additional layer of intelligibility and significance in the light of an interpretation of Sartre's theory and in particular the normative notion of praxis but this perspective also contributes to an understanding of that theory and its notion of praxis.

At that point Sartre's theory will have been rehearsed in a variety of ways. On the basis of that rehearsal it will become apparent that Sartrean ideas have an application that goes beyond the liberal-communitarian debate and can make a contribution to the work of other critics of certain sorts of liberalism and in particular to the work of those feminist theorists who espouse an ethics of care. It will also be seen that, as with the perspective from moral agency, the work of those feminist theorists can make a contribution to one's understanding of praxis.

Having established a developed view of the process of praxis, the final issue to be explored concerns the development of a dialectical method for inquiring into the nature of associations that is based solely on that process; the possibility of which Sartre asserts yet fails to demonstrate. It will be seen that not only is such a development possible but also that development will, as Sartre had hoped, reveal a structure for dialectical reason.

The major focus of this work has been the use of Sartre's theory of practical ensembles and his ideas on the intelligibility of history in correcting certain deficiencies in the communitarian account of community. These deficiencies, some of which have been commented on by defenders of liberal theory and which are identified in chapter three of this work, can be categorised into two groups. One group consists of all the things that communitarians do say about community but don't say particularly well. The other group consists of all those things that are aspects of the life of a community about which communitarians say little or nothing at all by way of offering a theory of their own.

Into the first group goes the communitarian failure to explain fully why and in what ways a community has a significant part to play in the life of the individual. From this fundamental failure arise all the other items in group one. Thus there is little by way of detail about the ways in which communities are constitutive of the identities of individuals, or of what gives rise to anyone's conception of the good or indeed what the good might be and this despite MacIntyre's views on virtues and human telos. Certainly attention is paid to the social meaning and just distribution of social goods. However, this attention is confined to the level of explaining what these things mean and hence why they are important. It does not explain how these things come into being and neither does it explain how, once in being, these things actually operate.

It is because Sartre does not seek to diminish the significance of the individual that he is able to explain how the community works. With all groups the individual is not simply a constituted member of the association but is also a constituting member of the association. As a constituted member of the group the individual is embedded or immanent but as a constituting member she is transcendent. In the group-in-fusion, the pledged group and the organisation the third party, as quasi-sovereign, regulates the actions of others who, in the exercise of their limited sovereignty, regulate her actions as part of the process of mutual dependency, enforcement and participation thus maintaining the relationship of the individual to the group as one of immanence-transcendence. This makes intelligible the communitarian idea that certain attachments cannot be set aside as they are constitutive features of our identities.

It has been argued that groups can arise when, in the face of a threat, or to satisfy some other need, individual praxis becomes common praxis and it is the common praxis that defines the group. The different praxis of each group can require the exercise of different dispositions. These dispositions, rooted in and exercised by praxis, contribute to the attainment of and are part of the good for each group. Indeed, a conception of the good which is found to be held in common can in itself produce a particular form of association. Human fulfilment itself, understood as the liquidation of seriality, overcoming the effects of scarcity, the satisfaction of needs, the promotion of freedom and the realisation of social justice, was seen to be a possibility in the pledged-organised group as a result of the constituting praxis that formed that group and which in so doing and in the continuing activity of sustaining the group constitutes the individual. It is in this sense that human fulfilment can be understood in terms of praxis.

Praxis also provides a basis for the generation of shared meanings concerning social goods and their just distribution. The example of the Chinese peasants and the nomads shows that the meaning of a social good can arise from praxis. In this particular case even though the peasants and the nomads were pursuing the same scarce social good, land, the different praxis of each group invested that social good with a different meaning. Indeed, as has been said, whatever else might establish the meaning of a social good, praxis always will. In fact, the meaning established by praxis can itself be constituting of a group. It is also the case that it is praxis that defines both the forms and terms of association and that part of that definition will be an understanding of the social goods that are sought and the meaning that is attached to the manner by which they are obtained. This provides the sense in which different forms of association may react to need in different sorts of ways and may, to some extent, seek different sorts of social goods. In so far as needs are indicators of values it means that different groups may have different values.

When communitarians claim that community is good for people it is not clear just what the nature of that claim might be. Buchanan, by way of a criticism of the nature of the claim, asks if it is to be thought of as a psychological claim requiring empirical evidence or as a normative claim requiring a theory of objective value.[1] Sartre's theory can be used to address this criticism and clear up the confusion by avoiding both of Buchanan's alternatives. The community is not to be understood as an objective value for two reasons. First, there are different sorts of communities and the value that they have is put there by the constituting praxis. It is, therefore, from the dialectical process of praxis, normatively conceived, that a normative claim arises, not from a theory of objective value. If communities are a fundamental ingredient in the good life for human beings, then they are so due to the constituting activity of praxis. Second, it is only from within the community that such a judgement may be exercised. In other words, in order to understand fully the good of community the individual must be part of the normative, dialectical process of praxis by which individuals constitute communities and by which, therefore, communities play their part in constituting individuals. As was seen in chapter two, this dialectical process can be intelligible only to the individual who is part of the process. Although membership of this group can be regarded as a way of life and thus the group becomes an end as well as a means, it is so only because of the constituting activity of its members and only for those members. Having established the way in which the community is good for human beings it follows that communitarians do not have to make a psychological claim at all in order to argue for the good, such as it might conceivably be, of community and are thus relieved of the burden of searching for empirical evidence.

If the nature of the claim that community is a good was unclear then so too would be the claims that sociality, sharing and relationships are good. In any event, claims as to the necessary good of sociality, sharing and relationships are contested by critics of communitarianism. Holmes criticises communitarians for investing words like 'social' and 'sharing' with positive value. He argues that the word 'social' can refer to bad as well as to good practices and that just because something is shared, that in itself does not make it admirable. What is shared could be a racist attitude and sociality can produce racial discrimination.[2] Similarly, the idea that all relationships are necessarily good is also contested.

---
[1] Buchanan, 1989, p. 857.
[2] Holmes, 'The Permanent Structure of Antiliberal Thought', in Rosenblum (ed.), 1989, p. 231.

Rosenblum[3] and Kymlicka[4] argue that belonging, attachments and relationships can be unpleasant and damaging experiences. Thus life in the institution might not be very pleasant at all and quite unlike life in an organised group. Sartre's analysis can be used to provide the communitarians with two lines of defence. Since both sets of criticism are provoked by the communitarian failure to differentiate between various forms of association the first would be to be more precise in identifying the form of association in which the sociality, sharing and belonging is to occur and hence to be more precise in the use of the word 'social' since different forms of association will embody different conceptions of the social. The different types of reciprocity to be found in different groups, whilst associated, indicate that sociality and belonging can be good for different reasons. The second line of defence, arising from the first, would be to refer to the reasons why certain sorts of groups are formed in the first place. There would, therefore, be a reference to the liquidation of seriality and with that the attempt to overcome the effects of certain forms of scarcity, satisfy needs and enhance human freedom.

The second line of defence provides the basis for justifying the communitarian claim that certain communal practices are the basis for a politics of the common good. Liberals object that it is not clear what these practices are.[5] They cannot automatically or inevitably be taken to be sociality or sharing. They can, however, be identified as those practices that would achieve the objectives that led to the formation of groups. Therefore, for members of the pledged group and the organisation certain practices can be identified. These would be practices that engender commitment and the performance of functions.

Kymlicka also questions the communitarian view that social practices are constitutive of the person.[6] He argues that communitarians find that they cannot reject the value that these social practices have for the person since, on the communitarian view, without these social practices there would be no person. Kymlicka's argument is that no matter how involved in a social practice the individual might be, she still has the capacity for questioning the value of that practice. Kymlicka's argument is correct and communitarians would have to acknowledge that it was correct since in criticising liberal practices they are providing the proof for that argument. As Sartre illustrates, without the capacity for questioning social practices there could be no escape from seriality. His description of the genesis of the group-in-fusion shows how an escape is possible. Furthermore, as a member of both the group-in-fusion and the pledged group the individual is both constituted and actively constituting, she is immanent or embedded within the group and yet at the same time transcendent and although she may have a particular function the fulfilment of that function requires the operation of her free praxis. In fact, Kymlicka appears to be reacting to one of

---

3   Rosenblum, 'Pluralism and Self-Defense', in Rosenblum (ed.), 1989, p. 216.
4   Kymlicka, 1990, p. 213.
5   Ibid., p. 226.
6   Ibid., p. 213.

communitarianism's more excessive claims. Actually, Sandel expresses some wariness at the notion of a radically situated self. In connection with Sartre's work it has been consistently necessary to claim that people are constituted only in part by their practices, attachments and so on and then only to the extent that people are themselves constituting of those practices and attachments.

Into the second group of deficiencies, those aspects of community life about which communitarians have little or nothing to say by way of offering a theory of their own, goes a communitarian account of rights and commitment. Communitarians do have things to say about rights and commitment but largely only by way of criticising liberal theories of rights and the liberal absence of commitment. Also into this group goes other aspects of communal life about which communitarians have little or nothing to say on their own account which are, specifically, issues to do with conflict, power and leadership, alienation, the interplay between the relationship that people have with the environment and the relationship that they have with each other and finally the issue of scarcity. The failure of communitarians to address these issues at all, or if addressed then only in a cursory fashion, partly explains their failure with regard to the items in the first group.

When communitarians do talk about rights it is usually to criticise liberalism for encouraging a proliferation of rights, or for having a mistaken view of the priority of rights and for producing people of a particular kind in a particular kind of society, which are the stances taken by, respectively, Etzioni and Sandel. MacIntyre argues that there are no such things as rights and when, despite his reluctance to talk about rights, Walzer does say something, it is to say that they are peculiar to particular settings. However, Gutmann,[7] Buchanan[8] and Kymlicka[9] point out that liberal rights serve to protect the interests of minorities and subordinate groups of all kinds. Sartre is not concerned with the number of rights that a person may be said to have nor with their priority. His concern is with how people may be said to have rights, in which concern he is similar to Walzer, and with the work that they do which is a concern that is similar to one that is held by Sandel. Thus for Sartre, rights arise from and are an expression of particular terms of association. He is critical of the liberal theory of rights because they are part of the terms of a particular form of association, seriality, and they perform a particular purpose, the maintenance of seriality. Sartre is clear that the interests of subordinate groups must be protected. Yet the existence of rights in a bourgeois liberal society will ultimately do nothing to end the subordinate status of certain groups since in practice these rights serve to maintain the status quo.

Behind the concern for the interests of subordinate groups lies the issue of the role of the State. Liberal theorists ask if it is the role of the State to protect

---

[7] Gutmann, 1985, p. 319.
[8] Buchanan, 1989, p. 858.
[9] Kymlicka, 1989, p. 902.

the freedom of the individual to pursue her own conception of the good or to encourage certain ways of life and discourage others and answer yes to the first part of the inquiry and no to the second. The liberal argument is that their theory of rights is one that protects the freedom of individuals to pursue their own ways of life, including the freedom to enter into associations of one's own choice, without undue interference. Sartre too, whilst questioning the legitimacy of the State, clearly favours the first option but argues that the individual can fully pursue her own conception of the good only within certain forms of association, that seriality is not such a form and that, furthermore, liberal democracies do encourage certain ways of life and discourage others. Sartre proposes a view of rights which are attached to functions and which are, as Etzioni and Glendon would wish, the equivalence of duties and which serve to protect both the individual and, as Sandel would wish, the community. Rights arise, therefore, from the contribution of individual praxis to common praxis and serve quite a different purpose to the rights that serial individuals are said to have. Viewed in this way rights can be seen as being part of the shared meanings of a particular community. They are also, for that particular community, a manifestation of the commitments that have been made by the members of that community. The origin of these commitments in the organised group lies in the praxis of taking the pledge and thus establishing an aspect of one's identity.

The commitment of the pledge is regarded by Sartre as the first step in the pursuit of the good life for human beings. However, the praxis of taking the pledge does not rule out the possibility of conflict occurring within the group. Indeed, in the pledged group it is the pledge itself that can provide the condition for the possibility of conflict. The individual has pledged to perform her function and, for the sake of the common goal, to perform it as well as possible. However, the excellence of her praxis threatens the group with seriality and hence conflict. Here conflict arises out of the very praxis that was designed to engender commitment to achieving the goals of the group. Conflict can also occur between sub-groups. In this case it is the attempt to preserve the unity of the group and protect the praxis of the sub-group that occasions the conflict. With sub-groups the origins of the conflict can also reside in the pledge. Yet the conflict itself can be the occasion for the development of shared meanings.

In the group-in-fusion and the pledged group everyone, by virtue of being a third party, can exercise a degree of power. Everyone can exercise a leadership role, albeit one that is limited by the regulatory actions of all the other third parties. This leadership role, or quasi-sovereignty, is strictly the result of the exercise of individual praxis and is regarded by Sartre as being entirely legitimate. Through her praxis the quasi-sovereign contributes to the meaning of social goods and to the self-understanding of the community. However, in the institution, understood as a degraded community, there is one sovereign praxis, the legitimacy of which may be called into question particularly if the sovereign fails to incarnate the end and wishes of the people and uses them as her instrument. The quasi-sovereignty of the individual in the organisation is an aspect of that individual's identity whereas the individual in the institution, understood as a degraded community, is passivised and becomes a mere tool. Thus in such an institution social alienation is reintroduced.

It is in the attempt to satisfy needs through her work that the individual becomes alienated. That alienation is compounded when the attempt is made by the serial individual in a milieu of scarcity. Yet as Rosenblum points out, 'alienation is absent from the communitarian vocabulary'.[10] Linda Bell points out that because Sartre identifies different kinds of alienation he can criticise societies in different ways. Thus because he denies that ontological alienation can ever be overcome in that it is associated with the nature of work, he can criticise societies who fail to acknowledge that fact and operate on the basis of 'idealistic voluntarism', claiming, in effect, that willing makes it so. In arguing that social alienation can be overcome, Sartre can criticise societies for failing to allow that to happen by keeping the people oppressed.[11]

Communitarians have tended to ignore the fact that the individuals who constitute communities have to be located somewhere and have some sort of relationship with their environment. There is, in other words, an environmental dimension to the notion of community. It has been seen that the way that people individually and collectively relate to the natural environment affects the way that people relate to each other as members of a community and the way that people relate to each other as members of a community affects the way that individually and collectively they relate to the natural environment. This dialectical movement can contribute to the self-understandings of a community, the meaning of social goods and conceptions of the good life. Therefore, the different praxes of the Chinese peasants and the nomads invests the land with different meanings and that is accompanied by different notions of the good. Thus the peasants and the nomads have a view of each other and of themselves which is a reflection of their relationship with the environment. In a different way the issue of identity also emerges from Sartre's discussion of the road-mender, the gardener and the intellectual. That discussion illustrates the idea that the constitution of an individual's identity resides in part with the relation that the individual has with the natural environment. This identity also contributes to the nature of the relationships that exist between people by virtue of the meaning that is ascribed to the relationship that the individual has with the natural environment. Moreover, the meaning that is attached to that relationship is one way of defining the community.

Sartre shows that a feature of humanity's original relationship with the natural environment and a feature of relationships between people as they are today is scarcity. Praxis operates to satisfy need in a milieu of scarcity and it is this that can occasion the attempt to liquidate seriality and establish different forms and

---

10 Rosenblum, 'Pluralism and Self-Defense', in Rosenblum (ed.), 1989, p. 216.
11 Linda Bell, 1979, pp. 418–19.

terms of association. This is because it is in the condition of seriality that the effects of scarcity are most pronounced. In that sense scarcity has a bearing on all of the items in both groups of concerns. The communitarian failure to address the issue of scarcity is all the more remarkable in the light of the fact that scarcity is one of the circumstances that informs Rawls's contract theory of which communitarians are so critical. On Sartre's account, an understanding of the good life for human beings requires an understanding of the effects of the milieu of scarcity and it is against the background of this milieu that the shared meanings of a community, including the meaning of social goods, arises.

There is a further criticism of communitarianism that is made by defenders of liberal theory which comes again not from what communitarians say but from what they do not say. Communitarians have failed to provide a political theory of their own.[12] There is, for example, no communitarian view on how a community can be created and sustained. Thus they have avoided the key issues of political theory such as the nature of the relationship between the individual and the community, and how to ensure that the power that results from human associations serves the well-being of the whole community.[13] These related criticisms are entirely valid and are also the reason why communitarians require Sartre's theory of practical ensembles and his ideas on the intelligibility of history both of which are rooted in a dialectical and normative notion of praxis.

At various points in this work praxis has been associated with the possession of certain dispositions. Sartre himself makes this association particularly in his examination of Stalin in the second volume of the *Critique*. It has been argued that the normative notion of praxis provides an account of how certain dispositions are both required by and developed by praxis and that these dispositions are exercised in the pursuit of human fulfilment and are part of what human fulfilment entails. It has been noted that the individual is constituted in part by associations and that associations are constituted in part by the individual. However, the means by which this occurs and the results that are obtained will vary from one form of association to another and they will vary because each form of association requires its own praxis and hence its own dispositions conceived as a quality whereby the individual invokes or otherwise experiences emotions of a certain kind and to a certain degree.

Sartre wisely, or at least consistently, distinguishes dispositions, which he calls qualities, from states.[14] A conception of dispositions that regarded them as fully settled states is one that invokes the notion of hexis. In the *Critique*, Sartre invests hexis with the idea of inertia in order to contrast hexis with praxis which is free and dynamic. In so far as the association of hexis with praxis is problematic then the association of dispositions, so conceived, with praxis would also be problematic. To regard dispositions as qualities avoids this problem. It

---

[12] Okin, 1989, p. 42. See also 'Humanist Liberalism', in Rosenblum (ed.), 1989, p. 46.
[13] Wallach, 1987, p. 601.
[14] Reinhardt Grossmann, 1984, p. 219. MacIntyre regards virtues as qualities, 1981, p. 178.

also supports Sartre's notion of freedom. In that connection Sartre's work on emotions themselves is relevant. In the *Notebooks* Sartre argues that, 'Ethical rationalism is correct to reject internal dispositions when they are pitfalls for action; it is wrong to consider them as moods, that is, as purely subjective agitations that procure only illusions about Being. Everything is *true*.'[15] In what can be taken as another deliberate reference to Kant, Sartre's view is that 'internal dispositions' are things that can lead us to, rather than away from, certain understandings and, moreover, not only do they not prevent freely chosen behaviour they are inherently an aspect of that behaviour. On this view dispositions are dynamic rather than inert and, not only may they be associated with praxis, it can be said that praxis involves dispositions.

So it is that the normative notion of praxis gives rise to another line of argument, that taken from the dispositions, which in its original form is not directly related to Sartre but which can also usefully be applied to some of the deficiencies in communitarianism. The strength of the argument from dispositions is that it provides a view of why and in what ways a community is a fundamental ingredient in the good life for human beings. It provides a view of what the good life means or involves. These are both areas where the communitarian account has proved to be deficient. It also provides a response to certain criticisms of communitarianism made by defenders of liberalism who raise the issues of the role of the State and of how the individual relates to the community. It will also be seen that this line of argument, which will require a review of certain of Aristotle's ideas, can be provided with additional explanatory force when set within the context of praxis and that simultaneously it serves as a reminder of an important dimension of praxis.

Before engaging on a review of certain of Aristotle's ideas, the significance of this line of argument for communitarianism is also indicated by Blum. Blum notes that communitarians have not attempted to develop a moral psychology to support or explain their position. He asks,

> What kinds of motivations, attitudes, sensitivities, and virtues are involved in the attachments, and the actions flowing from such attachments, to various communitarian entities? How do communitarian attachments in their various modes generate responsibilities and actions?[16]

These questions can now be answered with reference to praxis. It will be argued that praxis and the dispositions associated with praxis give rise to and are expressions of a way of life and understood as such the examination of the dispositions and the use of that examination in understanding the nature of associations will yield responses to the questions raised by Blum.

---

[15] NE, p. 488.
[16] Blum, 'Vocation, Friendship and Community: Limitations of the Personal-Impersonal Framework', 1994, p. 119. Reprinted from O. Flanagan Jr. and A. Rorty (eds), *Identity, Character, and Morality: Essays in Moral Psychology*, Mass: MIT Press, 1990.

The good life, the life of eudaimonia, for human beings is a flourishing or successful life. It consists off performing one's function in accordance with the highest standards of excellence. For Aristotle, the highest function for a human being is theoretical or contemplative reason. Thus eudaimonia involves intellectual virtues. However, human excellences cannot be practised by isolated individuals. Even a life of pure contemplation requires a community of some sort, albeit possibly only a language community. In any case, a life of pure contemplation is too high an aspiration for human beings as human beings are also social animals by nature. That is, human beings are biologically constituted as social beings. Thus eudaimonia consists of both intellectual and moral virtues, the latter being those virtues that will enable people to live well together. Virtues can be thought of as a particular kind of disposition, that is, as a certain disposition towards actions that are themselves good or bad. Of course, from the fact that people are by nature social beings it is not possible to prescribe what it is that they ought to do or which characteristics ought to be developed. However, although that fact does not logically entail anything it at least supports the idea that certain forms of association are desirable and that certain characteristics should be developed.[17]

The purpose of the polis is to ensure the life of eudaimonia. This is the end or telos towards which the individual's actions are aimed and it is one answer to Blum's question about communitarian motivation. The life of eudaimonia is not one of ephemeral delights. As Daniel Robinson says, '*Eudaimonia* is, then, not some mysterious condition of being that one somehow falls into as a result of good genes or sound instruction; it is an actually *conceived* state of being, towards which a person strives.'[18] Therefore, the judgement that one particular course of action is better than another is arrived at by reference to the individual's current conception of the life that is good for a human being to strive to realise. It is a conception that can constantly be informed and altered by circumstances.

To say that eudaimonia is a conceived state of being towards which a person strives and that it consists of performing one's function is to indicate an activity. The eudaimonic life is one that is lived in a certain way by a certain kind of person. Therefore, although the purpose of the polis is to ensure the life of eudaimonia, this end is not divorced from the actions themselves. In order to achieve excellence, it is necessary to practice excellence. Furthermore, one's virtues are exercised by the same kind of action as gave rise to them. For example, 'It is by refraining from pleasures that we become temperate, and it is when we become temperate that we are most able to abstain from pleasures.'[19] Since the eudaimonic life is a life that is lived in a certain way it means that

---

[17] It should be noted that the meaning of the virtues listed in *The Nichomachean Ethics*, IIii, p. 104, entails, requires or is derived from a social context.

[18] Daniel Robinson, 1989, p. 99.

[19] *The Nichomachean Ethics*, 1104a33–b20, p. 95.

flourishing involves doing things as opposed to being in a certain state. Eudaimonia means that human flourishing requires the exercise of certain of the faculties by which human life is defined and to exercise those faculties in accordance with excellence.

The exercise of the virtues by the individual is not only good for the individual, it is also good for the community and it follows, therefore, that the exercise of virtues by others in the community is also good for the individual. As James Wallace says,

> Such virtues as kindness, compassion and generosity tend to foster mutual feelings of good will among individuals in a community and to maintain individuals' sense of their own importance and worth. Such virtues as courage and restraint enable individuals to govern themselves, to pursue plans, to act on principles, and to participate fully in a life structured by intelligence, institutions, and conventions.[20]

This indicates a view of the relationship between the individual and the community.[21] The polis achieves its purpose when the people are flourishing and the people are flourishing when living the life of intellectual and moral virtue. The community, therefore, has a significant role in promoting the virtues. People are unlikely to become good unless the community and its terms of association are directed towards the achievement of human good.

---

[20] James Wallace, 1978, p. 15.

[21] This is a view that is in addition to the view that the polis is both natural for and prior to the individual. On the Aristotelian account all associations come into being for the sake of some good and the particular association that is the best of all will be the one that is most ardent and effective in pursuing the good and the best of all good. That association is the polis or the political association. (*The Politics* 1i, 1252a1–6, p. 7). To say that the polis is the best form of association is to say that the polis is natural. Aristotle sees the natural world as made up of different types or species of object both animate and inanimate, each with its own distinctive characteristics and capacities. Each species should develop and exercise its own natural characteristics. By doing so it realises its essence and performs its work or function. This is its particular good or end which condition is the final and formal cause of its development. It is the final cause because it is the final condition for the sake of which something occurs or is brought about, it is the end towards which the process of development is directed. It is the formal cause because it is identified with the form or nature which is realised when a particular thing is fully developed. It is in this sense that the polis, being the association that is most ardent and effective in pursuing the good and the best of all good, is the best form of association for human beings and that, therefore, the polis is natural for human beings.

However, the polis is not only natural but it is also prior to the individual (*The Politics* 1ii, 1253a25, p. 11). The polis is prior to the individual in two senses. First, what is posterior in the order of becoming is prior in the order of nature. This is part of Aristotle's teleological view of nature whereby any natural process of development is directed towards some end. The end, which is the realisation of the nature of the thing, is presupposed during the whole process of development and knowledge of the end is necessary for understanding the process. Second, a thing is also said to be prior to other things when its existence is the condition for the existence of those other things. In the case of the polis no particular individual can live a fully human life without the polis. The polis, however, can exist without any particular individual, though not without all of them.

Blum summarises much of the above by providing six links between at least certain virtues and community.[22] First, virtues can be learnt only within certain forms of social life. Second, they can be sustained only in communities. Dispositions or virtues such as empathy and loyalty cannot be exercised outside of the community. The development and implementation of the virtues in a complete human life require that such a life be lived out with others engaged in a common project of attempting to live the good life. Only the material and cultural resources of the community allow this to happen. Third, a person's moral identity and moral agency itself as that which realises virtue is, in part at least, constituted by the communities to which the person belongs. However, as MacIntyre points out and as Sartre had recognised with his thoughts on baptism, the fact that the self has to find its moral identity within the context of communities does not mean that the self has to accept the moral limitations of those forms of community. Nevertheless, those forms of community do provide a starting point for the search for the good. Having said that, again echoing Sartre, MacIntyre goes on to say that,

> particularity can never be simply left behind or obliterated. The notion of escaping from it into a realm of entirely universal maxims which belong to man as such, whether in its eighteenth-century Kantian form or in the presentation of some modern analytical moral philosophies, is an illusion and an illusion with painful consequences.[23]

So it is that MacIntyre is able to argue that the concept of a virtue 'always requires for its application the acceptance of some prior account of certain features of social and moral life in terms of which it has to be defined and explained'.[24] So, fourth, it is communal life that provides the possibility for having knowledge of what a virtue means in terms of action (thus what it means to be honourable could mean one thing in the organised group and something quite different in the institution) and fifth, it is communal life that recognises that certain qualities are virtues. Finally, some virtues, such as trust, sustain communities.

These six links, when accompanied by the earlier Aristotelian analysis, address certain deficiencies in the communitarian position. We are, therefore, provided with an understanding of why and in what ways a community of a certain sort is a fundamental ingredient in the good life for human beings. It is a fundamental ingredient because its purpose is to promote certain dispositions and it is in the acquisition and exercise of these dispositions that the good life consists. It is in this way that the individual acquires those qualities that are a part of her identity and which inform her of what she is to do. Moreover, we are provided with an idea of a function of the community and of the relationship

---

22 Blum, 1994, pp. 146–48
23 MacIntyre, 1981, pp. 205–206
24 Ibid., p. 174

between the individual and the community. A function of the community is, as has been said, to promote certain dispositions and in turn these dispositions will sustain the community.

Although each of the six links between virtue and community are explicable from within the Aristotelian framework, reference to the praxis account of dispositions may serve to provide that framework with even more explanatory power. It will also, at the same time, provide further answers to Blum's earlier questions on motivations, sensitivities, virtues and responsibilities. The argument so far is that the virtues are dispositions of a certain sort but they are not innate dispositions, or inherited traits of personality. In addition to upbringing, which is affected by the praxis of others, they are acquired by practice and reflection on practice, that is, praxis, and to a certain extent reveal what we have made of ourselves. Thus they express our moral way of being, and our moral outlook and they are not just things we happen to have. Certain virtues are, therefore, essentially dispositions which are acquired as a result of the process of praxis which, as was seen in chapter two, always has a social dimension.

In order to understand that certain virtues are essentially dispositions which are acquired as a result of the process of praxis it is necessary to invoke two complementary ideas, that of the movement of interiorisation and re-exteriorisation and that of the states of transcendence and immanence. We have seen that the mechanics of praxis can be explained in terms of interiorisation and re-exteriorisation. It is in this way that, as Sartre says, 'Praxis makes society.'[25] However, it need not make just any old society because praxis has a normative aspect. Interiorisation and re-exteriorisation need not be processes that are neutral with respect to values. Ultimately, they are processes which are concerned with human needs and needs are indicators of values. Furthermore, the satisfaction of needs with the accompanying notion of freedom both in pursuit of and as a result of that satisfaction is an aspect of human fulfilment. When praxis is directed towards human fulfilment it requires individuals to be people of a certain sort and other than the sort to be found in the series where people may lack genuine positive reciprocity and personal responsibility. Moreover, being the passive consumers of objects and the ideas and values of others, serial individuals are mediocre, that is, lacking in those excellences which may be fostered and which are required and exercised by other forms of association. In order to liquidate the series and form the group-in-fusion individual needs are felt as common needs. The awareness of the existence of a common need, an awareness that occurs through praxis, indicates the importance of certain dispositions and in particular the disposition for empathy. Since everyone within the group is a third party to all the others everyone requires and exercises that disposition. Here the notions of transcendence and immanence become important. The relations of transcendence and immanence that everyone

---

[25] CDR II, p. 142

has with the group means that everyone is both leader and led. This means that everyone in the group is responsible for and dependent upon the common praxis. Thus in the group-in-fusion the praxis of the third party as both constituted and constituting, or as both immanent and transcendent, heralds a development of the moral personality.

The moral personality developed further in the pledged group through the praxis of the pledge itself. This praxis was an act of commitment involving, in addition to empathy, loyalty. The pledge as praxis is a constituting activity which, in Sartre's example, is constituting the individual not to be a traitor. It is, therefore, on the basis of that praxis and in order to sustain that praxis that the moral personality emerges more fully. The pledge creates self-assumed obligations or commitments and it does so because dispositions such as empathy and loyalty are inherent in the praxis of the pledge. Thus the pledge becomes a particular way by which the individual transcends her previous state. The moral personality continues to emerge in the organisation where, with the allocation of functions and the equivalence of rights and duties, further dispositions towards excellence associated with the proper performance of a function that will contribute to the attainment of the goals of the group are required.

The inherence of dispositions within praxis reveals that dispositions are dynamic qualities. Therefore, the praxis notion of dispositions is one that is, in many significant ways, quite different from the view of dispositions as settled states or habits. On the praxis view, dispositions, being both required and exercised by praxis, might change as praxis itself changes. Of course, people can change their habits but a particularly useful explanation for that occurrence is in any case to be found in the operation of praxis.

The explanation for both the dynamism of dispositions and their inherence within praxis is, therefore, to be found in the process of interiorisation and re-exteriorisation, which can be regarded as a transcending movement and the states of immanence and transcendence understood as conditions or states of affairs that are brought about by that process. The relevance to the praxis notion of dispositions of interiorisation-re-exteriorisation and immanence-transcendence is illustrated by Sartre's portrayal of Stalin in the second volume of the *Critique* which was referred to earlier in this chapter and which was commented on in chapter two of this work. In chapter two it was noted that Sartre recalls the importance of psychoanalysis as one of the mediations necessary within the Marxist interpretation of society and history by drawing attention to Stalin's interiorisation of his harsh childhood. However, Stalin's development as a leader was not arrested at that point. Stalin is described as 'an iron-fisted opportunist'[26] and as 'hard and aggressive'[27] and these qualities are associated with the twenty years that he had spent as a party militant. However, the dialectic of praxis must be kept in mind. In connection with Stalin, 'the historical process sustains

---
[26] Ibid., p. 101.
[27] Ibid., p. 102.

and carries the man who makes it. Thus opponents become traitors. Danger is discovered and reinteriorised as hatred'.[28] Having described Stalin as an iron-fisted opportunist, Sartre goes on to say that the circumstances in the USSR 'demanded a sovereign who would be a dogmatic opportunist'.[29] One should not assume that these qualities associated with the years that Stalin had spent as a party militant are in fact due to those years, 'a happy chance that had supposedly provided the sovereign individual with these qualities'.[30] On the contrary, these qualities are due,

> to a certain way of having transcended and preserved the common past whose particularity appeared in the light of the current praxis as the *developed truth* of the former practice and experience. Thus not only did praxis require individuality inasmuch as this was forged by praxis ... and so require itself retrospectively; but it was also current action that gave its meaning and its truth to the practical experience of the individual it selected.[31]

There is, therefore, a sense of accumulation or development which may be explained by the transcending movement of interiorisation-re-exteriorisation. Transcendence here refers to a condition of the individual, namely, one who has acquired a particular quality and has thus transcended a particular state. Transcendence can also be regarded as a movement and as such refers to the exercise of that quality to produce a new state of immanence. This movement is present in praxis. The immanence of qualities acquired and exercised by past praxis will always be intelligible in the transcendence of current praxis, on which basis will be formed a new immanence. It is in this way that qualities are dynamic. In this way praxis has a consciousness-shaping effect which has an effect on future praxis. Moreover, the qualities required and exercised by praxis can, on account of that praxis, be regarded as a choice of a way of life.

So it is that the praxis account of dispositions may provide the Aristotelian framework with even more explanatory power with regard to Blum's six links between virtue and community and at the same time provide further answers to Blum's questions on motivations, sensitivities, virtues and responsibilities. Each of the six links between virtue and community can no doubt be explained in a variety of ways but here the explanation will refer to the process of interiorisation and re-exteriorisation, that is, the transcending movement of praxis.

First, virtues can be learnt only within certain forms of social life in the sense that virtues are inherent in praxis itself as it works on the world. The nature of these virtues will vary according to the nature of the work. The process that is to be described is one that works throughout the life of the individual

---

28 Ibid., p. 64.
29 Ibid., p. 215.
30 Ibid.
31 Ibid.

and starts from the time that the individual is able to engage in praxis. It is not to say that the description of the process that is to follow is a description of the only way in which virtues are learnt but it is one way of understanding such learning. The results of praxis are interiorised as part of the movement of transcendence. Since the meaning of praxis is in part the meaning of the result, that meaning is also interiorised. Part of the meaning will be the virtues required and exercised by praxis in order to achieve the result. Thus those virtues are interiorised. Since all praxis has a social dimension so it can be said that virtues can be learnt only within certain forms of social life and praxis is one such form. Moreover, when the work of praxis is constituting of groups such as the group-in-fusion or the pledged group, then the virtues that will be interiorised will be those that are required by the constituting of those groups.

Just as virtues may be learnt through other sorts of processes so too may other sorts of processes work alongside the praxis account of the other connections between virtues and the community. However, again, it is that account that is of concern to us here. Therefore, second, virtues can be sustained only in communities in that communities are sustained by praxis. Thus the virtues that are interiorised on the basis of the constituting work of praxis continue to be exercised in order to maintain the community and for as long as the community is maintained. It is in maintaining the community that virtues are sustained. This dialectical process also realises certain motivations and sensitivities. These are inherent within praxis itself, normatively conceived. Responsibility emerges in the praxis of the third party. So it is that each of the terms of Blum's questions can be identified and defined in the light of the form of association at which praxis is aiming or within which praxis occurs. Third, this explains, therefore, a way by which a person's moral identity and moral agency as that which realises virtue can be constituted in part by the community. Fourth, it is communal life that provides the possibility for having knowledge of what a virtue is in terms of action in the sense that the meaning of praxis is given in praxis and part of the meaning of praxis will be the virtues exercised by praxis. Therefore, knowledge of what a virtue is in terms of action is already given in praxis of which virtue is a part. In the case of praxis that is constituting the group, the knowledge of what is required, including which virtues, will depend on the nature of the group being constituted. Fifth, it is communal life that recognises that certain qualities are virtues and again what it is that receives that recognition will depend upon the nature of the community that is being constituted and maintained.

The sixth connection, which is that some virtues, such as trust, sustain communities, raises a problem that has already been resolved by reference to the praxis account of dispositions. The praxis account of dispositions permits an understanding of apparently disparate elements in the relationship between virtue and community. How can that which is sustained by the community also sustain the community? More particularly, how is it possible for that which arises from the community as a constituting aspect of the identity of the individual be that which also constitutes the community? The response would be that praxis requires and exercises those dispositions that are required by the form of community at which praxis is aiming. It is in this way that the virtues are acquired and become part of the individual's identity. With reference to the second of these six points, virtues sustain communities in so far as they are inherent in the sustaining work of praxis and it is through the praxis of maintaining a community that these virtues are sustained. It is in this sense that it can be said that virtues cannot be exercised outside of the community, whatever form that community might have. In other words, it is through the dialectic of normative praxis that it is possible to understand the relationship between, on the one hand, communities giving rise to and sustaining certain virtues and hence the moral identity of individuals within those communities and, on the other hand, virtues sustaining communities and becoming part of those communities' terms of association. Thus it may now be seen that, as suggested in chapter three, virtues such as empathy and loyalty constitute both the framework conditions for a community of the sort recommended by Sartre to maintain itself and an essential part of the form of life at which those communities are aiming.

It must also be said that the insights derived from the psychology of moral agency serve to highlight a component of praxis that has hitherto been understated. The emphasis on the dispositions that are required and developed by praxis calls attention to the fact that praxis has an emotional dimension. Dispositions summon emotions and emotions have important work to do. What that work is and how it is carried out becomes clear in Sartre's *Sketch for a Theory of the Emotions*. There Sartre describes emotion as a 'specific manner of apprehending the world',[32] as 'a transformation of the world'[33] and most importantly as 'an organised pattern of means directed to an end'.[34] The similarity between this description of emotion and Sartre's later description of praxis will not be overlooked. This is not to say that praxis is a type of emotion or even vice-versa. It does, however, provide an insight into the psychodynamics of praxis. We know that praxis gives rise to and exercises certain dispositions and so we are able to assert that, in as much as praxis gives rise to and exercises certain dispositions, praxis has an emotional dimension which contributes to the comprehension component of praxis which selects the appropriate means to attain the end and thus, in a particular sense, transforms the world and, of course, in so doing, transforms the individual. The world is also transformed in the sense that the emotional dimension of praxis provides a particular way of thinking about the world and the transformations that are required. This, therefore, develops further the point of difference between Sartre and Kant. For Kant, it is rational autonomous agency that occasions respect whereas the

---

[32] *Sketch for a Theory of the Emotions*, p. 57.
[33] Ibid., p. 63.
[34] Ibid., p. 41.

Sartrean view is that respect is occasioned by praxis. Now that praxis is seen to have an emotional dimension this particular difference is deepened.

At this point it becomes possible to extend the explanatory power provided by an understanding of the process of praxis by applying that understanding to a different context. This application will lead directly to the development of a dialectical method for inquiring into the nature of associations based on that process.

Communitarians are not the only theorists to propose an alternative to the view of the individual and society proposed by certain sorts of liberalism. Certain feminist theorists, I refer here to radical and Marxist feminists in particular, have also proposed an alternative vision. Since many feminist theorists espouse some communitarian ideals, particularly those to do with embeddedness and the constituting nature of associations, the intention here is to focus on those criticisms made by feminist theorists but not by communitarians. In any event, as will become clear, some feminist theorists are also critical of certain aspects of communitarian thinking. It is possible to identify two complementary criticisms of liberalism which appear in some feminist theory but not in communitarianism. The first criticism concerns what is regarded as the unjustifiable dichotomy between reason and emotion. The second, complementary, criticism concerns what is regarded as the unjustifiable dichotomy between the personal and the political.

The first criticism can begin by showing why feminist theorists believe that emotions have an important role to play in moral understanding. Virginia Held argues that,

> We value emotion not only in the way traditional moral theories do – as feelings to be cultivated to help us carry out the dictates of reason or as preferences setting goals toward which utilitarian calculations will recommend rational means. Although such theorists as Mills and Rawls applaud the cultivation of certain appropriate feelings, they value those feelings for their assistance in carrying out the requirements of morality, not in helping us to understand what those requirements are.[35]

A feminist argument is that the emotions have a vital part to play in helping people to understand what it is that morality recommends. Held admits that there are harmful emotions but to rid moral theory of harmful emotions by ignoring all emotions would be misguided. She also addresses the idea that the individual will have to acquire an understanding of which emotions are appropriate, given that some are harmful. She argues that the requirement of understanding which emotions are appropriate is no more difficult to achieve than the requirement to understand what train of reasoning is appropriate for morality.

The significance of the emotions does not, however, reside only in their capacity to inform. A further significance, as the quotation above indicates,

---

[35] Virginia Held, 1993, p. 29.

resides in their capacity to motivate. The claim is that universal rules of morality do not, on their own, motivate people into action. The dictates of reason can be defied. The rational and autonomous individual may not care enough to do anything moral. Taking the example of the mother, in the sense of the person who performs the role of a mother, and the child, it is argued that the child is not cared for and neither does the child care for the mother because of universal moral rules. The reciprocity of love and concern between the mother and the child, when all is as it should be, motivates the making of decisions about what one ought to do and motivates much of what one actually does. Things may not be all as they should be for a number of reasons, one of which would be the absence of an emotional attachment. Baier argues that for Hume, moral theory is not a matter of obedience to a universal law, but of cultivating proper character traits.[36] The traits, or virtues, that are most important are those concerning relations with others. It is proper, then, to emphasise the importance of sentiment and the sympathetic showing of sentiment, rather than universal reason alone. Therefore, morality rests ultimately on sentiment, on a special motivating feeling we come to have once we have exercised our capacity for sympathy with others' feelings. Reasoned judgement becomes important when conflicts arise between the different demands that may be occasioned by sympathy.

Arguments for the significance of the emotions directly contradict Kantian arguments which, with one exception, show that they have no moral significance whatsoever. The exception is respect for the moral law.[37] Part of the argument for the moral insignificance of the emotions concerns their summonability and efficaciousness.[38] However, the part of the argument that is of interest at this point is the Kantian equation of emotion with nature and the Kantian contrast between nature and freedom. The usual argument is that emotions are not things that people choose to have, yet choice is a key feature of moral agency. It is possible to dispute this argument on the Sartrean grounds that some emotions are indeed chosen, or are summonable. However, a feminist response to the argument concentrates on the moral significance of choice itself. Again using the example of the mother and the child, it is an example which certain feminist theorists frequently use, it is pointed out that their relationship is not an entirely voluntary one. Of course, one may choose to try to have a child and if one is successful one becomes a mother. One can also choose to abandon a child. In that case one ceases to be a mother, in the sense of one performing that role. One cannot both be a mother and choose to abandon the child. As Held argues,

---

[36] Baier, 'Hume, the Women's Moral Theorist?', in Eva Feder Kittay and Diana Meyers (eds), 1987, p. 40.

[37] It has been suggested that the claim that only acts which are done from duty are morally good is compatible with allowing that emotions other than respect for the moral law can be morally good since it is possible, for example, that one could be motivated to act from love of doing one's duty. (Justin Oakley, 1992, p.88. On the significance of duty see also Marcia Baron, 1984, pp. 197–220.)

[38] For a discussion on this see Blum, 1980, pp. 30–33.

> A recognition of how limited are the aspects of voluntariness in the relation between the mothering person and child may help us to gain a closer approximation to reality in our understanding of most human relations, especially at the global level, than we can gain from imagining the purely voluntary trades entered into by rational economic contractors to be characteristic of human relations in other domains.[39]

The contractarian model of morality as a matter of living up to freely-chosen commitments is going to run into difficulties both with duties of parents to their children and with duties of children towards their unchosen parents. As Baier observes, 'This relationship, and the obligations and virtues it involves, lack three central features of relations between moral agents as understood by Kantians and contractarians – it is intimate, it is unchosen, and it is between unequals.'[40] A feminist argument, therefore, is that what is required is a moral theory that is capable not only of addressing the freely chosen activities of autonomous individuals but also of addressing the unchosen activities of individuals who are constrained by circumstances. In the absence of such a theory, mothering and women's behaviour in general may be interpreted as natural, driven by instinct, a biological activity and, therefore, not a source of moral experience or moral sensitivity and irrelevant to morality conceived of solely as rationality.

The characterisation of women's experience as natural, instinctual or biological introduces the second and complementary criticism which points to the dichotomy between the personal and the political. It has to be said that this is not a criticism that is levelled only at certain sorts of liberalism but at a history of moral and political thought that goes back to Aristotle. However, in what is to come those elements of the criticism that do apply to liberalism, though not necessarily exclusively so, will be the main concern. Having said that, and in order to set the scene, it is necessary to recall the traditional notion that it is in the public-political domain that man transcends his animal nature and becomes truly human. Women are to remain in the private-personal domain, reproducing and nurturing. A feminist argument is that what occurs in the home does not occur as if in some mysterious way isolated from or insulated against public political decision-making. It has already been said that seriality can affect the family. The personal is very much affected by external political power. This political power sets some of the most important conditions for the personal life in terms of, for example, maternity leave and allowances, health care, child care, occupational opportunities, earning capacity and so on. Held points out that, 'The result of the distinction between public and private, as usually formulated, has been to privilege the points of view of men in the public domains

---

[39] Held, 'Non-contractual Society: A Feminist View', in Hanen and Nielsen (eds), 1987, p. 126.

[40] Baier, 'Hume, the Women's Moral Theorist?', in Eva Feder Kittay and Diana Meyers (eds), 1987, p. 44.

of state and law, and later in the marketplace, and to discount the experience of women.'[41]

The concept of equality that is associated with the formal individualism of liberalism ensures that every rational individual is entitled to equal rights regardless of, amongst other things, race, class and gender. However, feminist theorists argue that real human beings are not individuals abstracted from their circumstances but instead they are constituted in part by the particularities of their race, class and gender. As such, human beings have different needs. Alison Jaggar argues that, 'No adequate philosophical theory of human need can ignore the facts of human biology: our common need for air, water, food, warmth, etc. Far from being irrelevant to political philosophy, these facts must be its starting point.'[42] Since human beings have many biologically based needs, humans can be understood only in relation to a world in which these needs may be satisfied. Young agrees, linking the satisfaction of needs with social justice and democratic participation by arguing that, 'For a social condition to be just, it must enable all to meet their needs and exercise their freedom; thus justice requires that all be able to express their needs.'[43] Jaggar and Young are, of course, talking needs in general. However, certain features of women's biology may mean that occasionally their needs are different from those of men. Reproductive functions occasion needs for maternity leave, facilities for nursing and so on. The liberal insistence on formal equality makes it easy to ignore these needs, to deny that they are relevant and to argue that any attempt to meet these needs would amount to the granting of special privileges. From a feminist perspective, there is a hidden male bias in liberalism.

A feminist argument is that the mother-child model of social relations is a model that can include business transactions, economic arrangements and political affairs. However, the free market, rational contract, economic man model of social relations cannot include the mother-child relationship. People can imagine a society on the model of economic man, a society built on a contract between rationally self-interested persons because it is the model with which people are most familiar. They find it far more difficult to imagine society in any way resembling a group of people connected by relations of trust and care as with the mother-child model or to conceive of themselves as being in certain situations the 'mother' and in other situations the 'child'. In fact, these sorts of roles and relationships in addition to, as Jaggar says, the facts of human biology, transform the liberal problematic. Thus,

> Instead of community and cooperation being taken [by liberals] as phenomena whose existence and even possibility is puzzling, and sometimes even regarded as impossible, the existence of egoism, competitiveness and

---

[41] Held, 1993, p. 46.
[42] Alison Jaggar, 1983, p. 42.
[43] Young, 1990, p. 34.

conflict, phenomena which liberalism takes as endemic to the human condition, would themselves become puzzling and problematic.[44]

It is not enough to argue that it is perfectly legitimate for women to venture into the political domain. If women simply join men in that domain there will be no one left to speak for the personal domain. There will, moreover, be no one involved in the nurture of the next generation of self-interested contractors.

Sartre is not best known as a champion of women's perspectives. Grimshaw, for example, cites him, along with Aristotle and Schopenhauer, as a male philosopher whose view of women is a 'dreary one of misogyny'.[45] The argument here, however, is that the view of praxis developed on the basis of the *Critique* can perform useful functions for feminist theorists.

The nature of praxis sheds some light on the dichotomy between reason and emotion. As has been seen, dispositions are inherent within praxis. Praxis, therefore, has an emotional dimension. It also has rationality as one of its components in as much as praxis involves discerning the best means given existing circumstances towards an end which is itself given in praxis. Thus praxis contains within itself motive, cause and end and these will be influenced by both the rational and emotional aspects of praxis. Therefore, to talk of praxis is to talk of both rationality and emotion.

Moreover, to talk of praxis is, as Jaggar demands, to view needs as the starting point for political philosophy. A particular consequence of doing so will be examined in the discussion on the dichotomy between the personal and the political. However, in general terms, if needs become the starting point for political philosophy then the elements of a feminist critique of liberalism that arise from or are connected with a repudiation of the dichotomy between reason and emotion can be shown to be related. Thus the importance, morally speaking, of choice can be revisited in the light of one's own needs and in the light of the needs of concrete others to whom one might have an obligation to care and for whom the withholding of that care would be a mark of disrespect and an instance of injustice. An understanding of a person's needs involves a recommendation and a motivation for action. That is, they present certain demands that require a response. The idea that there are demands that require a response coupled with the reference to obligations and injustice means that there is a sense in which needs are morally significant. A perspective on praxis will take the related strands of the feminist argument which point to the moral significance of needs and will show that needs are morally significant in the sense that human fulfilment depends in part on their satisfaction and their satisfaction requires certain forms and terms of association. Therefore, the moral significance of needs resides in the fact that they point to certain ways of both acting and being in the sense of having certain dispositions, namely, those that constitute and sustain those forms

---

[44] Jaggar, p. 41.
[45] Grimshaw, 1986, pp. 36–37.

of association. The normative notion of praxis provides an account of how certain dispositions lead to human fulfilment and how they are part of what human fulfilment means. So it is that a perspective on praxis strengthens the argument from needs and in doing so adds a further strand to feminist arguments directed at the moral significance of the emotions.

Regarding the personal and the political, praxis performs two functions. As above it renders the dichotomy redundant at one level of understanding and, at another level of understanding, it also offers one explanation for its existence. An explanation for its existence involves the notion of interiorisation and re-exteriorisation. As Baldwin says, Sartre,

> holds that each of us typically interiorizes the conception of ourselves that others have of us, and since this conception is, broadly, a conception of our relationship to the forces of production, it is in terms of that relationship that we are prone to think of ourselves, even though these forces (tools, machines, etc.) only get their significance through the use we make of them. Thus, although productive machinery is such only because it is so used, the workers who use it typically define themselves in terms of their relationship to it because of their position within the relations of production.[46]

Precisely the same process can be seen in operation with regard to women. If anything the effects of the process are intensified since women may be regarded and may regard themselves as having no direct relationship with the forces of production and are thereby bereft of a position within the relations of production. When identity is conceived of largely in terms of such relations the individual who lacks an obvious relation of that sort may come to believe that she is, in the eyes of others, a non-person and so may become that in her own eyes. Thus notions of the roles of women, women's work, women's bodies are interiorised by both men and women and then re-exteriorised in terms of behaviours. These behaviours are interiorised in turn and so the process continues until it is halted by a moment of awareness followed by choice. With regard to women's work praxis has a special poignancy since, as with all work, women become instruments and as such suffer ontological alienation. This ontological alienation can lead to social alienation since not only does the worker objectify herself, she is also objectified by others. Where the realm of women's work is understood as the domain of the personal it means that, again, women effectively become invisible from the perspective of the political domain. This has further implications for reciprocity. Given that reciprocity is always concrete in that it depends on the work and goals of the individual, although reciprocity can be positive or negative, the invisibility of women means that the reciprocity with those in the political domain that is enjoyed by women in the personal domain will be negative. In other words, women's ends will not be served by the political domain and women become the means to the ends of those who occupy that domain.

---

[46] Baldwin, 1993, p. 212.

At another level of understanding it is also through praxis that the dichotomy between the personal and the political becomes redundant. The process of interiorisation is a process that fuels the movement between immanence and transcendence. It has been seen that communitarianism lacks an adequate notion of transcendence. Liberalism does too, although for a different reason. In liberalism, though not only in liberalism, transcendence is achieved by moving beyond the immanence of the home and becoming active in the political domain. Those who are confined to the domain of the personal are unable to engage in transcendence. However, this is a partial and, therefore, inadequate view of transcendence. In other words, if transcendence is defined as movement into the domain of the political then those who are unable to make that movement are deemed incapable of transcendence. However, once the dichotomy between the personal and the political has been rendered redundant a re-orientation of perspectives becomes a possibility. Thus reproduction and motherhood, traditionally regarded as natural or biological and hence entirely within the realm of the personal can be regarded as an act of transcendence for two reasons. First, the woman herself achieves transcendence, from not being to being a mother. As Held says, '*In both giving birth and mothering, the woman expresses the kind of woman she has chosen to be.*'[47] This is not simply transcendence within the domain of the personal. It is also a transcendence with political implications in terms of what the State expects from the mother and in terms of what she may expect from the State. In that sense mothering is a political act. Second, the process of conception and birth is perhaps the ultimate interiorisation and re-exteriorisation, the ultimate transcending movement. The emergence of new life impinges on the political domain in two ways. First, the new life also creates political demands in terms of health care, educational opportunities housing requirements and so on. Second, to quote Held, 'To give birth to a new human being capable of contributing to the transformation of human culture is to transcend what existed before.'[48]

Some feminist theorists have also been critical of certain aspects of communitarianism. They point out that communitarian communities will, by and large, be communities not only of men but also of women, and, it should be added, of other living and non-living things as well. The critics of communitarianism argue that communitarian communities offer no account of female needs. Nor, to use the language of this work, do they offer any account of female praxis or forms and terms of association. As Marilyn Friedman argues, 'Communitarians invoke a model of community which is focused particularly on families, neighborhoods, and nations. These sorts of communities have harboured social roles and structures which have been highly oppressive for women, as recent feminist critiques have shown.'[49] She points out that

---
[47] Held, 1993, p. 133.
[48] Ibid., p. 126.
[49] Marilyn Friedman, 1989, p. 277.

communitarians show no awareness of this state of affairs so that through their uncritical reference to community, communitarians may be regarded as propounding a philosophy which feminists should not wish to follow.

Okin elaborates on the oppressive roles and structures of which communitarians seem oblivious by arguing that the Aristotelian tradition espoused by MacIntyre is one that applauds not the good life, or even the good life for a human being but the good life for man. This was a life from which women, slaves and manual workers were excluded. In fact the good life 'not only excludes but *depends* upon the exclusion of the great majority of people, including all women'.[50] In other words, those with the leisure to engage in political and intellectual life had acquired that leisure on the back of the labours of others who were, on account of those labours, excluded from the good life. MacIntyre is criticised for not taking account of this. Furthermore, MacIntyre's suggestion in *Whose Justice? Which Rationality?* that there should be a redistribution of tasks does not go far enough.[51] What is required is a re-evaluation of the worth of those tasks. Such a redistribution and re-evaluation will require certain shared understandings. Okin is not optimistic about the possibility of this happening, pointing out that there are no shared understandings on the subject of gender.

The analysis of the forms and terms of association presented in this work would indicate that feminist theorists are justified in being sceptical of shared understandings and justified in believing, as Christine Sypnowich, supporting a Marxist position, says 'that it is only in community that individuals forge their personalities and define their interests, but not any community will do'.[52] However, without rehearsing the arguments yet again, both shared understandings and non-oppressive forms of community can arise from individual praxis combining with the praxes of others. It would appear that the form of association that comes closest to fulfilling the requirements of certain feminist theorists would be that of Sartre's organisation which has as its key terms of association quasi-sovereignty, mutual dependence, an equivalence of rights and duties, reciprocal participation and equality. As has already been indicated, that is the kind of association in which human fulfilment may be pursued and which might, in fact, be the result of that pursuit.

Not only can the view of praxis developed on the basis of the *Critique* perform a useful function for the feminist theorists but also the insights of the feminist theorists can contribute to an understanding of praxis in terms of how it develops. In the complete version of her article, 'What Do Women Want in a Moral Theory?', Baier argues that Rawls's account of the conditions for the development of a sense of justice needed for the maintenance of a just society 'takes it for granted that there will be loving parents rearing the children in

---

50   Okin, 1989, p. 52.
51   MacIntyre, 1988, p. 105.
52   Christine Sypnowich, 1993, p. 498.

whom the sense of justice is to develop'.[53] The same applies to praxis. It is important to remember that which Sartre accused Marx of forgetting, namely, that people do not come into the world as workers. In this case the thing to remember is that people are not born with a fully fledged capacity for praxis. That capacity is the result, in part, of a process of nurturing which is itself a praxis. This provides us with a different view of the social nature of praxis. It is not only that the praxis of any individual will have social implications. It is also the case that the capacity for praxis develops, in part, on the basis of a chain of praxes reaching back into the past.

To sum up, feminist theorists, therefore, provide a reminder of two particular dimensions of praxis. Again, we can refer to the example of mothering. First, the significance of the example of mothering as a praxis is partly dependent upon the significance of emotion as a source of understanding. However, as has already been indicated, the significance of the emotional component of praxis is not limited to understanding in any passive sense of understanding. In the case of mothering the understanding produces action. Second, although we should be alert to the idea that there is probably no single way of characterising motherhood, mothering can be considered as a paradigm for the satisfaction of needs, for the development and maintenance of human relationships, for care and concern and for movement into the future. Mothering is a series of decisions made and actions performed in the light of certain obligations. In other words, the example of motherhood serves to emphasise that which was mentioned in chapter two in connection with praxis's own understanding of the existence of a lack, in chapters four and six in connection with the relationship between cause and end, in chapter five in connection with the individual's awareness of his isolation and impotence and earlier in this chapter in connection with the dichotomy between reason and emotion, which is that praxis has a motivational dimension. It is this dimension of praxis that marks a further particular difference between Sartre's dialectic and the dialectic of both Hegel and Marx.

With the completed view of praxis as both dialectical and normative in character we arrive, incidentally, at a view of praxis as that activity which not only realises external goods, of the sort that will satisfy certain needs, but which will also realise internal goods and thus satisfy a wider range of needs. Given the argument in chapter five, this view of praxis reveals that there is a contradiction involved in treating any agent as a commodity. This is because, like practices, all praxis realises certain dispositions and involves an aspiration to attain that which is deemed to be of value. Therefore, the more that one is active the less one becomes a commodity. This is not to say that agents won't be treated as commodities. It is just that there is a contradiction involved when that happens.

---

[53] Baier, 1994, p. 6. 'What Do Women Want in a Moral Theory?' Originally published in *Nous*, vol. 19, no. 1, March 1985, pp. 53–63.

Having now established a fully developed view of process of praxis it is possible to examine the final issue. It has been seen that the process of praxis is a dialectical process. Throughout this work reference has been made to the dialectical method of inquiry and to the possibility of a dialectical reason. Sartre has argued that the dialectical method of inquiry is indistinguishable from the dialectical process of praxis, that the method can be derived from the process and that the condition for the possibility of dialectical reason is also that process. Yet, for the reasons given in chapter two, this was not something that he himself succeeded in demonstrating. The final issue to be explored, therefore, concerns the possibility of establishing the existence of dialectical reason or a dialectical method of inquiry on the basis of praxis, as opposed to any other kind of basis.

Sartre was himself unsure of the existence of dialectical reason. As was seen in chapter two, he qualifies his own references to it with the words, 'if it exists'[54] and nowhere does he claim that it does. The issue is a trifle confused because Sartre seems to draw the distinction made in the previous paragraph between dialectical reason and a dialectical method of inquiry. Clearly he writes as if there is a dialectical reason which may be distinguished from analytical reason. At other times, however, he writes of a dialectical method of inquiry as, for example, with his stated intention which is 'to establish the dialectic as the universal method and universal law of anthropology'.[55] Then again, his most frequent reference is simply to the dialectic which could mean one thing or the other, or possibly even both. Commentators can suffer from the same ambiguity. Stack, for example, argues that 'Sartre adopts a dialectical approach to social phenomena because he believes that the analytical conception of man and his social world treats man as a determinate object, a "thing" which can be understood in the same way in which a physical object is understood' and on the same page he writes of an 'analytical approach' and 'analytical reason'.[56] In another publication Stack concludes that Sartre 'does not describe the nature of dialectical thinking as distinguishable from inductive or deductive reasoning, but, rather, appeals to the nature of human experience in its actuality'.[57] As has been seen in chapter two, Stack goes on to set out the conditions for the possibility of dialectical reason, arguing that 'if a dialectical interpretation of individual or group *praxis* (and of the original dependent relationship of man upon the material world) is plausible, and if it is possible to grasp the complex reciprocity of social relationships and show their intelligibility, then dialectical reason is possible'.[58] It will be recalled from chapter two that Sartre also sets out the conditions for the possibility of dialectical reason saying that 'a dialectic exists if, in at least one ontological region, a totalisation is in progress which is

---

[54] CDR I, p. 44. See also ibid., p. 58.
[55] Ibid., p. 18.
[56] Stack, 1971, p. 396.
[57] Stack, 1977, p. 78.
[58] Ibid., p. 81.

immediately accessible to a thought which unceasingly totalises itself in its very comprehension of the totalisation from which it emanates and which makes itself its object'.[59]

The problem is compounded because, as was also seen in chapter two, Sartre defines dialectical reason in terms of its capacity for totalisation, arguing that totalisation does occur but that it cannot be grasped by analytical reason. The problem arises not so much because dialectical reason is said to exist by virtue of the failure of analytical reason but because Sartre's own example of a totalisation is history itself which, in the event, was a totalisation too grand even for Sartre. The indeterminateness of Sartre's chosen totalisation is such that it also eludes dialectical reason and, therefore, cannot serve to validate the existence of dialectical reason.

There is a final problem that must be resolved before progress may be made. As was seen in chapter two, one can discover the dialectic only by being involved in the dialectic as a process of either reason or inquiry, or possibly both and by being within that which is being investigated, that is, situated within that which is being investigated and not an external observer. The traditional, that is, Kantian, notion of a critique demands a separation of the knower and the known, or a de-situated knower. Therefore, the dialectical insistence on setting the knower within being could render a critique of dialectical reason a contradiction in terms. However, the dialectical method and/or reason is a mode of comprehension of social phenomena and the individual is able to understand the dialectical character of social phenomena because she both experiences that dialectical character and is, in her praxis, involved in its creation. Thus, according to Sartre, 'dialectical investigation (l'expérience dialectique) has emerged as *praxis* elucidating itself in order to control its own development'.[60] This is because, 'It is in praxis itself, in so far as it objectifies itself, that we will find the new moment of dialectical intelligibility, which constitutes the result of the negation of the undertaking'.[61]

So it is that progress may be made on the final issue to be explored. Praxis has a dialectical structure. However, does the existence of that structure establish the existence of a dialectical reason or a dialectical method of inquiry? The claims made by Sartre have been noted. What is required is attention to praxis itself. From this will come an attempt to elucidate the dialectical method, if not reason, and finally, the testing of that method on something that is a known social phenomenon to see if it reveals the kind of intelligibility that it claims. In short, the equivalence of praxis and the dialectical method will be tested against a manageable totalisation.

---

[59] CDR I, p. 44. Note that 'a dialectic' here can be taken to refer to dialectical reason since it follows directly from the passage in which Sartre questions the existence of dialectical reason.
[60] Ibid., p. 220.
[61] Ibid., p. 160.

The starting point is to identify the relevant features of praxis for determining the existence of dialectical reason or a dialectical method of inquiry and to go on to show that the processes at work will in themselves reveal a way of pursuing intelligibility. The relevant features of praxis for determining the existence of dialectical reason or a dialectical method of inquiry are that praxis stems from need, involves the negation of a negativity, operates according to a law by which, in a two-way movement, people are mediated by things to the extent that things are mediated by people, and involves a process of interiorisation and re-exteriorisation which is a process by which immanence and transcendence, understood as conditions or states of affairs, come into being since the process of interiorisation and re-exteriorisation is the dynamic of transcendence understood as the movement between those two states. Of course, we must remember that mention of two states is intended to aid clarity. As has already been said and as will be made more explicit, what is being considered is not two independent states but a totalisation in progress. The end, after all, is given in praxis. Both immanence and transcendence are known to praxis. Praxis has to have a motivational dimension and, therefore, must know that which is to be. The process of interiorisation is also the process by which the components of the states of immanence and transcendence and the relationships between them and their relationship with the totalisation, which is in any case part of their meaning and of the meaning of the totalisation, become known to praxis and the process of re-exteriorisation is the process by which those components, now changed and thus re-related with each other, produce the state of transcendence and hence a new state of immanence, that is, a new totalisation. The idea that praxis can reveal the components of the states of immanence and transcendence was flagged in the discussion on methodology in chapter two. It should be noted that these components may contradict or conflict with each other and these contradictions or conflicts will have to be resolved by praxis itself in the light of the internal factors such as dispositions and the external factors such as institutions, both of which are generated by praxis, and the relationship between these factors that might prevail. This point will become clearer through the use of an example which is to follow shortly. Thus praxis is also both transformative and totalising. In this portrayal of a dialectical method of inquiry, praxis will be described as a transcending movement or a movement of transcendence. That description encompasses the idea of praxis being both immanent and transcendent.

A criticism of Sartre's notion of the dialectic has been made by George Kline who argues that Sartre's dialectic is a 'truncated dialectic, a dialectic without synthesis, without reconciliation'.[62] However, as Bertell Ollman points out, illuminating another difference between Sartre's dialectic and that of Hegel, 'Dialectics is not a rock-ribbed triad of thesis – antithesis – synthesis that serves

---

[62] George Kline, 'The Existential Discovery of Hegel and Marx', in Warnock (ed.), 1971, p. 298.

as an all purpose explanation.'[63] Similarly, Roy Bhaskar denies that dialectical processes are 'invariably, or even typically, triadic in form'.[64] A response to Kline involves a reference to and an elaboration upon the notion of transcendence as a movement but not necessarily one of reconciliation. In order to establish the existence of a dialectical method of inquiry whose existence can be demonstrated through the operation of praxis it is necessary to refer to Sartre's notion of the negation of the negativity, first encountered in chapter two in connection with need and praxis. It has already been established that praxis is not something directed from outside by something material that remains exterior to it. Rather, a particular praxis inscribes itself on the material world and creates specific conditions. Its successor encounters the conditions created by the first praxis. Each praxis must cope with the results of the previous praxis as a situation to be transcended. This is a dialectic which, in the most general terms, proceeds from a state of affairs or condition, a state of immanence, in which it is possible to identify a lack or negativity, on to the negation of the negativity as the transformative action of praxis understood as a transcending movement, and so on to totalisation, a state of transcendence which is the result of the negation of the negativity. Each stage is marked and instigated by praxis. It should be noted that any condition or state of affairs is not simply what it appears at a particular time and place to a particular person. That condition, viewed under different circumstances or by another person, might produce quite a different conclusion. A clearer understanding of a particular state of affairs may require adjustments of viewpoint. This could become apparent when an individual praxis encountered the praxis of another, or if the individual decided to engage in the process of abstraction that is described below.

Although praxis is inherent in both immanence and transcendence as states and these states are two dimensions of the dialectic and although praxis is a transcending movement, which is the third dimension, it can also be considered as a fourth, cohering, dimension. This is not to say that it can be considered apart from either immanence or transcendence as states, any more than those states can be considered apart from praxis. It is to say that praxis achieves the states of immanence and transcendence through the transformative movement of transcendence yet it can never be reduced to those states. Bhaskar appears to argue along similar lines when he says that 'the character of human praxis as transformative agency mean[s] that, in making, we cannot replicate the conditions of our making, we must negate or absent, that is to say, change them'.[65] Thus praxis emerges as a fourth cohering dimension due to it also being a transcendent movement in so far as it links the states of immanence and transcendence even whilst engaged in change.

---

[63] Bertell Ollman, 1993, p. 10.
[64] Roy Bhaskar, 1993, p. 3.
[65] Ibid., pp. 190, 341.

Immanence can be regarded as a condition or a state of affairs in which the organism happens to be. However, the condition or the state of affairs that is now immanence was not always so. At some time that condition or state of affairs was a transcendent condition or state. So it is that immanence is never just immanence. To be understood an element of transcendence must be recognised within immanence, as the ground of immanence with immanence being recognised as the ground of transcendence. Similarly, transcendence is never simply transcendence because it must always refer to a state or condition, immanence, that is being transcended as well as to a future state or condition that will become immanence. Transcendence, therefore, contains both retrospectively and prospectively an element of immanence. However, these observations do not, by themselves, establish the existence of a dialectical method, far less a dialectical reason. These observations can be regarded as two analytical moments and if one is to take Sartre's argument seriously these moments must be located within a wider dialectical framework. That is to say, they must be motivationally connected producing the indistinction of immanence and transcendence mentioned in chapter two.

The notion of the indistinction of immanence and transcendence is useful in that it explains how the individual is within the known even as the known is being changed by the process of interiorisation and re-exteriorisation. The movement to the state of transcendence provides the knower with a critical capacity even whilst immanent to the known. In other words, there are not two independent states, one known and the other not known both of which, without any explanation, contain the knower. The two states are motivationally connected through praxis which allows the knowing to occur. However, the epistemological use of the notion of immanence-transcendence must itself be explained in terms of a movement. It is in *The Problem of Method* that a clue to the understanding of the nature of praxis as a transcending movement is to be found. Sartre argues that,

> In relation to the given, the praxis is negativity; but what is always involved is the negation of a negation. In relation to the object aimed at, *praxis* is positivity, but this positivity opens to the 'non-existent,' to what *has not yet been*. A flight and a leap ahead, at once a refusal and a realization, the project retains and unveils the surpassed reality which is refused by the very moment which surpassed it.[66]

Busch comments that 'Surpassing is still understood in terms of negation; the given is always encountered in terms of the temporal upsurge toward the future (the not yet). However, Sartre now adds the notion of *retention*, admitting thereby that the given leaves its mark upon the surpassing subject.'[67] Busch points out that Sartre emphasises the notion of retention by arguing that, 'To surpass . . . is

---

[66] *The Problem of Method*, p. 92.

also to preserve.'[68] As was seen earlier in this chapter, Stalin's qualities were due to the way in which the past had been transcended and preserved.[69] Thus the dialectic involves a movement into the future which will always retain something of the past and, indeed, this is one way in which praxis, encountering the results of previous praxis, may be understood. If the notion of preservation sits uneasily with the notion of transformation then it can be addressed with reference to the notion of motivation which is at the heart of the negation of a negativity or of transcendence as a movement and without which there would be no movement, no transcendence as a state and hence no dialectic as it is being currently conceived. Thus preservation might simply be the memory of what was, as is the case with the negative presence of seriality in the pledged group. In the event, of course, change is rarely total. Not even the existential notion of a choice of who to be is that radical, nor can it be if the notion of personhood itself is to be sustained. In order to complete the dialectic it must also be said that the present was itself, at one time, a movement into the future.

A more obviously Hegelian, in the sense of being triadic though not synthesising but reconciling, yet in terms of process relatively unmotivated, approach to the dialectic yields the same result with regard to transcendence as a movement and at the same time offers a slightly different perspective on the meaning of that movement. On the basis of the observations concerning immanence and transcendence that have been made so far it can be said that immanence and transcendence can be regarded as two temporally differentiated moments or states of affairs within the same process or movement of transcendence and every such movement will contain those states. So it is that one may begin to understand what that movement means. The negative of immanence as a state is transcendence and the negative of transcendence as a state is immanence and each state contains its respective negativity. The negativities of immanence and transcendence indicate the contradictory nature of each notion. Given the objections that attend the affirmation of a contradictory state of affairs it becomes necessary to avoid the contradiction contained within each notion.[70] It is necessary, therefore, to establish a further notion which contains within it the conceptual content of the two previous notions less their contradictory elements. In other words, the negative of the negative must be a positive result that preserves the two previous notions but avoids the contradictions that each

---

[67] Busch, 1991, p. 29.
[68] Ibid. See *The Problem of Method*, p. 101.
[69] CDR II, p. 215.
[70] Sartre himself points to the importance of recognising contradictions in talking of needs and the organic need for the inorganic. As was seen in chapter two, he argues that, 'The original negation, in fact, is an initial contradiction between the organic and the inorganic'. (CDR I, p. 80) The satisfaction of need or the negation of the negation in this case is achieved 'through the transcendence of the organic towards the inorganic' (ibid.) in a totalising movement that attends to the contradiction. It is this negation of a negation that, in non-Hegelian terms, constitutes the movement of transcendence towards the state of transcendence.

contains, thus uniting them by modifying their meaning and hence arriving at the meaning of transcendence as a movement which will contain those two states. Furthermore, the positive result must allow for more movement.

It is not easy to see what the outcome of this modification and unification might be. One candidate might be the category of being but it has to be rejected. Being clearly involves immanence but it could be argued that being is simply immanence and in itself allows for no transcendence to a new immanence. The category that most obviously embodies both immanence and transcendence, whilst avoiding their contradictoriness is becoming. Becoming must first embody immanence because its immanence consists in what is already there and second it must embody transcendence because that represents its fullest manifestation as a process. Moreover, leaving the Hegelian approach to the dialectic behind, the notion of becoming allows for new movement into the future, new notions of interiorisation and re-exteriorisation, new notions of immanence and transcendence and this is all based on praxis. It can, furthermore, be rooted in something concrete, namely need, from which stems praxis. It is, for that reason, a circular or spiralling process that avoids mystification. Thus the movement of transcendence can be regarded as the movement of becoming.

All that remains to be done to establish beyond doubt the existence of a dialectic as a valid form of methodology, as understood on the basis of praxis, is to see if it works. In other words, will it, as Stack demands, permit a particular interpretation of praxis and provide a grasp of the complex reciprocity of social relationships, and will it, as Sartre demands, provide an understanding of a totalisation in progress which is accessible to a thought which unceasingly totalises itself? To see if it works in accordance with those conditions attention will now be turned yet again to motherhood, the example we saw favoured by certain feminist theorists, as an example of an association, a complex social relationship and a totalisation in progress. In turning to a particular example it will be seen that a further aspect of this dialectical methodology, that concerning the components of states, will become clearer.

To the question, 'What is a mother?' the analytical approach might reply, 'A woman with a child,' or perhaps, 'Someone who has a certain relationship with a child and performs certain functions'. That approach might go on to list the characteristics of that relationship and go on to detail the functions performed. A dialectical approach provides quite a different set of responses, although, by now, due to both familiarity with the approach and, connected with that familiarity, more importantly for those who are in this position, an insider awareness of the praxis of mother-child relationships, none that should surprise. Whilst we should remember that there is probably no single way of characterising motherhood what should also become apparent is that what motherhood means for a particular individual will be revealed by praxis.

Motherhood has already been referred to as a state of transcendence but what that state means becomes clearer with the application of a dialectical method of inquiry as established by the process of praxis. The immanent state is one in which this particular woman perceives a negativity, not having a child. The perception of childlessness as a negativity is motivational. Through praxis the negativity is negated. The transformative work of praxis as the movement of transcendence produces a new totalisation, the state of transcendence in which the woman has a child. This transcendent state contains the immanence of both the past and the future; the woman who did not have a child now does and now will face further movement. In other words being a mother is not simply a changed state, it is also a state of changing as the child changes. Looked at another way, though with precisely the same result, having transcended the state of childlessness, one and the same woman enters the immanence of motherhood. However, this immanence once was transcendence and, more importantly, will be the ground for transcendence, a state that will change as the child changes and in accordance with the praxis of the particular mother. This reveals a further insight. The true state of mothering is revealed as one in which one does not have a child in the way that one can have a bicycle, or some other possession, and having had a child is not like having had a meal, in the sense that once had it is all over. Mothering is a state of becoming which allows for new movement into the future. Thus the mother will have a child who is not yet of school age and then is an adolescent and each stage contains its own transcending movement and so movement into the future occurs, possibly into the state of being mother-in-law, grandmother and so on. Mothering can, therefore, be seen as a state of changing as the child changes, that is, as the movement of transcendence. Motherhood is a process and a relation between the parent and the child and with the past and future of that parent herself. Moreover, it is a relation that is occupied by a particular person. Thus to talk simply of a mother is to invoke an abstraction. This invocation, although a useful device, must be related ultimately to a concrete situation, to a particular mother.

It becomes apparent that motherhood is not simply a relation between parent and child and parent and herself. The functions or components of motherhood such as feeding, cleaning and training, which are revealed along with other functions by the praxis of mothering, are also relations. In other words, components such as feeding, cleaning and training each has a relation with the totalisation that is motherhood and that relationship is part of the meaning of both the component and the totalisation. This is necessarily the case by virtue of the formal law of praxis, that the individual is mediated by things to the extent that things are mediated by the individual. The two-way movement of this dialectic means that as the mother makes the meal she is being made by the making of the meal into a mother. Furthermore, if any of the components were to change, or rather, in the case of motherhood, as each of these components changes, for example from breast to bottle feeding, from toilet training to training in literacy, so too does the character of motherhood change. Moreover, at any time any of the components can be related to any or all of the other components and the meaning of each component is, therefore, also in part, the incorporation of all the relations that it has with all of the other components and that too will, therefore, inform the relationship between the component and the totalisation and, therefore, the meaning of the totalisation, that is, the meaning of the relationship between the parent and her child and the parent and herself. We should note that the interlocking nature of functions, each affecting the other, has already been examined in connection with functions in the organised group.

Two notes of caution are appropriate here. First, of course, motherhood is not defined simply by these three components. These three components simply serve to illustrate a complex process. Second, we should also remember that although the totaliser is part of the totalising process, the totaliser is not absorbed into the totalisation. In the act of effecting the totalisation the mother is apart from the totalisation of the components, that is, she is doing something else. The agent cannot totalise herself because the very condition of totalisation, transcendence by praxis, precludes her being an object for herself. She is not radically situated.

It should be noted that motherhood and its attendant components involves relations that are both social and natural in kind and one kind can inform the other. Understanding is not best served by attempting to restrict the social and the natural to separate spheres. Furthermore, these components, with their social and natural aspects, will affect each other, if they do, in reciprocity rather in terms of cause and affect. Given that perspective there is no determining factor that is not in itself affected by that which it determines and no cause that is independent of that to which it gives rise. This is not to say, however, that at a particular moment one component could not be said to have no greater effect on the others, or on the totalisation, than they or it does on that component. Here we have an extension of the notion of the interlocking nature of functions first examined in connection with the organised group.

The degree and kind of relationship that any component has with any other may change over time and may even disappear altogether. This is where the analytical process of abstraction, identified in chapter two as the regressive method can become a useful tool in dialectical methodology. In fact, a dialectical methodology based on the process of praxis does not require abstraction. Nevertheless, for the sake of thoroughness, it should be said that abstracting is another way of dividing the nature of motherhood into components. Thus the analytical method, can be part of a dialectical method though not of the dialectical method that is being described in this work. However, that which is abstracted, a particular component has, on its own, only limited value. More important is what the abstraction reveals about a further set of relationships. Once abstracted or separated from the totalisation any component can be examined to reveal the nature of the relationship that component has with any or all of the other components and with the totalisation at any particular time. The process of abstraction enables the investigator to put into different kinds of focus the components of motherhood. Taking feeding as a component of motherhood it can be seen that this is an abstraction that has a number of dimensions. First, it is an event that occupies a particular time and place. In other words, feeding has a range of meanings depending on when and where the feeding is occurring. We are no longer hunter-gatherers. In some places today some people will never eat purely for pleasure. Here comes the Christmas dinner. The investigator is free to establish her own boundaries of time and place in accordance with the nature of the investigation. Second, feeding also has meanings according to who is doing the feeding and who is being fed. Thus one can establish a degree of specificity with regard to feeding according to whether one is interested in the feeding of all living things, people in general, children in general or at different ages, or this particular baby. Extending and collapsing of both the boundaries of time and place and the degree of specificity can help the investigator to make connections with other components. Having established the time and the place, here and now, in this room watching television, and the degree of specificity, this particular baby, one can establish the meaning of the feeding and, as part of that meaning, its relationship with other components. The baby cannot be trained because she is distracted by the television. The baby is easier to keep clean when she is in her special baby chair in the kitchen. Of course, this can also be revealed to the praxis of the investigator who is located within the investigation and if it is it will be the result of the process by which praxis becomes intelligible to itself.

Although feeding, cleaning and training are different components in that they have different characteristics, involve doing different things and have certain goals that are different, they are in fact the same in that they are all forms of nurturing. These components of nurturing constitute, in part, the terms of the particular form of association that exists between the mother and the child. As has been said, there will be other components involved in mothering, other components that constitute those terms. Here there is a recognition of what Bhaskar, following Hegel, calls 'identities-in-differences or unities-in-diversities'.[71] However, whatever else might reveal this identity, such as the process of abstraction just described, it should also be pointed out that it can certainly be revealed by praxis. It is revealed precisely through the processes of interiorisation and re-exteriorisation. Thus they are recognised as the same not by recognising them as separate and static components but by recognising the reciprocity between them as being part of the same praxis of motherhood. Viewed in that way certain aspects of these components may be regarded as being in conflict or in contradiction with each other, aspects of one tending to negate aspects of another. Thus feeding the child is not conducive to training the child to feed herself, whilst training the child by insisting that the child

---

[71] Bhaskar, 1993, p. 10. The process also works the other way so that it is possible to recognise 'differences-in-identity or diversities-in-unity'. (Ibid.)

feeds herself may accomplish little by way of feeding and either or both of those processes are unlikely to keep the child clean. Yet keeping the child clean may preclude the possibility of any feeding. It is the maintenance of these contradictions in a degree of equilibrium that constitutes nurturing and it is through nurturing, that is, through that particular praxis, that the contradiction is resolved. Thus the interiorisation of the demands of these components reveals the contradiction that is resolved, temporarily at least, in the re-exteriorisation that is nurturing which becomes a constant process of interiorisation and re-exteriorisation. The circularity of the process may be noted. The conflict or contradictions between the various components which are resolved by praxis are in fact brought about by praxis and can be recognised through praxis.

Of course, contradictions can be compounded by the juxtaposition of internal factors such as the disposition to nurture the child and external factors such as those institutions that have a professional interest in matters to do with diet, hygiene and education and all these factors are also components of motherhood. The internal factors need not conflict with all or indeed any of the external factors, but they could. Furthermore, the internal dispositions could conflict with each other and the external institutions could contradict each other. Once again, these conflicts and contradictions, which are wrought by praxis, will be resolved by praxis. Moreover, since praxis stems from need and in so far as needs are indicators of values then these conflicts and contradictions are conflicts and contradictions between values.

It can be seen that motherhood, the state of transcendence, is itself a changing state. The familiar idea that everything changes is enlivened by the application of the dialectical method of inquiry which, in terms of the social experience of human beings, provides an understanding of the manner and the extent of change and allows that the manner and the extent of the change is part of the meaning of the state under consideration. If mothering is a state that changes as the child changes, this dialectical methodology reveals the demands upon the individual that mothering entails. However, it reveals these demands in a way that is, in two important and related respects, different from the way in which demands are revealed by the analytical approach and it reveals different demands with regard to the notion of having a child. This confirms and validates the existence of a dialectical method of inquiry on the basis of the process of praxis.

For that confirmation and validation to be clear it should be understood that immanence and transcendence have been placed in juxtaposition as two states in order to attempt to make the methodology clear. In fact, as has been seen, each state contains elements of the other and any movement from one state to another will itself be a movement of transcendence and thus the two states will be connected. Nevertheless, it is important not to confuse the movement with the state because the movement informs the state and thus the movement itself must be understood. It is in relation to this movement that the dialectical method of inquiry developed in this work differs from the analytical approach. It is not that this dialectical method reveals that there is a movement and that this is something that the analytical approach is unable to do. The analytical approach can describe, up to a point, the state of immanence and the state of transcendence in terms of their components. The analytical approach can also identify the relationships between the components of a state of affairs. In describing the state of immanence and the state of transcendence the analytical approach also reveals a movement. Finally, the analytical approach can also reveal the nature of that movement in terms of identifying those features of immanence that produce transcendence. However, it is at this point that the first of the two important and related ways in which the analytical approach differs from the dialectical approach becomes apparent. In so far as the analytical approach can provide an understanding of a certain state of affairs only at a particular moment and of another state of affairs only at another moment, it cannot use the nature of the movement between those states of affairs to inform its description of those states. In other words, the movement that is inherent in those states must be absent from the analytical moment. The movement in this case concerns the changing relationship between the mother and the child, the child and the mother and the mother and herself. These relationships also embody the components of those relationships as revealed by either praxis or abstraction. These components may also be changing, some certainly will be. The changes in these components involves a change in their relationship to each other and a change in their relationship with the totalisation and the interiorisation and re-exteriorisation which recognises and brings about these changes is part of their meaning and part of the meaning of the totalisation. All of this must be absent from the analytical approach. The analytical approach must exclude, therefore, from its understanding of a state of affairs the transformative, totalising work of praxis as transcending movement and as constitutive of that state of affairs. Thus although the analytical approach can describe different sets of relationships at the level of both states and components at particular moments in time, its analysis of those moments cannot capture the reciprocity of these changing relationships through time as a totalisation in progress.

It has been seen that the dialectical method of inquiry established on the basis of praxis is concerned with change, or with transcendence as a movement. As Ollman says, the dialectical method 'takes change as the given and treats stability as that which needs to be explained'.[72] In fact the emphasis on praxis as the embodiment of this dialectic indicates that the subject of dialectics is both relationships and change at the level of the continuity of states or moments and at the level of the components of those states or moments. Regarding relationships, praxis reveals different forms of reciprocity and reveals that different forms of reciprocity are part of the meaning of any sort of relationship. However, in the words of Bhaskar's epigram, the analytical approach must exclude from its understanding of a state of affairs 'the coincidence of

---

[72] Ollman, 1993 p. 3.

distinctions and connections'.[73] Regarding change, Ollman talks of the way that change is usually studied in the social sciences and asks,

> But what is actually taken as 'change' in most of these works? It is not the continuous evolution and alteration that goes on in their subject matter, the social equivalent of the flowing water in Heraclitus' river. Rather, almost invariably, it is a comparison of two or more differentiated states in the development of the object or condition or group under examination.[74]

Ollman goes on to provide the example of how a study of the changes in the political thinking of the electorate gets translated into an account of how people voted in particular years. The differences revealed by the comparison of these particular moments in time is what is called change. Ollman comments that, 'It is not simply, and legitimately, that the one, the difference between the moments, gets taken as an indication of or evidence for the other, the process; rather, it stands in for the process itself.'[75] Therefore, the dialectical method based on praxis, in contrast to the analytical approach, shows that how a thing happens is part of what the thing is and this has a bearing on relationships.

The concern with relationships and change and with the idea that how change occurs is part of what a thing is invokes the second of the two important and related ways in which the analytical approach differs from the dialectical method based on praxis. The analytical approach locates the investigator apart from that which is to be investigated. This dialectical approach locates the investigator within the investigation. In this way, the notion of praxis as a form of comprehension becomes important. Thus, first, not only is there a totalisation in progress, second, this totalisation involves a complex reciprocity of social relationships and both of these things are comprehensible to praxis. So it is that this dialectical method of inquiry can emerge as praxis elucidating itself, providing a grasp of the complex reciprocity of social relationships and an understanding of a totalisation in progress which is accessible to a thought which unceasingly totalises itself. It is the inability of the analytical approach in these two respects, that of the capture of movement and the involvement of the investigator, that also limits its ability to describe, in full, the nature of a particular state or condition, even at a particular moment.[76]

The dialectic based on praxis, in moving beyond its contradictions, does indeed uncover the new in a different manner to that which might be available to the analytical approach on its own. Moreover, the validity of the methodology may be verified by the observer situated in interiority, that is, to one who conducts an investigation by employing the method and who is involved in what is to be

---
73 Bhaskar, 1993, p. 190.
74 Ollman, 1993, p. 29.
75 Ibid.
76 Sartre repeatedly insisted that the analytical approach makes sense only within a dialectical context. See CDR I, pp. 59, 502–504, 561; CDR II, pp. 28, 35, 102. That is not a claim that is being made in this work.

known, as one involved in mothering, as one involved in both mothering and being a child, or in being a child. That said, the process of praxis has established the existence of a dialectical method of inquiry. Furthermore, it is a method that, by being practised, provides a structure for the exercise of reason and in that sense it can be said that dialectical reason exists.

Having established the existence of a dialectical method of inquiry and having established that it is a method that provides a structure for the exercise of reason, all that remains is the application of that method and structure to the communitarian notion of community in order to demonstrate that it is a methodology that should be of interest to communitarians.

CHAPTER EIGHT

Conclusion: the dialectic and the communitarian community

The previous chapter concluded by demonstrating that the process of praxis reveals the existence of a dialectical method of inquiring into social experience which can be regarded as providing a structure for the exercise of reason. All that remains by way of a conclusion is to apply that method and structure to the idea of community. Unfortunately, since it is an idea of community rather than an actual community that is to be examined, no conclusions can be drawn with respect to real conditions or states of affairs. It will be necessary, therefore, to talk of community rather in the same way as in the previous chapter there was talk of motherhood, with no particular instance in mind. The application will, therefore, be limited in that respect. Moreover, just as there is probably no single way of characterising motherhood, so too is there no single way of characterising community. In the case of community, however, the problem can be ameliorated to some extent by deploying the characteristics deployed by communitarians. Thus part of the aim of this conclusion is to apply the dialectical method and structure for the exercise of reason to the communitarian idea of community, that is, to show what the dialectical method of inquiry reveals about the nature of communitarian community; how the various elements are related.

A key theme in the forms of communitarianism that have been the focus of attention in this work is that communities are important because they are constitutive of the identities of individuals, a source for the conception and pursuit of the good life and a forum for the generation of shared meanings concerning social goods and their just distribution. These are things that communities either do or should do. The meaning and mechanics of the elements of this theme have been examined during the course of this work. However, for the sake of brevity, these elements as presented by communitarians will be the focus of attention in this chapter. Accompanying and informing these descriptions and prescriptions is the basis of a normative theory of associations which provides a particular view of the community. According to this view, the community should put into place certain values and practices of the sort that, for example, enable its members to most effectively satisfy needs and, relatedly, enhance their freedom thus enabling them to pursue the goal of human fulfilment. The intention in this chapter is to apply the dialectical method of inquiry that has been established on the basis of praxis to these descriptive and normative views of community.

For the sake of argument let us say that communitarians perceive the state of immanence to be a state of seriality. That is the state that communitarians wish to transcend. The recognition of both immanence as it is and the state of transcendence as it will be is interiorised resulting in an awareness of the negativities associated with what the communitarians identify as the immanent state of seriality, namely, the absence of attachments, the absence of shared interests, meanings or goals, impotence and isolation resulting in the struggle to satisfy needs, and the absence of freedom. This interiorisation is re-exteriorised as the desire to negate these negativities. At this point the communitarian is confronted with a real world problem. Is it possible for her to negate all these negativities with the transformative action of praxis understood as a transcending movement, or must the negation of the negation proceed in piecemeal fashion? It is an empirical question which need not affect the process of application that is being conducted here and which, therefore, need not detain the inquiry but it is a question which should certainly inform communitarian policy, assuming that the communitarian project is to instigate change in the real world. It also serves as a reminder of the temporal dimension of change, that the transcending movement can extend over lengthy periods.

The awareness of negativities is motivational, informing the negation of the negation as the transformative action of praxis, involving the re-exteriorisation of the desire for a state of transcendence in terms of action in the form of the negation of seriality and understood as a transcending movement leading to a new totalisation, a state of transcendence. As was seen in chapter six, this state of transcendence, the communitarian community, will be sustained, in part at least, by the negative presence of seriality. In this way the state of transcendence preserves an element of the state of immanence. Of course, if that negative presence is not maintained then there will always be the possibility of a return to seriality which would be a new movement of transcendence. The totalisation is, therefore, always open to further transformation. Indeed, even if the whole world were somehow to be filled with genuinely intersubjective communities, the possibility of their relapsing into renewed seriality could never be eliminated. What is important, therefore, is not to have a blueprint for an ideal future but to have an understanding of the kinds of things that communities are.

The totalisation will be a community that is not only constitutive of the identities of individuals but also has a view of the good for human beings and of the virtues that are part of that good and that are exercised by the pursuit of that good, and is an assembly of shared meanings concerning social goods and their just distribution. Of course, since these components have been derived from the work of different theorists it is quite possible that any of the theorists might object to the components derived from the others and thus, for that theorist, the state of transcendence might not contain those components. However, it will certainly contain components of some kind and if not those components then probably something like them. Each of these components will have a relationship with the totalisation that is the communitarian community and this relationship is part of the meaning of both the component and the totalisation. Were any of these components to change, as might be the case with the meaning of a social good such as health care, then that would change the nature of the communitarian community.

The components can also relate to each other. At any time any of the components can be related to any or all of the other components. For example, the shared meaning of a social good will be an aspect of a person's identity in the sense that it is an understanding, possibly a value or a belief, that is held by that person. Were that shared meaning to change that would involve a change in the person's identity and also a change in the totalisation. Similarly, a change in a person's identity may effect a change in the meaning of a social good. Accidents, disabilities, epidemics can be the occasions for new understandings of health care. The reciprocity of the relations between these components could, in the examples supplied, also occasion changes in the idea of the good for human beings and, therefore, in the identification of the virtues that are part of that good and which are exercised by the pursuit of that good. Furthermore, any change in the idea of the good, either by itself or in relation with any other component, could effect changes to either or both of the other components and at any time any component could be more influential than either or both of the others thus affecting either or both of the others and the totalisation.

So it is that there are relationships between identity, ideas of the good and shared meanings with their social and environmental dimensions and the other components that have been identified, those of shared interests and attachments, enhanced freedom and so on. The praxis that is inherent in the totalisation would show that these components are all elements of the meanings generated by the community in the sense that they are generated by the members who constitute the community. It is also the case, however, that some of these components could come into conflict or contradiction. A notion of the good that dictated obligations to a non-voluntaristic attachment might be an unwanted aspect of one's identity which the individual with her enhanced freedom might, in the absence of other considerations, seek to remedy. This becomes a way in which conflict can enter into a communitarian community and this will affect the meaning of the totalisation. Of course, if these components do come into conflict or contradiction it will be because of praxis. It can be praxis that recognises conflicts and it will be praxis that will resolve them. The point is that the relationships between the components are not necessarily mutually supporting of each other. They could be relationships that are conflictual or contradictory.

It is also the case that the ingredients or the components of a component can come into conflict. This can be illustrated by examining the role of internal and external factors. Again for the sake of brevity, the one example of an internal factor and the one example of an external factor attending the transcending movement of praxis that has been acknowledged in the previous two chapters will be recalled only briefly. As an example of an internal factor, it was seen in chapter six that dispositions are inherent in praxis and are required and exercised by praxis in, for example, its constituting activity. These dispositions are, in turn, in the two-way movement of the dialectic of praxis, sustained by the sustaining action of praxis on the community. As an example of an external factor, it was seen in chapter five that institutions are also the work of praxis, in this case in preventing a return to seriality. Therefore, praxis produces the internal and the external factors within which praxis must operate by mediating a reciprocal relationship between them.

The transcending movement of praxis has to accommodate both internal and external factors. Therefore, where health care is institutionalised, which is itself a praxis, it may produce a praxis which is at odds with those who are disposed to practice health care and at odds with those who are disposed to seeing health care practised. Those so variously disposed might find their understandings of health care are challenged and their dispositions thwarted by the institutional nature of health care. If this creates tensions then those tensions will be part of the meaning of the totalisation. This is another way in which conflict, which is the product of praxis and which must be resolved by praxis, can be part of the communitarian community.

Moreover, the institutions serving the community can conflict with each other. The institution of health care could conflict with an institution of security such as defence even though both institutions can be understood as social goods. Thus health care could conflict with defence in terms of the resources required to sustain them, especially financial resources. Furthermore, practices within institutions could come into conflict. Paediatrics competes with gynaecology for scarce resources. Any community could be well disposed to both health care and to defence and to the practices within both institutions and thus suffer conflict. Furthermore, the conflict that occurs can be a manifestation of the community's efforts to achieve or maintain a degree of unity. Indeed, as a demonstration of the capacity of the dialectical method of inquiry to reveal contradictions, this conflict can be understood as a conflict of values. In so far as these components arise from praxis which stems from need and in so far as needs are indicators of values then it is possible to understand how, for any community, community values can come into conflict. More specifically, any individual member of the community could experience a conflict of dispositions in respect of these two institutions and in respect of the practices sustained by those institutions. The internality of dispositions obviously reveals the complicating presence within communities of constituting and constituted individuals, each of whom could have something to say about the good life for human beings and the shared meanings of social goods.

Another factor wrought by praxis and with which praxis must cope is the non-human environment in that the communitarian community and its attendant components involves relations with the non-human environment. The way that individually and collectively people relate to the environment affects the way that people relate to each other as members of a community and the way that people relate to each other as members of a community affects the way that individually and collectively people relate to the environment. This means that the components of the communitarian community which at least in part are wrought by praxis, and their relationship through praxis with each other and with the totalisation, which is the outcome of praxis, will be affected by and will in turn affect the environment through the two-way movement of the dialectic of praxis.

Attending to the components wrought by praxis raises one final issue. The transcending movement inevitably involves change. The nature of that change becomes part of the meaning of the totalisation, the communitarian community. For example, the changing relationships between the components during the transcending movement are themselves part of the meaning of the transcendent state. However, the precise meaning of that movement of transcendence which becomes part of the meaning of the totalisation and, therefore, also the precise meaning of the totalisation itself will be available only to the individual who is involved in the transcending movement and the totalisation.

The dialectical method of inquiry that has been established on the basis of praxis reveals four things, which are not obvious to certain communitarians, one of which is not revealed to the analytical approach. Hidden from the analytical approach is the insight that communities and the individuals that constitute and are constituted by them are dynamic in terms of the relationships and the changing nature of the relationships that define them as individuals and as communities and this dynamic and change is part of the meaning of the community. To fail to understand that is to fail to understand in full the community. For certain communitarians one thing that should be obvious is that it is as mistaken to emphasise the priority of the community as it is for certain liberals to emphasise the priority of the individual. Another thing that should be obvious is that even communitarian communities can experience conflict as well as harmony. The final thing is that, taking into account the previous three points, communities as networks of interlocking reciprocities which affect and are affected by issues concerning identity, notions of the good life, shared meanings and human fulfilment are vastly more complex than communitarianism appears to appreciate. Of course, we could always say that we knew these things. The praxis view of associations provides us with a particular way in which we know that we knew these things.

In chapter one reference was made to the argument presented by Bick who draws a distinction between political philosophy and political theory. She argues that at the level of political philosophy the communitarian methodology is holistic whereas at the level of political theory it is particularistic and that these two levels, thus characterised, are not incompatible. This is because the claim that the particularist methodology is important at the level of political theory is, at the level of political philosophy, a universal claim that communitarians make about their methodology.[1] Reference was also made in chapter one to the distinction, noted by Neal and Paris, between theory and practice.[2] The dialectical method of inquiry that has been established on the basis of praxis also recognises the distinction between the whole and its parts and it acknowledges different levels of inquiry. However, it has the additional feature of bringing the whole and its parts, different levels of inquiry, and theory and practice, together in a symbiotic relationship which provides a degree of intelligibility unavailable to a methodology committed to the maintenance of distinctions bereft of connections. It is this feature of this dialectical method of inquiry, coupled with the demonstration of its use, that indicates that this is a method of inquiry that should be of interest to communitarians.

The claim in this work is not that a praxis view of associations nor the dialectical method of inquiry that is derived from that view can provide communitarianism with a fully-fledged political theory of its own. More modestly, the claim is that a praxis view of associations and the corresponding dialectical method of inquiry will help communitarianism to address certain deficiencies in its account of community and it provides a response to certain criticisms made by the defenders of liberalism. It seeks to do this by providing a particular view of the nature of associations. Moreover, the conception of praxis as dialectical and normative provides a basis for a normative theory of associations which can serve to justify communitarian claims for a particular sort of community that should put into place certain values and practices. The inquiry is, of course, unfinished. It has yet to be applied to particular communities. Indeed, it gives rise to further investigations. For example, having been explicated from within the context of Sartrean social anarchism, ideas on the nature and function of interdependency can be used to develop the arguments of other social anarchists. Murray Bookchin comes to mind. Moreover, in the course of this work reference has been made to certain theories of normative ethics in an attempt to understand the relationships, that is, the forms and terms of association that should obtain between the individuals who constitute and who are constituted by various forms of association. The next step is to develop a dialectic of ethics itself.

---

[1] Bick, 1987, p. 137.
[2] Neal and Paris, 1990, pp. 422–23.

Bibliography

Anderson, T. C. (1979) *The Foundation and Structure of Sartrean Ethics* Kansas: Regents Press
— (1993) *Sartre's Two Ethics. From Authenticity to Integral Humanity* Chicago: Open Court
Aoudjit, A. (1987) *A Critique of Existential Marxism* unpublished PhD thesis, Georgetown University
Arblaster, A. (1984) *The Rise and Decline of Western Liberalism* Oxford: Basil Blackwell
Aristotle (1976) *The Ethics of Aristotle. The Nichomachean Ethics* trans. J. A. K. Thomson, Harmondsworth: Penguin
— (1995) *The Politics*, trans. E. Barker, revised with an Introduction and Notes by R. F. Stanley, Oxford: Oxford University Press
Aron, R. (1975) *History and the Dialectic of Violence. An Analysis of Sartre's Critique de la Raison Dialectique* Oxford: Basil Blackwell
Aronson, R. (1973) 'Sartre's Individualist Social Theory', *Telos*, **16** (Summer) 68–91
— (1980) *Jean-Paul Sartre – Philosophy in the World* London: Verso
— (1985) 'On Boxing: "Incarnation" in Critique II' *Revue Nationale De Philosophie* (152–153) 149–71
— (1996) 'Introduction', *Hope Now. The 1980 Interviews* trans. A. van den Hoven, London: University of Chicago Press
— (1987) *Sartre's Second Critique* Chicago: University of Chicago Press
Baier, A. C. (1985) 'What Do Women Want in a Moral Theory?', *Nous*, **14**, (1) March, 53–63
— (1987) 'Hume, the Women's Moral Theorist?', in E. F. Kittay and D. T. Meyers (eds) *Women and Moral Theory* New York: Rowman and Littlefield
— (1994) *Moral Prejudices. Essays on Ethics* Cambridge, MA: Harvard University Press
Bakunin, M. (1950) *Marxism, Freedom and the State* K. J. Kenofit (ed.) London: Freedom Press
— (1990) *Statism and Anarchy* trans. Marshall Shatz (ed.) Cambridge: Cambridge University Press
Baldwin, R. N. (ed.) (1968) *Kropotkin's Revolutionary Pamphlets. A Collection of Writings by Peter Kropotkin* London: Benjamin Blom
Baldwin, T. (1993) 'Sartre and Cohen on Marx', *Stanford French Review*, **17** (2–3) 207–19
Barnes, H. E. (1963) 'Introduction', *The Problem of Method* London: Methuen
— (1974) *Sartre* London: Quartet Books

— (1981) 'Sartre as Materialist', in P. A. Schilpp (ed.) *The Philosophy of Jean-Paul Sartre* La Salle, Illinois: Open Court

Baron, M. (1984) 'The Alleged Moral Repugnance of Acting from Duty', *The Journal of Philosophy*, **18**, 197–220

Beauvoir, Simone de (1984) *Adieux. A Farewell to Sartre* trans. P. O' Brian, London: Andre Deutsch and Weidenfeld and Nicolson

Bell, D. (1993) *Communitarianism and its Critics* Oxford: Clarendon Press

Bell, L. A. (1979) 'Sartre: Alienation and Society', *Philosophy and Social Criticism*, **6** (4) Winter, 409–22

Bernstein, R. J. (1972) *Praxis and Action* London: Duckworth

Bhaskar, R. (1993) *Dialectic. The Pulse of Freedom* London: Verso

Bick, M. (1987) *The Liberal-Communitarian Debate: A Defence of Holistic Individualism* unpublished D. Phil thesis, Balliol College

Birt, R. E. (1984) *Alienation in the Later Philosophy of Jean-Paul Sartre* unpublished PhD thesis, Vanderbilt University

Blum, L. A. (1980) *Friendship, Altruism and Morality* London: Routledge and Kegan Paul

— (1994) *Moral Perception and Particularity* Cambridge: Cambridge University Press

Bree, G. (1974) *Camus and Sartre. Crisis and Commitment* London: Calder and Boyars

Buchanan, A. E. (1982) *Marx and Justice. The Radical Critique of Liberalism* London: Methuen

— (1989) 'Assessing the Communitarian Critique of Liberalism', *Ethics*, **99** (July) 852–81

Busch, T. W. (1990) *The Power of Consciousness and the Force of Circumstances in Sartre's Philosophy* Indianapolis: Indiana University Press

— (1991) 'Sartre on Surpassing the Given', *Philosophy Today*, **35** (Spring) 26–31

Camus, A. (1995) 'The Artist and His Time', in *The Myth of Sisyphus* trans. J. O' Brien, London: Hamish Hamilton

— (1961) 'Preface to Algerian Reports', in *Resistance, Rebellion and Death* trans. J. O' Brien, New York: Alfred A. Knopf

Caney, S. (1991) 'Sandel's Critique of the Primacy of Justice: A Liberal Rejoinder', *British Journal of Political Science*, **21** (4) October 511–21

Cannon, B. (1991) *Sartre and Psychoanalysis. An Existential Challenge to Clinical Metatheory* Kansas: University of Kansas Press

Catalano, J. S. (1986) *A Commentary on Jean-Paul Sartre's Critique of Dialectical Reason. Volume 1, Theory of Practical Ensembles* Chicago: University of Chicago Press

Caws, P. (1984) *Sartre* London: Routledge and Kegan Paul

Chiodi, P. (1978) *Sartre and Marxism* trans. K. Soper, London: Harvester Press

Cohen-Solal, A. (1988) *Sartre: A Life* trans. A. Cancogni, London: Heinemann

Craib, I. (1976) *Existentialism and Sociology. A Study of Jean-Paul Sartre* Cambridge: Cambridge University Press
Cranston, M. (1973) *The Mask of Politics and Other Essays* London: Allen Unwin
Crocker, D. A. (1983) *Praxis and Democratic Socialism: The Critical Social Theory of Markovic and Stojanovic* New Jersey: Humanities Press
Crocker, L. G. (1968) *Rousseau's Social Contract. An Interpretive Essay* Cleveland: The Press of Case Western Reserve University
Cutler, R. M. (ed.) (1985) *From Out of the Dustbin. Bakunin's Basic Writings 1869–1871* trans. Robert M. Cutler, Ann Arbor: Ardis
De Lue, S. M. (1971) *On the Marxism of Jean-Paul Sartre in the Light of Jean-Jacques Rousseau: An Analysis of the 'Critique De La Raison Dialectique'* unpublished PhD thesis, Washington University
Denise, T. C. (1973) 'The Concept of Alienation: Some Critical Notices', in F. Johnson (ed.) *Alienation. Concept. Term and Meanings* New York: Seminar Press
Desan, W. (1965) *The Marxism of Jean-Paul Sartre* New York: Doubleday
Dobson, A. (1993) *Jean-Paul Sartre and the Politics of Reason. A Theory of History* Cambridge: Cambridge University Press
Dolgoff, S. (ed.) (1973) *Bakunin on Anarchy. Selected Works by the Activist Founder of World Anarchism* trans. Sam Dolgoff, London: George Allen & Unwin
Doppelt, G. (1988) 'Rawls' Kantian Ideal and the Viability Of Modern Liberalism', *Inquiry*, **31** (December) 413–49
— (1989) 'Is Rawls's Kantian Liberalism Coherent and Defensible?', *Ethics*, **99** (July) 315–51
— (1990) 'Beyond Liberalism and Communitarianism: Towards a Critical Theory of Social Justice', in D. Rasmussen (ed.), *Universalism vs. Communitarianism. Contemporary Debates in Ethics* Cambridge, MA: MIT Press
Downing, L. A. and Thigpen, R. B. (1986) 'Beyond Shared Understandings', *Political Theory*, **14** (3) August, 451–72
Doyal, L. and Gough, I. (1991) *A Theory of Human Need* London: Macmillan
Dufrenne, M. (1980) 'Sartre and Merleau-Ponty', in H. J. Silverman and F. A. Elliston (eds), *Jean-Paul Sartre. Contemporary Approaches to His Philosophy* trans. H. J. Silverman and F. A. Elliston, Brighton: Harvester Press
Edwards, S (ed.) (1970) *Selected Works of Pierre-Joseph Proudhon* trans. Elizabeth Fraser, London: Macmillan
Elliot, R. (ed.) (1995) *Environmental Ethics* Oxford: Oxford University Press
Elshtain, J. B. (1995) 'The Communitarian Individual', in A. Etzioni (ed.), *New Communitarian Thinking. Persons, Virtues, Institutions, and Communities* Charlottesville: University Press of Virginia

Etzioni, A. (1995a) 'Old Chestnuts and New Spurs', in A. Etzioni (ed.), *New Communitarian Thinking. Persons, Virtues, Institutions, and Communities* Charlottesville: University Press of Virginia

Etzioni, A. (1995b) *The Spirit of Community. Rights, Responsibilities and The Communitarian Agenda* London: Fontana

Festinger, L. (1950) 'Informal Social Communication', *Psychological Review*, **57**, 271–82

Fitzgerald, R. (1977) *Human Needs and Politics* Oxford: Pergamon

Flynn, T. R. (1981) 'Mediated Reciprocity and the Genius of the Third', in P. A. Schilpp (ed.), *The Philosophy of Jean-Paul Sartre* La Salle, Illinois: Open Court

— (1986) *Sartre and Marxist Existentialism* Chicago: University of Chicago Press

Forsyth, D. R. (1987) *Social Psychology* Monterey: Brooks/Cole

Frazer, E. and Lacey, N. (1993) *The Politics of Community. A Feminist Critique of Liberal Communitarian Debate* London: Harvester Wheatsheaf

Fretz, L. (1980) 'An Interview With Jean-Paul Sartre', in H. J. Silverman and F. A. Elliston (eds) *Jean-Paul Sartre. Contemporary Approaches to His Philosophy* trans. G. Berger, Brighton: Harvester Press

— (1992) 'Individuality in Sartre's Philosophy', in C. Howells (ed.), *The Cambridge Companion To Sartre* Cambridge: Cambridge University Press

Friedman, M. (1989) 'Feminism and Modern Friendship: Dislocating the Community', *Ethics*, **99** (January) 275–90

Galston, W. A. (1980) *Justice and the Human Good* Chicago: University of Chicago Press

— (1991) *Liberal Purposes. Goods, Virtues, and Diversity in the Liberal State* Cambridge: Cambridge University Press

Garaudy, R. (1970) *Marxism in the Twentieth Century* trans. R. Hague, London: Collins

Gauthier, D. (1986) *Morals By Agreement* Oxford: Clarendon Press

— (1993) 'Between Hobbes and Rawls', in D. Gauthier and R. Sugden (eds) *Rationality, Justice and the Social Contract. Themes from Morals by Agreement* Hemel Hempstead: Harvester Wheatsheaf

Gauthier, D. and Sugden, R. (eds) (1993) *Rationality, Justice and the Social Contract. Themes from Morals by Agreement* Hemel Hempstead: Harvester Wheatsheaf

Giddens, A. (1973) *The Class Structure of the Advanced Societies* London: Hutchinson

Glendon, M. A. (1991) *Rights Talk. The Impoverishment of Political Discourse* New York: The Free Press

Goldman, A. H. (1990) *Moral Knowledge* London: Routledge

Gordon, H. and Gordon, R. (1995) *Sartre and Evil. Guidelines for a Struggle* Westport, Conn: Greenwood Press

Gorz, A. (1980) *Ecology and Politics* trans. P. Vigderman and J. Cloud, London: Pluto Press
Gough, J. W. (1957) *The Social Contract. A Critical Study of its Development* Oxford: Clarendon Press
Gray, J. (1995) *Liberalism* Buckingham: Open University Press
Grene, M. (1973) *Sartre* New York: New Viewpoints
Grimshaw, J. (1986) *Feminist Philosophers. Women's Perspectives on Philosophical Traditions* London: Harvester Wheatsheaf
Gross, R. (1987) *Psychology. The Science of Mind and Behaviour* London: Hodder and Stoughton
Grossman, R. (1984) *Phenomenology and Existentialism. An Introduction* London: Routledge and Kegan Paul
Gutmann, A. (1985) 'Communitarian Critics of Liberalism', *Philosophy and Public Affairs*, **14** (1985) 308–22
Hampton, J. (1980) 'Contracts and Choices: Does Rawls Have a Social Contract Theory?', *The Journal of Philosophy*, **LXXVII** (6) (June) 315–38
— (1986) *Hobbes and the Social Contract Tradition* Cambridge: Cambridge University Press
Hanen, M. and Nielsen, K. (eds) (1987) *Science, Morality and Feminist Theory* Calgary: The University of Calgary Press
Hartmann, K., 'Praxis: A Ground for Social Theory?' (1970) *The Journal for the British Society for Phenomenology*, **1** (2) (May) 47–58
— (1981) 'Sartre's Theory of Ensembles', in P. A. Schilpp (ed.) *The Philosophy of Jean-Paul Sartre* La Salle, Illinois: Open Court
Hayim, G. J. (1980) *The Existential Sociology of Jean-Paul Sartre* Amherst: University of Massachusetts Press
Held, V. (1987) 'Non-contractual Society: A Feminist View', in M. Hanen and K. Nielsen (eds) *Science, Morality and Feminist Theory* Calgary: The University of Calgary Press
— (1993) *Feminist Morality: Transforming Culture, Society, and Politics* Chicago: University of Chicago Press
Heller, A. (1976) *The Theory of Need in Marx* London: Allison and Busby
Hirsch, H. N., 'The Threnody of Liberalism', *Political Theory*, **14** (3) August, 423–49
Hobbes, T. (1994) *Leviathan* London: Everyman
Holmes, S., 'The Permanent Structure of Antiliberal Thought', in N. Rosenblum (ed.) *Liberalism and the Moral Life*, Cambridge, MA: Harvard University Press
Horton. J and Mendus, S. (eds) (1994) *After MacIntyre. Critical Perspectives on the Work of Alasdair MacIntyre* Cambridge: Polity Press
Howells, C. (ed.) (1992) *The Cambridge Companion To Sartre* Cambridge: Cambridge University Press

Jaggar, A. M. (1983) *Feminist Politics and Human Nature* Brighton: Harvester Press
Johnson, F. (ed.) (1973) *Alienation. Concept. Term and Meanings* New York: Seminar Press
Kittay, E. F. and Meyers, D. T. (eds) (1987) *Women and Moral Theory* New York: Rowman and Littlefield
Kline, G. L. (1971) 'The Existential Discovery of Hegel and Marx', in M. Warnock (ed.) *Sartre. A Collection of Critical Essays,* New York: Anchor Books
Knecht, I. (1980) 'Seriality: A Ground for Social Alienation?', in H. J. Silverman and F. A. Elliston (eds) *Jean-Paul Sartre. Contemporary Approaches to His Philosophy* trans. J. Bernauer and H. J. Silverman, Brighton: Harvester Press
Kropotkin, P. (1995) *The Conquest of Bread and Other Writings* Marshall Shatz (ed.), Cambridge: Cambridge University Press
— (1913) *Anarchist Communism: Its Basis and Principles* London: Freedom Press
Kukathas, C. and Pettit, P. (1990) *Rawls: A Theory of Justice and its Critics* Cambridge: Polity Press
Kymlicka W. (1989) 'Liberal Individualism and Liberal Neutrality', *Ethics*, **99** (July) 883–905
— (1990) *Contemporary Political Philosophy. An Introduction* Oxford: Oxford University Press
— (1991) *Liberalism, Community and Culture* Oxford: Clarendon Press
La Capra, D. (1979) *A Preface to Sartre* London: Methuen
Langer, M. M. (1989) *Merleau-Ponty's Phenomenology of Perception. A Guide and Commentary* London: Macmillan
Larmore, C. E. (1987) *Patterns of Moral Complexity* Cambridge: Cambridge University Press
Lehning, A. (ed.) (1974) *Michael Bakunin: Selected Writings,* trans. Steven Cox and Olive Stevens, New York: Grove Press
Lessnoff, M. (ed.) (1990) *Social Contract Theory* New York: New York University Press
Lottman, H. R. (1981) *Albert Camus. A Biography* London: Picador
MacIntyre, A. (1981) *After Virtue. A Study in Moral Theory* London: Duckworth
— (1988) *Whose Justice? Which Rationality?* London: Duckworth
Malatesta, E. (1942) *Anarchy* London: Freedom Press
Manser, A. (1967) *Sartre. A Philosophical Study* London: Athlone Press
— (1971) 'Praxis and Dialectic in Sartre's Critique', in M. Warnock (ed.) *Sartre. A Collection of Critical Essays* New York: Anchor Books
Maundrell, R. (1992) *Sartre and Liberalism* unpublished PhD thesis, University of Waterloo
Maximoff, G. P. (ed.) (1953) *The Political Philosophy of Bakunin: Scientific Anarchism* London: Collier-Macmillan

McBride, W. L. (1991) *Sartre's Political Theory* Indiana: Indiana University Press
McLellan, D. (1977) *Karl Marx. Selected Writings* Oxford: Oxford University Press
Meadows, D. H. and D. L. and Randers, J. (1992) *Beyond the Limits. Global Collapse or a Sustainable Future* London: Earthscan Publications
Merleau-Ponty, M. (1974) *Adventures of the Dialectic* trans. J. Bien, London: Heinemann
Midgley, M. (1995) 'Duties Concerning Islands', in R. Elliot (ed.) *Environmental Ethics* Oxford: Oxford University Press
Miller, D. (1984) *Anarchism* London: J. M. Dent and Sons Ltd.
— (1995) 'Introduction', *Pluralism, Justice, and Equality* D. Miller and M. Walzer (eds), Oxford: Oxford University Press
Miller, D. and Walzer, M. (eds) (1995) *Pluralism, Justice, and, Equality* Oxford: Oxford University Press
Mouffe, C. (1990) 'Rawls: Political Philosophy Without Politics', in D. Rasmussen (ed.) *Universalism vs Communitarianism. Contemporary Debates in Ethics* Cambridge, MA: MIT Press
Mulhall, S. and Swift, A. (1992) *Liberals and Communitarians* Oxford: Blackwell
Neal, P. and Paris, D. (1990) 'Liberalism and the Communitarian Critique: A Guide for the Perplexed', *Canadian Journal of Political Science*, **XXIII** (3) September, 419–39
Noddings, N. (1984) *Caring: A Feminine Approach to Ethics and Moral Education* Berkeley: University of California Press
— (1990) 'A Response', *Hypatia*, **5** (1) Spring, 120–26
Noone Jr., J. B. (1980) *Rousseau's Social Contract. A Conceptual Analysis* Athens: University of Georgia Press
Oakley, J. (1992) *Morality and The Emotions* London: Routledge
Okin, S. M. (1989) *Justice, Gender, and the Family* New York: Basic Books
— (1989) 'Humanist Liberalism' in N. Rosenblum (ed.) *Liberalism and the Moral life* Cambridge, MA: Harvard University Press
Ollman, B. (1993) *Dialectical Investigations* London: Routledge
Pateman, C. (1979) *The Problem of Political Obligation* Chichester: John Wiley and Sons
Pepper, D. (1989) *The Roots of Modern Environmentalism* London: Routledge
Peterson, J. (1981) *Towards A Concrete Sartrean Moral Philosophy* unpublished PhD thesis, University of Colorado: Boulder
Plamenatz, J. P. (1968) *Consent, Freedom and Political Obligation* London: Oxford University Press
Poster, M. (1979) *Sartre's Marxism* London: Pluto Press
Proudhon, P-J. (1979) *The Principles of Federalism* trans. Richard Vernon, Toronto: University of Toronto Press

Rasmussen, D. (ed.) (1990) *Universalism vs Communitarianism. Contemporary Debates in Ethics* Cambridge, MA: MIT Press

Raven, B. H. and Jeffrey, J. R. (1982) *Social Psychology* Chichester: John Wiley and Sons

Rawls, J. (1971) *A Theory of Justice* Oxford: Oxford University Press

— (1985) 'Justice as Fairness: Political not Metaphysical', *Philosophy and Public Affairs*, **14** (3) Summer 223–51

— (1988) 'The Priority of Right and Ideas of the Good', *Philosophy and Public Affairs*, **17** (4) Fall 251–76

— (1993) *Political Liberalism* New York: Columbia University Press

Rabbie, J. M. and Horwitz, M. (1969) 'Arousal of ingroup – outgroup bias by a chance win or loss', *Journal of Personality and Social Psychology*, **13** (3) 269–77

Richards, V. (ed.) (1965) *His Life and Ideas* London: Freedom Press

Robinson, D. N. (1989) *Aristotle's Psychology* New York: Columbia University Press

Rosenblum, N. L. (1989) 'Pluralism and Self-Defense', in N. Rosenblum (ed.) *Liberalism and the Moral Life* Cambridge, MA: Harvard University Press:

Rousseau, J-J. *The First and Second Discourses* ed. R. D. Masters, trans. R. D. and J. R. Masters, New York: St. Martin's Press

— (1968) *The Social Contract* trans. M. Cranston, Harmondsworth: Penguin

— (1973) *The Social Contract and Discourses*, trans. G. D. H. Cole, London: Everyman

Salvan, J. L. (1967) *The Scandalous Ghost. Sartre's Existentialism as Related to Vitalism, Humanism, Mysticism, Marxism* Detroit: Wayne State University Press

Sandel, M. J. (1982) *Liberalism and the Limits of Justice* Cambridge: Cambridge University Press

— (1984a) 'The Procedural Republic and the Unencumbered Self', *Political Theory*, **12** (1) February 81–96

— (1984b) 'Morality and the Liberal Ideal', *The New Republic* 15–17 May

Sartre, Jean-Paul (1963) *The Problem of Method* trans. H. E Barnes, London: Methuen

— (1965) *Anti-Semite and Jew* trans. George J. Becker, New York: Schocken Books

— (1969) *Being and Nothingness* trans. H. E. Barnes, London

— (1970) *Existentialism and Humanism* trans. P. Mairet, London: Methuen

— (1971) *Sketch for a Theory of the Emotions* trans. P. Mairet, London: Methuen

— (1974) 'The Itinerary of a Thought', in *Between Existentialism and Marxism* trans. J. Mathews, New York: Pantheon

— (1978) 'Elections: A Trap for Fools', in *Sartre in the Seventies. Interviews and Essays* trans. Paul Auster and Lydia Davis, London: Andre Deutsch

— (1991) *Critique of Dialectical Reason* vol. 1. *Theory of Practical Ensembles* trans. A. Sheridan-Smith, London: Verso
— (1991) *Critique of Dialectical Reason* vol. II. (Unfinished) *The Intelligibility of History* trans. Q. Hoare, London: Verso
— (1992) *Notebooks for an Ethics* trans. D. Pellauer, Chicago: University of Chicago Press. Originally published as *Cahiers pour une morale* (Editions Gallimard: Paris, 1983)
Sartre, Jean-Paul and Levy, B. (1996) *Hope Now. The 1980 Interviews* trans. A. van den Hoven, London: University of Chicago Press
Schacht, R. (1972) *Alienation* London: George Allen and Unwin
Schilpp, P. A. (ed.) (1981) *The Philosophy of Jean-Paul Sartre* La Salle, Illinois: Open Court
Seitz, B. (1991) 'The Identity of the Subject, After Sartre. An Identity masked by the Denial of Identity', *Philosophy Today*, **35** (4) Winter 362–71
Shklar, J. N. (1989) 'The Liberalism of Fear', in N. Rosenblum *Liberalism and the Moral Life* cambridge, MA: Harvard University Press
Silverman, H. J. and Elliston, F. A. (eds) (1980) *Jean-Paul Sartre. Contemporary Approaches to His Philosophy* Brighton: Harvester Press
Sorell, T. (1991) *Hobbes* London: Routledge
Stack, G. J. (1971) 'Sartre's Dialectic of Social relations', *Philosophy and Phenomenological Research*, **31** (3) March 394–408
— (1977) *Sartre's Philosophy of Social Existence* St. Louis: Warren H. Green
Sugden, R. (1993) 'Rationality and impartiality: Is the contractarian enterprise possible?', in D. Gauthier and R. Sugden (eds) *Rationality, Justice and the Social Contract. Themes from Morals by Agreement* Hemel Hempstead: Harvester Wheatsheaf
Sypnowich, C. (1993) 'Justice, Community and the Antinomies of Feminist Theory', *Political Theory*, **21** (3) 484–506
Thomson, G. (1987) *Needs* London: Routledge and Kegan Paul
Valady, M. (1988) *The Development of Sartre's Notion of Freedom*, unpublished PhD thesis, University of Texas
Waldron, J. (ed.) (1987) *Nonsense Upon Stilts. Bentham, Burke and Marx on the Rights of Man* London: Methuen
Wallace, J. D. (1978) *Virtues and Vices* Ithaca: Cornell University Press
Wallach, J. R. (1987) 'Communitarians and the Tasks of Political Theory', *Political Theory*, **15** (4) November 581–611
Walzer, M. (1983) *Spheres of Justice. A Defence of Pluralism and Equality* Oxford: Martin Robinson
— (1984) 'Liberalism and the Art of Separation', *Political Theory*, **12** (3) August 315–30
— (1989) *The Company of Critics. Social Criticism and Political Commitment in the Twentieth Century* London: Peter Halban

— (1990) 'The Communitarian Critique of Liberalism', *Political Theory*, **18** (1) 6–23 February

Wardman, H. W. (1992) *Jean-Paul Sartre. The Evolution of his Thought and Art* Lampeter: Edwin Mellen Press

Warnock, M. (1965) *The Philosophy of Sartre* London: Hutchinson

Warnock, M. (ed.) (1971) *Sartre. A Collection of Critical Essays* New York: Anchor Books

Waters, A. (1976) *Alienation in the Philosophy of Jean-Paul Sartre*, unpublished PhD thesis, University of Missouri

Xenos, N. (1987) 'Liberalism and the Postulate of Scarcity', *Political Theory*, **15** (2) (May) 225–43

Young, I. M. (1990) *Justice and the Politics of Difference* Princeton: Princeton University Press

— (1997) *Intersecting Voices. Dilemmas of Gender, Political Philosophy and Policy* Princeton: Princeton University Press

Index

alienation 10, 25, 31, 71, 90–93, 96, 105, 119, 132, 156, 162–3, 209, 225
analytical reason 33, 36, 134–5, 229–30
anarchism 3–7, 13, 32, 130–31, 133, 139, 148, 158, 161, 168, 172–7
antecedently individuated self 42–4, 46, 90, 105, 127, 187
Aristotle 10, 16, 30, 50, 52, 211–12, 222, 224
Aronson, R. 7–8, 24, 26, 28–9, 105, 119, 191
autonomous individual 42, 58, 73, 85, 127, 188, 219, 221–2
autonomy 17, 39, 89, 116

Bakunin, M. 3–4, 34, 99, 113, 135, 140, 149, 158–9, 161, 172–4, 176, 186–7, 197
Barnes, H. E. 22, 27, 105, 110
Blum, L. A. 58–59, 164, 200, 211–12, 214–15, 217–18
bourgeois 5, 88–9, 113–14, 119, 124–6, 134
  bourgeoisie 97, 115, 119, 134–5

capitalism 6, 25, 114, 122, 124
capitalist 7, 22, 40, 62, 66, 89, 93, 98–9, 110, 113–15, 118, 122, 124, 130
Catalano, J. 21, 24, 96
Chiodi, P. 7, 23, 110
circularity 24, 27, 29, 31, 81, 95, 100, 104, 110, 136, 239
circumstances of justice 26, 48, 74, 128
citizen 3, 16, 50, 56–7, 62, 67–8, 78, 114, 131–2, 135, 150, 168, 186
class 5, 19, 25, 40, 93, 96–7, 103, 110, 112, 119, 121, 124–6, 130, 132, 134, 223
communist 4–5, 140
communitarianism 1–2, 9, 58–9, 63, 70–71, 75, 138, 145–6, 154, 174, 190, 196, 200–01, 203, 205–7, 210–11, 220, 226, 243, 247–8
community 1–2, 4–13, 20, 38–40, 44–7, 49, 51–3, 55, 57–71, 73–7, 79

competition
  bourgeois/capitalist 40, 119, 124, 126, 134
  economic 66, 113
  and forms and terms of association 121, 126
  and scarcity 22, 25–7, 49, 74, 83, 92, 110, 112, 114, 162, 246
complex equality 62, 119
conception(s) of the good 41–2, 49, 51, 63, 70, 84, 127, 144, 199, 204, 208–9; *see also* eudaimonia
  competing conceptions of the good 41, 63
concrete universal, *see* universal
conflict 7–8, 20, 23, 25–6, 40, 55, 60, 63, 74, 83, 100, 113, 115, 118–19, 121, 134, 137, 149, 163, 175, 190–91, 193, 207–8, 221, 224, 231, 239, 245–7
consent 124, 143, 151, 153, 155, 166–8, 171–2, 174, 179, 198
constituted
  individual 8, 42, 44–5, 69, 75, 77, 110–11, 121, 139, 148, 151, 154, 156, 165, 169, 172, 175, 180, 187–9, 194, 201, 204, 207, 210, 214, 216, 218–20, 223, 246–8
  community 8, 45, 79, 104, 111, 144–5, 151, 155–6, 165, 169, 172, 175, 201–2, 204–6, 210, 216, 218–19, 246
constitutive
  of individual identity 1, 28, 40, 44, 46–7, 49, 51, 55, 71–2, 75–6, 88, 90, 103, 121, 125–6, 145, 150–51, 155, 157, 165, 184, 194, 204, 206, 243–4; *see also* identity
  of community 34, 47, 50, 145, 187, 202
contract 12, 31, 39, 42, 47, 63, 77, 85, 92, 116–19, 121, 125, 130–31, 135, 141–2, 145, 166–07, 169, 171, 173–4, 196, 198, 210, 222–4; *see also* social contract
co-operate 5, 8, 26, 49, 140, 158, 163, 176
co-operation 5, 20, 26, 112, 142, 163, 170

259

deforestation 82, 85, 112
Desan, W. 8, 83, 89, 122, 143, 195
desert 46–7, 57, 187; *see also* talents
dialectic 8, 20, 29, 32–3, 35–6, 38, 64, 78–9, 81–2, 90, 94, 96, 103, 130, 134–5, 146, 165, 174, 185, 188, 216, 219, 228–30, 232, 234–6, 240–41, 246, 248
dialectical method 2, 8, 11, 32–7, 68, 76, 82, 134–6, 189, 203, 220, 229–31, 233, 235, 237, 239–43, 246–48
dialectical reason 11, 32, 35–7, 134–5, 203, 229–31, 233, 242
disposition(s) 10, 27, 30–31, 52, 56, 84, 106, 141, 172, 184, 189, 200–204, 210–12, 214–19, 224–5, 231, 239, 246; *see also* virtue

emotion 211, 219–21, 224–5, 228
Engels, F. 93, 130, 185
equality 6, 38, 60, 62–3, 66, 87, 94, 114, 122, 166–8, 175, 186–7, 199, 223, 227; *see also* complex equality
Etzioni, A. 71–2, 149, 207–8
eudaimonia 58, 212–13; *see also* conception(s) of the good
exploitation 19, 25, 31, 87, 110, 112–13, 118–19, 122, 124, 185–6
external goods 53–4, 194, 228; *see also* internal goods

feminist 203, 220–24, 226–8, 235
freedom 2, 4, 19–20, 30, 38–40, 66–7, 73, 81, 84–5, 87, 95, 111–12, 114, 116–22, 131, 135, 148, 150, 152–3, 156, 160–62, 164–9, 171, 173–5, 177, 179–80, 182, 185–6, 189–90, 194, 196, 202, 204, 206, 208, 211, 215, 221, 223, 243, 245
free market 86, 122, 223
fused group 149, 156; *see also* group-in-fusion

Gauthier, D. 23, 163, 171, 179, 183
gender 109–10, 223, 227
Glendon, M. A. 115, 149, 208
group-in-fusion 103, 139, 142–5, 149–51, 156, 159, 161, 164, 171–2, 174, 179, 180–81, 183, 190, 199–201, 204, 206, 208, 215–16, 218; *see also* fused group

Hampton, J. 117, 129, 137
Hegel, G. F. W. 8, 32–4, 81, 83, 91, 28, 231, 234–5, 238
Held, V. 220–22, 226
hexis 210; *see also* inertia
hierarchy 6, 148
hierarchical 7, 87, 148
Hobbes, T. 9–10, 12, 21, 23, 27, 31, 39, 54, 92, 128–130, 137, 152, 156, 159–60, 163–4, 168, 170–72, 185, 190, 196
Hope Now 18, 132, 157, 168
Hume, D. 26, 48, 50, 57, 221
hyperorganism 144–5, 147–8, 178

identity 1, 20, 40, 42, 44–5, 47, 49, 51, 55, 57–9, 71, 75–6, 80, 88–90, 99, 103, 110, 127, 133, 151, 166, 169, 175, 180–181, 184, 186, 188, 200–01, 208–9, 214, 218–19, 225, 238, 244–5; *see also* constituted, constitutive
immanence, immanent 19, 36–7, 81, 148, 151, 171–2, 181, 204, 206, 215–7, 226, 231–6, 239–40, 244
inertia 80, 89, 100, 160, 195, 200, 210; *see also* hexis
institution, the 193–201, 206, 209, 214
interdependency 6–7, 176–7, 189, 248
interiorisation 15, 24, 28–9, 65, 80, 94, 100, 111–12, 156, 165, 215–7, 225–6, 231, 233, 235, 238–40, 244
internal goods 53, 58, 96, 120, 228; *see also* external goods
Jaggar, A. M. 223–4
justice 9, 26, 41–2, 44, 46–8, 50–1, 55, 57, 60–1, 63–5, 68–8, 73–5, 78, 84–5, 116, 128, 133, 168, 178, 186–7, 189, 194, 197, 204, 223–4, 227

Kant, I. 1, 9, 17, 33, 37, 40, 42–3, 48, 89–91, 107, 127, 173, 188, 211, 214, 219, 221–2, 230
Kropotkin, P. 5–6, 13–14, 22, 133, 136, 143, 176
kulaks 99
Kymlicka, W. 1, 71–3, 125, 206–7

labour 17, 30, 60, 79, 83, 89, 92–4, 110, 119–20, 130–31, 173, 176, 227

Index

legitimacy, political 87, 132, 155, 167, 198, 208
liberalism 1, 10, 25, 39, 50–1, 58, 60, 63, 66–7, 69, 74, 77, 83, 88, 101, 108, 113, 115, 120, 127, 135, 138, 154, 173, 183, 203, 207, 211, 220, 222–4, 226, 248,
   deonotological/Kantian-Rawlsian 1, 9, 40–41, 72, 89–90, 105, 117, 171
   laissez-faire 2, 9, 59, 76, 85–7, 89, 105, 121, 124, 134, 169, 181

MacIntyre, A. 1, 9, 38, 43, 51–2, 54–60, 72, 74–6, 96, 105, 127, 136, 138, 141, 184, 194–5, 199, 204, 207, 214, 227
Malatesta, E. 3–5, 22, 32, 173, 176–7, 197
Marx, K. 4–5, 7–8, 14, 16, 19–20, 25, 27, 30, 32, 34, 60, 63, 67, 81, 85, 91–3, 114, 125, 136, 228
Marxist 7, 15, 25, 32, 35, 66, 74, 78, 88, 113, 130, 142, 216, 220, 227
material world 28, 35, 80–82, 89–90, 106, 229, 252
matter 14, 19, 22, 28, 79, 81–3, 89, 91–2, 94–5, 100
   inert matter 34, 80–81
   organic matter 30
   worked matter 28, 96, 100, 177
McBride, W. L. 8, 107–8, 128, 151, 158
mediated reciprocity 146, 148, 166, 174, 189, 246
moral agency 10, 31, 51, 171, 203, 214, 218–19, 221
motherhood 221–3, 226, 228, 235–40, 242
motivation 8, 25, 36, 43, 50, 76, 128, 140, 152, 211–12, 215, 217–18, 221, 224, 228, 231, 233–4, 236, 244

negation 14–15, 18–19, 45, 65, 93, 108, 136, 150, 156, 161, 230–34, 244
nomads 83–4, 93, 98, 127, 199, 204, 209
Notebooks for an Ethics 13, 19, 32–3, 115, 211

obligation, political 78, 116, 132, 153, 159, 162, 166–8, 170–72, 177, 185, 188, 196, 216
oppression 31, 93, 111–12, 122, 124, 130

organic matter; *see* matter
organised group 142, 175, 177, 188, 190–91, 193–5, 198, 202, 204, 206, 208, 214, 237
original position 42, 47–8, 117, 154; *see also* veil of ignorance

Pateman, C. 87, 167–8
peasants, Chinese 82–5, 98–9, 112, 127, 145, 157, 199, 204, 209
pledge, the 153, 155–60, 162–9, 171–2, 174, 178–9, 181–2, 186, 191, 200, 202, 208, 216
pledged group 103, 155–9, 161, 163–6, 169, 171–2, 174–5, 179–180, 182–3, 186, 190–191, 199, 204, 206, 208, 216, 218, 234
practice 52–6, 58, 74, 76, 85, 96, 120, 184, 194–5, 228, 246
practico-inert 19–21, 26, 28, 31, 35, 45, 76, 81, 96, 106–7, 109–11, 142, 152, 194, 202
Problem of Method, The 27, 36, 233
proletariat 120, 134
Proudhon, P.-J. 3–4, 133, 163, 174

quasi-sovereign(ty) 180, 189, 193, 195, 199, 208–9, 227
queue(s), as series 105–8, 122–3, 130, 136, 139, 149

rational agents 42, 51, 63, 71, 89, 127, 170–71, 174, 183, 188, 219, 221–3
Rawls, J. 41–9, 51, 57, 60, 63–4, 74, 116–17, 128, 141, 154, 165–6, 168, 179, 187, 210, 220, 227
reciprocity 26, 35, 38, 59, 82, 89, 91, 103, 106, 110, 116, 118, 123, 136, 146–8, 153, 159, 166, 174–5, 178, 181, 183, 187, 189, 193, 206, 215, 221, 225, 227, 229, 235, 237–8, 240–41, 245–7
re-exteriorisation 15, 24, 26, 28–9, 111, 165, 215–17, 225–6, 231, 233, 235, 238–40, 244
rights 12, 39, 42, 46, 57, 60, 67, 69, 72–3, 78, 85, 87, 101, 113–15, 118, 135, 149, 158–9, 162–3, 175, 178, 182, 185, 187, 189, 207–8, 216, 223, 227
Rousseau, J-J. 10, 80, 87, 92, 110, 124, 131, 137, 150–55, 160, 163, 166, 168, 172–3, 190, 196

same, the 146–150, 166, 178
Sandel, M. J. 1, 9, 40, 48–51, 59–60, 69, 72–6, 105, 116–17, 121, 127–8, 138, 149, 154, 166, 171, 187, 207–8
scarcity 8–9, 12–13, 20–28, 48–9, 64–6, 74, 79, 82–8, 92–4, 96, 103, 110, 112, 115, 121, 123, 125–31, 135, 143–5, 156, 158, 160, 162, 164, 169, 172, 174–5, 180, 185, 190, 199, 202, 204, 206–7, 209
self-interest 27, 31, 93, 112, 143, 154, 170–72, 196, 223–4
seriality 104, 113, 119, 122–3, 125, 127–30, 132, 134–40, 142, 144–5, 148, 150, 154, 156–7, 162–4, 168–9, 175, 178, 182, 185, 190–91, 193–9, 202, 204, 206–9, 222, 234, 244, 246
  series 103–5, 107–10, 118, 121–3, 125–7, 132, 143, 150, 168, 178, 215, 228
shared meaning 1, 12, 50, 65, 68–71, 84, 99–100, 122–7, 134, 144, 151, 154–5, 161, 169, 178, 192–3, 199, 202, 204, 208, 210, 243, 245–7
social contract 39, 42, 63, 92, 130–131, 154, 160, 163, 171–4, 196; *see also* contract
social goods 1, 20, 26, 59–61, 63–5, 69–70, 74–6, 84, 99, 103, 124–6, 144, 186, 190, 199–201, 204–5, 208, 210, 243–6
Stalin, J. 15, 98, 111, 122, 210, 216, 234
State, the 3, 5, 40, 56, 63, 66–7, 73–4, 78, 103, 130–33, 139, 153, 158, 166, 168, 173–4, 196, 198, 207–8, 211, 226

talents 46–7, 175, 180, 187–8, 193, 198, 201; *see also* desert

telos 38, 52, 58, 75, 84, 204, 212
terror 7, 145, 156–7, 159, 190
third party 146–54, 157, 159, 171–2, 180–82, 192, 198, 201, 204, 208, 215–6, 218
top ten 108, 132, 136
totalisation 14, 17–18, 36, 122, 135, 147, 150, 181, 190, 229–32, 235
totality 14, 16–18, 34, 36, 193, 236–7, 240–41, 244–7
transcendence, transcendent 15–16, 18, 20–21, 30, 36–7, 81, 83, 90, 94, 148, 151, 156, 164–5, 171–2, 181, 204, 206, 215–7, 222, 226, 231, 233–7, 239–40, 244, 246–7

universal 33, 51, 57, 60, 64, 68–9, 91, 113, 149, 214, 221
utilitarian 41, 142, 220

values 10, 15, 17, 20, 30, 32, 38, 59, 64, 69–70, 79, 100, 109, 126, 139, 144, 155, 164–5, 187, 189, 199–200, 205, 215, 239, 243, 246, 248
veil of ignorance 47, 63, 117; *see also* original position
violence 24, 93, 112–13, 119, 125, 128, 142, 156–7, 192, 195
virtues 38, 44, 48–59, 62, 69, 75–6, 85, 96, 106, 120, 142, 173, 184–5, 194, 199, 201, 204, 211–12, 215, 217–18, 221–2, 244–5; *see also* disposition(s)

Walzer, M. 1, 9, 60–69, 72, 74–5, 84, 126, 138, 154, 185–6, 190, 198, 207
Warnock, M. 16, 89–90, 128, 159
worked matter; *see* matter
Young, I. M. 69, 102, 136, 223